HANDBOOK *of the* TEACHING *of* PSYCHOLOGY

For Chris Cardone, our long-time friend and trusted advisor

Handbook of the Teaching of Psychology

Edited by

William Buskist and Stephen F. Davis

BLACKWELL PUBLISHING
350 Main Street, Malden, MA 02148-5020, USA
9600 Garsington Road, Oxford OX4 2DQ, UK
550 Swanston Street, Carlton, Victoria 3053, Australia

First published 2006 by Blackwell Publishing Ltd

1   2006

Library of Congress Cataloging-in-Publication Data
Handbook of the teaching of psychology / edited by William Buskist and Stephen F. Davis.
p. cm.
Includes bibliographical references and indexes.
ISBN-13: 978-1-4051-3204-6 (hardcover : alk. paper)
ISBN-10: 1-4051-3204-3 (hardcover : alk. paper)
ISBN-13: 978-1-4051-3801-7 (pbk. : alk. paper)
ISBN-10: 1-4051-3801-7 (pbk. : alk. paper)   1. Psychology—Study and teaching.   I.
Buskist, William.   II. Davis, Stephen F.

BF77.H268 2005
150′.71′1—dc22

2005014828

A catalogue record for this title is available from the British Library.

Set in 10.5/12.5pt Adobe Garamond
by Graphicraft Limited, Hong Kong
Printed and bound in Great Britain
by TJ International, Padstow, Cornwall

For further information on
Blackwell Publishing, visit our website:
www.blackwellpublishing.com

Contents

Contents

Contents

Contents

Preface

Psychology is one of the few academic disciplines that places an overwhelming degree of importance on teaching. To be sure, the teaching of psychology is a vibrant and burgeoning subfield within the larger parent discipline of scientific psychology. It is a field that emphasizes both scholarly teaching and the scholarship of teaching. It fuses basic pedagogical research with the practical exigencies faced by classroom teachers. Just as importantly, the field includes an expansive and supportive community of teachers in high schools, two-year colleges, baccalaureate and master's institutions, and major research universities.

As testimony to the field's vitality, consider the venues within this community for sharing research findings and practical ideas to enhance the teaching of psychology:

- **The Society for the Teaching of Psychology** (STP; Division Two of the American Psychological Association [APA]), which boasts over 2,500 annual members, publishes a widely known and highly respected journal, *Teaching of Psychology*, and sponsors a lively series of invited addresses, symposia and panel discussions, and posters at each annual meeting of the APA. STP also sponsors an annual "Best Practices" conference each fall that centers on central issues and topics within the field. STP publishes a monthly e-column called "Excellence in Teaching." Each year the column editors compile these essays in book form and post them to the STP home page (www.teachpsych.org). In addition, STP publishes e-books on the teaching of psychology, which also are available on its home page.
- **The National Institute on the Teaching of Psychology** (NITOP) is held each January in St. Petersburg Beach, Florida (see www.nitop.org). NITOP is a 3-day meeting featuring an abundance of plenary speakers representing all subfields of psychology, participant idea exchange sessions, and posters. NITOP is currently compiling many of its plenary addresses into a multivolume series to be published by the American Psychological Society (APS).

- **APS** features a day-long preconference institute on the teaching of psychology and includes a teaching track within its larger annual conference program. *The Observer*, a monthly publication of the APS, includes a highly touted column called *Teaching Tips*. Periodically, APS reproduces columns in book form. To date, APS has published two volumes of *Tips* columns – *Lessons Learned: Practical Advice for the Teaching of Psychology*. In addition to these national venues, several annual regional conferences exist that focus exclusively on the teaching of psychology. The conferences generally span 1 to 2 days and feature plenary speakers, symposia, workshops, and paper and poster sessions.

This extensive discipline-wide interest in the teaching of psychology provides the underpinning for this book. Its major aim is to provide readers with comprehensive coverage and analysis of current trends and issues, basic mechanics, and important contextual variables related to effective teaching in psychology. By incorporating short and primarily prescriptive chapters, this book is both lively and informative and covers the gamut of topics currently of interest to all teachers of psychology. The book's 57 chapters span 10 sections or parts.

Books do not write, or in our case, edit, themselves. To be sure, a volume the size of this one requires considerable teamwork to create, edit, and produce. We gratefully acknowledge the excellent work of all our authors who, although they worked in relative isolation from each other, nonetheless collaborated in helping us fashion this extensive treatment of the teaching of psychology. We also warmly appreciate the enthusiastic support and guidance of Chris Cardone, Senior Acquisitions Editor in Psychology at Blackwell Publishing. Thanks, too, to Sarah Coleman, Associate Development Editor, Linguistics and Psychology, at Blackwell Publishing, who shepherded us through the development and publication process.

Bill Buskist, Auburn, AL
Steve Davis, Lindale, TX

part I

Ψ

Introduction to the Teaching of Psychology

This section provides a broad overview of the teaching of psychology and features chapters on basic elements of teaching and learning, the place of the psychology curriculum in the context of modern higher education, the scholarship of teaching in psychology, and the Society for the Teaching of Psychology.

1
What Teachers Need to Know about Teaching and Learning

Ψ

Stephen F. Davis & William Buskist
Texas Wesleyan University & Auburn University

The two of us have been teaching over 50 years; during that time, we have spent countless hours preparing thousands of classroom presentations to share with thousands of students. We have evaluated thousands of quizzes and examinations, critiqued thousands of term papers, and given thousands of final grades. In turn, our students have offered thousands of critiques of our teaching – some glowing, some scathing, and some very helpful. Somewhere among all the preparation, lecturing, grading, and evaluating, we both also found time to study how teachers teach and how students learn. However, even when we put our minds together we do not know everything there is to know about teaching and learning. Nonetheless, we have learned a few insightful tidbits about these processes over the half-century we have been in the academy. In this chapter we briefly describe 21 things that we believe all teachers should know about teaching and learning – and thus about themselves and their students. Many of these issues are covered in greater depth in the separate chapters in this book.

 The Basics

Know Why You Teach

Our advice is not just to *think* about this issue; after you have finished thinking, write down the reasons why you teach and review them periodically. Here are some questions that may assist your thought processes: What do you find rewarding about teaching? Are you teaching what you want in the way you want? Are you satisfied with your teaching and your students' performance; what still needs to be accomplished? Answers to these questions will form the core of your teaching philosophy (Korn, 2002; 2004).

Know the Goals You Have for Teaching

Another key element of your teaching philosophy centers around your teaching goals. What do you want your students to learn: knowledge of facts, excitement about the subject matter, applicability of the material to the real world and their lives, preparation for subsequent classes, all of these things? Are you interested in having your students learn other skills, such as writing, ethics, critical thinking? Have you documented your goals in your teaching portfolio (see chapter 51)?

Know the Methods You Will Use to Achieve Your Teaching Goals

Once you have determined your teaching goals, the next step is to determine how you will achieve them. With which teaching strategies are you most comfortable and which do you like to use most often? Why do you choose to use these methods as opposed to other methods? Which of your current teaching strategies are not as effective as you would like? How will you improve them? What would an observer in your classroom see and hear when you are doing your best teaching (see Bain, 2004)?

Know Your Stuff

Both students and faculty agree that the most effective teachers are knowledgeable about their subject matter (see e.g., Schaeffer, Epting, Zinn, & Buskist, 2003). To be knowledgeable means that teachers possess both depth in their understanding of the subject matter and breadth in their understanding of how it relates to other topics, including the real world. Teachers reveal their knowledge when they speak extemporaneously during class without having to rely on notes or the text, use clear examples to underscore important points, and easily answer student questions regarding the subject matter or how it relates to other topics and student experience (Buskist, Sikorski, Buckley, & Saville, 2002).

Know Your Students

Knowing your students – your audience – is critical for understanding the important backdrops to your classroom presentations: their level of understanding of the course content and their educational goals, professional aspirations, personal interests, and life experiences. Knowing and appreciating any or all of these student variables provides teachers with useful points of contact – topics to which key course concepts can be made relevant for students. The best way to get to know your students is to spend time talking with them: before and after class, during office hours, and in the hallways and on campus – wherever you happen to bump into them (see, e.g., Sturnick & Conners, 1995).

Know that Preparation Matters

Although knowing that you should be prepared for your classes seems common sense, we encourage you to take your preparation for your teaching seriously (see McKeachie, 2002). How many times have faculty members (you?) been cajoled into teaching a class that they were not prepared to teach that started the next day? How many junior faculty at the bottom of the pecking-order teach those "unwanted" classes that they are not really prepared to teach? How prepared are you when you walk into each class that you teach? Students will appreciate your being prepared to the best of your ability for each class.

Know How to Set Appropriate Academic Standards

In dealing with this issue, we suggest that you begin with the question, "Are your standards very high, high, or average?" Once you have answered this question, then ask yourself if you have included such factors as the nature of your institution and the nature of the students you teach in your answer. If you included these and other related factors, then your standards most likely are appropriate. If your answer did not include a consideration of these factors, you probably should examine your standards a bit more closely and make appropriate adjustments. We also encourage you to reconsider this question from time to time – your academic standards are not static (Brewer, 2002).

Know that Students Rise to the Level of Your Expectations

Your students are one reason that your academic standards are dynamic. Keep in mind that your students will raise (or lower, if you have low standards) their level of performance to meet your expectations (Brewer, 2002). Of course, the tricky part is to keep your expectations within the reach of your students.

In the Classroom and Beyond

Know that Teaching Critical Thinking Trumps Teaching Only Knowledge

Like other scientific disciplines, the knowledge base of psychology has a relatively short shelf life. Showing students only the "facts of psychology" teaches them little about how psychologists developed such knowledge, how to evaluate its merits and applications, and how psychologists, or for that matter, students, might consider expanding it. A more effective strategy is to teach students how to think critically about psychological knowledge so they can use information in creative and practical ways to deepen their understanding of both knowledge and the science that produced it (Halpern, 2003).

Know that Active Learning is Superior to Passive Learning

We know from research in cognitive psychology that people who process information at a deep level learn and retain information more effectively than people who process information at shallower levels. Thus, anything that teachers might do to encourage their students to process information about course content at deep levels, for example, infusing their classes with active learning techniques, is likely to enhance student learning (see chapters 9 through 15; 21 and 22). Many teaching experts (e.g., Davis, 1993; McKeachie, 2002) argue persuasively that active learning exercises such as written assignments, discussion, and involvement in research are effective in producing higher levels of learning than passive learning techniques such as listening to a lecture.

Know that Teaching and Learning Occur in Context

Despite the opinion of some critics and legislators, a course taught at one particular college or university is not identical to this course taught at another institution. Different institutions create different teaching contexts. Moreover, the context, including campus politics, may change from time to time within institutional boundaries (see chapter 52). Monday classes differ from Friday classes; classes at the beginning of the semester are not the same as classes at the end of the semester or just before a holiday. Moreover, campus events, such as winning (or losing) an important athletic contest, or a widely publicized student tragedy, can alter the context of your classes significantly. Likewise, the factors impacting you, such as health, finances, family responsibilities, professional demands, and so forth, will influence your teaching and could impact your students' learning. Be alert to such contextual changes.

Know How to Establish Rapport with Your Students

A powerful approach to creating a warm and inviting classroom learning environment is to establish rapport with your students. Building rapport rests squarely on showing your students that they can trust you (see chapter 7). For example, by addressing your students by name, treating them courteously in and out of class, commenting favorably on their good works and effort, and by smiling while you teach, you increase the likelihood that students will attend to – and get – your message (Buskist & Saville, 2004; Lowman, 1995).

Know How to Care for Your Students

Caring for students means that you are concerned about what students are learning in your classes and that you monitor factors that might influence their academic performance (Baiocco & DeWaters, 1998; Lowman, 1995). Showing that you care involves knowing students' names, talking to them about what they are learning, rewarding them for making comments and asking questions in class, and letting them know you are available to help them when they encounter difficulty with their coursework.

Know How to Make Your Subject Matter Relevant

In his presidential address to the Society for the Teaching of Psychology in 1999, Neil Lutsky noted that "success in teaching depends mainly in capturing and organizing students' attention." There is perhaps no better way of "capturing and organizing students' attention" than making your subject matter bear on important issues in your students' lives. Connecting your subject matter with students' interests, experiences, and aspirations often piques their curiosity about psychology and provides a plausible framework for helping them construct meaning from your courses.

Know How to Show Your Passion for Teaching and Learning

A reading of the literature on master teaching leaves the indelible impression that one of the most important qualities of excellent teachers is the passion or enthusiasm that they show for their subject matter, their students' learning, and for teaching *per se* (see e.g., Baiocco & DeWaters, 1998; Roth, 1997). Indeed, Charles Brewer (2002), one of psychology's most famous master teachers, has argued that such passion is what "separates adequate from exceptional teachers" (p. 505). Although there is no single recipe for how to demonstrate your passion in the classroom – the expression of this quality is as unique as each individual teacher – students often perceive changes in facial expression, vocal inflection and tone, body posture, and hand gestures of their teachers as conveying interest in the subject matter and enthusiasm for teaching (Buskist et al., 2002).

Know that Learning Occurs Outside of the Classroom

Certainly your students do not stop learning as they exit the doors to your classroom. If your concern for student learning follows them as they leave your classroom, then you can have a significant impact on your students. Are there internships from which they might benefit? What about becoming involved in research (see chapter 22) or in service-learning (see chapter 23)? Do not forget to encourage your students to participate in professional development activities such as attending or presenting a paper at a student research conference or preparing a paper for submission to a student journal (see chapters 53 and 55). Your students will learn a *great* deal from these extracurricular experiences.

Becoming a More Effective Teacher

Know How to Create Learning Opportunities for Yourself and Your Students

Effective teachers provide realistic opportunities for their students to acquire new knowledge and develop critical thinking skills that they can use both in college and life. Through careful preparation for their courses, these teachers also provide opportunities for themselves to deepen their knowledge base and sharpen their cognitive skills (Beidler, 1997). They cultivate such opportunities by creating challenges – problems to be solved, issues to be understood, dilemmas to be discerned – posing them to their students, and then working together with students to develop informed judgments (Buskist, 2002).

Know that Effective Teaching Entails Calculated Risks

One of the marvelous things about classroom teaching is that it is live. Anything might happen over the course of a class period – and probably will if you teach long enough. Coupling this sort of uncertainty with the presentation of new ideas, examples, and demonstrations that you may want to experiment with in class makes teaching a risky, and to be sure, messy, business (Kreiner, 2002). Nonetheless, to become a better teacher, adjusting to unpredictable classroom dynamics and tinkering with innovative teaching methods in an effort to improve your teaching is a necessary and key element of professional development.

Know How to Assess Your Teaching Effectiveness

Understanding and believing that you should assess your teaching effectiveness is key to becoming a more effective teacher. Once you have accepted this tenet, you will find a multitude of useful assessment techniques at your command. Among these techniques are the numerous in class assessment strategies (see chapter 47; Angelo & Cross, 1993), student evaluation tactics (see chapter 48), videotaping approaches (see chapter 50), and peer observation and feedback methods (see chapter 49). Rather than expand on these techniques at this point, we encourage you to read the appropriate chapters in this volume and then develop and implement your own assessment program.

Know How to Become a Reflective Teacher

An often overlooked aspect of authentic teaching assessment is stepping back from both classroom teaching and its assessment and looking at them from afar – that is, reflecting over what it is that you do as teacher and how effective it may or may not be in benefiting your students' learning. Korn (2002; 2004) has argued that perhaps the best way to gain such perspective is to write a statement of your teaching philosophy and then periodically revisit it – both to revise and update it as well as to contemplate its meaning as you face new challenges in your teaching. As Brookfield (1995) noted, reflection should be as critical as it is pensive.

Know that You are Human and so are Your Students

You should have no difficulty understanding the nature of this issue; teachers and students alike are subject to the same problems and turmoil with which the rest of the human race struggles. The trick is to remember this fact and act accordingly!

Conclusion

Clearly, teachers have a lot to consider regarding what they do in – and out of – the classroom and how they go about doing it. The best teachers make teaching look easy and natural. These teachers know, though, that mastering their craft took years to achieve and not without some hard-won personal struggles with the issues we have just described. Indeed, truly effective teachers realize that their work is ongoing – that each new class they teach is a new and different opportunity to influence in no small way the course of their students' intellectual, personal, and professional lives. They also realize that it is difficult, if not impossible, to teach at the top of their game year in and year out. Perhaps it is this awareness that helps motivate the great teachers to keep exploring and tinkering with their craft – always knowing that excellence in teaching is more of a journey than it is a destination.

ACKNOWLEDGMENTS

We thank Carrie Burke, Amber Henslee, Jared Keeley, and Ryan Siney for carefully reading and commenting on an earlier version of this chapter.

REFERENCES

Angelo, T. A., & Cross, K. P. (1993). *Classroom assessment techniques: A handbook for college faculty* (2nd ed.). San Francisco: Jossey-Bass.

Bain, K. (2004). *What the best college teachers do.* Cambridge, MA: Harvard University Press.

Baiocco, S. A., & DeWaters, J. N. (1998). *Successful college teaching: Problem-solving strategies of distinguished professors.* Boston: Allyn & Bacon.

Beidler, P. G. (1997). What makes a good teacher? In J. K. Roth (ed.), *Inspiring teaching: Carnegie Professors of the Year speak* (pp. 2–12). Bolton, MA: Anker.

Brewer, C. L. (2002). Reflections on an academic career: From which side of the looking glass? In S. F. Davis & W. Buskist (eds.), *The teaching of psychology: Essays in honor of Wilbert J. McKeachie and Charles L. Brewer* (pp. 499–507). Mahwah, NJ: Erlbaum.

Brookfield, S. D. (1995). *Becoming a critically reflective teacher.* San Francisco: Jossey-Bass.

Buskist, W. (2002). Effective teaching: Perspectives and insights from Division Two's 2- and 4-year awardees. *Teaching of Psychology, 29,* 188–93.

Buskist, W., & Saville, B. K. (2004). Rapport-building: Creating positive emotional contexts for enhancing teaching and learning. In B. Perlman, L. I. McCann, & S. H. McFadden (eds.), *Lessons learned: Practical advice for the teaching of psychology* (pp. 149–55), vol. 2. Washington, DC: American Psychological Society

Buskist, W., Sikorski, J., Buckley, T., & Saville, B. K. (2002). Elements of master teaching. In S. F. Davis & W. Buskist (eds.), *The teaching of psychology: Essays in honor of Wilbert J. McKeachie and Charles L. Brewer* (pp. 27–39). Mahwah, NJ: Erlbaum.

Davis, B. G. (1993). *Tools for teaching.* San Francisco: Jossey-Bass.

Halpern, D. F. (2003). *Thought & knowledge: An introduction to critical thinking* (4th ed.). Mahwah, NJ: Erlbaum.

Korn, J. H. (2002). Beyond tenure: The teaching portfolio for reflection and change. In S. F. Davis & W. Buskist (eds.), *The teaching of psychology: Essays in honor of Wilbert J. McKeachie and Charles L. Brewer* (pp. 203–13). Mahwah, NJ: Erlbaum.

Korn, J. H. (2004). Writing a philosophy of teaching. In W. Buskist, V. W. Hevern, B. K. Saville, & T. Zinn (eds.), *Essays from e-xcellence in teaching* (vol. 3). Retrieved Oct. 23, from http://teachpsych.lemoyne.edu/teachpsych/eit/eit2003/bio.html#horn

Kreiner, D. S. (2002). Taking risks as a teacher. In W. Buskist, V. W. Hevern, & G. W. Hill, IV (eds.), *Essays from e-xcellence in teaching* (vol. 1). Retrieved Oct. 23, 2004, from http://teachpsych.lemoyne.edu/teachpsych/eit/eit2000/eit00-20.rtf.

Lowman, J. (1995). *Mastering the techniques of teaching* (2nd ed.). San Francisco: Jossey-Bass.

Lutsky, N. (1999, Aug.). Not on the exam: Teaching, psychology, and the examined life. Presidential Address, Society for the Teaching of Psychology, presented at the annual meeting of the American Psychological Association.

McKeachie, W. J. (2002). *Teaching tips: Strategies, research, and theory for college and university teachers* (11th ed.). Boston: Houghton Mifflin.

Roth, J. K. (1997). What this book teaches me. In J. K. Roth (ed.), *Inspiring teaching: Carnegie Professors of the Year speak* (pp. 226–32). Bolton, MA: Anker.

Schaeffer, G., Epting, K., Zinn, T., & Buskist, W. (2003). Student and faculty perceptions of effective teaching. A successful replication. *Teaching of Psychology, 30,* 133–6.

Sturnick, J. A., & Conners, K. J. (1995). Good practice encourages student–faculty contact. In S. R. Hatfield (ed.), *The seven principles in action: Improving undergraduate education* (pp. 9–21). Bolton, MA: Anker.

2

The Scholarship of Teaching
and Pedagogy

Ψ

Bernard C. Beins
Ithaca College

Academic psychologists are teachers as well as scholars. However, only recently have people noted the feasibility and the importance of linking the two (e.g., Halpern et al., 1998; Mathie et al., 2004; Schulman, 2000). As Schulman commented, academics are members of two professions: our chosen discipline and the educational community. As a result, there should be a natural connection between those two professions.

Halpern et al. (1998) pointed out that scholarship has not been associated with the teaching enterprise in the past half century. Rather, the emphasis in scholarly attainment has focused on producing new knowledge in a way that divorced it from pedagogy. Since the publication of Boyer's (1990) reconsideration of scholarship, psychologists have striven to bring pedagogy and scholarship together.

The task remains of defining those behaviors associated with the scholarship of teaching and pedagogy that institutions will recognize as valuable contributions to the academy; that is, what will earn tenure and promotion. Clearly, the traditional scholarship of discovery with publications in peer-reviewed journals remains the most obvious, but not the only, path to tenure and promotion.

A two-pronged path that is highly relevant to the present discussion involves the scholarship of pedagogy and the scholarship of teaching. The scholarship of pedagogy includes research on teaching and learning at all levels. This approach can differ little from the scholarship of discovery, although it extends into application as well. Based on its roots, one could regard psychology as the science of learning. Consequently, the scholarship of pedagogy falls firmly within the realm of psychological inquiry. In a different vein, the scholarship of teaching involves original contributions to teaching per se that have an impact on other teachers (Halpern et al., 1998; Reis-Bergan, 2002).

Reis-Bergan has cogently pointed out the difference between the scholarship of teaching and scholarly teaching. Scholarly teaching builds on existing knowledge, but it may not involve expertise in the domain of interest, or the scholarly teacher may not make it available for peer review. As Reis-Bergan noted, the scholarly teacher has significant impact on students, whereas the teacher as scholar affects the teaching profession.

Exactly what constitutes such scholarship has generated discussion, but the principles are fairly simple. The scholarship of teaching and of pedagogy both comprise those qualities that constitute good science: it is objective, data driven, verifiable, public, and peer reviewed. Other writers add further characteristics, specifying that scholarship involves self-reflection, relates to discipline-specific knowledge, shows innovation, and has significant impact (Diamond & Adam, 1995; Glassick, Huber, & Maeroff, 1997; Reis-Bergan, 2002).

Applying the Criteria for Scholarship

It is hard to believe that any conscientious teacher of psychology has not developed novel techniques or adapted existing pedagogical techniques in the classroom. Whenever we, as teachers, implement new strategies to enhance student learning, we are taking the first steps toward the scholarship of pedagogy. The most obvious way to move from scholarly teaching to the scholarship of pedagogy and of teaching is through dissemination, as with conference presentations and publication in peer-reviewed journals.

The journal of the Society for the Teaching of Psychology (STP), *Teaching of Psychology* (*ToP*), is the most obvious peer-reviewed publication devoted to the scholarship of pedagogy and learning for psychologists. *ToP* fields articles ranging from quite narrow pedagogical techniques to general articles of broad impact. A consistent feature of *ToP* articles is assessment of the activity. Historically, student evaluations of an innovation have been sufficient for identifying the success of the approach, but a manuscript with data on learning outcomes will have more impact. *ToP*'s stated policy now favors data on student learning. Manuscripts without adequate assessment of learning outcomes will not pass muster in the journal.

Publishing in *ToP* requires the same assiduous attention to detail required for any high-level peer-reviewed journal. Lack of such attention will obviate publication. The acceptance rate for journal articles is less than 20 percent, but the editorial process emphasizes working with authors to produce publishable manuscripts. Manuscripts must (a) contain literature reviews that indicate how the manuscript relates to work previously published, (b) address important practical or theoretical issues, (c) provide adequate documentation of results and generate a discussion of strengths and limitations of the innovation, and (d) conform fastidiously to the style set forth in the *Publication Manual of the American Psychological Association* (5th ed., American Psychological Association, 2001).

When high-quality, pedagogically oriented projects do not meet the criteria for publication in *ToP*, there are other options. Specifically, STP's Office of Teaching Resources in Psychology (OTRP) offers a peer-reviewed forum for manuscripts that are not as empirically based as those that appear in *ToP*. For instance, Project Syllabus proffers a set of exemplary syllabi in virtually every course in the psychology curriculum. If accepted by the OTRP editor, the syllabus will appear on the STP website. Project

Syllabus may allow the instructor to illustrate the application of knowledge as a form of scholarship.

This activity goes beyond good teaching in that the innovation is evaluated by professionals and made public, two important criteria for the scholarship of pedagogy and teaching. Resources made available on OTRP can have notable impact: The OTRP website received over 100,000 hits during the 2003–4 academic year and over 70,000 downloads.

Teachers of psychology who submit materials to OTRP need to remember that the focus of materials published in OTRP is utilitarian. Theoretical justification for the project and the background literature are less important for resources in OTRP (Janet Carlson, personal communication, Aug. 10, 2004).

In Project Syllabus, submissions receive most positive reviews when they show creativity that separates them from other syllabi, when they are written clearly, and when they have a positive (rather than intimidating) tone (Jeanne Slattery, personal communication, Aug. 11, 2004). Unless the instructor produces a syllabus that meets these criteria and successfully progresses through the review process, it may reflect good teaching but will not reflect scholarship in its multifaceted definition.

Another plausible option for scholarship through STP is by means of the creation of electronic books that are available on the STP website. In the past few years, STP has fostered the development of several electronically published volumes. Peer review can be a component of such volumes; all proposals for such e-books receive scrutiny by the Society before acceptance. STP is likely to publish numerous other electronic books that will benefit psychology's teaching community.

For topics involving the scholarship of teaching that might not fit comfortably into *Teaching of Psychology*, in OTRP, or as an STP e-book, other outlets exist. For instance, the relatively new *Journal of Scholarship of Teaching and Learning* (*JoSTaL*) provides a broader look at the scholarship issues arising in higher education. As a peer-reviewed journal, *JoSTaL* provides an interesting forum for the ideas of many teachers of psychology. Much as in the case of *ToP*, manuscripts involve empirical reports of action research in the classroom, case studies, and other work involving the scholarship of teaching. Like other academic journals, *JoSTaL* reviews submissions based on the quality of a project and its ideas and on the appeal of the ideas for the likely audience. In addition, this journal specifically requires authors to reflect on the content of their work.

Less technical offerings are appropriate for academically oriented newsletters. For instance, STP's newsletter includes substantive articles that are of benefit to psychology teachers; relevant manuscripts are those that, for a variety of reasons, may not be suitable for publication in *ToP*. These articles are reviewed for suitability, although they may not follow the protocol of review beyond the editor's judgment.

Outside of psychology, other newsletters disseminate broader ideas developed by teachers. Magna Publications publishes several newsletters pertinent to the scholarship of teaching and learning, including *The Teaching Professor*, *Online Classroom*, and *Distance Education Report*. As their titles suggest, these periodicals retain a broader aspect than single-discipline publications like *ToP*. Guidelines for these outlets specify that writing should be more informal and accessible than is often the case with academic journals. (Making life easier for psychologists, these publications request that references appear in APA format.)

What Counts as Scholarship?

Halpern et al. (1998) identified criteria for scholarship, as noted previously. The development of classroom-based action research that is ultimately published or presented at a professional conference fulfills these criteria. The extent to which tenure and promotion committees regard such work as sufficient is another matter entirely. Rice (1991) traced the change in the definition of scholarship since the Second World War. Readers will not be astonished to learn that denizens of the academic world have created a fairly myopic definition of scholarship – the creation of new knowledge, called the scholarship of discovery by Boyer (1990).

How does the expanded definition discussed by Halpern et al. (1998) fit into the picture? The answer is highly contextual, depending in large part on the culture and the mission of a college or university. Some institutions define published manuscripts as appropriate only when a certain number of peers have evaluated the paper. Members of a tenure and promotion committee would thus view articles in *Teaching of Psychology* as scholarly, although such publications might receive less weight than more theoretically-based articles in nonteaching journals. At such universities, presentations at professional conferences receive minimal recognition and presentations at teaching-oriented conferences count even less. Fortunately, schools that place a premium on teaching, usually smaller liberal arts colleges, often recognize the importance of pedagogical research for their students and for the wider academic community.

The status of e-books is still evolving. For instance, STP's *The Many Faces of Psychological Research in the 21st Century* (Halonen & Davis, 2001) is an edited volume on the varieties of research in our discipline. The volume contains scholarly chapters but it is in an electronic format and was not published by a traditional academic press. It is likely that as STP's experience and reputation as an e-publisher grows, its offerings will attain greater status. Because of the increasing prevalence of online journals, academics will undoubtedly accord greater status to electronic publication.

Conclusion

The paramount characteristic that defines the scholarship of teaching and pedagogy is its quality. Peer evaluation guarantees that this scholarship will be as rich in quality as any other form of scholarship. As scholars produce their work, however, they must attend to the type of scholarship they create and identify the appropriate forum providing the best match with the scholarship. For instance, in STP's flagship publication, *Teaching of Psychology*, emphasis rests on work that has been empirically validated. Within this context, articles in *ToP* fall into the domain of scholarship of pedagogy. On the other hand, the various teaching handbooks that have appeared rely less on empirical assessment than on cogent presentation of ideas and pedagogical techniques. Similarly OTRP offers many resources of a very practical nature. Such work often falls in the realm of the scholarship of teaching.

The STP e-books that have grown in number reveal a different perspective. They often reflect larger issues in teaching rather than specific empirical articles or explications of innovations in teaching techniques. For example, the three volumes of *Essays from e-xcellence in teaching* on the STP website comprise diverse, provocative essays about teaching.

Each forum has a particular goal, and its audience has certain expectations regarding what it will find. The various outlets specify the nature of acceptable work, and authors must work within the paradigm of each venue. The differences across outlets point to the diversity that constitutes scholarship within the expanded rubric fostered by Boyer (1990). Fortunately for scholars who have adopted this broad perspective of scholarship, scholarship emerges in vastly different forms, with the new scholarship being comparably rigorous in relation to traditional forms of scholarship.

The number of periodicals, websites, and other outlets that focus on the scholarship of teaching and pedagogy has grown notably in the past decade and is likely to continue to increase. These outlets will form a congenial home for teaching-related scholarship.

References

American Psychological Association. (2001). *Publication manual of the American Psychological Association* (5th ed.). Washington, DC: Author.

Boyer, E. L. (1990). *Scholarship reconsidered: Priorities of the professorate.* Princeton, NJ: The Carnegie Foundation for the Advancement of Teaching.

Diamond, R., & Adam, B. (1995). *Recognizing faculty work: Reward system for the year 2000. New directions for higher education.* San Francisco: Jossey-Bass.

Glassick, C. E., Huber, M. T., & Maeroff, G. I. (1997). *Scholarship assessed.* San Francisco: Jossey-Bass.

Halonen, J. S., & Davis, S. F. (eds.) (2001). *The many faces of psychological research in the 21st century.* Retrieved Aug. 16, 2004, from the Society for the Teaching of Psychology website: http://teachpsych.lemoyne.edu/teachpsych/faces/script/index.html

Halpern, D. F., Smothergill, D. W., Allen, M., Baker, S., Baum, Cy., Best, D., Ferrari, J., Geisinger, K. F., Gilden, E. R., Hester, M., Keith-Spiegel, P., Kierniesky, N. C., McGovern, T. V., McKeachie, W. J., Prokasy, W. F., Szuchman, L. T., Vasta, R., & Weaver, K. A. (1998). Scholarship in psychology: A paradigm for the twenty-first century. *American Psychologist, 53,* 1292–7.

Mathie, V. A., Buskist, W., Carlson, J. F., Davis, S. F., Johnson, D. E., & Smith, R. A. Expanding the boundaries of scholarship in psychology through teaching, research, service, and administration. *Teaching of Psychology, 31,* 233–41.

Reis-Bergan, M. (2002). On the distinction between the scholarship of teaching and scholarly teaching. In W. Buskist, V. W. Hevern, & G. W. Hill (eds.), *Essays from e-xcellence in teaching, 2002* (ch. 12). Retrieved Nov. 3, 2004, from the Society for the Teaching of Psychology website: http://teachpsych.lemoyne.edu/teachpsych/eit/index.html

Rice, R. E. (1991). The new American scholar: Scholarship and the purposes of the university. *Metropolitan Universities, 1,* 7–18.

Schulman, L. S. (2000). From Minsk to Pinsk: Why a scholarship of teaching and learning? *The Journal of Scholarship of Teaching and Learning, 1,* 48–52.

3

Psychology Curricula and the New Liberal Arts

Ψ

Thomas V. McGovern
Arizona State University West

In this brief history of undergraduate psychology education, I offer synopses of:

1. American higher education
2. Evolution of disciplinary curricula
3. Courses versus learning outcomes for diverse students, and
4. Postmillennial and postdisciplinary liberal arts.

Teacher–scholars and program developers will find theoretical conceptualizations, historical and empirically based models, and blue-ribbon panel recommendations for best practices in Lloyd and Brewer (1992); Brewer et al. (1993); McGovern (1992, 1993, 2004); McGovern and Brewer (2003, 2005); McGovern and Hawks (1984, 1986, 1988); and McGovern, Furumoto, Halpern, Kimble, and McKeachie (1991). Three edited texts on the curriculum, pedagogy, and assessment are Davis and Buskist (2002); Dunn, Mehrotra, and Halonen (2004); and Puente, Matthews, and Brewer (1992). *Teaching of Psychology* devoted three special editions to undergraduate psychology in the next decade (Morris, 1982), writing across the curriculum (Nodine, 1990), and critical thinking (Halpern & Nummedal, 1995).

American Higher Education

For Rudolph (1977), "curricular history is American history and therefore carries the burden of revealing the central purposes and driving directions of American society" (p. 24). Since the mid-seventeenth century, undergraduate education has combined liberal arts learning and preparation for specific vocational interests. Veysey (1973) concluded that after higher education diversified institutional missions and degrees during the nineteenth century, three catalytic forces crystallized during the Progressive era

(1870–1910) and propelled the changes of the twentieth century. These often conflicting forces were pragmatic tradition, which dictated that higher education's professional programs advance its utilitarian needs; increasingly sophisticated scientific knowledge and methods that fostered widespread expectations for empirical arguments to inform decision-makers; and public belief that the liberal arts shaped moral character for an articulate citizenry. I link these forces to specific milestones: creation of land grant institutions (1862; 1890), graduate research university specialization models and their mirror images in the undergraduate "major" (1875–), advent of professional societies and disciplinary associations (1890–1920), Wisconsin concept of "service to the community" and extended education programs (1904–), and creation of urban and municipal universities (1920–) that elevated the arts, social sciences, and human services professional programs.

After the Second World War, similar forces kicked into high gear again to include more and diverse peoples in new programs, and then to deal with the intended and unintended curricular consequences: the GI Bill (1945), community colleges (1960–), Civil Rights and Women's Movements (1960s–), proliferation of courses and unstructured curricula (1970s), general education debates and the cultural canon wars (1980–), external demands for accountability and assessment of student learning outcomes (1985–), distance education and technological changes to pedagogy (1990–), and education for global societies (2000–).

In the new millennium, teacher–scholars debated how to create, communicate, apply, and integrate knowledge in an information society with multiple discourse community audiences. We lamented having too few schemas and literacies to synthesize a plethora of information and its dizzying transformations. Psychologists spent the twentieth century constructing their disciplinary paradigm within the scientific tradition; twenty-first century curricular derivatives now are less clear.

Evolution of Disciplinary Curricula

Ratcliff (1997) analyzed "discipline" thus:

> Disciplines can provide a conceptual framework for understanding what knowledge is and how it is acquired. Disciplinary learning provides a logical structure to relationships between concepts, propositions, common paradigms, and organizing principles. Disciplines develop themes, canons, and grand narratives to join different streams of research in the field and to provide meaningful conceptualizations and frameworks for further analysis . . . impart truth criteria . . . set parameters on the methods employed in discovering and analyzing knowledge . . . (p. 14)

Calkins (1910), Sanford (1910), and Whipple (1910) audited the psychology curriculum and began a tradition of mapping undergraduate education via catalog studies: Henry (1938); Sanford and Fleishman (1950); Daniel, Dunham, and Morris (1965); Lux and Daniel (1978); and Perlman and McCann (1999a, 1999b). Like other academic faculties, psychologists supplemented their evolving canon of required courses with special topics from their research. They resisted a splintering effect by periodically sharpening their vocabulary, principles, methods, and preferred modes of inquiry. The Cornell Conference (Buxton et al., 1952), the Michigan Conference (McKeachie & Milholland, 1961), Kulik (1973), the APA/Association of American Colleges Project on Liberal Learning, Study-in-Depth, and the Arts and Sciences Major (McGovern et al., 1991), and the St. Mary's College of Maryland Conference (McGovern, 1993) examined the central tendencies of what is now the most popular, single-discipline major in higher education. In 2001–2, 76,671 undergraduates received baccalaureate degrees in psychology ("Almanac," 2004), with no single curriculum for undergraduate education in the discipline.

Perlman and McCann (1999a) summarized the structures of the undergraduate curriculum in their review of 500 sampled catalogs:

> The Cornell report's (Buxton et al., 1952) emphasis on teaching psychology as a scientific discipline in the liberal arts tradition remains current. The required core as recommended by the St. Mary's report (Brewer et al., 1993) as implemented by departments seems to cover "both natural science and social science aspects of psychology." (p. 439, pp. 175–6)

In a companion piece on course content, Perlman and McCann (1999b) concluded:

> Many frequently offered courses have been found for decades and 13 such courses first listed by Henry (1938) are in the present Top 30. Some courses are slowly being replaced. Thus, the curriculum reflects both continuity and slow change, perhaps due to the time that it takes for theory, research, and discourse to define new subdiscipline areas or perhaps due to department inertia and resistance to modifying the curriculum. (p. 181)

Their comparative tables tracking historical changes are especially informative.

Courses versus Learning Outcomes

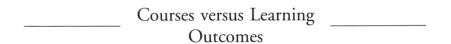

Proliferation of courses and unstructured requirements in the 1970s led to heated debates in the mid-1980s about general education and about assessment and accountability mandates. Based on recommendations from the APA/AAC project (McGovern et al., 1991) and the Saint Mary's Conference (Halpern et al., 1993; McGovern, 1993), the APA approved the *Quality Principles for Undergraduate Psychology Education* (McGovern & Reich, 1996). After continuing work by many members of the Society for the Teaching of Psychology, the Board of Educational Affairs endorsed the Undergraduate Psychology Major Learning Goals and Outcomes (Halonen, 2002); Dunn et al. (2004) spotlighted best practices in assessment for undergraduate program renewal.

As part of an interdisciplinary project on liberal learning, McGovern et al. (1991) identified eight common goals for psychology curricula: knowledge base, thinking skills, language skills, information-gathering and synthesis skills, research methods and statistical skills, interpersonal skills, history of psychology, and ethics and values. Halpern et al.'s (1993) desired outcomes included: knowledge base (content areas, methods, theory, and history); intellectual skills (thinking, communication, information-gathering and synthesis skills, and quantitative, scientific, and technological skills); and personal characteristics (interpersonal and intrapersonal skills, motivation, ethics, and sensitivity to people and cultures). This study group advocated a multimethod, matrix approach to assessment, using data from archives, classroom assessments, standardized testing, course-embedded measures, portfolio analyses, interviews, external examiners, and performance-based strategies.

The Undergraduate Psychology Major Learning Goals and Outcomes (Halonen, 2002) specified 48 student learning outcomes for 10 common goals organized into two categories: knowledge, skills, and values consistent with the science and application of disciplinary psychology (Goals 1 to 5), and those consistent with liberal arts education that are further developed by psychology (Goals 6 to 10). The five expectations for student learning of the discipline included: knowledge of major concepts, theoretical perspectives, empirical findings, and historical trends; understanding the applications of the research methods of design, data analysis, and interpretation in psychology; capacity to use critical and creative thinking, skeptical inquiry, and the scientific approach to solving problems related to behavior and mental processes; demonstrated ability to apply psychological principles to personal, social, and organizational issues; and capacity to weigh evidence, tolerate ambiguity, act ethically, and reflect values of psychology as a disciplined science. The five liberal arts goals included: information competencies and ability to use computers and technology; effective communication using various formats; understanding and respect for the complexities of sociocultural and international diversity; insight into one's own and others' behavior and mental processes with effective strategies of self-management and self-improvement; and knowing how to implement psychological knowledge, skills, and values in various occupational pursuits and settings. This differentiation between discipline-based outcomes and those outcomes that synergize with broader liberal arts education hearkens back to McKeachie and Milholland (1961), who first articulated goals for diverse learners. We may no longer have course-content driven curricula; outcomes-based programs lead directly to my final topic in this review.

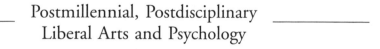

Postmillennial, Postdisciplinary Liberal Arts and Psychology

Higher education debates continue about the nature and forms of general education and students' areas of concentration. Schneider and Schoenberg (1998) saw the emerging liberal arts as: "acquiring intellectual skills or capacities," "understanding multiple modes of inquiry and approaches to knowledge," "developing societal, civic, and global knowledge," "gaining self-knowledge and grounded values," with a "concentration and integration of learning in a major" (pp. 7–8). The Greater Expectations National Panel (2002) proposed that a contemporary liberal arts curriculum should prepare all students for successful careers, enriched lives, and engaged US and global citizenship; develop self-directed, integrative, intentional learners who are reflective about their educations;

be based on a practical liberal education in which students apply their learning in multiple ways to complex problems; be characterized by diversity of perspectives; be informed by technology and develop information literacy; and set high standards of performance, without prescribing a standardized path.

Responding to such daunting, committee-based definitions, I find Nussbaum's (1997) classical defense of liberal education more compelling. Her interdisciplinary analyses excavated the roots of the sciences, social sciences, and humanities in the Greek and Roman academies. All apply directly to psychology's recently defined outcomes, yet prescribed no formulaic requirements. Socrates' critically examined life accepted no belief or perspective as authoritative without reason's rigorous scrutiny and respectful arguments. Aristotle's reflective citizenship advocated interdependence as central for an increasingly pluralistic and global society. Greek and Roman emphases on narrative imagination fostered educated persons' capacity for empathy, being able to see the world through others' eyes and not just their own locally bound visions or experiences.

In the last chapter of *Measuring Up*, I wrote that "the rainbow demographics of American society, its complex problems, and the interconnectivity that persons create and technology enables all suggest the need for a twenty-first century, postdisciplinary liberal arts in higher education" (McGovern, 2004, p. 270). Interdisciplinary expectations, the recent APA statement on student learning outcomes, and the rich material in the following chapters of this book will be psychology faculty's challenge to integrate. We must create empathic and intellectually rich environments for students drawn to our faculty and courses of study, setting high expectations for them as they advance their lifelong learning. Curriculum was, is, and will continue to be the social construction of teacher–scholars.

REFERENCES

Almanac: Earned degrees conferred, 2001–2002. (2004, Aug. 27). *The Chronicle of Higher Education*, p. 22.

Brewer, C. L., Hopkins, J. R., Kimble, G. A., Matlin, M. W., McCann, L. I., McNeil, O. V., Nodine, B. F., Quinn, V. N., & Saundra. (1993). Curriculum. In T. V. McGovern (ed.), *Handbook for enhancing undergraduate education in psychology* (pp. 161–82). Washington, DC: American Psychological Association.

Buxton, C. E., Cofer, C. N., Gustad, J. W., MacLeod, R. B., McKeachie, W. J., & Wolfle, D. (1952). *Improving undergraduate instruction in psychology*. New York: Macmillan.

Calkins, M. W. (1910). The teaching of elementary psychology in colleges supposed to have no laboratory. *Psychological Monographs, 12* (4, Whole No. 51), 41–53.

Daniel, R. S., Dunham, P. J., & Morris, C. J. (1965). Undergraduate courses in psychology: 14 years later. *Psychological Record, 15*, 25–31.

Davis, S. F., & Buskist, W. (eds.) (2002). *The teaching of psychology: Essays in honor of Wilbert J. McKeachie and Charles L. Brewer*. Mahwah, NJ: Erlbaum.

Dunn, D. S., Mehrotra, C. M., & Halonen, J. S. (eds.) (2004). *Measuring up: Assessment challenges and practices for psychology*. Washington, DC: American Psychological Association.

Greater Expectations National Panel (2002). *Greater expectations: A new vision for learning as a nation goes to college*. Washington, DC: Association of American Colleges and Universities.

Halonen, J. S. (ed.) (2002). *Undergraduate psychology major learning goals and outcomes: A report.* Washington, DC: American Psychological Association. (Available at: www.apa.org/ed/pcue/taskforcereport2.pdf.)

Halpern, D. F., Appleby, D. C., Beers, S. E., Cowan, C. L., Furedy, J. J., Halonen, J. S., Horton, C. S., Peden, B. F., & Pittenger, D. J. (1993). Targeting outcomes: Covering your assessment concerns and needs. In T. V. McGovern (ed.), *Handbook for enhancing undergraduate education in psychology* (pp. 23–46). Washington, DC: American Psychological Association.

Halpern, D. F., & Nummedal, S. G. (eds.) (1995). Psychologists teach critical thinking [Special issue]. *Teaching of Psychology, 22* (1).

Henry, E. R. (1938). A survey of courses in psychology offered by undergraduate colleges of liberal arts. *Psychological Bulletin, 35,* 430–5.

Kulik, J. (1973). *Undergraduate education in psychology.* Washington, DC: American Psychological Association.

Lloyd, M. A., & Brewer, C. L. (1992). National conferences on undergraduate psychology. In A. E. Puente, J. R. Matthews, & C. L. Brewer (eds.), *Teaching psychology in America: A history* (pp. 263–84). Washington, DC: American Psychological Association.

Lux, D. F., & Daniel, R. S. (1978). Which courses are most frequently listed by psychology departments? *Teaching of Psychology, 5,* 13–16.

McGovern, T. V. (1992). Evolution of undergraduate curricula in psychology, 1892–1992. In A. E. Puente, J. R. Matthews, & C. L. Brewer (eds.), *Teaching psychology in America: A history* (pp. 13–38). Washington, DC: American Psychological Association.

McGovern, T. V. (1993). Transforming undergraduate psychology for the next century. In T. V. McGovern (ed.), *Handbook for enhancing undergraduate education in psychology* (pp. 217–38). Washington, DC: American Psychological Association.

McGovern, T. V. (2004). Liberal arts, diverse lives, and assessing psychology. In D. S. Dunn, C. M. Mehrotra, & J. S. Halonen (eds.), *Measuring up: Assessment challenges and practices for psychology* (pp. 259–75). Washington, DC: American Psychological Association.

McGovern, T. V., & Brewer, C. L. (2003). Undergraduate education. In D. K. Freedheim (ed.), *History of psychology* (pp. 465–81). Vol. 1 in I. B. Weiner (Editor-in-Chief), *Handbook of psychology.* New York: Wiley.

McGovern, T. V., & Brewer, C. L. (2005). Paradigms, narratives and pluralism in undergraduate psychology. In R. Sternberg (ed.), *Unity in psychology* (pp. 125–43). Washington, DC: American Psychological Association.

McGovern, T. V., Furumoto, L., Halpern, D. F., Kimble, G. A., & McKeachie, W. J. (1991). Liberal education, study in depth, and the arts and sciences major – Psychology. *American Psychologist, 46,* 598–605.

McGovern, T. V., & Hawks, B. K. (1984). Transitions and renewal of an undergraduate psychology program. *Teaching of Psychology, 11,* 70–5.

McGovern, T. V., & Hawks, B. K. (1986). The varieties of undergraduate experience. *Teaching of Psychology, 13,* 174–81.

McGovern, T. V., & Hawks, B. K. (1988). The liberating science and art of undergraduate psychology. *American Psychologist, 43,* 108–14.

McGovern, T. V., & Reich, J. N. (1996). A comment on the "Quality Principles." *American Psychologist, 51,* 252–5.

McKeachie, W. J., & Milholland, J. E. (1961). *Undergraduate curricula in psychology.* Glenview, IL: Scott, Foresman.

Morris, C. G. (ed.) (1982). Undergraduate psychology in the next decade [Special Issue]. *Teaching of Psychology, 9* (1).

Nodine, B. F. (ed.) (1990). Psychologists teach writing [Special issue]. *Teaching of Psychology*, *17* (1).

Nussbaum, M. C. (1999). *Cultivating humanity: A classical defense of reform in liberal education.* Cambridge, MA: Harvard University Press.

Perlman, B., & McCann, L. I. (1999a). The most frequently listed courses in the undergraduate psychology curriculum. *Teaching of Psychology*, *26*, 177–82.

Perlman, B., & McCann, L. I. (1999b). The structure of the undergraduate psychology curriculum. *Teaching of Psychology*, *26*, 171–6.

Puente, A. E., Matthews, J. R., & Brewer, C. L. (eds.) (1992). *Teaching psychology in America: A history.* Washington, DC: American Psychological Association.

Ratcliff, J. L. (1997). What is a curriculum and what should it be? In J. G. Gaff, J. L. Ratcliff, & Associates (eds.), *Handbook of the undergraduate curriculum: A comprehensive guide to purposes, structures, practices, and change* (pp. 5–29). San Francisco: Jossey-Bass.

Rudolph, F. (1977). *Curriculum: A history of the American undergraduate course of study since 1636.* San Francisco: Jossey-Bass.

Sanford, E. C. (1910). The teaching of elementary psychology in colleges and universities with laboratories. *Psychological Monographs*, *12* (4, Whole No. 51), 54–71.

Sanford, F. H., & Fleishman, E. A. (1950). A survey of undergraduate psychology courses in American colleges and universities. *American Psychologist*, *5*, 33–7.

Schneider, C. G., & Schoenberg, R. (1998). *Contemporary understandings of liberal education.* Washington, DC: Association of American Colleges & Universities.

Veysey, L. (1973). Stability and experiment in the American undergraduate curriculum. In C. Kaysen (ed.), *Content and context: Essays on college education* (pp. 1–63). New York: McGraw-Hill.

Whipple, G. M. (1910). The teaching of psychology in normal schools. *Psychological Monographs*, *12* (4, Whole No. 51), 2–40.

4

The Society for the Teaching of Psychology: A Psychology Teacher's Best Friend

Ψ

G. William Hill IV
Kennesaw State University

Established in 1945 as one the original 19 divisions of the American Psychological Association (APA), the Society for the Teaching of Psychology (STP) is the oldest and most active national organization for psychology teachers. Although STP struggled with its identity in its early years (see Wight & Davis, 1992), throughout its history STP has played a leadership role in advancing excellence in the teaching of psychology. STP's mission focuses on developing and disseminating resources for teachers, collaborating with other organizations, advocating for the needs of teachers at all educational levels, and promoting the scholarship of teaching and learning (see STP bylaws, STP, 2004a).

Membership in STP

Although STP is still affiliated with APA as its Division 2, a common misconception is that one must be an APA member to join STP and that non-APA members lack voting privileges. STP initiated affiliate membership in 1985 for non-APA members and in 1990 affiliate members were given voting rights. The 1999 bylaws eliminated the designation of "affiliate membership" (STP, 1999) and all STP members, regardless of APA membership status (including students, high-school teachers, and other individuals interested in the teaching of psychology), are now full members of STP.

However, because STP is an APA Division, there are a few limitations for non-APA STP members with respect to voting, offices they can hold, and Fellow status recognition. In concordance with APA bylaws, the only elected office that cannot be held by or voted on by a non-APA member are the STP representatives to the APA Council of Representatives (STP, 2004a). Because STP Fellow status is simultaneously Fellow status in APA, all Fellows must be APA members (STP, 2004a).

The current annual dues rate for STP membership is US$15 for students and $25 for nonstudents (STP, 2004b). Another misconception is the belief that APA receives some of this revenue. All dues income goes toward member benefits and services. Membership is an exceptional deal because a major membership benefit is an annual subscription to STP's journal *Teaching of Psychology* (*ToP*). Members receive a substantial savings on their *ToP* subscription compared to the non-STP member subscription rate.

Joining STP is easily accomplished by accessing the online membership application (STP, 2004b). Although currently applications must be mailed, STP plans to institute an online application and payment option in the near future.

Member-Only Benefits

Teaching of Psychology (*ToP*)

ToP evolved from the original STP Newsletter into a journal in 1974 (see Daniel, 1992, for a history of *ToP*). Published quarterly, *ToP* primarily includes articles reflecting the highest-quality scholarship of teaching and learning in psychology and has been recognized as one of the preeminent journals on pedagogy (Weimer, 1993).

Emphasizing a strong empirical research basis for its articles, *ToP* has four sections: *Topical Articles*, which address a wide variety of teaching issues; *Methods and Techniques*, focusing on innovative teaching activities and course content; *Faculty Forum*, short articles that center on techniques, commentary, or opinion; and *Computers in Teaching*, focusing on innovative uses of computers in teaching, evaluations of computer-assisted instruction, and software reviews (Beins, 2004). *ToP* also includes *The Generalist's Corner*, interviews with prominent researchers focusing on incorporating cutting-edge research into classroom teaching, *News Tips* (e.g., information on upcoming conferences, new resources for teachers), and *STP News* (e.g., STP President's column, official STP reports). Regardless of what you teach, *ToP* probably publishes articles related to your courses or teaching interests.

If you are a new subscriber to *ToP*, there are two resources for finding previously published articles relevant to your interests. *ToP*'s autumn issue includes an annotated bibliography for the past year. In addition, the STP Office of Teaching Resources in Psychology (OTRP) has a free downloadable database and index of all *ToP* articles through 2001 (Johnson, 2002).

STP Newsletter

Members of STP are mailed a copy of the biannual (fall and spring) *Newsletter of the Society for the Teaching of Psychology*. The newsletter includes up-to-date information on STP resources and initiatives, announcements of interest to teachers of psychology from other organizations dedicated to the teaching of psychology (e.g., the APA Education Directorate), and columns and commentary by the STP president and others. In recent years the newsletter has expanded its content to include invited short essays on teaching.

TOPNEWS-Online

TOPNEWS-Online is a monthly email sent to all STP members. Providing members with the most current information on initiatives and events sponsored both by STP and other organizations, it includes a brief description and online links to detailed information about new resources, grant opportunities, and upcoming conferences of interest to psychology teachers.

———————— STP's Free Services ————————

In his well-known APA presidential address, George Miller charged psychologists to "give psychology away" through sharing research with the public and addressing how it is applicable to everyday lives (Miller, 1969). This philosophy guides STP's development and distribution of resources for psychology teachers, especially since the advent of the internet. I have summarized current STP online resources below. However, because STP is continuously adding new resources, I encourage you to visit and review the news notices on the STP Home Page regularly (http://teachpsych.lemoyne.edu/teachpsych/div/divindex.html).

Online Resources

Office of Teaching Resources in Psychology (OTRP). In 1992, STP established OTRP to coordinate the development and dissemination of resources for psychology teachers. Initially, resources were only available by mail order and required a fee for printing and mailing costs. In 1997, STP unveiled the OTRP website (http://www.lemoyne.edu/OTRP/index.html). This website includes free downloadable copies, regardless of STP membership status, of most current OTRP resources as well as information on other STP services for psychology teachers (i.e., Departmental Consulting Service, which is a joint service with the APA Education Directorate; Instructional Resource Awards, annual competitive grants for the development of instructional resources; and a faculty mentoring service).

All OTRP resources are peer-reviewed prior to posting. Representative current resource areas include: Project Syllabus (a repository of exemplary syllabi for a wide variety of psychology courses), advising, teaching diversity and cross-cultural issues, ethical issues in teaching, teaching history of psychology, teaching introductory psychology, and writing letters of recommendation.

STP Home Page. The STP Home Page (http://teachpsych.lemoyne.edu/teachpsych/div/divindex.html) also provides a rich resource for psychology teachers. In addition to posting information on current STP initiatives and developments, it includes content of more general interest such as the list of general and teaching-focused psychology conferences.

E-Books. For many years *ToP* was the only STP publication. However, the internet provided yet another opportunity for STP to publish and disseminate material through free downloadable online e-books. STP's first e-book was *The Many Faces of Psychological Research in the 21st Century* (Halonen & Davis, 2001). Three e-book volumes of essays on teaching, which collect the monthly E-xcellence in Teaching essays posted on the PsychTeacher discussion list, have followed (see http://teachpsych.lemoyne.edu/teachpsych/eit/index.html) and additional e-books are being developed, including *Preparing the New Psychology Professoriate: Training Graduate Students to Become Competent Teachers.*

PsychTeacher. In 1999, STP started a listserv discussion list open to all psychology teachers. Unlike other discussion lists that allow open posting of messages, PsychTeacher is a moderated list where messages are initially reviewed by a moderator, who acts as an editor to insure that messages meet list guidelines. Thus, the list keeps its focus on the teaching of psychology and avoids posting personal or commercial messages. Additional information on PsychTeacher, including subscription information, is available online at http://teachpsych.lemoyne.edu/teachpsych/div/psychteacher.html.

Conferences

Historically the only STP conference and workshop programming was its divisional hours at the APA Convention. Although STP continues to offer a significant block of teaching-related programming and coordinates the G. Stanley Hall lectures at the APA convention, it has expanded its programming offerings in recent years. STP has sponsored or co-sponsored a number of workshops on teaching (e.g., co-sponsoring with the APA Education Directorate the Preparing the New Professoriate preconference workshops at many regional psychology conferences; a preconference teaching workshop at the annual Society for Personality and Social Psychology meeting). In 2002, the American Psychological Society (APS) invited STP to assume co-sponsorship and coordination of the annual APS preconference teaching institute and to also offer teaching-related programming as part of the main APS convention. Finally, STP, the National Institute for the Teaching of Psychology, and the Kennesaw State University Center for Excellence in Teaching and Learning have co-sponsored a popular series of conferences on "best practices" in teaching psychology. These annual conferences focus on a specific issue or course in the psychology curriculum, with the first three in the series addressing assessment in psychology education, teaching introductory psychology, and teaching research methods and statistics.

Recognizing Excellence in Teaching and Scholarship

Through its affiliated Fund for Excellence in the Teaching of Psychology, STP annually recognizes outstanding teachers in four categories: university/four-year college (the Robert S. Daniel Award), high school (the Moffett Memorial Award), two-year colleges (currently unnamed), and graduate student teaching (the Wilbert McKeachie Early Career Award). These awards are bestowed annually at the APA Convention and recipients receive a cash award and plaque.

Because STP values and encourages the scholarship of teaching and learning, it also sponsors a poster award program at most regional psychology meetings and national and regional teaching conferences. The poster award recognizes an outstanding poster exemplifying the scholarship of teaching and learning with a cash prize and an invitation to present the poster as part of STP's poster session at the annual APA convention.

Joining a Community of Psychology Teachers

Given all the free STP resources, you might be inclined to consider STP membership as unnecessary. If this is your conclusion, I want to suggest several reasons for you to reconsider. First, STP needs dues-paying members. Realistically, without dues income STP can lose some of its ability to develop and disseminate free resources. Although many resources were developed by volunteer efforts of faculty like yourself, dues funding is critical to underwrite STP's operations.

Another important reason to join is the opportunity to connect with a community of dedicated psychology teachers. Development and coordination of STP's initiatives and resources require membership involvement, and without them STP's contributions cannot continue indefinitely. Many faculty dedicated to the scholarship of teaching often find themselves either isolated at smaller institutions or within departments that place a greater emphasis on more traditional scholarship. Thus, another benefit of getting involved in STP is the opportunity to develop lasting friendships and collaborations.

Because of the extensive information found on STP's homepage, getting involved is easier than you think. All you have to do is review the current list of officers, committee chairs, and task force chairs and email one of them about your interest. Another possibility is to attend one of STP's workshops or conferences. Because many STP members attend these sessions, you have the opportunity to meet them and discover shared interests. I invite you to act today and join STP.

REFERENCES

Beins, B. C. (2004). *Types of articles published.* Retrieved Aug. 21, 2004, from the Teaching of Psychology homepage: http://www.ithaca.edu/beins/top/top.htm

Daniel, R. S. (1992). *Teaching of Psychology,* the journal. In A. E. Puente, J. R. Matthews, & C. L. Brewer (eds.), *Teaching psychology in America: A history* (pp. 433–52). Washington: American Psychological Association.

Halonen, J. S., & Davis, S. F. (eds.) (2001). *The many faces of psychological research in the 21st century.* Retrieved Aug. 21, 2004, from the Society for the Teaching of Psychology website: http://teachpsych.lemoyne.edu/teachpsych/faces/script/index.html

Johnson, D. E. (2002). *Teaching of Psychology database & index.* Retrieved Aug. 21, 2004, from the Office of Teaching Resources in Psychology Online website: http://www.lemoyne.edu/OTRP/ToP/ToPdb.html

Miller, G. A. (1969). Psychology as a means of promoting human welfare. *American Psychologist, 24,* 1063–75.

Society for the Teaching of Psychology. (1999). *By-laws of the Society for the Teaching of Psychology*. Retrieved Aug. 21, 2004, from the STP: Operations, Reports & Documents webpage: http://teachpsych.lemoyne.edu/teachpsych/div/documents.html

Society for the Teaching of Psychology. (2004a). *By-laws of the Society for the Teaching of Psychology*. Retrieved Aug. 21, 2004, from the STP: Operations, Reports & Documents webpage: http://teachpsych.lemoyne.edu/teachpsych/div/documents.html

Society for the Teaching of Psychology. (2004b). *How to Join (or Renew Membership in) the Society for the Teaching of Psychology*. Retrieved Aug. 21, 2004, from the STP homepage: http://teachpsych.lemoyne.edu/teachpsych/div/howjoin.html

Weimer, M. (1993, Nov./Dec.). The disciplinary journals on pedagogy. *Change, 25* (6), 44–51.

Wight, R. D., & Davis, S. F. (1992). Division in search of self: A history of APA Division 2, the division of the teaching of psychology. In A. E. Puente, J. R. Matthews, & C. L. Brewer (eds.), *Teaching psychology in America: A history* (pp. 365–84). Washington: American Psychological Association.

part II

Ψ

Preparing for Teaching

This section includes three chapters on important activities involved in getting ready to teach a class – course planning and syllabus considerations, selecting a text and courseware, and first day of class activities.

5

Options for Planning a Course and Developing a Syllabus

Ψ

Anne-Marie Suddreth & Amy T. Galloway
Appalachian State University

One of the unique benefits of teaching is that teachers create their own workplace atmosphere in the classroom. Unlike many other professions in which new employees feel pressure to conform to the preexisting workplace culture, in the classroom your behavior and approach to your work determine how relaxed or structured your students perceive your class to be. In other words, you can tailor your workplace environment so that it fits comfortably with your personality.

You begin creating your workspace from the time you start planning your course (Forsyth, 2003). In this chapter, we provide practical suggestions for planning your class and syllabus. We focus on three general points: course content, class environment, and grading. Although no amount of planning can prepare you for everything that can (and will) happen in your class, following these suggestions provides you with a solid foundation.

Course Content

In planning a new course, many accomplished teachers begin by deciding what they want their students to gain from the course (McKeachie, 2002). One technique for achieving your student learning outcomes is to develop a theme (or two, or three) for the class (Davis, 1993). A theme is an overarching idea that you can use to tie your classes together conceptually. With proper repetition, explanation, and reiteration, it may just be the one idea your students take away from the class. For example:

1. Abnormal Psychology. What is abnormal is relative; abnormal only means "disordered" if it causes distress and impairment.

2. Social Psychology. Social Psychologists cannot predict what any given individual will do in a certain situation, but they can predict what most individuals are more likely to do in certain situations.
3. Cognitive Psychology. The brain strives for efficiency of thought.

You also may want to consider reading the American Psychological Association's list of learning goals and outcomes for suggestions of theme ideas (available at www.apa.org/ed/pcue/taskforcereport.pdf). After you determine your themes, consider making them explicit in your syllabus. Try to repeat them at least once in each class. Ask exam questions related to them. Ask your students to relate the day's topic to your theme during class or in homework.

It is also wise to avoid the common mistake of trying to cover too much material in a semester (Boice, 1990). How much is too much? Most of the time, the entire textbook is too much. Practical limitations require you to pick and choose which material to cover. Here are a few suggestions to get you started:

1. Find out from your department chair what you may be required to cover. Some topics are obvious; for example, obedience studies in a social psychology class, working memory in a cognitive class, and Freud in a personality class.
2. Look at your list of topics and note which ones you find personally most interesting. After all, if the material interests you, chances are you will make it interesting for your students. You will also enjoy your time in class more.
3. Review syllabi for the class from previous semesters. Make an effort to obtain and review syllabi from seasoned instructors and others whose teaching styles appeal to you. Note what topics they covered, how much time they devoted to each topic, and the format and assignments they used. Remember, a syllabus that does not appeal to you can be helpful as well.

Class Environment

In planning for your class it is helpful to visualize yourself in the classroom. What do you want your class time to be like? How do you picture a "typical" class period? Your responses to these questions may seem difficult to formulate if you are new to teaching. If so, think about what kind of classes you enjoyed being in as a student. How were your favorite classes organized? What made you feel comfortable and engaged as a student? Below are some more detailed points to consider for your classroom.

Think About How You Want to Present Your Material in Class

This process begins by first considering what you want students to learn (Bain, 2004). Some teachers are excellent lecturers, managing to engage their students effectively in a lecture format. Other teachers adopt an active learning approach with minimal lecture. Consider what alternatives or supplements to lecturing, such as group activities or demonstrations, you may wish to use, and what your comfort level with or interest in each may be. Each alternative has its own unique benefits for the classroom and challenges for the instructor. For example:

1. Discussion. How comfortable are you with leading a class discussion? For some teachers leading a discussion will take practice; other teachers seem to be very natural at effectively directing the flow of discussion.
2. Group work. What are your opinions of group work? Will you use it to evaluate students? If so, how? How will you monitor groups to make sure they are working effectively?
3. Video. Video is easy to present, to be sure, but how will you incorporate it into class material? Will you want to have students write about what they learned from the video? Will you test on video material or use it only as a demonstration?
4. Class activities. How much time do you want to devote to class activities? Would you prefer one highly involved class activity or shorter demonstration activities?

Consider How You Want to Structure Your Class

Although a degree of structure is a necessary element for a successful classroom experience, there is plenty of room for personal style and practicality to customize your class. There are dozens of possibilities, but consider two examples:

1. Each day of class follows the same structure: class business, review of old material, new material, alternative to lecture (i.e., discussion, group work, etc.), summary.
2. Each week or topic follows the same structure: one day of lecture, one day of supplementary material (articles, videos) and discussion, one day for review and quiz, then overview of new material.

Providing balance between structure and spontaneity will appeal to students who have preferences for one or the other. It is wise to plan what you will do if a particular topic takes longer than expected or what you will do if the class gets behind.

Grading

There are many ways to evaluate student performance, but we suggest that your assessment methods correspond to your course objectives (Bernstein & Lucas, 2003). In addition, practical considerations and personal style come into play when deciding what methods of evaluation you will use for grading. Consider the following issues:

1. Quizzes. Quizzes come in all shapes and sizes, such as more frequent quizzes that weigh less in the overall grading scheme, pop quizzes, or several big quizzes in place of "exams." Quizzes encourage students to keep up with the material; their preparedness, in turn, facilitates engagement during class. Additionally, quizzes provide frequent

opportunities for feedback to students. However, quiz construction, grading, and in-class review can be time consuming.

2. Exams. Do you want to follow the mid-term and final exam format? This format is less time-consuming for the instructor but may foster test anxiety for students. More frequent exams provide more frequent assessment and feedback and allow students to do poorly on one exam without failing the course. Consider, too, the exam review: Do you want to use class time for the review, give a written handout, or skip a review entirely?

3. Writing assignments. Writing assignments can foster critical thinking skills and provide a creative alternative to exams. To reduce subjectivity in grading written assignments, create a grading rubric and present it to the class to make your expectations clear. Also, be cognizant of the time it takes to grade written assignments. If you assign so many written assignments that you cannot return them in a timely manner, your students will not benefit, they will not be happy with you, and you will be constantly stressed by the accumulation of materials you need to grade.

4. Final papers and projects. Final papers and projects allow students to explore their own relevant interests and require them to synthesize concepts and facts they may have absorbed in class. Do you want them to give a presentation on it, as well? How will you grade it: Will you grade each element separately or give one final grade? Keep in mind that grading large projects is time-consuming and can be stressful as end of semester obligations pile up.

5. Out-of-class time. In most cases, you will be expecting your students to read class material. Do you want to give them credit for their efforts by offering a grade for their work? If so, how will you evaluate it?

Syllabus Nitty-Gritty

Many miscellaneous items can be included in your syllabus to make it more inclusive and helpful to your students (Appleby, 1994). We provide a list of points that you can or should note in your syllabus.

1. Contact information: your name, office number, phone number, email address, office hours, and website address (if applicable). Some departments will encourage giving your home phone number, others will not. If you have a preferred method for contact, state it.

2. Student learning objectives.

3. Required texts and supplemental readings.

4. Classroom rules (or etiquette): for example, turning off cellphones in class. You may also want to note that you expect your students to show respect for one another in class, particularly if you will be discussing sensitive topics.

5. Special needs: You may want to invite students with special needs to see you during office hours or after class if they would like to discuss their needs. This invitation conveys the idea that you will not pry but are willing to be accommodating if need be.

6. Class schedule: Consider your ideas about how your class will be structured. Do you want to give a day-by-day account of topics to be covered, or would you prefer to state it in a week-by-week format? You should include due dates and exam dates in the syllabus regardless of how you detail topic coverage.
7. Academic honesty policy.
8. It is a good idea to note that the instructor reserves the right to make changes to the syllabus as becomes necessary.

Conclusion

Creating a comfortable classroom is more than a luxury; it is a necessity. If you strive to be strict and organized down to the smallest detail when you are naturally a more go-with-the-flow individual, you may well end up with a mess in the classroom when you cannot maintain the structure you created. Likewise, if you are a very rule- and schedule-oriented person and you try to structure your class more loosely, you may become frustrated with the degree of uncertainty you may experience in your classroom. Thus, plan your class in such a way that you feel as confident and comfortable in your teaching role as possible.

REFERENCES

Appleby, D. C. (1994). How to improve your teaching with the course syllabus. In B. Perlmann, L. I. McCann, & S. H. McFadden (eds.), *Lessons learned: Practical advice for the teaching of psychology* (pp. 19–24). Washington, DC: American Psychological Society.

Bain, K. (2004). *What the best college teachers do.* Cambridge, MA: Harvard University Press.

Bernstein, D. A., & Lucas, S. G. (2003). Tips for effective teaching. In J. M. Darley, M. P. Zanna, & H. L. Roediger (eds.), *The compleat academic: A career guide* (2nd ed., pp. 79–116). Washington, DC: American Psychological Association.

Boice, R. (1990). *Advice for new faculty members.* Boston: Allyn & Bacon.

Davis, B. G. (1993). *Tools for teaching.* San Francisco: Jossey-Bass.

Forsyth, D. R. (2003). *The professor's guide to teaching: Psychological principles and practices.* Washington, DC: American Psychological Association.

McKeachie, W. J. (2002). *McKeachie's teaching tips: Strategies, research, and theory for college and university teachers* (11th ed.). Boston: Houghton Mifflin.

6

Selecting a Text and Using Publisher-Produced Courseware: Some Suggestions and Warnings

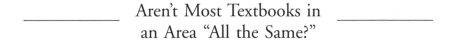

Andrew Christopher
Albion College

Selecting a textbook, particularly for a course you have never taught, can be as intimidating a process as it is an important process. Indeed, it may well be the case that the best predictor of student learning in a given course is the textbook used (McKeachie, 2002). The purpose of this chapter is to provide some suggestions for selecting a primary course textbook (not primary source readings), and how to integrate (or ignore) textbook supplements into your classroom teaching.

Aren't Most Textbooks in an Area "All the Same?"

I admit that when I try to familiarize myself with the texts available for a new course I am teaching, on the surface, they do look quite similar. However, such an impression is simply an example of the fallibility of human cognition. Several empirical studies strongly suggest that, irrespective of the course in question, texts differ in many ways. For example, Griggs and Marek (2001), in an examination of introductory psychology texts, found that although chapter topics and organization were similar across most texts, the texts were heterogeneous across core concepts, key terms, pedagogical aids, data graphs, critical thinking programs, reference citations, and level of difficulty. Such results are not limited to introductory texts. Christopher, Griggs, and Hagans (2000) found similar diversity among texts for social and abnormal content area courses (see also Jackson, Lugo, & Griggs, 2001; Marek & Griggs, 2001 for other research on textbook heterogeneity).

To me, perhaps the most important variable in selecting a textbook is finding one whose level of difficulty corresponds to the students' ability level.[1] Particularly when starting at a new school, it is hard to ascertain your students' capabilities (even after being in the same place for three years, I still find this consideration to be a challenge). Ask around and see what introductory texts are being used in your department (assume your more experienced colleagues can read students' ability level correctly). You can view an assessment of the level of difficulty for these texts at www.lemoyne.edu/OTRP/introtexts.html (Koenig, Daly, Griggs, Marek, & Christopher, 2004), and then use Griggs's (1999) formula for determining textbook difficulty level for texts used in other courses.

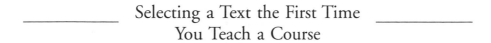

Selecting a Text the First Time You Teach a Course

The phrase "new prep" is one that can be particularly anxiety-provoking, especially for new faculty. Preparing for a new course is a multifaceted process in which choice of text is key. When teaching a course for the first time, select a limited number of texts to consider because too many choices can lead to overload and make a stressful situation even worse. To select your texts to review, rely on colleagues both at your institution and elsewhere who have taught the class. In addition, contact your local book representatives, tell them what information you want a textbook for the course to include, and allow them to "find" you texts to review. In limiting the number of texts to review, you may feel as though you are potentially "missing out" on the perfect text. Certainly, it can be comforting to have a plethora of supplementary texts at your disposal to make sure you do not run out of class material. However, the costs of overloading yourself with too many textbook options may minimize such benefits. Besides, as anyone who has taught a course can attest, you rarely need to worry about "running out" of material to cover in class (quite the opposite, actually). Although perhaps easier said than done, try to limit your choice to between five and seven textbooks your first time teaching a course. Certainly, as you revise and update the course, you will review other texts, and perhaps find that perfect one.

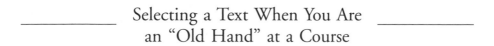

Selecting a Text When You Are an "Old Hand" at a Course

I must confess that outside of introductory psychology and statistics, I am not an "old hand" at much of anything when it comes to teaching. With that caveat in mind, I have changed texts in both of these classes when a couple of warning signs appeared. I suspect we all experience such warning signs, but we must be alert to what they are saying. I had used the same text in introductory psychology for six years, having taught at least one section of the course every semester but one. Then, last fall, something happened. The text came out in a new edition, and I found I really did not want to read the updated version (I did so, but not as intently as perhaps I should have). That semester, I had two sections of exceptionally bright and motivated students who asked a number of good questions, some of which I had actually encountered before. Yet, at times, I felt unsure of myself in some of my responses. In fact, after admitting on a few occasions that I did not know the answer to a question, I realized that upon searching for the answer I actually had known it, but could not recall it easily. Something had to change. The next semester, using a new introductory text, these sorts of incidents did not occur. Although I have no evidence to support this observation, it did seem as though a greater proportion of students came to class having read the material I asked them to read. When teachers have that little edge of enthusiasm on our side, our students pick up on it and behave accordingly.

What About All Those "Extras" That Come With the Text?

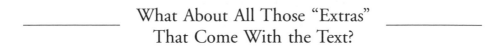

Student study guides, test banks, instructor manuals, prepared lecture outlines on PowerPoint are some of the supplements that are available with many texts, especially for introductory classes. I must admit that I am captivated by many of these "extras." However, I have found some caution must be taken to use these products effectively.

When I first began teaching, I figured study guides would be an excellent resource for students. After all, they usually include the major points covered in the text, and often contain questions that allow students to test their understanding of what they read in the text. However, it took me only until after the first test I ever gave to realize that I was badly mistaken about how well students use study guides. First, some students (often the less able ones, from my informal observations) use the study guide instead of the textbook. It is perhaps human nature for people to maximize outputs while minimizing inputs into a given task, and if students perceive a study guide will allow this process to occur, teachers should not be surprised or upset by such behavior. Second, students falsely assume that the questions contained in the study guide are representative of questions I will ask them on exams. Examine the study guide carefully to see if such questions are representative of test questions. If so, wonderful. If not, I am not sure it is advisable or even ethical to require the study guide. At the very least, students need to be warned that study guide questions are not always representative of actual test questions, as research suggests that students rely on aids that help them prepare for tests (e.g., Marek, Griggs, & Christopher, 1999).

Test banks contain potential exam questions, usually of multiple-choice format, which are drawn from information presented in the textbook. I have a love–hate relationship with test banks. On the one hand, when particularly pressed for time, I have liberally used test bank questions. However, the psychometric quality of exams I created directly from test banks has been, quite candidly, bad. Test banks have the potential to be a wonderful resource, depending on how a teacher uses them. With a little time and energy, it is possible to alter test bank questions to make them more reliable and valid indicators of student learning. To do so, as soon as possible after each class meeting, you should draft (not necessarily in final form) five or so test questions from your lecture and class discussions. The test bank can provide a starting point for doing so. Gradual construction of exam questions is particularly important when giving multiple-choice items on exams. The choice of plausible, appealing distractors is a critical but difficult task in constructing a psychometrically sound exam.

Instructor's manuals, like test banks, are two-edged swords. They can certainly help a teacher prepare for class, but rarely are they complete enough that the teacher can rely exclusively on them to carry them through a class. Instructor's manuals are generally structured solely around information contained in the text; thus, if the teacher wants to bring in material outside of the text, these manuals may be of minimal value. Likewise, instructor's manuals vary greatly in the extent of resources provided. A few manuals contain more information than can be covered in a year-long course, let alone a one-semester or one-quarter course! At the other extreme, some manuals contain outlines of the text material and perhaps a lone suggested activity. I always consult the instructors' manuals for any text I adopt, although I tend to use only a small portion of what they contain. Rather, as with test banks, I use them as a springboard to generate other ideas for class meetings.

On the surface, it would seem that "prepackaged lectures," perhaps in the form of PowerPoint slides, would be a huge timesaver. For some teachers, perhaps so. Certainly, such a resource can, like the others discussed, provide a starting point for an important task (e.g., organizing class sessions) in teaching a course. However, prepackaged lectures often follow the text verbatim, leaving the teacher with little wiggle room to include information not in the text or to skip over information that is in the text. Another problem is that, assuming students read the text, using prepackaged lectures will be largely a repeat of what they have already read in the text, not an extension of it. As with study guides, test banks, and instructor's manuals, "prepackaged lectures" can be an asset, but only if used as a cog in the wheel of teaching, not as the wheel itself.

Conclusion

In sum, there are many considerations in choosing a textbook and using the accompaniments available with each one. To complicate matters further, teachers must ponder such considerations with respect to their teaching styles. As is the case with most every other aspect of teaching, there is no "one size that fits all." I am reminded of Halonen's Corollary, "What works well for some teachers fails miserably for others" (Halonen, 2001). The choice of a textbook and use of publisher-produced courseware is no exception to this rule.

NOTE

1   Although beyond the scope of the current chapter, Griggs (1999) developed an objective formula to determine textbook difficulty level that can be used to assess the difficulty level of any textbook.

REFERENCES

Christopher, A. N., Griggs, R. A., & Hagans, C. L. (2000). Social and abnormal psychology textbooks: An objective analysis. *Teaching of Psychology, 27,* 180–9.

Griggs, R. A. (1999). Introductory psychology textbooks: Assessing levels of difficulty. *Teaching of Psychology, 26*, 248–53.

Griggs R. A., & Marek, P. (2001). Similarity of introductory psychology textbooks: Reality or illusion? *Teaching of Psychology, 28*, 254–6.

Halonen, J. (2001, Aug.). *Beyond sages & guides: A postmodern teacher's typology.* Harry Kirke Wolfe Lecture at the annual convention of the American Psychological Association, San Francisco, CA.

Jackson, S. L., Lugo, S. M., & Griggs, R. A. (2001). Research methods textbooks: An objective analysis. *Teaching of Psychology, 28*, 282–8.

Koenig, C. S., Daly, K. D., Griggs, R. A., Marek, P., & Christopher, A. N. (2004). *A compendium of introductory psychology texts (2003).* Retrieved March 10, 2004, from www.lemoyne.edu/OTRP/introtexts.html

Marek, P., & Griggs, R. A. (2001). Useful analyses for selecting a cognitive psychology textbook. *Teaching of Psychology, 28*, 40–4.

Marek, P., Griggs, R. A., & Christopher, A. N. (1999). Pedagogical aids in textbooks: Do college students' perceptions justify their prevalence? *Teaching of Psychology, 26*, 11–19.

McKeachie, W. J. (2002) *Teaching tips* (11th ed.). Boston: Houghton Mifflin.

7

The First Day of Class and the Rest of the Semester

Ψ

Sandra Goss Lucas

University of Illinois, Urbana-Champaign

What would your "best" class look like? Would students be enthusiastically discussing scintillating topics, while you subtly guided the discussion? Would students be sitting in a circle or working in a group? Would they be making presentations? Would they be sitting in rows, notebooks open, pens poised, as you presented material?

"Best" or "ideal" classes don't just magically occur. The seeds for an "ideal" class are planted on the first day of class. Although the first day of class is the most important day of the semester, many instructors use it as a "throw-away" class. Whether because of their own anxiety or because they don't see it as a "real" class session, few instructors prepare and plan for the first day as well as they do later class sessions. However, from your students' perspective the structure of the first class becomes the "norm" for the rest of the semester. Because most students have many instructors and because these instructors seldom explicitly state what student behaviors they value, students become experts at inferring instructor preferences. They take their biggest cue from how you present yourself the first day.

Establishing the normative structure of the class in the first week, makes it almost impossible to deviate from that structure. I learned this lesson the hard way. After "redoing" the first unit of my course, I got so caught up in the material that I ignored the fact that I was only lecturing. When I tried later to get students to participate in the course, I was unsuccessful: I had already established my students' expectations of the role they were to play in the class.

A typical first-day scenario involves the instructor walking into the classroom as the bell is ringing, distributing and reading the syllabus, and dismissing class. As a student in that class I would infer that: "The teacher doesn't really like to teach. The instructor is not interested in getting to know me. Class time is not important."

Contrast that with this first-day scenario: The instructor is in the classroom early. Her name, the course title/number, and an outline of that day's class are on the board or overhead. She greets students as they enter and makes small-talk with them before class begins. When class begins she introduces herself, telling students about herself, personally and academically. Students introduce themselves. She has all of the required materials to show to students. She asks for questions and scans the class with sufficient wait time. She covers the syllabus, which is well thought out and includes a list of "her" rules regarding arriving late for class, eating in class, attendance and so on. She shares with students why she is excited about teaching this course and begins to teach the material. She uses teaching techniques that will lead to the development of her "ideal" class. As a student in this class, I would infer that the material is exciting, my teacher cares about me as an individual, and class time is important.

Laying the Groundwork

Determining what your "ideal" class looks like involves deciding what your goals are for this class. If you are not sure of your goals or your goals are vague (such as, "doing a good job," "teaching the material," "being fair"), you might complete the Teaching Goals Inventory (TGI), which is available in print (Angelo & Cross, 1993), or online at www.uiowa.edu/~centeach/tgi/. The TGI is useful in itself, but may also stimulate you to think about additional goals. Once you know your goals, you need to decide how to translate them into classroom material and presentation style.

To have as smooth and exciting a first day as possible, there are some essential details to which you need to attend. At least a week before the new term begins, visit each classroom in which you will be teaching and familiarize yourself with its layout and systems. Pay attention to all the details. If the room is normally locked, be sure you have a key. Locate the switches for lighting, projection screens, temperature, and other aspects of the classroom environment that you will need to control during class. Does everything work properly? Is there a podium or table for your notes and other teaching materials? If not, contact the appropriate campus office to report malfunctions or request items you will need.

If the room is equipped with instructional technology, be sure you know how to use it. If you are not sure, ask about them in your department or campus office that services instructional equipment. Also ask for information on how to get keys or combinations for equipment that is in locked storage in your classroom. If you will be bringing your own projector, laptop computer, or other equipment, locate electrical outlets for plugging them in, and any connections you will need to gain access to a campus computer network. If you will need to use window shades to darken the room during audiovisual presentations, be sure they work properly.

If you plan to use a chalkboard, dry-erase board, or flip chart, confirm that there is chalk or felt-tipped pens, and just in case, plan to bring your own. Finally, be sure that there is enough seating in the room to accommodate the number of students enrolled in your class.

Consider, too, how well the room's seating fits your instructional style (Chism & Bickford, 2002). For example, many teachers feel that in small classes a circular seating arrangement is the most conducive to student–faculty communication (Billson & Tiberius, 1998). If you plan to create a seating circle, be sure that the chairs can be arranged in this way. If you are planning to have small-group discussions, determine how you will set up chairs during these activities – especially if the seats are connected or attached to the floor.

What Should I Say and Do?

Many students arrive on the first day of class with four questions in mind: "Will this class meet my needs?" "Is the teacher competent?" "Will the teacher be fair" and "Will the teacher care about me?" (Ericksen, 1974; Scholl-Buckwald, 1985). They may have other questions and concerns too, but it is vital to begin to address these four, through word and deed, during the first class session.

Introduce Yourself

You begin to answer these four questions when you introduce yourself. Telling students about your academic interests helps them to understand your connection with the course's subject matter. Telling students about your personal interests helps you become more human in their view. Be sure to let your students know how they should address you – as Dr., Ms., Professor, or by your first name.

Express Interest in the Students

For most instructors, having students actively participate in the class is important. Because many students' default expectation is that the course will be taught via lecture, it becomes vital that students are active the first day. Demonstrating that your class will be interactive can be achieved through a variety of activities during the first class.

In a smaller class, have students give their name (you can check attendance as they do so), any nickname, or abbreviated name they prefer, and some information about themselves. In larger classes, you can simply ask students to introduce themselves to those students seated nearby and exchange email addresses. If you plan to include group activities in your course, you might set the stage by asking pairs of students to interview each other for a few minutes and then introduce their partner to the class (Scholl-Buckwald, 1985).

You can also use "ice-breaker" activities to help students become more comfortable with each other, and with you, on the first day of class (e.g. Billison & Tiberius, 1998; Davis, 1993; Scholl-Buckwald, 1985). Put students into small groups and ask them to write a course-related question they would like you to answer. Collect the questions; respond to some, and save the rest for later in the course. This method helps students to meet each other and promotes cooperative learning (Erickson & Strommer, 1991). Alternatively, you could ask the small groups to respond to a course-related question such as "Which psychologist would you most like to have dinner with, and why?" or "What do you think psychologists do all day?"

You can also develop a list of attributes relating to your course content and ask students to circulate and find other students possessing those attributes (e.g., for an introductory course: Took an introductory psychology course in high school. Is a psychology major. Slept at least 8 hours last night. Ate breakfast this morning). Each student is allowed to sign next to only one item. This activity encourages students to meet as many other students as possible (for other suggestions for ice-breakers, see McGlynn, 2001).

Learning Students' Names

Start learning your students' names the very first class session. Knowing names makes the classroom more comfortable for you and the students. Trying to learn names, even if you make mistakes, shows students that you care about them. Also, students who feel a connection with instructors are more likely to do well in classes and approach teachers when they encounter difficulty (Erikson & Strommer, 1991).

Covering Content on the First Day

Depending on how much time you have available, you can begin your first lecture, or pose some questions for students to answer (perhaps in small groups), or perhaps even administer a short quiz designed to test students' knowledge of, or misconceptions about, the content of your psychology course. This experience helps to motivate students to begin their reading, and to come back to the next class.

Giving students a taste of the course material to come encourages them to leave that first class thinking about course content. Don't forget to remind students of their reading assignment for the next class, as well as of any other homework you have set for them – including the return of information cards or other material for which you may have asked.

Bringing class to an organized conclusion is important for every session, not just the first one. As the end of class approaches, don't just let time run out. Reserve a few minutes to summarize the main points you have covered and to say a few words about the material you will address the next time (Billison & Tiberius, 1998). You might even use the final 2 minutes to have your students jot down and turn in their reactions to the day's material. This exercise shows that you care what your students think and it also provides you with immediate feedback on the class (McKeachie, 2002).

Conclusion

It is normal to feel anxious on the first day of class. Once you and your students get to know each other and begin to form a working relationship over the first few class sessions, you will probably find that teaching becomes much less stressful, and a lot more enjoyable and productive. By preparing well for the first day of class you sow the seeds for many future "ideal" classes. Best of luck!

REFERENCES

Angelo, T., & Cross, K. P. (1993). *Classroom assessment techniques: A handbook for college teachers* (2nd ed.). San Francisco: Jossey-Bass.

Billson, J., & Tiberius, R. (1998). Effective social arrangements for teaching and learning. In K. Feldman & M. Paulsen (eds.), *Teaching and learning in the college classroom* (pp. 561–76). Boston: Pearson.

Chism, N., & Bickford, D. (eds.) (2002). *The importance of physical space in creating supportive learning environments: New directions for teaching and learning.* San Francisco: Jossey-Bass.

Davis, B. G. (1993). *Tools for teaching.* San Francisco: Jossey-Bass.

Ericksen, S. (1974). *Motivation for learning.* Ann Arbor, MI: University of Michigan Press.

Erickson, B., & Strommer, D. (1991). *Teaching college freshmen.* San Francisco: Jossey-Bass.

McGlynn, A. (2001). *Successful beginnings for college teaching: Engaging your students from the first day.* Madison, WI: Atwood Publishing.

McKeachie, W. J. (2002). *Teaching tips: Strategies, research, and theory for college and university teachers* (11th ed.). Boston: Houghton Mifflin.

Scholl-Buckwald, S. (1985). The first meeting of the class. In J. Katz (ed.), *Teaching as though students mattered: New directions for teaching and learning* (pp. 13–21). San Francisco: Jossey-Bass.

part III

Ψ

Techniques of Teaching: Approaches and Strategies

Part III contains 11 chapters centering on specific teaching and learning activities: lecturing, writing, team teaching, collaborative learning, problem-based learning, critical thinking, leading discussions, using classroom demonstrations, using technology in the classroom, using the internet in teaching, and using electronic databases.

8

The Classroom Lecture

Ψ

Stephen H. Hobbs
Augusta State University

Despite its antiquity and questionable utility, the live lecture has survived challenges from such innovations as the printing press, television, videotape, and the internet (McKeachie, 2002). Lectures continue to dominate the typical student's collegiate experience, and lecture preparation and delivery continue to dominate the teaching portion of the typical college professor's life. Classes are selected and promotions are earned, in part, on the basis of presentational reputation.

It is no wonder that perceived lecturing responsibilities can intimidate both novice and experienced instructors. Concerns range from "I'm not an expert on everything this course is supposed to cover, so what if I end up teaching something that's wrong?" to "What if this is the only psychology course these students ever take and I can't get them to even distinguish between pop and scientific psychology?"

The Lecture in Context

Consider a rather simple approach that can make lecturing less intimidating and a more effective learning tool: Carefully select the course's text (or collections of readings, journal articles, etc.), and make it, not the lectures, the center of the course. Establishing a focus on outside-of-class reading overcomes many of the commonly acknowledged limitations of the lecture, such as cognitive passivity, insufficient class time to cover necessary material, and wandering attention by even the best of students listening to the best of lecturers. In an extreme form of this approach, noted psychologist and educator Fred Keller (personal communication, 1978) would not permit students to attend his lectures unless they had passed a test over assigned readings on the scheduled lecture topic. Attendance was not required, but the lecture room was always full of students.

Some critics of a reading-dependent course will say that they can't get their students to read, or that student reading comprehension is too poor. Perhaps, but I think there are effective, although not perfect, means for dealing with these challenges. Unfortunately, to do so is beyond the scope of this short chapter. Other critics of a reading-dependent course may fear that it diminishes their instructional role. A changed role? Yes. A diminished one? Certainly not. Indeed, this approach can be very liberating.

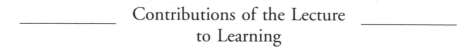

Contributions of the Lecture to Learning

No longer burdened by the must-cover-it-all mentality, the instructor is freed to use the lecture for what the lecture can do best. The language of the profession is heard, not just read. The lecturer becomes a live role model who can inspire. The lecturer can impart material that the text author excluded, or that is more recently available. The lecturer can clarify difficult issues or offer alternative approaches to understanding a concept. The reading-focused course offers more opportunity to engage students in problem-solving and the scientific enterprise, to interject timely and regionally relevant "real world" examples and applications, to focus on the big issues, and to emphasize relations across units of material and disciplinary boundaries.

The prototype of the outstanding lecture may be of a powerful speaker mesmerizing the audience across the entire class period. However, also consider the professor whose style is so subtle and interactive that students are often unaware of how much material has been presented or how much they are learning. In support of this less formal technique, there is much to be gained from interspersing lectures with panels, videos, discussions, in-class assignments, student presentations, hands-on activities, demonstrations, and the like. The best mix is usually dictated by the course level, student demographics, and class size.

The Successful Lecturer

A professor of mine once began his course by claiming that research had shown that we retain only about 20 percent of what a teacher says in class. Therefore, he explained, he would double his rate of speech so that we would take from the course twice as much information! You can imagine how that turned out. We may not all be gifted lecturers, but there is no excuse for being a bad lecturer. The key ingredients are known and they can be learned.

Course Preparation

Lecture preparation begins with course design. Why does this course exist? How does it relate to the general education curriculum, to the major, to professional development, to living life? What knowledge and skills do your students need to have at the end of the course, and in years to come? This exercise should provide the core lecture topics around which to build the course with other presentations, special activities, reviews, tests, and the like. Plan for proper pacing of the course so that lectures just before tests or near the end of the course are not rushed and filled with excessive material.

Lecture Preparation

For each lecture, select the two or three most important concepts or ideas you want to introduce – less is more. Because you are no longer compelled to be the learner's main source of detailed information, you can elaborate on the central ideas with linkages to the main course goals and other material, with anecdotes and recent research, and with special attention to difficult material. The lecture should help learners create conceptual frameworks or "compartments" wherein they can file facts, nuances, and exceptions.

Good organization is essential to accomplishing this task. I'm convinced that PowerPoint has improved many presentations, including my own, not by adding pizzazz, but by forcing some structure on what had become a collage of unwieldy notes. Improved flow across the lecture's structure can be achieved by casting it as an unraveling story or by adding an underlying theme. For example, I may use "serendipitous discovery" as a theme to help introduce students to the emergence of psychotherapeutic medications.

Professors often fear that their authority and expertise will be suspect if they do not fill every minute of the lecture period or if they provide time for students to ask questions for which they have no ready response. Such an attitude is contrary to our mission of maximizing student learning. Most experienced teachers can recall a particularly effective presentation that occurred when circumstances prevented them from preparing as thoroughly as usual. Allow time in every lecture for spontaneity, student reflection, questions, and interesting diversions. Include in your notes reminders to emphasize the main lecture points at the beginning, during, and at the conclusion of the lecture. Retention may be enhanced by actively involving students in this last step via oral questions or a short task, such as, "Write down the main things you learned in today's class."

Let me elaborate: Do not make students guess at what you think is most important. Learning is not a game to be won or lost on the exam. You can emphasize important material by linking the lecture to the text's learning objectives, providing a handout, putting key points on the board, or simply saying to the class, "If you don't remember anything else, remember this:_____."

Lecture Delivery

Capture the audience from the outset. Charles Brewer is noted for making direct and stern eye contact with everyone – yes, every one – in the audience before he utters his first word. Speaking so softly when beginning that complete classroom silence is required is another approach. Other successful lecturers start with a powerful case study, anecdote, slide, or demonstration. Continue to monitor the audience throughout the presentation. Watch students' expressions and body language. Periodically ask questions to check for student understanding of what you are covering. Glance at what students are writing in their notes.

Nearly everyone agrees that an essential component of delivery is enthusiasm, or what Benjamin (2002) called passion. Hopefully you are lecturing on material in, or related to, your chosen discipline and specialty, so share your fascination with your students. Be bold about it: Jim Kalat unabashedly introduced one of his textbooks with "Biological psychology is the most interesting topic in the world" (Kalat, 2004). Try starting with something like, "Today's lecture will introduce you to two means of solving problems that you can use throughout your life. Yes, your entire life!" Maintain as much eye contact with students as possible. Vary and exaggerate loudness, tone, gestures, and movement about the room. Doing so may feel awkward at first, but it will help convey your enthusiasm and will support your message.

Routine fosters inattention. Intersperse your presentation with thought-provoking questions. Give a stretch break during long classes. Take a poll by asking students to raise their hands. Involve the class in a demonstration. Go to the board and write or draw something.

Humor can be extremely helpful but it requires tact (see Pollio, 2002). My own preference is for cartoons and amusing stories of real behavior, as opposed to "telling jokes." Dry and subtle humor can be effective in gauging student attention and under-standing. I once concluded a summary of the functions of a particular brain structure by saying it was obviously the seat of the superego. Showing no comprehension at all, a handful of students wrote that down verbatim! When using classroom humor, by all means, avoid the vulgar or offensive. Any possible benefit is small in comparison with potential risks.

Technology can greatly enhance both the lecture and learning outside the classroom, but you must use these tools wisely. Talking to a PowerPoint slide while students madly try to capture the screen's text in their notes is not effective instruction.

Assessment and Reflection

Evaluating what works well and what does not work actually begins with rehearsals prior to delivery, and continues into the presentation itself and beyond. Make mental notes of student eye contact, facial and bodily expressions, note-taking behavior, and types of questions asked. After class but before the day is over, jot down your insights and thoughts about the presentation in your lecture notes so that they will be available when you next need to prepare for that topic. On occasion I have had students make daily ratings of each lecture in a column provided on their course schedule for collection at the end of the term. These ratings and more standard course evaluations by students can be very helpful in improving lectures. If your institution's course evaluations do not ask useful questions, develop your own. All lecturers should have themselves videotaped periodically for self-examination.

Resources

Experienced colleagues, textbook ancillaries, and faculty-support specialists available at some universities can be very helpful, along with technique-rich information in articles and texts (e.g., Benjamin, 2002; Davis, 1993; Forsyth, 2003, McKeachie, 2002; and Satterfield, 1978). You are probably your own best resource: Recall what your finest and weakest lecturers did and did not do when you were a student.

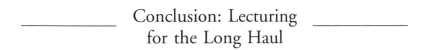

Conclusion: Lecturing for the Long Haul

It is not possible always to give peak performances: no one becomes an accomplished lecturer overnight; and even a noted lecturer's glow will fade if enthusiasm wanes and content becomes dated. To make a difference for students across academic terms and across the years, lecturers must understand what the classroom presentation can do best, constantly seek to improve and refine, and keep the learner's needs in plain view. An approach such as this will reap rewards well beyond the presentations themselves for learners and lecturers alike.

REFERENCES

Benjamin, Jr., L. T. (2002). Lecturing. In S. F. Davis & W. Buskist (eds.), *The teaching of psychology: Essays in honor of Wilbert J. McKeachie and Charles L. Brewer* (pp. 57–67). Mahwah, NJ: Lawrence Erlbaum.

Davis, B. G. (1993). *Tools for teaching.* San Francisco: Jossey-Bass. [Electronic version of chapter *Delivering a lecture* retrieved on Aug. 30, 2004, from University of California, Berkeley, website: http://teaching.berkeley.edu/bgd/delivering.html

Forsyth, D. R. (2003). *The professor's guide to teaching: Psychological principles and practices.* Washington, DC: American Psychological Association.

Kalat, J. W. (2004). *Biological psychology* (8th ed.). Belmont, CA: Wadsworth.

McKeachie, W. J. (2002). *Teaching tips: Strategies, research and theory for college and university teachers* (11th ed.). Boston: Houghton Mifflin.

Pollio, H. R. (2002). Humor and college teaching. In S. F. Davis & W. Buskist (eds.), *The teaching of psychology: Essays in honor of Wilbert J. McKeachie and Charles L. Brewer* (pp. 69–80). Mahwah, NJ: Lawrence Erlbaum.

Satterfield, J. (1978). Lecturing. In O. Milton (ed.), *On college teaching: A guide to contemporary practices* (pp. 34–61). San Francisco: Jossey-Bass.

9

Writing in Psychology

Ψ

Robin K. Morgan & David L. Morgan
Indiana University Southeast & Spalding University

Assigning student writing is not without significant peril. We suspect there is not a psychology instructor who has not received a student paper that is poorly written, full of inaccuracies, and completely off topic. Instructors can, however, create writing assignments that will produce more relevant and well-written products from the majority of students (Brent & Felder, 1992). As Nodine (1990) reported, writing is "a process that can be learned and for which strategies should be taught" (p. 4).

Why ask students to complete a writing assignment? McGovern and Hogshead (1990) described four primary objectives in student writing: assess student knowledge; promote learning; develop student writing skills; and facilitate analytic, creative-thinking, and problem-solving skills. Consider the following writing assignment:

> Read an article from a psychological journal. Summarize the article using American Psychological Association (APA) format. The paper is due on the last day of class and is worth 25% of your grade.

This assignment may have many potential uses. The instructor may wish students to become familiar with scientific writing in psychology. Alternatively, the instructor may be interested in students learning the various sections of a research article or how to use APA format. The instructor may be interested in students expanding their knowledge of a particular topic in psychology or demonstrating the ability to think critically about psychological research. Any of these possible objectives are quite legitimate. However, the assignment, as written, does not provide students with any understanding of the instructor's objective(s), creating the impression that the assignment is simply busy work.

When creating such a writing assignment, then, it is vital that students understand how this particular assignment fits into the overall course objectives (Brent & Felder, 1992). One possible way to change the above assignment to fit the course objectives might be the following:

One objective in this course is for you to be able to summarize the various sections of a research article in psychology. You will be provided with a list of articles, each one describing a research study that utilizes the sections of a report that we will be discussing in class. In addition, the subject matter of each study will parallel the topics we will be discussing in class. Your task will be to choose one article and summarize each section of the research study you select using the sections of a paper we are studying (i.e., Introduction, Methods, Results, and Discussion), and then to compare your study with what we have discussed in class or what you have read in your text about this topic. The paper is due on the last day of class and is worth 25% of your grade.

This version of the writing assignment is significantly improved but still not sufficient. One-shot writing assignments do not provide students with the structure and guidance needed to allow them to develop their writing and thinking abilities (Price, 1990). Instructors typically use two processes for shaping students' writing. One process is the traditional writing assignment that allows for, at a minimum, a required rough draft and the final paper. The instructor provides feedback on the rough draft, allowing students ample time to revise before submitting the final graded paper. A second process, called progressive writing, breaks the writing assignment into identified subsections and students must successfully complete the first subsection before proceeding to the next subsection (Finken & Cooney, 2003; Poe, 1990).

Regardless of the writing approach utilized, instructors must carefully review the process planned for assigning feedback and grades. Bloom's taxonomy, for instance, may be especially useful in identifying the instructor's desired level of writing on a particular assignment (Bloom, 1967). We recommend the creation of a rubric, provided on the syllabus, that explicitly details the expectations of the assignment. There are many ways to create rubrics (e.g., Madigan & Brosamer, 1991). Whatever the style, the rubric should assign the highest point values to those aspects of the assignment the instructor deems most important. The rubric should match what you have told students you value in terms of your stated course objectives (Yes, be redundant!). By following the rubric, students should be able to get an "A" on the assignment. The rubric should be detailed enough that peer reviewers, friends, or tutors would know what to look for in reviewing a draft. Finally, the rubric should facilitate rapid grading. Completing the rubric provides feedback to the student and saves instructors from writing the same comments on each assignment. For example:

One objective in this course is for you to be able to summarize the various sections of a research article in psychology. You will be provided with a list of articles, each one describing a research study that utilizes the sections of a report that we will be discussing in class. In addition, the subject matter of each study will parallel the topics we will be discussing in class. Your task will be to choose one article and summarize each section of the research study you select using the sections of a paper we are studying (i.e., Introduction, Methods, Results, and Conclusion) and then to compare your study with what we have discussed in class or what you have read in your text about this topic. To provide you with a chance to improve your writing, a required rough draft (ungraded but required for passing the final draft) will be due on XXX; the final draft will be due XXX. The rubric below will be used for grading both the rough draft and the final draft:

Rough Draft	Instructor simply indicates with a check if completed accurately.

Student has selected an appropriate article ____

Student has summarized each section ____

Student has attempted to compare study with material covered in class or text: Material compared is accurate ____

Underlying psychological principles described and discussed ____

Limitations of current knowledge outlined ____

Final Draft

Absence of typographical errors or grammatical problems	5%
Writing style conforms to APA guidelines	20%
Summary of each section is detailed and accurate	30%
Comparison of present study with course material reflects:	
Accurate reporting of article and course material	15%
Description of psychological principles underlying topic	15%
Understanding of limitations of current knowledge in the field	15%

Creating effective writing assignments may seem overwhelming, at least initially. However, once instructors begin developing such assignments, they can revise each assignment to accommodate differing course expectations and changes in course structure. Examples of types of writing assignments abound in the teaching of psychology research literature. Chrisler (1990), for example, had students read a novel and then describe the psychological symptoms of the main character, provide a diagnosis, and describe treatment. This assignment led to greater critical thinking and empathy for characters diagnosed with psychological disorders. In contrast, Czuchry and Dansereau (1996) described a spatial-verbal technique they called node-link mapping. Students view the creating of knowledge maps as more interesting than traditional writing assignments, and the mapping assignment led to greater learning of the material than a traditional writing assignment. In addition, students reported that the knowledge maps allowed them to be more creative and expressive and to organize and remember information more effectively.

When compiling writing assignments for your own course, remember that each course you teach should have multiple points of assessment. Just as giving only one exam is less effective than giving multiple exams, using only one writing assignment is less effective than using multiple writing assignments. Two possible student characteristics may be useful to remember: student motivation and student anxiety. A simple way to increase student motivation to complete writing assignments is to allow them a choice in terms of what writing assignments they complete. For example, Wade (1995) reported success with allowing students to complete six of a series of writing assignments, any of which met course objectives. Boice (1982) highlighted the importance of recognizing students' anxiety levels. He suggested that students' writing improves when students submit several small writing assignments rather than one large, traditional term paper. Rickabaugh (1993) also found that providing students with a series of weekly writing assignments integrated with course content led to improved writing quality, increased critical thinking about course content, and decreased student procrastination and anxiety. Ideally, each course should contain at least two to three writing assignments of varying lengths and complexity.

Finally, instructors do not need to grade every writing assignment. Indeed, writing assignments may be most effective if ungraded. For example, asking students at the end of a class session to write a question about the material covered is a very effective tool, as it allows the instructor to determine what students have not understood and aids them in expressing their thoughts in writing about course material. Journal writing is another strategy for encouraging students to put their thoughts on paper in a systematic manner. Students may be more comfortable writing journals if their instructors do not grade them, especially if the journals include sensitive information. Many instructors simply comment on the entries and require completion of the journal (see Connor-Greene [2000] for an example of a simple method of using and assessing journal writing that improves student learning).

Although adding writing assignments to your course may seem formidable, especially in large undergraduate courses, the addition of such assignments need not lead to endless hours of grading poor-quality papers. Spiegel, Cameron, Evans, and Nodine (1980) described several "writing for learning" exercises that do not significantly increase demands on instructors. When a question or issue arises in class, for example, instructors may ask students to write their understanding of the issue and then share that understanding with peers or the class. Instructors need to consider combining graded and ungraded writing assignments, varying the length and complexity of assigned writing, and creating rubrics to simplify the grading process. Most importantly, the selected writing assignments for a course should develop naturally from the objectives you have chosen for that course. Utilizing these principles will increase the odds that student papers will achieve your course objectives.

REFERENCES

Bloom, B. S. (ed.) (1967). *Taxonomy of educational objectives: Handbook I: Cognitive domain.* New York: David McKay.

Boice, R. (1982). Teaching of writing in psychology: A review of sources. *Teaching of Psychology, 9,* 143–7.

Brent, R., & Felder, R. M. (1992). Writing assignments: Pathways to connections, clarity, creativity. *College Teaching, 40,* 43–8.

Chrisler, J. C. (1990). Novels as case-study materials for psychology students. *Teaching of Psychology, 17,* 55–7.

Connor-Greene, P. A. (2000). Making connections: Evaluating the effectiveness of journal writing in enhancing student learning. *Teaching of Psychology, 27,* 44–6.

Czuchry, M., & Dansereau, D. F. (1996). Node-link mapping as an alternative to traditional writing assignments in undergraduate psychology courses. *Teaching of Psychology, 23,* 91–6.

Finken, L. L., & Cooney, R. R. (2003). A comparison of progressive and two-draft writing assignments in introductory psychology courses. *Teaching of Psychology, 30,* 246–8.

Madigan, R. J., & Brosamer, J. J. (1991). Holistic grading of written work in introductory psychology: Reliability, validity, and efficiency. *Teaching of Psychology, 18,* 91–4.

McGovern, T. V., & Hogshead, D. L. (1990). Learning about writing, thinking about teaching. *Teaching of Psychology, 17,* 5–10.

Nodine, B. F. (ed.) (1990). Psychologists teach writing (Special issue). *Teaching of Psychology, 17 (1)*, 1–61.

Poe, R. E. (1990). A strategy for improving literature reviews in psychology courses. *Teaching of Psychology, 17*, 54–5.

Price, D. W. W. (1990). A model for reading and writing about primary sources: The case of introductory psychology. *Teaching of Psychology, 17*, 48–53.

Rickabaugh, C. A. (1993). The psychology portfolio: Promoting writing and critical thinking about psychology. *Teaching of Psychology, 20*, 170–2.

Spiegel, T. A., Cameron, S. M., Evans, R., & Nodine, B. F. (1980). Integrating writing into the teaching of psychology: An alternative to Calhoun and Selby. *Teaching of Psychology, 7*, 242–3.

Wade, C. (1995). Using writing to develop and assess critical thinking. *Teaching of Psychology, 22*, 24–8.

10

Let the Concert Begin:
The Music of Team Teaching

Ψ

Kenneth D. Keith
University of San Diego

It happens not so much on schedule
as at those moments when
something with something else
beautifully collides . . .
– William Kloefkorn (1993, p. 51)

We are sitting in a circle in a small classroom, talking now about our reactions to the film version of John Steinbeck's (1945) *Cannery Row*. More specifically, we are each trying to articulate an ethical issue raised by the story, and our proposals are diverse – including, among others, the plight of Mack and his largely unemployed comrades, the rights of the frogs captured by these fellows for their friend Doc, and the relative virtues of the goings-on at Dora's "sporting house." Our group includes about 18 individuals, mostly first-year university students, plus a three-member teaching team: a psychologist, a philosopher, and a senior undergraduate student. It is my first try at team teaching.

Our course, "Ethics and Morality," is one of the offerings in a program designed to introduce new students to university life. Universities have assigned various labels to such programs, including preceptorials, liberal arts seminars, and first-year experience. My co-teachers are as new to this as I am, but the philosopher and I will go on to offer this course four times, each with a new student co-instructor, and I will subsequently design another first-year course, named for Carl Sagan's (1996) *The Demon-Haunted World: Science as a Candle in the Dark*, also team taught each time with a senior undergraduate instructor. However, on this day, struggling to generate a discussion of the ethics of *Cannery Row*, I do not yet know that these classes will be some of my most memorable experiences in teaching.

Team Teaching: What Is It?

Team teaching can range from delivery of courses planned by several professors, but implemented by one at a time, each individually teaching one or more sessions, to two or more teachers working together to plan and deliver material in concert (Davis, 1997). I have come to believe that the former approach – individuals implementing a team plan – is not really team teaching. Instead, I agree with the approach advocated by Blythe and Sweet (2004), who discussed the merits of sharing the full load of planning, preparation, and presentation, including appearance in the classroom by all team members at every class session. Other psychologists (Flanagan & Ralston, 1983; Hammer & Giordano, 2001; Selby & Calhoun, 1990) have also used this approach to good advantage, suggesting that total collaboration is essential to true team teaching.

Team teaching can properly denote the pedagogical efforts of a professor–student team; that is, the team need not consist only of faculty-level teaching members. Gray and Harrison (2003), for example, reported the benefits (and a few problems) associated with a fairly large project evaluating effectiveness of faculty–student team teaching, and my own experience includes a number of gratifying opportunities to team teach with students.

Throughout the remainder of this chapter, when I use the term "team teaching" I mean to imply fully collaborative efforts in which all members of the team are jointly involved at all stages, from course planning to daily in-class teaching. I also intend to include not only faculty–faculty teams, but faculty–student teaching teams as well.

What Do I Need to Know?

Good Teams

Good teams require careful planning and nurturing. Basketball fans recognize that American men's teams have experienced difficulty in winning international competitions in recent years – a fact that analysts attribute to an overemphasis on individual play and a corresponding lack of teamwork. There is a message in this analysis for team teachers. Eisen (2000) likened team teaching to family systems, which include a variety of relationship models. She concluded that for development and implementation of new courses, team teachers should seek a committed relationship.

Trust Is Essential

Work with someone you trust and who will be committed to the time and effort required to develop and teach an effective course. Team teaching does not offer an alternative to the hard work and preparation time required for any form of good teaching, and in fact may complicate your life by demanding more coordination and planning than would normally accompany a conventional single-teacher course. Grading, for example, requires close coordination and agreement between team members (Hammer & Giordano, 2001).

Keep Your Passion

We cannot avoid – nor should we, Myers (1997) suggested in his discussion of "professing with passion" – bringing our own values and ideas to our teaching. Passion characterizes effective teachers (L. T. Benjamin, 2002). Brewer (1996) argued that good teachers have several passions, among them preparation, excellence, parsimony, and patience. Team teaching requires the same commitment to excellence, and the same enthusiasm, which outstanding teachers identify as essential to their work (e.g., Buskist, 2002).

What Do I Need to Do?

During the course of several years of team teaching I have come to believe that a number of day-to-day behaviors are essential to the success of team-taught courses. Here are five:

1. Be prepared. It is never a good idea to assume that your partner will carry your weight. For the team to engage in, and to lead, effective in-class exchanges, everyone needs to be prepared every day.
2. Have the courage to disagree. One of the compelling advantages of team teaching is the opportunity for faculty to model intellectual discourse at a level not always directly available to students. If you and your partner(s) are prepared to articulate discrepant points of view in a meaningful, cogent way, you can elevate the classroom atmosphere to new heights. The consequence of mustering the courage to disagree, of course, is that sometimes you may be wrong. Don't be afraid of that, either; students can gain from the opportunity to see how we handle our own fallibility, and we can learn much from Bronowski's (1973) moving advice to make ourselves aware of the possibility we may be wrong.
3. Allow silence to be your friend. Sometimes new ideas or rhetorical questions require a little time to percolate, and students need opportunity to think before responding. When two or more faculty are in the room, it becomes especially important that you all understand the need to let thought ferment for a bit. Resist the urge to leap into the lurch simply because you find a few moments of silence uncomfortable.
4. Talk about student evaluation and reach a sensible agreement on the procedures you will use. A plan, a rubric, a template – whatever the specific process and your name for it – can help to ensure that you respond to student writing, exams, and class participation in a manner that your students will see as fair and reasonable.
5. Show your enthusiasm. It is one thing (and an important one) to be enthusiastic in traditional single-instructor teaching. It is yet another to take good advantage of the synergy made possible by two or more models of excitement and love of learning and subject matter. When you do it well, enthusiastic team teaching affirms Selby and Calhoun's (1990) use of the "concert" metaphor.

—————— ## What's In It For Me? ——————

Just as music can sometimes be discordant, some days in the classroom are better than others; and team teaching has the potential to make the discord more obvious, the struggling teacher more vulnerable. The planning, coordination, and consultation required for effective team teaching, some would assert, take time away from other activities, including the scholarship demanded by so many of our institutions. Is the return worth the risk? I believe it is, and I will attempt to say why, first in the concrete world of scholarship, and second in the more nebulous realm of risk, vulnerability, and possible failure.

Scholarship of Team Teaching

In recent years, faculty have increasingly recognized the scholarly nature of teaching and of research extending our knowledge of teaching. Although acknowledging some potential pitfalls, Johnson (2002) made a compelling case for the scholarship of the teaching of psychology, suggesting that it can meet many, if not all, the criteria typically applied to research conducted within the content areas of the academic disciplines. Boyer (1990) made a similar argument, more broadly applied, and many institutions have subsequently accepted, at least to some degree, the merits of the scholarship of teaching.

Critics of our science have claimed that individualism has distorted our understanding (Grumet, 1994), giving rise to what Sullivan (1994) called the "myth of the independent scholar." However, just as collaboration has become the norm in many areas of basic science, the value of collaboration in pedagogy has also begun to come into its own. J. Benjamin (2000), for example, used data from five disciplines (psychology, biology, medicine, economics, and law) to demonstrate that the scholarship of teaching can be found in teaching teams as well as in independent teachers, and that a multidimensional model of the scholarship of teaching can be used to conceptualize such work. I have no doubt there are rich possibilities to be explored in pedagogical research on team teaching, and that psychologists can be in the forefront of this form of scholarship.

The Music of Failure

L. T. Benjamin (2002) pointed out that one of the surest roads to failure is to fail to be yourself in the classroom. I agree with this sentiment as it applies to solo teaching, and I believe it also applies, perhaps even more clearly, in team teaching. Allowing yourself to be natural may increase feelings of vulnerability, but avoiding an artificial act also reduces the likelihood of forgetting your lines. Students appreciate honesty and sincerity, and even if you need some time to find your way in concert with your teaching partner(s), you will eventually make your best music if you each speak in your own true voice.

Ultimately, your effectiveness will not depend so much on the polish of your presentation as the legitimate effort, integrity, and care that go into your teaching. Holm

(1985), in describing the farm woman who was his first piano teacher, acknowledged that her music was not particularly artful; but this, he said, made no difference. What became memorable was her passion, her love of the music, and the fact that she was unafraid of making mistakes. Thus, Holm said, "in every artery of my body, and in yours too, that music of failure plays – continually. It sounds like Bach to me, and you must make up your mind what it sounds like to you" (p. 86). Effective collaboration may be aptly described as a symphony (Kennedy, Marback, & McManus, 1994), and I now realize that on that day when my colleagues, our students, and I were deconstructing Steinbeck we were at the same time constructing our own form of music, assembling the parts in a pleasing way made possible only by our collaboration.

Coda

The good teachers whom I know love to learn and they love to see the results when others learn. Team teaching, entered into with planning, cooperation, and hard work, can elevate the teaching–learning relationship to a new level. It offers collaborative opportunities in the best spirit of the liberal arts tradition, along with new possibilities for pedagogical scholarship. It is, in short, tailor-made to provide great satisfaction for willing teachers and learners alike.

Find a capable, congenial partner, engage in a meaningful dialogue, and before long you will generate myriad possibilities for team-taught subjects. This process has, in my case, led naturally to meaningful collaborative discussions in a wide range of settings: kitchens, pubs, hiking trails, and automobiles, among others. This experience is not unique; other collaborators of various sorts (e.g., Latimer & Spoto, 1994) have reported similar effects. Immersed in the process, you may make music that will play well beyond the walls of the classroom and the end of the semester.

> On a bright late-September morning
> two trumpets in sunlight blare softly . . .
> I stay to hear the silver duo perform
> far beyond the moment
> when the music's done . . .
> – William Kloefkorn (1996, p. 45)

References

Benjamin, J. (2000). The scholarship of teaching in teams: What does it look like in practice? *Higher Education Research & Development, 19,* 191–204.

Benjamin, L. T., Jr. (2002). Lecturing. In S. F. Davis & W. Buskist (eds.), *The teaching of psychology: Essays in honor of Wilbert J. McKeachie and Charles L. Brewer* (pp. 57–67). Mahwah, NJ: Erlbaum.

Blythe, H., & Sweet, C. (2004). Total team teaching – Sharing teaching duties equally. *The Teaching Professor, 18 (3),* 1, 5.

Boyer, E. L. (1990). *Scholarship revisited: Priorities of the professoriate.* Princeton, NJ: Carnegie Foundation.

Brewer, C. L. (1996). A talk to teachers: Bending twigs and affecting eternity. *Platte Valley Review, 24 (2)*, 12–23.

Bronowski, J. (1973). *The ascent of man.* Boston: Little, Brown & Co.

Buskist, W. (2002). Effective teaching: Perspectives and insights from Division Two's 2- and 4-year awardees. *Teaching of Psychology, 29*, 188–93.

Davis, J. R. (1997). *Interdisciplinary courses and team teaching.* Phoenix: American Council on Education.

Eisen, M. J. (2000). The many faces of team teaching and learning: An overview. *New Directions for Adult and Continuing Education, 87*, 5–14.

Flanagan, M. F., & Ralston, D. A. (1983). Intra-coordinated team teaching: Benefits for both students and instructors. *Teaching of Psychology, 10*, 116–17.

Gray, T., & Harrison, P. (2003). Team teach with a student: A pilot study in criminal justice. *Journal of Criminal Justice Education, 14*, 163–80.

Grumet, M. R. (1994). Foreword. In S. B. Reagan, T. Fox, & D. Bleich (eds.), *Writing with: New directions in collaborative teaching, learning, and research* (pp. vii–viii). Albany, NY: State University of New York Press.

Hammer, E. Y., & Giordano, P. J. (2001). Dual-gender team-teaching human sexuality: Pedagogical and practical issues. *Teaching of Psychology, 28*, 132–3.

Holm, B. (1985). *The music of failure.* Marshall, MN: Plains Press.

Johnson, D. E. (2002). Teaching, research, and scholarship. In S. F. Davis & W. Buskist (eds.), *The teaching of psychology: Essays in honor of Wilbert J. McKeachie and Charles L. Brewer* (pp. 153–62). Mahwah, NJ: Erlbaum.

Kennedy, S., Marback, R., & McManus, E. (1994). A melting pot of brains? Metaphors for collaboration and diversity. In S. B. Reagan, T. Fox, & D. Bleich (eds.), *Writing with: New directions in collaborative teaching, learning, and research* (pp. 157–77). Albany, NY: State University of New York Press.

Kloefkorn, W. (1993). *Going out, coming back.* Fredonia, NY: White Pine Press.

Kloefkorn, W. (1996). *Treehouse: New & selected poems.* Fredonia, NY: White Pine Press.

Latimer, M. A., & Spoto, P. (1994). Collaboration and world view. In S. B. Reagan, T. Fox, & D. Bleich (eds.), *Writing with: New directions in collaborative teaching, learning, and research* (pp. 265–81). Albany, NY: State University of New York Press.

Myers, D. G. (1997). Professing psychology with passion. In R. J. Sternberg (ed.), *Teaching introductory psychology: Survival tips from the experts* (pp. 107–18). Washington, DC: American Psychological Association.

Sagan, C. (1996). *The demon-haunted world: Science as a candle in the dark.* New York: Random House.

Selby, J. W., & Calhoun, L. G. (1990). Concert teaching: An alternative strategy. In J. Hartley & W. J. McKeachie (eds.), *Teaching psychology: A handbook* (pp. 104–5). Hillsdale, NJ: Erlbaum.

Steinbeck, J. (1945). *Cannery row.* New York: Viking Press.

Sullivan, P. A. (1994). Revising the myth of the independent scholar. In S. B. Reagan, T. Fox, & D. Bleich (eds.), *Writing with: New directions in collaborative teaching, learning, and research* (pp. 11–29). Albany, NY: State University of New York Press.

11

Collaborative Learning: Maximizing Students' Potential for Success

Ψ

Tina Vazin & Phyllis Reile
Alabama State University

Most educators know from experience that regardless of how familiar they are with a particular subject matter, teaching it to others gives them a deeper and broader understanding of it. This benefit comes from, among other things, spending time thinking of ways to make the information more understandable, devising clear examples, figuring out strategies to avoid common points of confusion, thinking of different approaches to presenting the information, showing students how the new information fits into existing knowledge.

Given that educators know the benefits of explaining, demonstrating, and discussing information, it seems reasonable for them to create opportunities for students to capitalize on the effects of "teaching" to facilitate learning. Collaborative learning is an instructional approach that allows students to realize these benefits by working with other students in small groups toward a common learning goal. In addition to facilitating learning of the course material, well-designed collaborative learning activities have the potential of offering additional advantages such as (a) instilling in students a sense of responsibility for their learning that develops the requisite skills, mindset, and desire to become lifelong learners, (b) developing a respect for diversity of ideas and alternative interpretations, and (c) introducing the importance of professional teamwork in areas such as laboratory research (Eccles, 1994).

You should not think of these additional benefits as "icing on the cake" for academic programs that wish to produce scholarly candidates for graduate studies, as most undergraduate psychology programs aspire to do. Rather, curricula should include a variety of courses that include collaborative learning activities that have as their explicit goal the development of these professional attributes. Students who develop a sense of accountability for their education, value diversity of thought, and appreciate the unique product of teamwork in addition to excelling in their knowledge of psychology will have received an education that has maximized their potential for success. In the words of Paul Pinet, a Geology professor at Colgate, "college must educate students, not merely inform them" (as quoted in Bruffee, 2003, p. 20).

Essential Components of Collaborative Learning

Although collaborative learning activities have much to offer students, many instructors who have incorporated these activities into their courses can recount instances of disastrous outcomes due to poor design. Students regard collaborative learning projects that are not well conceived or poorly implemented as busy work or as a time-consuming nuisance. In fact, most of faculty can recall from their undergraduate experiences being victims of such course requirements, referred to as "group assignments," which resulted in either us taking the bull by the horns and completing the entire assignment ourselves or being ostracized by the group and being denied the opportunity to make any contributions. Either way, the experience often left us with ill feelings toward our peers and contempt for our instructor for assigning a project that we perceived as an unfair test of our ability. For collaborative learning projects to be effective, (a) students must be led to value both process and outcome, (b) the projects must require a significant amount of communication among students, (c) students must feel that they are individually responsible for and have contributed significantly to the outcome, and (d) the members must feel that the end product is superior to what any one member could have produced individually. An examination of the teaching of psychology literature and suggestions offered on the PSYCHTEACH listserv (www.psychteach.list.kennesaw.edu) is an excellent starting point for stimulating your thinking about ideas for collaborative learning projects.

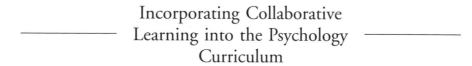

Incorporating Collaborative Learning into the Psychology Curriculum

Efforts to incorporate collaborative learning into a curriculum should begin with determining if the collaborations will extend across courses or will be contained within each course. Learning communities or learning cohorts where students enroll in a sequence or block of courses together are designed to provide collaborative learning opportunities with a particular group of students across courses and semesters. Student cohorts establish learning communities that "provide settings in which students feel comfortable enough with one another that they begin putting academic concepts in their own terms, teaching one another, and grappling with ideas together" (Lundberg, 2003, p. 10). Once a learning community is established with a relatively small student cohort, collaborative learning assignments become less necessary as the members of the group become more interdependent, and discussing, arguing, demonstrating, and explaining become a natural extension of all classes.

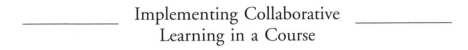

Implementing Collaborative Learning in a Course

Establishing student cohorts is not a viable option for many programs, so teachers are left to devise methods to encourage collaborative learning within a particular course. In designing collaborative learning projects instructors need to consider (a) how to achieve collaborative learning, (b) the type of assignments to be used, and (c) how to evaluate the project.

Process is Key

It is important to remember that the process of doing collaborative learning assignments – the actual collaboration amongst students – is the desired outcome. The final product is partial evidence of the process, but it is not necessarily evidence of the quality of student collaboration. For example, if a group of students submit a perfect project, but they did not discuss the material, explain their interpretation, argue points, and ponder important concepts together, collaborative learning did not occur.

Designing assignments and evaluations with the process in mind instead of the final product is a new and challenging approach for many instructors. Some ideas that instructors might consider to get students started thinking about collaboration include (a) beginning the semester with discussions distinguishing group tasks and group processes and the importance of effective group processes; (b) putting students into groups on the first day of class, having them read the syllabus, and asking each group to generate at least one question about its content; and (c) having groups generate guidelines that should help them function effectively, generate a composite list of guidelines, and distribute it to the entire class (Giordano & Hammer, 1999).

Types of Collaborative Learning Activities

The next consideration is whether collaborative learning will be achieved through in-class assignments, out-of-class assignments, or Web-based activities. In-class activities can be as simple as asking students to brainstorm with each other about a point made in class. For example, Mazur, a Harvard physicist, routinely asked at different points throughout the lecture for students to compare what they thought the main point of the lecture was with the person sitting next to them. He found that this technique significantly improved test results (Bruffee, 2003). Halpern (2004) extended this exercise by having the two students explain their interpretation of the main point to a third student. In another example, instead of lecturing about Kant, a philosophy instructor organized his students into small groups and asked them to examine short passages and explain how the passages fit into the portion of Kant's argument that had been discussed. The instructor described the scene as, "Listen to them. They are not talking about Kant. They are talking Kant. They are using Kant's language and concepts to penetrate Kantian problems" (Bruffee, 2003). In both types of activities, the collaboration is relatively easy to monitor and evaluate without the instructor spending much time and effort.

Out-of-class collaborative learning assignments are more difficult to monitor and usually demand more effort by both students and the instructor. Common assignments include having (a) different student groups conduct a research project in which each member collects data individually and the group works together to organize, analyze, and present the results to the class; (b) students individually write brief papers about a common topic and work together to put all the information together into one presentation or paper; and (c) students individually view a movie related to a class theme, prepare an analysis of the characters, and, as a group, write and prepare a summary for the class.

Another method growing in popularity involves using the internet to form computer-supported groups (Oliver & Omari, 2001). This method may be especially convenient for students who are separated by distance, work full-time, or are registered for online courses. Although the internet offers unlimited possibilities for creative works, the tendency is for educators to use these powerful new technologies in traditional ways. The possibilities for instructors are limited only by their ability to create and design challenging projects and, of course, having the time to do so. For example, consider the following ideas: (a) instructors forming international collaborations with other faculty so that students from different cultures work on projects together (this idea is especially applicable to social psychology and multicultural psychology projects); and (b) having students create online surveys to collect data from hard-to-access populations such as victims of stigmatized diseases, localized natural disasters, or members of small ethnic groups.

Evaluation of Collaborative Learning

Another consideration is determining how to evaluate the collaborative learning process. Most instructors require a tangible final product as evidence of collaboration for out-of-class and Web-based activities. Other than a final paper or research project, instructors may (a) require group members to keep a daily journal describing the form and outcome of group collaborations, (b) ask group members to assess the contribution of each group member, and (c) appoint a student in each group to be the "collaboration monitor" who submits a brief report to the instructor on the quality of group's collaboration. All of these tactics remind students of the importance of each member's contribution to their group's outcome. However, to some students collaborative learning may be more effortful than it is enjoyable. The challenge for instructors is to enlighten students to the value of collaboration so that it will become a desirable activity in which to participate.

Conclusion

There is little doubt that infusing collaborative learning into psychology courses promotes learning of course objectives as well as useful skills for lifelong learning. Collaborative learning projects range in complexity from spending a few minutes in class discussing an issue with another student to completing projects that extend across semesters. In addition, the internet offers many new avenues to explore that could go as far as having students from Nigeria, China, Italy, and the US collaborating to investigate interesting cultural differences in, for example, music preferences of college students. However, the important thing for instructors to keep in mind as they design and evaluate collaborative learning activities is that just as the "proof is in the pudding," the value of collaborative learning lies in the processes involved in students working together to complete a meaningful project.

REFERENCES

Bruffee, K. A. (2003). Cultivating the craft of interdependence: Collaborative learning and the college curriculum. *About Campus, 17*, 17–23.

Eccles, J. S. (1994). Understanding women's educational and occupational choices: Applying the Eccles et al. model of achievement-related choices. *Psychology of Women Quarterly, 18*, 585–609.

Giordano, P. J., & Hammer, E. Y. (1999). In-class collaborative learning: Practical suggestions from the teaching trenches. *Teaching of Psychology, 26*, 42–4.

Halpern, D. F. (2004). Creating cooperative learning environments. In B. Perlman, L. I. McCann, & S. H. McFadden (eds.), *Lessons learned: Practical advice for the teaching of psychology* (pp. 165–73). Washington, DC: American Psychological Society.

Lundberg, C. A. (2003). Nontraditional college students and the role of collaborative learning as a tool for science mastery. *School Science and Mathematics, 103*, 8–18.

Oliver, R., & Omari, A. (2001). Student responses to collaborating and learning in a web-based environment. *Journal of Computer Assisted Learning, 17*, 34–47.

12

Problem-Based Learning

Ψ

Patricia A. Connor-Greene
Clemson University

The term "problem-based learning" (PBL) originated in the 1960s at McMaster University's School of Medicine in Canada (Neufeld & Barrows, 1974). In response to problems drawn from real or hypothetical cases, students combine individual and collaborative research to locate and evaluate resources for effective solutions, gaining expertise in problem-solving, critical thinking, and communication. PBL is student- rather than teacher-directed (Vernon & Blake, 1993; Wilkerson & Gijselaers, 1996), requiring students to seek solutions actively rather than to receive information passively from the teacher. PBL's premise is that much of the content of today's classes becomes obsolete in a matter of weeks, months, or years, while the transferable higher-level skills acquired through the active *process* of solving problems endure over time.

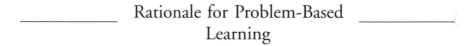

Rationale for Problem-Based Learning

The proliferation of information on the internet heightens the need for students to develop and use strong critical-thinking skills, learning to evaluate both the quality and the relevance of information (Regan, 1998). For students in the twenty-first century, finding information is effortless. In contrast, synthesizing and evaluating resources to solve problems involves a more complex, effortful, and essential set of skills (Halpern, 1998).

Given the overwhelming volume of information available to students, faculty are more essential than ever as teachers of the analytic and evaluative skills involved in critical thinking. However, higher-level cognitive skills are not an automatic byproduct of standard educational practices (de Sanchez, 1995; Nummedal & Halpern, 1995). Halpern and Nummedal (1995) called for teachers to make critical thinking a primary goal of education. With its goal of enhancing students' flexible, relevant knowledge base, problem-solving and reasoning, self-directed learning, and effective collaboration within a team (Kelson & Distlehorst, 2000), PBL is one way to enhance critical thinking.

PBL engages students in critical and creative thinking, 1 of the 10 goals outlined by the APA Task Force on Undergraduate Psychology Major Competencies (Halonen et al., 2002). The Steering Committee of the American Psychological Association's National Conference on Enhancing the Quality of Undergraduate Education in Psychology designated active, collaborative learning as one of its quality principles (McGovern & Reich, 1996).

Active engagement and personal investment are powerful means of maximizing student learning (Angelo, 1995). PBL enlivens class material, creating a context for "connected" rather than "separate" knowing (Enns, 1993) and fostering active skills of inquiry rather than passive receipt of information. Assigning real-world, meaningful activities increases the relevance of learning for students (Halonen et al., 2003), encouraging students to move from factual knowledge ("knowing what") to procedural knowledge ("knowing how") (Eyler, Root, & Giles, 1998, p. 86). Students are more likely to retain knowledge learned and applied in a realistic context (McKeachie, 2002). PBL closely mirrors the way professionals solve problems (Duch, 2001), giving students experience grappling with the complexities, ambiguities, and challenges of real-world problems that are often missing from traditional academic lectures or textbooks.

When using PBL, students move beyond knowledge and comprehension into the higher cognitive levels of application, analysis, synthesis, and evaluation (Bloom, 1956). PBL fosters critical thinking by enhancing students' ability to: (a) analyze and solve real-world, complex problems; (b) locate, evaluate, and apply relevant learning resources; (c) collaborate with others in solving problems; (d) demonstrate effective communication skills, and (e) acquire and use skills that characterize lifelong learners (Duch, Groh, & Allen, 2001). As Hildebidle (1991) wrote, "the word *learning* is, properly, a verb masquerading as a noun: an activity, not a substance; something we do, not something we have" (p. 270).

Despite an extensive body of PBL literature, there are few published examples of PBL in psychology classes (Hays & Vincent, 2004). Problem-based exercises in psychology range from a single assignment with some elements of PBL (e.g., Connor-Greene & Greene, 2002), to a semester-long, problem-based service learning project integrated into a course (e.g., Connor-Greene, 2000; 2002), to a series of PBL assignments interspersed throughout a course (e.g., Wells, 2003), to an entire course structured as PBL (e.g., Hays & Vincent, 2004).

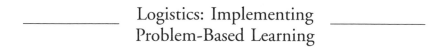

Logistics: Implementing Problem-Based Learning

Resources

In addition to books and articles, a wealth of PBL information is available on the internet. The University of Delaware (www.udel.edu/pbl/) and Samford University (www.samford.edu/pbl/index.html) have excellent websites that contain PBL resources and guidelines, links to other websites, information on training and conferences, and sample courses and syllabi.

Class Format and Structure

The PBL medical-school model typically involves groups of 8–10 students, although smaller groups of 4–5 students increase individual accountability, communication, and ease of scheduling group meetings (Duch, 2001). The management of groups becomes more complex as class size increases, although Shipman and Duch (2001) reported using PBL in classes as large as 340. Groups work under the guidance of a tutor or facilitator (faculty member, graduate student, or advanced undergraduate student). The group identifies "learning issues," concepts needing research as part of solving the problem (Bereiter & Scardamalia, 2000; Hmelo & Evensen, 2000). Combining individual and group work both within and outside of the classroom requires teamwork, communication, and individual and group research (Wood, 2003). Typically, PBL involves: (a) reading and discussing the problem, (b) identifying and discussing prior related knowledge, (c) identifying and prioritizing learning issues, (d) identifying and dividing research responsibilities, (e) doing individual out-of-class research, (f) reporting to the group, (g) applying prior knowledge to new material and refining learning issues, (h) determining and dividing new research responsibilities, (i) doing individual out-of-class research, (j) reporting to group members, and (k) deciding on a solution and producing a final product (Donham, Schmieg, & Allen, 2001).

Constructing Meaningful Problems

The heart of PBL is a relevant, engaging, and challenging problem (Wood, 2003). Good PBL problems require true collaboration among group members rather than a "divide and conquer" approach (Duch & Allen, 1996, p. 25). Sources of problems include real-life scenarios, video-clips, experimental or clinical data, newspaper articles, and journal articles (Wood, 2003). The University of Delaware maintains a Problem-Based Learning Clearinghouse, which includes a database of sample problems categorized by academic disciplines (www.mis4.udel.edu/Pbl/). Samford University's PBL website contains a rubric and guidelines for designing problems (www.samford.edu/pbl/process_probdesign.html), and recommends that problems should be engaging and real-world relevant, stimulate multiple hypotheses, require collaboration, relate to desired learning outcomes, build upon prior knowledge and experience, and promote higher-level cognitive skills of application, analysis, synthesis, and evaluation.

Duch (2001) outlined steps for writing PBL problems: (a) select a concept central to the course; (b) identify a real-world context for that concept using newspapers, magazines, and journals; (c) determine the structure and scope of the problem (e.g., how many class periods will it take? What learning issues should students identify? What resources will students need?); (d) prepare a schedule (e.g., mini-lectures, small group and whole-class discussions); and (e) identify several good resources to get students started.

Assessing Student Performance

Teachers who want students to develop strong problem-solving skills may unwittingly test basic knowledge rather than higher-level thinking (Bol & Strage, 1996). If instructors want students to develop higher-level skills, it is essential to evaluate and reward those skills (Elton & Laurillard, 1979; Goldberg, Roswell, & Michaels, 1996). Halonen et al. (2003) proposed a rubric for qualitative assessment of student learning, which could be valuable in assessing PBL.

Key PBL assessment issues include: What will students produce as evidence of their work? Will grading be individual or group? How can a teacher promote group learning while assessing individual work? How can exams incorporate problem-based learning? Should grades reflect group and communication skills? (Duch & Groh, 2001).

Outcome Studies

Benefits of Problem-Based Learning

In comparison to traditional classrooms, students who participate in PBL report more satisfaction with their learning environment (Lancaster et al., 1997) and better connect theory to practice (Shelton & Smith, 1998). By integrating new information with existing knowledge, PBL produces stronger and more enduring understanding of concepts than lecture or discussion alone (Capon & Kuhn, 2004). Students rated PBL higher in promoting interactions between faculty and students, developing critical thinking, research, and oral presentation skills, and helping them grasp concepts (Hays & Vincent, 2004). Both students and faculty perceive PBL as enhancing the development of students' self-directed learning (Blumberg, 2000; Hmelo & Evensen, 2000). For meta-analyses and reviews of PBL, see Albanese and Mitchell (1993), Barrows (1996), Berkson (1993), Dochy, Segers, Van de Bossche, and Gijbels (2002), and Vernon and Blake (1993).

Challenges in Using Problem-Based Learning

Despite its many positive outcomes, PBL's lack of structure and absence of a "right answer" can increase anxiety, especially for students highly successful in traditional classes (Evensen, Salisbury-Glennon, & Glenn, 2001; Glasgow, 1997). Medical students using PBL reported uncertainty about the breadth and depth of knowledge required, concerns about the time required for self-directed study, misunderstanding of the faculty role in PBL, and lack of confidence to succeed (Solomon & Finch, 1998). Because PBL represents a departure from the traditional ways of learning with which students are most familiar, students may experience disjunction, defined as frustration, confusion, and desire for "right answers" (Savin-Baden, 2000). It is important that teachers recognize disjunction as a starting point for learning (Jarvis, 1987) and a natural part of the process of grappling with complex problems, rather than a sign that PBL is ineffective.

Encouraging student engagement rather than withdrawal in the face of complexity, challenge, and ambiguity is an important part of facilitating PBL (Savin-Baden, 2000).

The most common concerns of PBL students are uncertainty in the face of loosely defined problems, unexpected challenges, logistical problems of working in groups, and the perception that there is no end to what they "need to know." Interestingly, these are the same challenges inherent in solving real-world problems. No profession enables an individual to rely only on the information acquired as a student, and PBL helps students develop problem-solving skills and perseverance to continue to acquire information on their own (Lieux, 2001).

From the teacher's perspective, PBL can be challenging to manage (Glasgow, 1997). Finding the right balance to foster student-directed learning can be difficult at times; teachers may be tempted to be too directive and intervene when a group is floundering (Dolmans, Wolfhagen, van der Vleuten, & Wijnen, 2001). Because group learning is central to PBL, teachers can benefit from resources that address problems and solutions in managing groups (e.g., Yamane, 1996). For example, Kitto and Griffiths (2001) published a form for group members to evaluate each other's performance. As a guideline for group facilitators, Allen and White (2001) developed a checklist of behaviors that impair group process.

Conclusion

PBL represents a paradigm shift in students' responsibility for learning. Making this shift requires reframing on the part of both teacher and students. In PBL, the role of teachers is to select engaging, meaningful problems and encourage and guide students toward self-directed learning. Complex, real-world problems defy a simple "right answer," and the uncertainty, ambiguity, and false starts inherent in PBL are part of a rich process of learning.

REFERENCES

Albanese, M. A., & Mitchell, S. (1993). Problem-based learning: A review of literature on its outcomes and implementation issues. *Academic Medicine, 68*, 52–81.

Allen, D. E., & White, H. B. III (2001). Undergraduate group facilitators to meet the challenges of multiple classroom groups. In B. J. Duch, S. E. Groh, & D. E. Allen (eds.), *The power of problem-based learning* (pp. 79–94). Sterling, VA: Stylus Publishing.

Angelo, T. A. (1995). Classroom assessment for critical thinking. *Teaching of Psychology, 22*, 6–7.

Barrows, H. S. (1996). Problem-based learning in medicine and beyond: A brief overview. In L. Wilkerson & W. Gijselaers (eds.), *Bringing problem-based learning to higher education: Theory and practice* (pp. 3–12). San Francisco: Jossey-Bass.

Bereiter, C., & Scardamalia, M. (2000). Commentary on Part 1: Process and product in problem-based learning (PBL) research. In D. H. Evensen & C. E. Hmelo (eds.), *Problem-based learning: A research perspective on learning interactions* (pp. 185–95). Mahwah, NJ: Erlbaum.

Berkson, L. (1993, Oct. Supplement). Problem-based learning: Have the expectations been met? *Academic Medicine, 68*, S79–88.

Bloom, B. S. (ed.) (1956). *Taxonomy of educational objectives. Handbook I: Cognitive domain.* New York: David McKay.

Blumberg, P. (2000). Evaluating the evidence that problem-based learners are self-directed learn-ers: A review of the literature. In D. H. Evensen & C. E. Hmelo (eds.), *Problem-based learning: A research perspective on learning interactions* (pp. 199–226). Mahwah, NJ: Erlbaum.

Bol, L., & Strage, A. (1996). The contradiction between teachers' instructional goals and their assessment practices in high school biology courses. *Science Education, 80,* 145–63.

Capon, N., & Kuhn, D. (2004). What's so good about problem-based learning? *Cognition and Instruction, 22,* 61–79.

Connor-Greene, P. A. (2000). Psychology. In S. Madden (ed.), *Service learning across the curriculum* (pp. 9–22). Blue Ridge Summit, PA: University Press of America.

Connor-Greene, P. A. (2002). Problem-based service learning: The evolution of a team project. *Teaching of Psychology, 29,* 193–7.

Connor-Greene, P. A., & Greene, D. J. (2002). Science or snake oil? Teaching critical evaluation of "research" reports on the Internet. *Teaching of Psychology, 29,* 321–4.

de Sanchez, M. A. (1995). Using critical-thinking principles as a guide to college-level instruction. *Teaching of Psychology, 22,* 72–4.

Dochy, F., Segers, M., Van de Bossche, P., & Gijbels, D. (2002). Effects of problem-based learning: A meta-analysis. *Learning and Instruction, 13,* 533–68.

Dolmans, D., Wolfhagen, I., van der Vleuten, C., Wijnen, W. (2001). Solving problems with group work in problem-based learning: Hold on to the philosophy. *Medical Education, 35,* 884–9.

Donham, R. S., Schmieg, F. I., & Allen, D. E. (2001). The large and small of it. In B. J. Duch, S. E. Groh, & D. E. Allen (eds.), *The power of problem-based learning* (pp. 179–90). Sterling, VA: Stylus Publishing.

Duch, B. J. (2001). Models for problem-based instruction in undergraduate courses. In B. J. Duch, S. E. Groh, & D. E. Allen (eds.), *The power of problem-based learning* (pp. 39–45). Sterling, VA: Stylus Publishing.

Duch, B. J., & Allen, D. E. (1996, Spring). Problems: A key factor in PBL. *About Teaching, 50,* 25–8.

Duch, B. J., & Groh, S. E. (2001). Assessment strategies in a problem-based learning course. In B. J. Duch, S. E. Groh, & D. E. Allen (eds.), *The power of problem-based learning* (pp. 95–106). Sterling, VA: Stylus Publishing.

Duch, B. J., Groh, S. E., & Allen, D. E. (2001). Why problem-based learning? A case study of institutional change in undergraduate education. In B. J. Duch, S. E. Groh, & D. E. Allen (eds.), *The power of problem-based learning* (pp. 3–11). Sterling, VA: Stylus Publishing.

Elton, L. R. B., & Laurillard, D. M. (1979). Trends in research on student learning. *Studies in Higher Education, 4,* 87–102.

Enns, C. Z. (1993). Integrating separate and connected knowing: The experiential learning model. *Teaching of Psychology, 20,* 7–13.

Evensen, D. H., Salisbury-Glennon, J. D., & Glenn, J. (2001). A qualitative study of six medical students in a problem-based curriculum: Toward a situated model of self-regulation. *Journal of Educational Psychology, 93,* 659–76.

Eyler, J., Root, S., & Giles, D. E., Jr. (1998). Service-learning and the development of expert citizens: Service-learning and cognitive science. In R. G. Bringle & D. K. Duffy (eds.), *With service in mind: Concepts and models for service-learning in psychology* (pp. 85–100). Washington, DC: American Association for Higher Education.

Glasgow, N. A. (1997). *New curriculum for new times: A guide to student-centered, problem-based learning.* Thousand Oaks, CA: Corwin Press.

Goldberg, G. L., Roswell, B. S., & Michaels, H. (1996). Empirical investigations: Can assessment mirror instruction? A look at peer response and revision in a large-scale writing test. *Educational Assessment, 3,* 287–314.

Halpern, D. F. (1998). Teaching critical thinking for transfer across domains. *American Psychologist, 53,* 449–55.

Halpern, D. F., & Nummedal, S. G. (1995). Closing thoughts about helping students improve how they think. *Teaching of Psychology, 22,* 82–3.

Halonen, J. S., Appleby, D. C., Brewer, C. L., Buskist, W., Gillem, A. R., Halpern, D., et al. (2002, March). Undergraduate Psychology major learning goals and outcomes: A report (APA Task Force on Undergraduate Psychology Major Competencies). Retrieved Aug. 31, 2004, from www.apa.org/ed/pcue/reports.html

Halonen, J. S., Bosack, T., Clay, S., McCarthy, M., Dunn, D. S., Hill, G. W., et al. (2003). A rubric for learning, teaching, and assessing scientific inquiry in psychology. *Teaching of Psychology, 30,* 196–208.

Hays, J. R., & Vincent, J. P. (2004). Students' evaluation of problem-based learning in graduate psychology courses. *Teaching of Psychology, 31,* 124–6.

Hildebidle, J. (1991). Having it by heart: Some reflections on knowing too much. In C. R. Christensen, D. A. Garvin, & A. Sweet (eds.), *Education for judgment* (pp. 265–74). Boston, MA: Harvard Business School Press.

Hmelo, C. E., & Evensen, D. H. (2000). Problem-based learning: Gaining insights on learning interactions through multiple methods of inquiry. In D. H. Evensen & C. E. Hmelo (eds.), *Problem-based learning: A research perspective on learning interactions* (pp. 1–16). Mahwah, NJ: Erlbaum.

Jarvis, P. (1987). *Adult learning in the social context.* London: Croom Helm.

Kelson, A. C. M., & Distlehorst, L. H. (2000). Groups in problem-based learning (PBL): Essential elements in theory and practice. In D. H. Evensen & C. E. Hmelo (eds.), *Problem-based learning: A research perspective on learning interactions* (pp. 167–84). Mahwah, NJ: Erlbaum.

Kitto, S. L., & Griffiths, L. G. (2001). The evolution of problem-based learning in a biotechnology class. In B. J. Duch, S. E. Groh, & D. E. Allen (eds.), *The power of problem-based learning* (pp. 121–30). Sterling, VA: Stylus Publishing.

Lancaster, C. J., Bradley, E., Smith, I. K., Chessman, A., Stroup-Benham, C. A., & Camp, M. G. (1997). The effect of PBL on students' perception of learning environment. *Academic Medicine, 72* (Suppl. 1), S10–12.

Lieux, E. M. (2001). A skeptic's look at PBL. In B. J. Duch, S. E. Groh, & D. E. Allen (eds.), *The power of problem-based learning* (pp. 223–35). Sterling, VA: Stylus Publishing.

McGovern, T. V., & Reich, J. N. (1996). A comment on the Quality Principles. *American Psychologist, 51,* 252–5.

McKeachie, W. J. (2002). *Teaching tips: Strategies, research, and theory for college and university teachers* (11th ed.). Boston: Houghton Mifflin.

Neufeld, V. R., & Barrows, H. S. (1974). The "McMaster Philosophy": An approach to medical education. *Journal of Medical Education, 49,* 1040–50.

Nummedal, S. G., & Halpern, D. F. (1995). Introduction: Making the case for "Psychologists teach critical thinking." *Teaching of Psychology, 22,* 4–5.

Regan, T. (1998). On the Web, speed instead of accuracy. *Nieman Reports, 52,* 81.

Savin-Baden, M. (2000). *Problem-based learning in higher education: Untold stories.* Philadelphia, PA: Open University Press.

Shelton, J. B., & Smith, R. F. (1998). Problem-based learning in analytical science undergraduate teaching. *Research in Science and Technical Education, 16,* 19–29.

Shipman, H. L., & Duch, B. J. (2001). Problem-based learning in large and very large classes. In B. J. Duch, S. E. Groh, & D. E. Allen (eds.), *The power of problem-based learning* (pp. 39–45). Sterling, VA: Stylus Publishing.

Solomon, P., & Finch, E. (1998). A qualitative study identifying stressors associated with adapting to problem-based learning. *Teaching and Learning in Medicine, 10*, 58–64.

Vernon, D. T., & Blake, R. L. (1993). Does problem-based learning work? A meta-analysis of evaluative research. *Academic Medicine, 68*, 550–63.

Wells, C. V. (2003). Service learning and problem-based learning in a Conflict Resolution class. *Teaching of Psychology, 30*, 260–3.

Wilkerson, L., & Gijselaers, W. H. (1996). *Bringing problem-based learning to higher education: Theory and practice.* San Francisco: Jossey-Bass.

Wood, D. F. (2003). ABCs of learning and teaching in medicine: Problem based learning. *British Medical Journal, 326*, 328–30.

Yamane, D. (1996). Collaboration and its discontents: Steps toward overcoming barriers to successful group projects. *Teaching Sociology, 24*, 378–83.

13
Understanding Human Thought: Educating Students as Critical Thinkers

Ψ

Heidi R. Riggio & Diane F. Halpern
Claremont McKenna College

Undergraduates often interpret the term "critical thinking" quite literally, with emphasis on the word "critical" as involving criticism, negativity, opposition, or argumentativeness. This type of interpretation is unfortunate, mainly because it may bias students' approach to a class that they perceive to be teaching them to be "critical," especially of strongly held personal beliefs. It is perhaps advisable then that instructors emphasize early in the semester what the term "critical thinking" actually means in the context of psychology: effortful, careful, consciously controlled processing that maximizes the use of all available evidence and cognitive strategies, and purposefully strives to overcome individual biases. Such thinking maximizes student learning both in course work and daily life; increases the likelihood of accurate, well-informed, successful judgments and decisions; and encourages development of rich, sophisticated knowledge.

The term "critical" may be compared to the word "skeptical," which means thoughtful. We should encourage our students to be skeptical, or thoughtful, in their evaluation of incoming information and development of judgments and decisions. Skepticism (habitual thoughtfulness) and its application in the real world (critical thinking) are not cynical – skepticism is a positive trait that contributes to individual and societal well-being through its carefulness, awareness, and evidentiary basis. The word "critical" also implies a negative emotional tone. Undergraduates must be made aware that truly critical thought is emotion-free – free of biases or preferences for one outcome over others because of emotions. Of course, no one is ever *completely* free of emotions, especially when thinking about controversial topics like abortion, the death penalty, and affirmative action, but we can be more rational, and that is a step in the right direction.

Critical thinking instruction is an imperative in contemporary society because adults who think critically – who carefully evaluate information provided by science, the media, government, religion, education – compose the "informed populace" that is a primary ingredient of rule by the people (or democracy). Skeptical undergraduates will also experience greater understanding and success throughout their coursework, suggesting that undergraduates should be exposed to critical thinking instruction early in their education (Messer & Griggs, 1989; Scott & Markert, 1994).

Arguably, the most successful development of critical thinking skills in undergraduates requires the transfer of these skills into their everyday lives (Halpern, 2003). How is this process best accomplished? In addition to direct instruction and practice, it seems essential that undergraduates understand that course material focuses on basic human information-processing qualities that are *universal.* In other words, undergraduates should internalize research evidence on human thinking as characteristic of their *own* individual thought processes. Most undergraduates are fascinated with the efficiency, complexity, and inherently functional nature of human cognition – they are equally fascinated by systematic errors resulting from that efficiency and automaticity. When they understand how their minds work in understanding the world around them, and the powerful influence of psychological and situational factors on their processing of information, they are likely to become more careful in their judgments. Knowledge of biases, automatic and unconscious thought processes, social influence, and the importance of evidence in making logical, informed judgments will encourage more careful, skeptical student thinking, especially if they enjoy learning about these things.

The Power of Emotions

Undergraduates need to be made aware of the powerful influence of their emotions on their processing of information. Emotional responses to issues, positive or negative, are the primary foundation for biased judgments. Truly impartial judgment does not involve favor for any particular outcome, but favor for careful examination of evidence supporting and detracting from each side. When you teach course material illustrating the power of emotions in thought, including presentations of research, you can draw material from feelings of certainty in making judgments (Werth & Strack, 2003); belief in a just world (Lerner, 1980); hindsight bias (Wasserman, Lempert, & Hastie, 1991); counterfactual thinking (Roese, Hur, & Pennington, 1999); self-serving biases in attribution (Campbell & Sedikides, 1999) and memory (Bahrick, Hall, & Berger, 1996); effects of mood on thought and social behavior (Forgas, 1998); and so on. It is especially important that undergraduates understand that these cognitive biases occur because they provide feelings of comfort and security in understanding the world, and thus people are motivated to use them, even if they are not consciously aware of the motivation (Sanna, Chang, & Meier, 2001).

A teaching tool one author (HR) uses is the O. J. Simpson murder trial, and the strong emotional component inherent in individual evaluation of the case. An exercise involves undergraduates as jurors who evaluate trial evidence (see Bugliosi, 1996; Darden, 1996, for reviews), deliberate, and reach a verdict. Discussion of the trial includes the perceptions of the actual jurors and the various opinions/reactions of black and white Americans to the not-guilty verdict (based on emotion, including widespread familiarity and liking of Simpson). An excellent video documentary,[1] which provides students with an "inside" view of the case (including interviews with actual jurors), complements the discussion.

You can further discuss the jury system as requiring decision-making divorced of emotion, using other controversial, emotional cases that have received widespread media attention. One example is the case of Andrea Yates, the Texas mother who drowned her five children in the bathtub, and the jury's conviction of her on first-degree murder, despite her extensive history of mental illness, including psychosis, suicide attempts, hospitalization, and so on (the veracity of the decision is nicely questioned when a comparison is made to Lorena Bobbitt, who was acquitted by reason of insanity for cutting off her husband's penis while he was sleeping). Another interesting example is Louise Woodward, the British nanny convicted of second-degree murder by a jury in the shaking death of her infant charge. The jury's decision was overturned by the trial judge (a very infrequent event) and changed to involuntary manslaughter because second-degree murder requires intent to kill.[2]

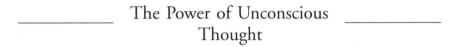

The Power of Unconscious Thought

Understanding human thought and learning to maximize its analytical abilities requires recognition of unconscious psychological processes, many of which occur rather automatically in response to situational cues (see Wegner & Bargh, 1998). When discussing how unconscious thought can affect rational thought, teachers may focus on material illustrating effects of automatic processes on judgment and decision-making, including confirmation biases in social behavior (Yzerbyt, Rocher, & Schadron, 1996) and memory (Halpern, 1985); automaticity of stereotypes (Vonk & van Knippenberg, 1995); priming of schemas, including aggression (Anderson, Benjamin, & Bartholow, 1998); snap judgments, including physical attractiveness biases (Casey & Ritter, 1996); self-fulfilling prophecy (Rosenthal & Jacobsen, 1968); and over-reliance on heuristics (Tversky & Kahneman, 1973).

One interesting area of research to highlight is unconscious mimicking of nonverbal behavior in interpersonal interactions (Chartrand & Bargh, 1999). Some individuals have a greater tendency to mimic the emotional expressions of others during interaction (of which they express no conscious recognition). In turn, individuals who engage in more mimicry tend to be liked more by their interaction partners, who are equally unlikely to recognize nonverbal mimicry as an important factor affecting liking (Dimberg, Thunberg, & Elmehed, 2001). Becoming conscious of unconscious processes allows (and perhaps encourages) undergraduates to exert greater control over their information processing and subsequent social behavior.

The Power of Social Influence

Teachers must present undergraduates with research documenting the powerful influence of situational factors and other people in influencing their thoughts and decisions. You should describe both informational and normative social influence (e.g., Sherif, 1936, versus Asch, 1952), including their different outcomes (conformity versus conversion). Milgram's (1974) classic obedience studies are also worth mention. Students also enjoy learning about research on compliance techniques and how they are used to manipulate consumers (Cialdini, 2001). Teachers may also discuss argument tactics and fallacies, including those based on emotions (virtue by association, bandwagon techniques, etc.).

A teaching tool one author (HR) uses is a documentary video of the People's Temple and the Jonestown murders/suicides.[3] Most undergraduates have never heard of Jonestown, and if they have they assume the event was a mass suicide. The video is rather graphic, including an audiotape of Jonestown during the killings (Jim Jones, his verbal persuasion during the event, children's cries, screams, etc.). Almost invariably, when asked to identify the causes of Jonestown, undergraduates demonstrate the fundamental attribution error and focus on the personal traits of Jones and his followers in explaining the event (e.g., "He was crazy"; "Those people were stupid"). A discussion following the video focuses on the multitude of very powerful situational factors affecting the behaviors of the people in Jonestown (e.g., physical, social, and informational isolation; sleep deprivation; hard labor; malnutrition; physical and sexual abuse, etc.; see Layton, 1998, for a survivor's autobiography). This consideration leads to a deeper discussion about commonalities among cult groups focusing on manipulation and social-influence tactics (including deindividuation techniques; Prentice-Dunn & Rogers, 1982), as well as the power of dissent (including singular dissent) in fighting normative social influence (Allen & Levine, 1971). Teachers should model the role of the lone dissenter in fostering resistance to normative influence, particularly effective early in the group encounter (Morris, Miller, & Spangenberg, 1977), to undergraduates as skeptical thinkers who are dependent on evidence rather than emotion and social outcomes.

The Power of Evidence

Critical-thinking instruction should involve an emphasis on maximizing the use of quality information in thinking. Course material may focus on logic and reasoning; scientific research methods; and divergent thinking, including relations with creativity and minority social influence (Peterson & Nemeth, 1996). One teaching tool one author (HR) has used is the film *The Crucible*, which undergraduates are often familiar with but which they may not have analyzed in terms of critical thinking and evidentiary value. Another tool used is an "exorcism" filmed by *Dateline NBC*, which is discussed in terms of the "evidence" of possession available in the film, hypothesis testing, and disconfirmation.[4] An excellent source for detailed discussion on superstitious thinking, including beliefs in astrology, alien abduction, parapsychology, "holocaust deniers," and so on is Shermer (1997), as well as the classic video "Secrets of the Psychics" starring the Amazing James Randi.[5]

The Power of Behavior

Instructors must teach students practical tools and skills to use in solving problems critically, including use of graphs, flow charts, diagrams, etc.; planning skills; metacognition; mnemonic and other memory devices; argument analysis; creative thinking and problem-solving skills; and above all, evidence evaluation skills (see Halpern, 2003). Instructors will find an abundance of critical thinking and problem-solving workbooks available (e.g., Halpern & Riggio, 2003).

Conclusion

In our experience, undergraduates sometimes display a general reluctance to engage in critical thinking, especially when class discussion turns to controversial issues (e.g., abortion, religion, the meaning of life, etc.). Teachers should try to convince them how important it is to habitually and *effortfully* evaluate information from the media, government, other social institutions, and sometimes the people around us. Emphasize the importance of critical thinking to a solid undergraduate education, including as mandated by groups of educators (Diamond, 1997) and policy-makers (National Commission of Excellence in Education, 1983). The future of the world is quite literally in the hands of our young adults; let them be critical thinkers, so that important decisions involved in government, education, and public policy do not involve illogical beliefs based on emotions that are unsupported by direct evidence.

NOTES

1 "Why O. J. Simpson Won" (1996). A&E Home Video, Cat. No. AAE-16022.
2 *Massachusetts v. Woodward*, available at www.courttv.com/trials/woodward/zobel.html.
3 "Jonestown: Mystery of a Massacre" (1996). A&E Home Video, Cat. No. AAE-17275.
4 *Dateline NBC*, 11/13/2001, Item #NBDL011113.
5 NOVA: "Secrets of the Psychics" (1974, re-released 1996). ASIN 6304463189.

REFERENCES

Allen, V. L., & Levine, J. M. (1971). Social support and conformity: The role of independent assessment of reality. *Journal of Experimental Social Psychology*, 7, 48–58.

Anderson, C. A., Benjamin, A. J., & Bartholow, B. D. (1998). Does the gun pull the trigger? Automatic priming effects of weapon pictures and weapon names. *Psychological Science*, 9, 308–14.

Asch, S. E. (1952). *Social psychology*. New York: Prentice-Hall.

Bahrick, H. P., Hall, L. K., & Berger, S. A. (1996). Accuracy and distortion in memory for high school grades. *Psychological Science*, 7, 265–71.

Bugliosi, V. (1996). *Outrage: The five reasons why O. J. Simpson got away with murder*. New York: W. W. Norton.

Campbell, W. K., & Sedikides, C. (1999). Self-threat magnifies the self-serving bias: A meta-analytic integration. *Review of General Psychology, 3*, 23–43.

Casey, R. J., & Ritter, J. M. (1996). How infant appearance informs: Child care providers' responses to babies in varying appearance of age and attractiveness. *Journal of Applied Developmental Psychology, 17*, 495–518.

Chartrand, T. L., & Bargh, J. A. (1999). The chameleon effect: The perception–behavior link and social interaction. *Journal of Personality and Social Psychology, 76*, 893–910.

Cialdini, R. B. (2001). *Influence: Science and practice* (4th ed.). New York: Longman.

Darden, C. (1996). *In contempt*. New York: Harper Collins.

Diamond, R. M. (1997). *Curriculum reform needed if students are to master core concepts* [webpage], at http://chronicle.com/search97cgi/s97_cgi? [2000, Dec. 28].

Dimberg, U., Thunberg, M., & Elmehed, K. (2000). Unconscious facial reactions to emotional facial expressions. *Psychological Science, 11*, 86–9.

Forgas, J. P. (1998). Asking nicely? The effects of mood on responding to more or less polite requests. *Personality and Social Psychology Bulletin, 24*, 173–85.

Halpern, D. F. (1985). The influence of sex-role stereotypes on prose recall. *Sex Roles, 12*, 363–75.

Halpern, D. F. (2003). *Thought and knowledge: An introduction to critical thinking* (4th ed.). Mahwah, NJ: Erlbaum.

Halpern, D. F., & Riggio, H. R. (2003). *Thinking critically about critical thinking: Workbook to accompany Thought and knowledge: An introduction to critical thinking* (4th ed.). Mahwah, NJ: Erlbaum.

Layton, D. (1998). *Seductive poison*. New York: Doubleday.

Lerner, M. J. (1980). *The belief in a just world: A fundamental delusion*. New York: Plenum.

Messer, W. S., & Griggs, R. A. (1989). Student belief and involvement in the paranormal and performance in introductory psychology. *Teaching of Psychology, 16*, 187–91.

Milgram, S. (1974). *Obedience to authority: An experimental view*. New York: Harper & Row.

Morris, W. N., Miller, R. S., & Spangenberg, S. (1977). The effects of dissenter position and task difficulty on conformity and response to conflict. *Journal of Personality, 45*, 251–66.

National Commission on Excellence in Education. (1983). *A nation at risk: The imperative for educational reform*. Washington, DC: Author.

Peterson, R. S., & Nemeth, C. J. (1996). Focus versus flexibility: Majority and minority influence can both improve performance. *Personality and Social Psychology Bulletin, 22*, 14–23.

Prentice-Dunn, S., & Rogers, R. W. (1982). Effects of public and private self-awareness on deindividuation and aggression. *Journal of Personality and Social Psychology, 43*, 503–13.

Roese, N. J., Hur, T., & Pennington, G. L. (1999). Counterfactual thinking and regulatory focus: Implications for action versus inaction and sufficiency versus necessity. *Journal of Personality and Social Psychology, 77*, 1109–20.

Rosenthal, R., & Jacobson, L. (1968). *Pygmalion in the classroom: Teacher expectation and pupils' intellectual development*. New York: Holt.

Sanna, L. J., Chang, E. C., & Meier, S. (2001). Counterfactual thinking and self-motives. *Personality and Social Psychology Bulletin, 27*, 1023–34.

Scott, J. N., & Markert, R. J. (1994). Relationship between critical thinking skills and success in preclinical courses. *Academic Medicine, 69*, 920–4.

Sherif, M. (1936). *The psychology of social norms*. New York: Harper.

Shermer, M. (1997). *Why people believe weird things: Pseudoscience, superstition, and other confusions of our time*. New York: Holt.

Tversky, A., & Kahneman, D. (1973). Availability: A heuristic for judging frequency and probability. *Cognitive Psychology, 5*, 207–32.

Vonk, R., & van Knippenberg, A. (1995). Processing attitude statements from in-group and out-group members: Effects of within-group and within-person inconsistencies on reading times. *Journal of Personality and Social Psychology, 68*, 215–27.

Wasserman, D., Lempert, R. O., & Hastie, R. (1991). Hindsight and causality. *Personality and Social Psychology Bulletin, 17*, 30–5.

Wegner, D. M., & Bargh, J. A. (1998). Control and automaticity in social life. In D. T. Gilbert, S. T. Fiske, & G. Lindzey (eds.), *The handbook of social psychology* (4th ed., vol. 1, pp. 446–96). New York: Oxford University Press.

Werth, L., & Strack, F. (2003). An inferential approach to the knew-it-all-along phenomenon. *Memory, 11*, 411–19.

Yzerbyt, V. Y., Rocher, S., & Schadron, G. (1996). Stereotypes as explanations: A subjective essentialistic view of group perception. In R. Spears, P. J. Oakes, N. Ellemers, & S. A. Haslam (eds.), *The social psychology of stereotyping and group life* (pp. 20–50). Malden, MA: Blackwell.

14
Leading Discussions and Asking Questions

Ψ

Tracy E. Zinn & Bryan K. Saville
James Madison University

Dubbed "the Velveeta of teaching methods" (Benjamin, 2002, p. 57), the lecture is the most widely utilized approach to classroom instruction, remaining the method of choice for over 80 percent of college instructors. Although lecturing can be a valuable tool in certain contexts (e.g., Davis, 1993; McKeachie, 2002; Zakrajsck, 1999), considerable research shows that it is less effective than other alternative methods of classroom instruction (e.g., Buskist, Cush, & DeGrandpre, 1991; Kulik, Kulik, & Cohen, 1979; Saville, Zinn, & Elliott, 2005).

One effective alternative to the lecture is the discussion method. In contrast with traditional lecture method, which typically treats students as passive, empty receptacles waiting to be filled with knowledge imparted by an erudite instructor, discussion promotes active learning and allows students to obtain knowledge and utilize critical thinking skills by engaging in a lively exchange of information and ideas. As Davis (1993) stated, "A good give-and-take discussion can produce unmatched learning experiences as students articulate their ideas, respond to their classmates' points, and develop skills in evaluating the evidence for their own and others' positions" (p. 63). The remainder of this chapter will provide a prescription for effectively facilitating in-class discussions.

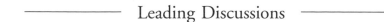 Leading Discussions

Preparation

Although discussion is often free-spirited and capricious, it is imperative that you spend some time preparing beforehand. Several days prior to a class discussion, you may want to hand out a "preparation guide" that provides the content to be discussed, and gives students the opportunity to think about topics in advance. You also should consider how you will start the discussion. Some possibilities include (a) asking students to respond directly to specific questions, factual and analytical, from the preparation guide; (b) opening with a controversial topic that is likely to pique students' interests; (c) asking students to pose questions that they considered while reviewing the preparation guide; and (d) raising questions based on common student experiences (see also Davis, 1993; McKeachie, 2002).

Once you have spent some time preparing, you will need to set ground rules for the discussion. First, make clear to students the purpose of the discussion. Whether your goal is to help students develop critical thinking skills, tolerate other students' opinions, or understand better their own views on a given topic, discussion will flow better if students appreciate the purpose of the discussion. Second, explain what behavior is acceptable during discussion. For example, can students speak freely at any time or must they raise their hands? You might wish to allocate some class time to teaching effective participation skills, and it might be useful to include students in the development of a set of rules that will define appropriate behavior (e.g., see Kramer & Korn, 2001). Finally, you should make it clear that your job is to guide the conversation, not dominate it.

Facilitating Discussion

Once you have taken the time to prepare your discussion questions and subsequently laid the ground rules for appropriate behavior, you still need to provide a context in which students are comfortable engaging in conversation. You can accomplish this objective by incorporating several simple, but effective, practices.

Promoting social interaction. One tactic for increasing participation is to have students become familiar with one another. You can achieve this goal simply by having students move their desks into a circle and introduce themselves to one another. If your classroom's structure does not allow for this rearrangement, students can at least turn in their seats to face one another, or you may ask them to break into smaller groups. By changing the layout of the classroom, you are no longer the center of attention, and students are more likely to engage each other in conversation. Thus, students are more likely to become acquainted. Consequently, when students – especially shy students – feel they are among friends, they are more likely to speak up (McKeachie, 2002).

Attending to nonverbal behavior. Students' body language will tell you if they are on-task (e.g., gazing off into space vs. looking intently at the speaker), have a question or comment (e.g., raising their hands), or are annoyed by a discussion monopolizer (e.g., rolling their eyes). Using students' nonverbal behaviors as a guide, you can assess the situation and quickly make changes to the discussion, when necessary.

Awareness of your own nonverbal behavior also is important. For example, if you have a discussion monopolizer, it may help to assess whether you are encouraging long-winded or irrelevant comments through subtle nonverbal behaviors such as nodding in agreement or smiling. These seemingly trivial behaviors can have a major impact on the quality of discussion. Similarly, you also can use your own nonverbal behavior to control the direction of the discourse. For example, moving around the classroom can energize the discussion, and quietly stepping between confrontational students can quickly defuse a heated argument. In sum, increased awareness of both your students' and your own nonverbal behavior can make for a more productive discussion.

Responding to students' comments and questions. The way that you respond verbally to students is perhaps the most important component of effectively facilitating discussion. First, be sure that the tone of your response is positive and constructive even if the question or comment is "off-track" or clearly wrong (e.g., Palmer, 1998). For example, if a student asks a question that would take the class off-topic, instead of saying, "That's not important," remark on the quality of the question and invite him to discuss it with you after class. Or, if a student addresses a topic that you will cover later in the semester, remark "That's a good point. Be sure to bring that up when we discuss chapter 6." You should always model respectful behavior and make it clear that the discussions are part of a cooperative endeavor (McKeachie, 2002).

Second, when responding to students' comments or questions, be specific rather than general. For example, saying "You did a good job relating those two concepts" is better than "Thanks" or "Good." These types of responses show that you are interested in what students have to say, help shape students' future comments, and create a supportive atmosphere.

Intervene only when necessary. During a discussion, you should "let students do the talking" (Finkel, 2000, p. 31). There are times, however, when you will need to speak up. If students are debating a concept they clearly misunderstand or the discussion is lagging or becoming too emotional, you may need to step in and remedy the situation. In addition, if the discussion is stagnant, you will need to change the direction or format. Nonetheless, you do not want to dominate the conversation or neutralize every disagreement. Use your authority judiciously.

Asking Questions

Although discussion should be student-centered and student-driven, leading an effective discussion will necessarily require you to ask appropriate questions. Whether asking a question simply to initiate the discussion or to redirect the discussion to a more appropriate topic, we have found the following tips to be helpful.

Ask questions of varying content and difficulty. Bloom's (1956) taxonomy of thinking skills may be helpful in this regard: Lower-level questions that focus on knowledge and comprehension (e.g., "What are the stages in Piaget's theory of cognitive development?") help assess students' understanding of the material, whereas higher-level questions that underscore application, analysis, synthesis, and evaluation (e.g., "How did Piaget's theory subsequently influence Kohlberg's theory of moral reasoning?") help develop critical thinking skills.

Ask only one question at a time. Students may become confused if you string together several questions. Also, students may hesitate to answer if they know the answer to the first question, but not the second. By breaking complex questions or problems into sub-problems, discussion is likely to be more effective, because students will be responding to the same part of the problem or question (Maier & Maier, 1957; McKeachie, 2002).

Avoid questions that require one-word answers. Sustained discussion is difficult if students can answer questions with a single word or phrase. Try instead to ask questions that require explanation or interpretation, or questions that may have more than one correct answer (Davis, 1993).

Be patient. One problem instructors often have when asking questions is that they do not allow students enough time to formulate a response (McKeachie, 2002). When asking complex questions, give students some time to think. In fact, by explicitly stating that you want them to contemplate their answers before responding, you are making it clear that you expect some silence between question and response.

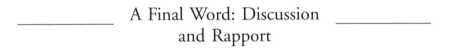

Evaluating Discussion

One problem with discussion is that students often have trouble ascertaining what, if anything, they learned during discussion. To address this problem, take 5 minutes at the end of class and ask students to reflect on the topics covered in the discussion, summarize the main points, and indicate what concepts the discussion did not address. You can also have students write down a "gem," the most interesting thing they learned that day, and ask them to submit it along with any ideas for improving discussion. This technique enhances learning and helps develop student–instructor rapport (Zinn, 2003). During the next class period, you can review the comments with the class and use them as a springboard to initiate that day's discussion.

A Final Word: Discussion and Rapport

Discussion will be much more successful if instructors have taken the time to develop rapport with their students (e.g., Buskist & Saville, 2004; Forsyth, 2003; Lowman, 1995). If students have experienced the increases in classroom self-efficacy and self-worth that often emerge as a function of increased student–instructor rapport, they will be more likely to "put themselves out there" and explore the uncertainties that often come with learning in discussion-based environments. As such, instructors may wish to consult Buskist and Saville (2004), who provided tips for developing classroom rapport and concluded that "[e]ffective teaching involves tinkering with [the] environment so that we maximize the chances that students will learn from our courses" (p. 155). Time spent rapport-building is likely to produce an amiable relationship between student and teacher, which will ultimately result in more stimulating and effective in-class discussions.

REFERENCES

Benjamin, L. T., Jr. (2002). Lecturing. In S. F. Davis & W. Buskist (eds.), *The teaching of psychology: Essays in honor of Wilbert J. McKeachie and Charles L. Brewer* (pp. 57–67). Mahwah, NJ: Erlbaum.

Bloom, B. S. (ed.) (1956). *Taxonomy of educational objectives, Vol. 1: Cognitive domain.* New York: Longmans, Green.

Buskist, W., Cush, D., & DeGrandpre, R. J. (1991). The life and times of PSI. *Journal of Behavioral Education, 1,* 215–34.

Buskist, W., & Saville, B. K. (2004). Rapport-building: Creating positive emotional contexts for enhancing teaching and learning. In B. Perlman, L. I. McCann, & S. H. McFadden (eds.), *Lessons learned, Vol. 2: Practical advice for the teaching of psychology* (pp. 149–55). Washington, DC: American Psychological Society.

Davis, B. G. (1993). *Tools for teaching.* San Francisco: Jossey-Bass.

Finkel, D. (2000). *Teaching with your mouth shut.* Portsmouth, NH: Heinemann.

Forsyth, D. R. (2003). *The professor's guide to teaching: Psychological principles and practices.* Washington, DC: American Psychological Association.

Kramer, T. J., & Korn, J. H. (1999). Class discussions: Promoting participation and preventing problems. In B. Perlman, L. I. McCann, & S. H. McFadden (eds.), *Lessons learned: Practical advice for the teaching of psychology* (pp. 99–104). Washington, DC: American Psychological Society.

Kulik, J. A., Kulik, C. C., & Cohen, P. A. (1979). A meta-analysis of outcome studies of Keller's personalized system of instruction. *American Psychologist, 34,* 307–18.

Lowman, J. (1995). *Mastering the techniques of teaching* (2nd ed.). San Francisco: Jossey-Bass.

Maier, N. R. F., & Maier, L. A. (1957). An experimental test of the effects of "developmental" vs. "free" discussion on the quality of group decisions. *Journal of Applied Psychology, 41,* 320–3.

McKeachie, W. (2002). *Teaching tips: Strategies, research, and theory for college and university teachers* (11th ed.). Boston: Houghton Mifflin Company.

Palmer, P. J. (1998). *The courage to teach: Exploring the inner landscape of a teacher's life.* San Francisco: Jossey-Bass.

Saville, B. K., Zinn, T. E., & Elliott, M. P. (2005). Interteaching vs. traditional methods of instruction: A preliminary analysis. *Teaching of Psychology, 32,* 160–2.

Zakrajsek, T. (1999). Developing effective lectures. In B. Perlman, L. I. McCann, & S. H. McFadden (eds.), *Lessons learned: Practical advice for the teaching of psychology* (pp. 81–6). Washington, DC: American Psychological Society.

Zinn, T. E. (2003, Feb.). Using frequent student feedback to modify and improve course content. Poster presented at the 15th annual Southeastern Conference on the Teaching of Psychology, Atlanta, GA.

15

Building a Repertoire of Effective Classroom Demonstrations

Ψ

Douglas A. Bernstein
University of South Florida

In an article called "Tell and Show: The Merits of Classroom Demonstrations" (Bernstein, 1994), I listed what I saw (and still see) as four main advantages of using demonstrations to promote and enliven the teaching of psychology: First, demonstrations attract and hold students' attention when they might otherwise tend to drift away mentally. Second, demonstrations that involve the entire class create active learning experiences that make demonstrated principles and phenomena especially memorable. Third, by bringing course material to life in the classroom, demonstrations help to motivate students to learn that material on their own, outside the classroom. (This is a vital benefit, because there is never enough class time to cover anywhere near as much material as we wish we could.) Fourth, effective demonstrations serve as course highlights that students can enjoy and that we teachers can anticipate with pleasure, whether it is the first or the umpteenth time we have taught the course. In short, I believe that having an extensive repertoire of good demonstrations not only helps our students to learn, but increases their motivation for learning while helping us to maintain our enthusiasm for teaching (Goss Lucas & Bernstein, 2005).

Finding Demonstrations

It is easy to find effective classroom demonstrations for psychology courses. The instructor's resource manuals and publisher websites associated with most major psychology textbooks are filled with them. Dozens more are available in numerous activities handbooks (e.g. Benjamin & Lowman, 1981; Benjamin, Nodine, Ernst, & Blair-Broeker 1999; Makosky, Whittemore, & Rogers, 1987; Makosky, Sileo, Whittemore, Landry, & Skutley 1990; Ware & Johnson, 2000a, 2000b, 2000c). Still other ideas for effective classroom demonstrations appear regularly in the APS *Observer* Teaching Tips column, in the journal *Teaching of Psychology*, and in postings to various teaching-related psychology mailgroups such as *TIPS* (Teaching in the Psychological Sciences; www.frostburg.edu/dept/psyc/southerly/tips/instruct.htm) and *PsychTeacher* (http://teachpsych.lemoyne.edu/teachpsych/div/psychteacher.html).

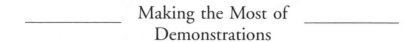

Making the Most of Demonstrations

Finding good demonstrations is one thing. Using them effectively can be quite another. To assure a smooth and professional demonstration, it is vital to practice performing it with friends or colleagues before using it in the classroom. If something *can* go wrong with a demonstration – even an apparently simple one – it *will*, or at least it might. Many psychology faculty have discovered this principle the hard way. One teacher I know wanted to spice up his introductory psychology lecture on learning by demonstrating how operant-conditioning principles are applied in police work. His plan was to have an officer from the local canine unit put a police dog through its paces on the stage of the auditorium where the class met. Unfortunately, schedule conflicts prevented a dry run before class, so when the officer and dog arrived they were immediately stationed at one side of the stage. A student volunteer, wearing a protective cuff, stood at the other. At the "attack" command, the animal sprinted for the student and, at the "halt" command, attempted to stop. A rehearsal would have revealed that the stopping distance for a large dog hurtling across a highly polished floor is a lot longer than one might think. Contrary to plan, the dog actually reached the student, who was a bit shaken (though unhurt) by the experience.

A second prerequisite for effective use of demonstrations is to establish a clear link between each demonstration and the concept, principle, or phenomenon you are trying to illustrate. This step is especially important when a demonstration is engaging enough, and enjoyable enough, to stand alone as a pleasant diversion from the "regular" course material. Consider the "rumor chain," for example. In this demonstration, a story is passed from one student to another until its content is markedly altered in the retelling. This exercise can nicely illustrate memory phenomena such as leveling and sharpening, distinctiveness, constructive/false memories, and the influence of gender and ethnic stereotypes on encoding and retrieval processes. However, if the teacher doesn't prepare students to listen for and take note of changes in the story, and if afterward there is no opportunity for students to identify the principles illustrated by those changes, the time spent on the demonstration, though enjoyable, may have done little to promote learning. In other words, failure to establish a link between a demonstration and its meaning can render even the most dramatic, active, and entertaining classroom activity ineffective as a teaching device.

Integrating Demonstrations into Lectures

How do you decide whether, and where, to include demonstrations in your courses? I think the best way to answer this question is to ask yourself another one: Are there lectures that you don't look forward to delivering because they feel stale or don't seem to interest your students? If the answer is yes, there are probably demonstrations that could break up and enliven the presentation – for you as well as for your class. In fact, I think that virtually any lecture can be enhanced by weaving some new demonstrations into it.

To decide exactly where to put new demonstrations, ask yourself where, in a particular lecture, things seem to bog down – where you might tend to lose a little enthusiasm and your students' interest might tend to wane; those are the spots on which to focus. Read over your lecture notes and ask yourself how you might better illustrate a particular phenomenon or principle instead of just talking about it. Better yet, think about the possibility of creating an illustration that actively involves the entire class. Then review the resources mentioned earlier and think about how you might use what you find there to turn some of your least favorite classes into sessions you'll look forward to, or at least not dread.

Don't hesitate to allow your creativity to come into play by using published demonstrations in new ways and by trying out demonstrations of your own devising. For example, when I started teaching abnormal psychology in the late 1960s, my lectures on various diagnostic categories were built around the filmed or tape-recorded interviews with mental patients that were available at the time. However, to help students understand some of the threats to the reliability of psychiatric diagnosis, I turned these presentations into an active learning exercise called "Name That Disorder" in which each student attempted to diagnose each patient. After an interview was presented, I read out the names of each major diagnostic category (e.g., schizophrenia, anxiety disorders, mood disorders). The students had been given a handout summarizing the features of these categories, and they were to raise a hand when I read the one they thought was correct. By looking around the room, the students could get an idea of the reliability of their diagnosis. I then read the names of various subcategories (e.g., conversion disorder, obsessive-compulsive disorder) and again asked for diagnostic votes by a show of hands. The result of this procedure was that students not only saw and heard behaviors that had been labeled as disordered, but experienced first hand the fact that interjudge agreement about major diagnostic categories is likely to be higher than it is for specific categories.

The idea for "Name That Disorder" came to me as I focused on how to improve my course, but ideas for expanding or creating demonstrations can come out of the blue, too. Years ago, my introductory psychology lecture on research methods contained only a passing mention of life records (diaries, school grades, etc.) as a research tool, and nothing about this data source was particularly memorable. Then, while reviewing my checkbook register in preparation for filing my income-tax return, it occurred to me that these records always brought back memories of the past year's events. Check registers, I realized, were a form of life record. From then on, I not only mentioned these records in my research methods lectures, but in the personality section of the course, I devised what became a very popular small-group active learning demonstration. Students in each group first review the checkbook registers of a (volunteer) student, and then try to draw inferences from it about the owner's life and personality. Afterward, there is a class discussion about the value and meaning of such inferences in comparison to other sources of data in personality assessment.

Another time, when the flash of a camera left a dark afterimage before my eyes, it dawned on me that if I created the same kind of image in a perception lecture I could illustrate Emmert's law (i.e., that the perceived size of an image is equal to the size of the retinal image multiplied by the perceived distance). I now bring a flash attachment with me to class, and after using it to create an afterimage, I ask my students to notice that this fixed-size image appears smaller when viewed against their outstretched hands (short perceived distance) than against a distant wall. Just the other day, I was reading *Games* magazine and noticed a drawing of a street scene that the reader is to scan for 30 seconds before trying to answer questions about the scene's details. It is a perfect stimulus for a classroom demonstration of the strengths and weaknesses of eyewitness testimony, and you can bet I will be using it the next time I teach the memory unit of introductory psychology. In other words, you can never tell when you will get a good idea for creating or improving a classroom demonstration, so be ready to write them down as soon as they occur to you. I have sometimes failed to do this because I was so sure I would remember my latest brainwave when I got home or arrived at the office. However, I didn't remember, and you might not either.

In summary, a repertoire of effective classroom demonstrations is a valuable component of your teaching, and you can strengthen it year by year simply by being open to the resources that are out there for the taking, and open as well to creating demonstrations that are uniquely your own. I must confess that it is often the prospect of conducting demonstrations, and the anticipation of my students' reactions to them, that makes my heart beat a little faster as I walk to class. I hope that some of the ideas I have offered here will help you to approach your own classroom with eagerness, too.

REFERENCES

Benjamin, L. T., Jr., & Lowman, K. (eds.) (1981). *Activities handbook for the teaching of psychology* (vol. 1). Washington, DC: The American Psychological Association.

Benjamin, L. T., Jr., Nodine, B., Ernst, R., & Blair-Broeker, C. (eds.) (1999). *Activities handbook for the teaching of psychology* (vol. 4). Washington, DC: The American Psychological Association.

Bernstein, D. A. (1994). Tell and show: The merits of classroom demonstrations. *APS Observer*, July/Aug. [Reprinted in B. Perlman, L. I. McCann, & S. H. McFadden (eds.) (1999). *Lessons learned: Practical advice for the teaching of psychology*. (vol. 1; pp. 105–8). Washington, DC: American Psychological Society.]

Goss Lucas, S., & Bernstein, D. A. (2005). *Teaching psychology: A step by step guide*. Mahwah, NJ: Erlbaum.

Makosky, V., Whittemore, L., & Rogers, A. (eds.) (1987). *Activities handbook for the teaching of psychology* (vol. 2). Washington, DC: The American Psychological Association.

Makosky, V., Sileo, C., Whittemore, L., Landry, C., & Skutley, M. (eds.) (1990). *Activities handbook for the teaching of psychology* (vol. 3). Washington, DC: The American Psychological Association.

Ware, M., & Johnson, R. (eds.) (2000a). *Handbook of demonstrations and activities in the teaching of psychology (Vol. 1: Introductory, Statistics, Research Methods, and History)* (2nd ed.) Mahwah, NJ: Erlbaum.

Ware, M., & Johnson, R. (eds.) (2000b). *Handbook of demonstrations and activities in the teaching of psychology (Vol. 2: Physiological-Comparative, Perception, Learning, Cognitive, and Developmental)* (2nd ed.) Mahwah, NJ: Erlbaum.

Ware, M., & Johnson, R. (eds.) (2000c). *Handbook of demonstrations and activities in the teaching of psychology (Vol. 3: Personality, Abnormal, Clinical-Counseling, and Social)* (2nd ed.) Mahwah, NJ: Erlbaum.

16

Lessons Learned Using PowerPoint in the Classroom

Ψ

Timothy J. Huelsman
Appalachian State University

I am not a techno-geek. I like technology and use plenty of it, but I do not really know how an LCD projector works or what the Level 2 cache on my new iMac does. Fortunately, you do not need to be a techno-geek to use classroom technology effectively. In fact, you don't really even need to like technology to use it well. All that is required is your willingness to learn a little and to prepare in advance.

"Technology . . . is a queer thing. It brings you great gifts with one hand, and it stabs you in the back with the other" (Snow as quoted in Lewis, 1971, p. 37). One of these gifts might be PowerPoint.[1] I have used PowerPoint for about 10 years. I have experienced both elements of Snow's description and I would like you to benefit from my experience. Thus, I have two objectives in this chapter. The first objective is to describe the lessons I have learned using this software. I will emphasize Microsoft's ubiquitous PowerPoint, but other presentation software is available (e.g., Apple's Keynote). The second objective is to describe how this great gift may stab us in our backs. Fortunately, appropriate preparation may help us lessen this pain.

Using the Great Gift: Teaching with PowerPoint

Critics have described many problems with PowerPoint. One problem is that given the limited amount of information appropriately presented on each slide, PowerPoint requires many slides to communicate complex information. Further, information "stacked in time" loses context, making relations difficult to evaluate (Tufte, 2003b). Another criticism rues the loss of real communication as presentations degrade into endless progressions of slides read by someone using PowerPoint as a teleprompter (Godin, 2001).

Given the popularity of PowerPoint and the ubiquity of bad PowerPoint presentations (we have all seen them; I will even admit to delivering one or two), I will dwell no longer on the ills of the method. Rather, I will describe some ways to use PowerPoint effectively.

Unfortunately, there is little research on what makes a good PowerPoint presentation, and the extant research misses the point. For instance, Cassady (1998) and Perry and Perry (1998) demonstrated that students prefer PowerPoint to other presentation methods (although I wonder if this is still the case now that some of the novelty has worn off). Closer to the issue, Bartsch and Cobern (2003) found that students' recall and recognition for information was worse when text and irrelevant pictures were presented on PowerPoint slides (versus text only and text with relevant pictures). Aside from these findings and a few dissertations, most of our knowledge is based on graphic-design principles and perception-oriented research regarding graphical display of information dating from the 1950s – work not specific to projected images in the classroom. However, although we may lack empirical data, we have no shortage of "best practices" lists for PowerPoint.[2] Although I will not produce yet another of these lists, I will offer five general guidelines that I have developed over the years.

First, do not use transitions between slides (e.g., dissolves), do not use animations to present text (e.g., each bullet point flies in), and do not use sound effects (e.g., "ka-ching"). The novelty of these techniques wears off quickly and they will ultimately detract from your message. Also, do not use PowerPoint's Auto-Content Wizard or sample presentations (these features generally employ many transitions, animations, and sounds).

Second, the information that you put in your slides should be relevant. This point is true not only for graphics (Bartsch & Cobern, 2003), but for verbal information as well. Students assume that "if it's on a PowerPoint slide, it's important." They make this inference for good reason. When you lecture, hold a discussion, or use an active learning exercise, you imply that the ideas are important enough to merit some of your limited class time. In this regard, PowerPoint is no different from these other classroom techniques.

Third, do not attempt to put everything in your slides. If you do, why should your students come to class? Very detailed slides lead to boring, complex presentations, and student withdrawal. Additionally, you will be more likely simply to read the slides. The slides should facilitate a deeper level of communication including stories, illustrations, examples, and your knowledge and experience. The slides should not substitute for these other teaching tools.

Fourth, consider providing slides to your students in advance. For several years I have made versions of my slides available via the internet, with good results. I require students to print these slides and bring them to class. I am frequently asked, "Don't your students skip class or read ahead rather than pay attention?" My answer is "generally, no." My slides are skeleton outlines; they do not include all the information I want my students to know (see the third guideline, above). I use PowerPoint to present information that would otherwise be difficult or time-consuming for students to put into their notes. For instance, when presenting complex graphical models, having the slide allows students to think about the ideas rather than feverishly drawing the picture. When I present a long definition, I don't have to repeat it 14 times while students try to reproduce it verbatim. Having the slides in advance also helps students prepare better for class. Students can preview my presentation using the notes as an "advanced organizer," and the slides help students anticipate what I will not cover in class, so they can ask for information.

Fifth, take advantage of the unique strengths of PowerPoint. Despite the lack of imagination with which many people use it, PowerPoint is a versatile software program. One strength is that I can quickly update my PowerPoint presentations. For example, if I hear a relevant story on National Public Radio, I can easily modify that morning's presentation to include the information or even use a hyperlink to the audio through NPR's website. With overheads, I found it to be just too much work to change the presentation in the few minutes just before class.

Another unique strength of PowerPoint is its ability to include other objects, in context, within the presentation. I can seamlessly incorporate audio, video, figures, pictures, spreadsheet data and charts, hyperlinks, and other objects from within the PowerPoint presentation. Inserting these objects is generally as easy as a quick drag-and-drop.

Yet another PowerPoint strength is its ability to keep me organized. In a survey of "best practices" for college teaching (Butt & Reutzel, 1997), students rated "giving lectures that are clear and well organized" as the most important thing an instructor can do to facilitate student learning. In my Organizational Psychology course, I frequently use my consulting experiences and student work experiences to illustrate material. These stories often lead us off the topic, but by reminding me what comes next, my slides always lead me back to the right place. Another organizational aid is the note-taking feature available in PowerPoint's "Normal View." Though students see only the information on the slide, each slide has a set of detailed notes that students do not see but the presenter does. These notes provide all the information I need to present the material (e.g., references, examples, data).

Finally, although PowerPoint is mostly linear, the dynamic, nonlinear presentation of visual information is possible. Let me provide two examples. When I describe national work cultures I present a slide illustrating the flags of 16 nations. I ask students where they would like to go and when a student says "Japan," I click on the flag to reveal a slide that describes contemporary Japanese work culture. When another student wants to look at the work culture in South Africa, I click on the flag to go to the appropriate slide. I use another dynamic set of slides to illustrate Lewin's Force Field Model. The slide that students see in the presentation is actually a series of four slides. In each, the elements in the figure are animated to illustrate the relation between driving forces and restraining forces, and their impact on the status quo. Neither of these demonstrations is possible with a chalkboard or overheads.

Do Not Get Stabbed in the Back: Some Avoidable Problems

Aside from the issues I have already noted, several additional problems deserve mention. The most important problem is the failure of technology. Technology, no matter how simple, will occasionally fail (even overhead projector bulbs burn out). Unfortunately, complex technologies may fail more frequently, and these failures can be more devastating and more difficult to correct. If you use PowerPoint you will eventually need to resort to "Plan B" – be prepared. My "Plan B" is the chalkboard and the printed versions of my presentation that students bring to class.

If you provide notes to your students in advance, you must make several decisions regarding these notes. One is whether you will provide paper copies or electronic ones. I use electronic copies to give students more flexibility. Another related issue is the format of these notes. Many students are not PowerPoint savvy, which may create difficulties when they try to print the notes. I save my presentations as PDF documents because most computers will easily open and print these files. I also make two versions of the presentations available: a version with one slide per page and a version with three slides per page. Students choose the format that is best for their note-taking styles.

Another difficulty derives from the fact that computers come in a dizzying array of configurations. Specifically, the computer you use to create the slides will probably not be the one you use to present the slides. The more different the authoring computer is from the presentation computer, the more likely you are to encounter difficulties. For example, unusual fonts must be loaded onto both machines for the presentation to work as intended. Other difficulties may arise when using different versions of the PowerPoint software. Although PowerPoint is not as bad as some programs, I do not need to remind Macintosh users of the difficulties of working in a Windows-dominated world. My advice for all of these compatibility-related issues is the same: test your presentation before you deliver it.

My final word of advice for using PowerPoint is to find people you can consider technology resources. Though I am not a techno-geek, I know people who are. Over the years I have become very good at solving my own problems, but I still encounter difficulties. When I do, I know exactly who to contact. You should too.

At this point, you might ask, "Should I use PowerPoint?" I will not argue that you should, but I will suggest that you should explore what it can do for you and your teaching. PowerPoint can be an evil back-stabber, but it can also be a great gift.

NOTES

1 Space will not allow me to describe other applications of computers and projection technology, nor can I describe other, more "exotic" technologies that may be used in classroom teaching (e.g., interactive whiteboards, handheld computers, and course management software).

2 Victor Chen's presentation (available online at www.vetmed.iastate.edu/vetzone/pdfanddocs/ Effective_presentation.ppt), Lutsky's (1997) article on using a "low-tech" approach to teaching, and the University of Notre Dame PowerPoint website (www.nd.edu/~learning/powerpoint/) provide useful guidelines.

REFERENCES

Bartsch, R. A., & Cobern, K. M. (2003). Effectiveness of PowerPoint presentations in lectures. *Computers & Education, 41*, 77–86.

Butt, D., & Reutzel, E. (1997). *Professors review best teaching practices.* Retrieved Aug. 6, 2004, from Pennsylvania State University, Department of Engineering Science and Mechanics website: www.psu.edu/practices.html

Cassady, J. D. (1998). Student and instructor perceptions of the efficacy of computer-aided lectures in undergraduate university courses. *Journal of Educational Computing Research, 19,* 175–89.

Godin, S. (2001). *Really bad PowerPoint (and how to avoid it)* [Electronic booklet]. Retrieved Aug. 6, 2004, from Amazon.com website: www.amazon.com/exec/obidos/ASIN/B00005R2F7/ qid=1093874569/sr=ka-1/ref=pd_ka_1/104-0403653-6457524

Lewis, A. (1971, Mar. 15). Dear Scoop Jackson. *New York Times,* p. 37.

Lutsky, N. (1997, May/June). Teaching with overheads: Low tech, high impact. *APS Observer, 10 (3),* 26–8.

Perry, T., & Perry, L. A. (1998). University students' attitudes towards multimedia presentations. *British Journal of Educational Technology, 29,* 375–7.

Tufte, E. (2003a). *The cognitive style of PowerPoint* [Essay]. Retrieved Aug. 6, 2004, from The Work of Edward Tufte and Graphics Press: www.edwardtufte.com/tufte/books_pp

Tufte, E. (2003b, Sept.). PowerPoint is evil. *Wired Magazine,* 11.09. Retrieved Aug. 6, 2004, from www.wired.com/wired/archive/11.09/ppt2.html

17

Using the Internet Effectively: Homepages and Email

Ψ

Vincent W. Hevern
Le Moyne College

For over a century, innovations in technology have influenced how teachers teach and students learn (Reiser, 2001a,b). Whether within the classroom or more indirectly through their effect upon the sociocultural context in which learning takes place, modern mass media in particular have challenged faculty to understand how they function and what they accomplish. In doing so, educators hope to harness their pedagogical potential by discriminating significant and helpful from trivial or malignant uses of such media (Postman, 1998). Among the mass media, the internet (Net) has emerged as perhaps the most revolutionary technological change confronting schools since the invention of printing (Choi, Stahl, & Whinston, 1998). As Paul Metz (1995) observed, "[e]lectronic communications . . . will fundamentally *change* scientific and scholarly communications. We have seen only the beginning and there is no turning back." Students have embraced the Net, often employing it as the major information source outside the classroom related to their learning (Metzger, Flanagin, & Zwarun, 2003).

Two of the most prominent tools of internet communication involve electronic mail (email) and pages on the World Wide Web. For over 20 years faculty have used some form of email for scholarly and pedagogical communication (Hyman, 2003) and, since the mid-1990s, they have authored individual webpages as well (Jordan, 1999). This chapter suggests ways that faculty might deploy these communication portals more effectively while avoiding significant pitfalls and errors. Note, though, that I will not discuss the use of the Net for "distance learning" (i.e., for teaching taking place either exclusively or predominantly online). Other sources can help instructors seeking guidance on a topic too complex for review here (Moore & Anderson, 2003; see also Duell, ch. 24 this volume).

Homepages

Individually authored homepages function broadly as a teacher's "face to the world" in cyberspace – both as a potential medium of instruction and student advisement and a more personal creation subject to evaluation and critique by professional peers (Erickson, 1996).[1] So, in preparing such pages, teachers should think about how they wish to present themselves to their students and colleagues as well as how to promote learning via the Net.

Instructional Uses

General. Recent studies suggest that faculty homepages should offer basic personal and contact information even though students and instructors often set different priorities about what is essential and what is optimal for inclusion on such pages (e.g., Dehoney & Reeves, 1999; Palmiter & Renjilian, 2003). This information should consist minimally of an instructor's office location and postal address, telephone number, email address, and office hours. Further desirable information includes academic rank, a list of courses taught, academic background, research interests, scholarly publications, professional memberships, and significant service and professional development experiences (e.g., postdoctoral placements, clinical internships). Inclusion of a photographic portrait may personalize a site and help visitors "know" an instructor better (Palmiter & Renjilian, 2003).

Student advisement. Teachers may offer advisement materials online, especially when these materials are notably absent from departmental pages (Hevern, 1997). These materials may include links to campus-based resources such as a job-placement or career office, student health and counseling services, and student organizations such as Psi Chi. Especially helpful may be links to specialized sites providing students with information about careers and graduate education (e.g., *Marky Lloyd's Careers in Psychology Page*, psychwww.com/careers, or Melissa Himelein's [1999] *Student Guide to Careers in the Helping Professions*, www.lemoyne.edu/OTRP/otrpresources/helping-online.html). Regularly distributed handouts are candidates for posting as well, including checklists of required or suggested courses for the psychology major, graduate school requirements, and the like.

Course-related considerations. Faculty construct course-related webpages reflective of their instructional philosophy (Gillani, 2000). They may use the Web principally as a one-way electronic distribution system: course syllabi, calendars, and lecture notes may be posted rather than printed. Students appreciate the availability of such materials (Palmiter & Renjilian, 2003). However, students appear to learn better when online materials are elaborated via hyperlinked multiformatted resources such as lecture objectives and outlines, review materials, and sample quizzes and test questions (Evans, Gibbons, Shah, & Griffin, 2004). Course sites should offer ease of use and navigation while also showing some level of playfulness or humor, such as linking important psychological concepts to true but off-beat or unusual examples (Slem, 2004). A promising Web feature is its ability to link students directly to available electronic journal articles and book chapters. Students can easily use primary research sources while avoiding access problems inherent in library-based reserve systems (Langston & Tyler, 2004).

Teachers should note that not all students find Web-based learning congenial (Nachimas & Segev, 2003; Thompson & Lynch, 2003). Such students may need special assistance or instruction to increase their efficacy working in a digital environment.

Design and Practical Issues

This essay cannot offer comprehensive design guidelines for webpages. Excellent printed and Web-based resources already offer such guidance (e.g., Horton, 2000; Lynch & Horton, 2001; Nielsen, 2000). However, several essential design rules generally govern construction of homepages:

1. *Keep it simple and visually consistent.* Use an easily readable and single typeface; don't mix multiple or odd-sized typefaces. Settle on a simple or muted color scheme. Avoid garish colors or using images as backgrounds, especially when printed text is superimposed or low color contrast makes reading effortful. Do not crowd pages with text and images: provide adequate blank space and ample margins. Design pages for a screen width of 800 pixels or less, a recognized Net standard.

2. *Keep it simple technically.* Complementing the comments on accessibility below, remember that homepages with high technical complexity (e.g., the latest Java applet) are more likely to be incompatible with readers' own computers or ability to display data.

3. *Give your reader choices.* Break very long pages into sets of shorter subpages. Warn your reader about the size and format of links to downloadable documents. Never force Web visitors to listen to background music.

4. *Provide clear navigation landmarks.* When using multiple subpages, place a navigation bar at the top of each page (or in a framed sidebar) to permit rapid movement within the site. Avoid "dead-end" pages; provide an exit (or "Home") link on every subpage.

5. *Date your work.* Include a creation and a "last revised" date for all subpages. This information allows you (and your site visitors) to evaluate the recency of posted materials and the possible need for updating.

Legal Issues

Copyright. US law generally limits the "fair use" of copyrighted materials by schools to "face-to-face" teaching activities (Copyright Law, 1976). Because the Net reaches far beyond the classroom, the retransmission of copyrighted materials online is impermissible without authorization by copyright owners (Capone, 1999).

Accessibility. Disabled students under US law have a right to accessible teaching materials including those posted online (Paul, 2000). Section 508 of the Rehabilitation Act (1998) requires federal agencies to make information technology accessible. State-supported schools must and other institutions ought to consider following these guidelines as well. Two forms of impairment – visual (blindness, low vision, lack of color perception) and mobility (limited strength or reach, tremor, manipulation difficulties) – especially challenge teachers to devise accessible materials. Multiple online resources can aid in crafting accessible webpages (e.g., DisabilityInfo.gov or www.section508.gov).

Privacy. The Federal Educational Rights and Privacy Act (1974) in the US prohibits the dissemination of student educational records without the student's explicit permission.

Faculty should obtain written authorization before posting online any student names, grades, or other personally identifiable educational data. Teachers in other countries may face similar limits.

Email

Faculty spend a great deal of time using electronic means to communicate: in some estimates, 40 percent of in-office work concerns email (e.g., Bonk, 2001; Marine, 2000). Are there any ways in which teachers can approach email more effectively? The guidelines below offer some important considerations.

Two General Principles

The ease of communicating by email has doubtless fostered its rapid growth across educational institutions. However, the facility of this medium hides pitfalls that suggest correspondents approach email cautiously.

1. *Treat all messages as permanent and potentially shareable.* Avoid saying anything in an email message that you would be unwilling to have made public. You do not control what happens to email after you press the "Send" key.

2. *Email is not a face-to-face mode of communication and lacks those visual and auditory cues of conversation that give nuance and context to messages.* Email is easily misconstrued. Authors may sound harsh or accusatory when they never intended to convey such overtones. Readers should give email authors the "benefit of the doubt" if they find themselves responding angrily or defensively to messages. "Flaming" – highly emotional or argumentative text – is almost never appropriate for teachers responding to students or scholars to their peers. Note that THE USE OF CAPITAL LETTERS AND MULTIPLE EXCLAMATION POINTS (!!!???) is considered the equivalent of loud screaming, usually an inappropriate practice.

Instructional Uses

Email can fulfill multiple instructional purposes. For example, teachers may clarify assignments, answer questions or provide feedback to individual students, or make last-minute changes to course activities via email (Cummings, Bonk, & Jacobs, 2002). You can easily return drafts of papers in standard formats such as "rich text" to students with your comments embedded directly in the draft (Monroe, 2003). Students may preview outline materials about upcoming lectures via email several days ahead of class (Yu & Hsin-Ju, 2002). Faculty may request reflective "one-minute" essays from students by email as feedback on class lectures, guest speakers, or other presentations (Angelo & Cross, 1993). Students who are quiet in the classroom setting may feel more comfortable voicing their opinions via email rather than in person when given the option (Wingard, 2004).

Practical Issues

As students we learned different rules for composing and sending business letters versus personal correspondence. Teachers can update those guidelines for email messages by considering these suggestions:

1. *Use an informative but modest signature.* The end of a message ought to contain a full name, postal address, and email address to facilitate responses. However, including personally meaningful quotations or slogans in professional email is often inappropriate.

2. *Avoid sending unsolicited attachments to others.* Fear of computer viruses and the inconvenience of slow downloading on dial-up lines should limit how attachments (e.g., documents, photos) are distributed. Be sure that your computer has the latest antiviral software and that you scan any attachment with that software prior to mailing.

3. *Use Subject: lines intelligently.* In a world of many junk messages, subject lines should be succinct but meaningful. They allow readers to decide whether to open a message. Avoid changing subject lines in electronic discussion lists: Use a new subject line only when a major shift occurs in the focus of a discussion. Teachers may require students to include a course catalog number in email to facilitate identification of such mail (e.g., "SUBJECT: PSY 101-02 Question about tomorrow's quiz").

4. *Edit quoted materials.* In replying to email from others (especially on electronic discussion lists), quote only the relevant portions of a message and edit out extraneous materials. The message's reader will appreciate your effort to highlight the focus of your response and may better understand what you are saying in your reply.

Legal Issues

The rapid growth of email as a medium of communication has generated a host of unsettled legal issues and the need for thoughtful practices in return (Schachter, 2002). Faculty should consider some basic legal considerations in their use of email (Flynn & Kahn, 2003):

1. *Authors of email messages "own" their writing for copyright purposes.* Faculty should not use or quote student messages publicly without their consent.

2. *In the US, messages stored on school-based mass storage drives should not be considered privileged or confidential.* They are generally subject to subpoena and discovery procedures in legal disputes.

3. *Libelous, defamatory, or slanderous materials in email are potentially actionable.* Faculty should exercise caution in how they characterize others in writing, particularly in describing private persons such as academic peers or students with language that may hurt their good name or reputation.

———— Conclusion ————

In the late 1990s, an academic colleague at a meeting heard another teacher exclaim, "Oh, I just don't have any time to pay attention to the internet." Startled, that colleague replied a bit contentiously, "I am reminded of those students of mine who say, 'I just don't have any time to go the college library!'" As this exchange suggests, different faculty have adapted to the new learning ecology of cyberspace with more or less enthusiasm. Yet, as Metz (1995) predicted, there really is no turning back as education moves into the twenty-first century. With some guidance and patience, most faculty can learn to use the basic tools of that environment quite well. I offer this chapter as a resource to help other teachers do so more confidently and effectively.

NOTE

1   Schools often dictate that faculty data appear in a standardized institutional Web directory and may invite their teachers to supply short biographical and other descriptive statements for inclusion on such pages. This review does not address these institutional pages, but those directly authored by individual teachers.

REFERENCES

Angelo, T. A., & Cross, K. P. (1993). *Classroom assessment techniques* (2nd ed.). San Francisco: Jossey-Bass.

Bonk, C. J. (2001). *Online teaching in an online world.* Bloomington, IN: CourseShare.com. Retrieved Sept. 9, 2004 from the website: http://php.indiana.edu/~cjbonk/faculty_survey_report.pdf

Capone, III, L. (1999). *Copyright law and distance learning.* Retrieved Sept. 12, 2004, at www.uncg.edu/cha/UNIVERSITY_COUNSEL/FAQ/distlrn.html

Choi, S.-Y., Stahl, D. O., & Whinston, A. B. (1998, January). Gutenberg and the digital revolution: Will printed books disappear? *Journal of Internet Banking and Commerce, 3 (1).* Retrieved Sept. 2, 2004, from http://www.arraydev.com/commerce/jibc/9801-4.htm

Copyright Law of the United States. 17 U.S.C. § 110(1). (1976). Retrieved Sept. 12, 2004, at www.copyright.gov/title17/92chap1.html

Cummings, J. A., Bonk, C. J., & Jacobs, F. R. (2002). Twenty-first century college syllabi: Options for online communications and interactivity. *Internet and Higher Education, 5,* 1–19.

Dehoney, J., & Reeves, T. C. (1999). Instructional and social dimensions of class web pages. *Journal of Computing in Higher Education, 10,* 19–41.

Erickson, T. (1996). The World Wide Web as social hypertext [Electronic version]. *Communications of the ACM, 39* (1), 15–17. Retrieved Sept. 12, 2004, from www.pliant.org/personal/Tom_Erickson/SocialHypertext.html

Evans, C., Gibbons, N. J., Shah, K., & Griffin, D. K. (2004). Virtual learning in the biological sciences: Pitfalls of simply "putting notes on the web." *Computers and Education, 43,* 49–61.

Federal Educational Rights and Privacy Act, 20 U.S.C. § 1232g. (1974). Retrieved Sept. 19, 2004, at www4.law.cornell.edu/uscode/20/1232g.html

Flynn, N., & Kahn, R. (2003). *Email rules: A business guide to managing policies, security, and legal issues for email and digital communications.* New York: American Management Association.

Gillani, B. B. (2000). Using the Web to create student-centered curriculum. In R. A. Cole (ed.), *Issues in Web-based pedagogy* (pp. 161–81). Westport, CT: Greenwood Press.

Hevern, V. W. (1997, Aug.). Developing a departmental online resource guide for psychology students. In M. K. Lloyd (Chair), *Advising online: Internet resources for psychology advisors and students.* Symposium conducted at the annual meeting of the American Psychological Association, Chicago, IL.

Himelein, M. (1999). *A student's guide to careers in the helping professions.* Society for the Teaching of Psychology: Office of Teaching Resources in Psychology. Retrieved Sept. 10, 2004, at www.lemoyne.edu/OTRP/otrpresources/helping.html

Horton, S. (2000). *Web teaching guide: A practical approach to creating course Web sites.* New Haven, CT: Yale University Press. [Also, retrieved the companion site on Sept. 12, 2004, at www.webteachingguide.com/]

Hyman, A. (2003). Twenty years of ListServ as an academic tool. *Internet and Higher Education,* 6, 17–24.

Jordan, T. (1999). *Cyberpower: The culture and politics of cyberspace and the Internet.* London: Routledge.

Langston, M., & Tyler, J. (2004). Linking to journal articles in an online teaching environment: The persistent link, DOI, and OpenURL. *Internet and Higher Education,* 7, 51–8.

Lynch, P. J., & Horton, S. (2001). *Web style guide: Basic design principles for creating web sites.* New Haven, CT: Yale University Press. [Also available online at www.webstyleguide.com/]

Marine, R. J. (2002, Summer). A systems framework for evaluation of faculty Web-work. *New Directions for Institutional Research,* No. 114, 63–71.

Metz, P. (1995, Jan./Feb.). The view from a library university: Revolutionary change in scholarly and scientific communications [Electronic version]. *Change, 27 (1),* 28–33.

Metzger, M. J., Flanagin, A. J., & Zwarun, L. (2003). College student Web use, perceptions of information credibility, and verification behavior. *Computers & Education, 41,* 271–90.

Monroe, B. (2003). How email can give you back your life. *English Journal, 92,* 116–18.

Moore, M. G., & Anderson, W. G. (eds.). (2003). *Handbook of distance education.* Mahwah, NJ: Erlbaum.

Nachimas, R., & Segev, L. (2003). Students' use of content in Web-supported academic courses. *Internet and Higher Education, 6,* 145–57.

Nielsen, J. (2000). *Designing Web usability: The practice of simplicity.* Indianapolis, IN: New Riders. [Also, retrieved the companion site on Sept. 12, 2004, at www.useit.com/]

Palmiter, D., Jr., & Renjilian, D. (2003). Improving your psychology faculty homepage: Results of a student-faculty online survey. *Teaching of Psychology, 30,* 163–6.

Paul, S. (2000). Students with disabilities in higher education: A review of the literature [Electronic version]. *College Student Journal, 34,* 200–10.

Postman, N. (1998). *Five things we need to know about technological change.* Paper presented at the New Tech 98 Conference, Denver, Colorado, March 27, 1998. Retrieved Sept. 11, 2004, from http://itrs.scu.edu/tshanks/pages/Comm12/12Postman.htm

Rehabilitation Act. Section 508. 29 U.S.C. 794d (1998). Retrieved Sept. 12, 2004, at www4.law.cornell.edu/uscode/29/794d.html

Reiser, R. A. (2001a). A history of instructional design and technology: Part I: A history of instructional media. *Educational Technology, Research and Development, 49,* 53–64.

Reiser, R. A. (2001b). A history of instructional design and technology: Part II: A history of instructional design. *Educational Technology, Research and Development, 49,* 57–67.

Schachter, M. (2002). *Law of Internet speech* (2nd ed.) Durham, NC: Carolina Academic Press.

Slem, C. M. (2004, July). *Principles for developing Web-based resources that students actually use.* Poster presented at the annual meeting of the American Psychological Association, Honolulu, Hawaii. Retrieved Sept. 9, 2004, from the California Polytechnic State University, San Luis Obispo website: http://cla.libart.calpoly.edu/~cslem/Slem/Research/apa2004.html

Thompson, L. F., & Lynch, B. J. (2003). Web-based instruction: Who is inclined to resist it and why? *Journal of Educational Computing Research, 29,* 275–85.

Wingard, R. B. (2004). Classroom teaching changes in Web-enhanced courses: A multi-institutional study [Electronic version]. *Educause Quarterly 27* (1), 26–35. Retrieved Sept. 2, 2004, from www.educause.edu/ir/library/pdf/EQM0414.pdf

Yu, F.-Y., & Hsin-Ju, J. Y. (2002). Incorporating email into the learning process: Its impact on student academic achievement and attitudes. *Computers & Education, 38,* 117–26.

18
Teaching Students to Use Electronic Databases

Ψ

Maureen McCarthy & Thomas P. Pusateri
Kennesaw State University and American Psychological Association
& Florida Atlantic University

Student learning outcomes, as articulated in the Undergraduate Psychology Major Learning Goals and Outcomes (American Psychological Association [APA], 2002), explicitly state that students should be able to: "Locate and use relevant databases, research, and theory to plan, conduct, and interpret results of research studies." In order for students to develop these skills fully, faculty should help students to become critical consumers of information. Information-literate students should be able to, "recognize when information is needed and have the ability to locate, evaluate, and use effectively the needed information" (Association of College & Research Libraries [ACRL], 2000). ACRL further explicated outcomes related to information literacy that include: (a) developing a research plan, (b) identifying keywords and related terms, (c) carefully selecting terms relative to the database, and (d) using appropriate commands (e.g., Boolean operators, truncation, and proximity for search engines; internal organizers such as indexes for books). Merriam, LaBaugh, and Butterfield (1992) proposed minimum training guidelines for instructing psychology students on library skills. In this chapter, we will provide faculty with recommendations and resources for teaching students how to develop skills in information literacy related to psychology.

Instructing Students About Available Electronic Databases

Several electronic databases contain information relevant to psychology. When designing classroom assignments, we suggest that you require students to use more than one database to familiarize themselves with similarities and differences among the databases. Databases differ with respect to the journals searchable within the database and the information about each article obtained from a search (e.g., full text or abstract only). For example, PsycARTICLES®, www.apa.org/psycarticles/, is a full-text compilation of APA published journals, whereas PsycINFO®, www.apa.org/psycinfo/, contains abstracts of published psychological literature. ERIC® (Educational Resources Information Center), www.eric.ed.gov/index.html, provides abstracts of educational literature with full-text access via ERIC Document Reproduction Service, and MedlinePlus®, http://medlineplus.gov/, contains abstracts of articles from sources that publish biomedical research.

Databases also differ with respect to the keywords and search strategies that may be used to locate articles, some of which will be described below. Kidd, Meyer, and Olesko (2000) developed *An Instructor's Guide to Electronic Databases of Indexed Professional Literature* that describes 20 databases relevant to psychology and strategies for using each database. This instructor's guide is available free for download from the website of the Office for Teaching Resources in Psychology (www.lemoyne.edu/OTRP/index.html).

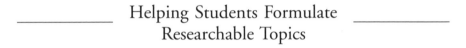

Helping Students Formulate Researchable Topics

Identification of appropriate search terms is a critical first step in helping students to become effective researchers. Students often select terms that are either too broad or too narrow, thus coming to the erroneous conclusions that there is either too much information to process or not enough information available about their topic. One way to illustrate an appropriate search strategy is to use an introductory psychology text to demonstrate the process of narrowing a topic. Introductory textbooks typically outline the subfields of psychology, whereas sections within each chapter focus on specific areas of study within the subfield, and key terms (e.g., in boldface or italics) narrow those areas further. For example, a chapter on social psychology typically includes sections on conformity and obedience, interpersonal attraction, prejudice, and causal attribution. We recommend advising students to begin their searches by using terms similar to those used in chapter sections and narrowing their search by using key terms. They may also want to compare these terms with those in the *Thesaurus of Psychological Index Terms* (American Psychological Association, 2004), which provides the keywords used in the PsycINFO® and PsycARTICLES® databases.

Another method for demonstrating an appropriate search strategy is to use a student's research question to facilitate selection of search terms. For example, a student interested in the question "What causes people to develop a snake phobia?" could begin by identifying the introductory textbook chapter that would include this topic (i.e., psychological disorders). Subsequent narrowing of the search might be accomplished by using terms such as "anxiety disorder," "phobia," and "snake phobia." Additionally, students could compare the specific term with that listed in the *Thesaurus of Psychological Index Terms*. This example helps students to understand the process for selecting appropriate terminology.

Selecting Appropriate Language
for the Search

Using keywords to search a database is among the most comprehensive approaches to searching for information. However, the search sometimes produces too many results; thus, it is often more efficient to use delimiters in the search process. It is important that a search produces results that include the necessary information, but not extraneous entries. Therefore, a thorough search requires careful attention to key terms. For example, it is often, but not always, useful to include all derivatives of a key term (e.g., "develop," "development," "developing"). Truncation and use of a wildcard will produce the largest number of entries for a given search. For example, if students wanted to obtain information pertaining to a cognitive development, they might search using the key term "develop*" in some databases. "Develop" represents a truncation of the key term and the asterisk is the wildcard that requests all derivatives of the term such as "develop," "develops," "developing," and "development." The wildcard varies depending on the database being used, but is quite often an asterisk, question-mark, or dollar sign. Some wildcards represent exactly one character (e.g., "phobi?" might represent the words "phobia" and "phobic"), whereas others represent any number of characters (e.g., "phobi*" might include additional words such as "phobias" and "phobics"). Most databases have instructions available online to assist students in selecting appropriate wildcards.

In addition to use of individual terms, you should instruct students in the use of combining terms in order to refine their search. Boolean logic, or use of specific combinations, is critical in the use of keywords in most databases. For example, the terms "and," "or," and "not" constitute terms that we now describe as Boolean search terms. Each of these terms performs a specific function within the search process; "and" narrows the search, "or" broadens the search, and "not" excludes terms from the search. Students who are able to apply this logic will become proficient in the use of most electronic databases.

In addition to instruction about individual terms and combinations, it is important to educate students about the more advanced functions of searching electronic databases. It is possible to impose hierarchical search strategies to search a database more efficiently. Most databases permit a process called nesting. Nesting involves the use of parentheses to group concepts and prioritize the terms that are entered first into the search. It is important to instruct students that delimiters have an explicit order. Application of delimiters uses the following order: NOT, AND, OR. Additionally, students should only group like items within the parentheses. For example, a student interested in conducting research on adolescent or adult memory may use the following search string "(adults OR adolescents) AND memory." Use of the parentheses will instruct the search to obtain entries for adults and adolescents, and then reduce the search to include only those items related to memory. Nesting is often used to refine an initial search and to reduce the number of records to a manageable size.

Many databases offer the option of using standard fields (e.g., author, title, journal, and year) to further limit a search. We recommend that you instruct students who have located a relevant article to use information from that article strategically to improve their search strategies. For example, students might review the reference section of an article for additional citations related to the topic they are researching. The student could then return to the electronic database and search on the basis of the name of an author, a specific journal, or terms derived from the title of the article. These strategies may assist students in obtaining results from electronic searches that include more relevant, and fewer irrelevant, articles.

We have provided a general framework for search strategies that can be employed with electronic databases. Our recommendations are similar to those offered by Joswick (1994), when she made her initial recommendations for using PsycLIT. Perhaps the most important recommendation is that faculty should always contact librarians because they possess the most current knowledge about a variety of databases. Librarians frequently are willing to provide specific instruction about information literacy and specific databases. We recommend instructors meet with a librarian to discuss the purpose and specific instructions for their assignments. Librarians can often offer additional suggestions for improving the instructions so that the assignment is clearer to students, and they may suggest ways to improve assignments to increase the likelihood that the assignment will achieve its stated purpose.

Using the Results of the Search

Instruction about use of electronic databases often concludes when students print a set of potential references. In order to achieve information and technological literacy as a specific learning outcome, the next instructional goal should be to teach students to choose relevant sources from among the references they locate. Databases provide information about accessing the printed resource, and you should provide students with additional instruction about using campus-based holdings for both journals and texts. Similarly, you should encourage students to obtain materials that might not be immediately available on campus. Libraries are increasingly linking databases to local holdings or to interlibrary loan requests. The crucial step is to help students to use abstracts to identify which resources might be most useful to their work and to follow through with obtaining those resources.

In some instances, students will not need to access a print version of a reference through traditional methods of locating a physical copy of the document within the library. Some databases now provide access to full-text articles in different formats, most typically as HTML or PDF files. We recommend you encourage students to choose the PDF file because it will print the article most similarly to the way the article appeared in its original source (e.g., pages in a journal). The HTML version is likely to contain numerous typographical errors and may exclude or alter the appearance of relevant tables, graphs, or other material when compared to the original source.

It is also important to instruct students in advance to record all relevant information they will need to create a reference for the electronic media they collect. Refer students to pages 278–80 of the *Publication Manual of the American Psychological Association* (2001), particularly examples 88 and 90, for instructions. Encourage students to print a copy of the database page from which they retrieved the article and to keep it with their copy of the article. This page usually includes all of the information students will need to construct a reference. Warn students that it may be difficult to reconstruct this information later (e.g., recalling which database they used and how they initially located the article).

Encourage students to keep a log of their search strategies. This log could include the following: (a) date of their search, (b) name of the electronic database, (c) search terms used (including quotations, wildcards, etc.), and (d) notes on the success of each search term (e.g., number of hits, quality of articles). If you learn that a student is having difficulty with the search for articles, examining this log may help you make recommendations for improving the student's search strategies.

Information literacy is an important instructional goal. The ACRL provides specific skills that students should be able to use, and the APA Undergraduate Psychology Major Learning Goals and Outcomes extend the instructional goals such that students should not only be able to conduct an efficient search of the literature, but they also should be able generalize their skills and become critical consumers of information. Students who employ the general strategies that are provided in this chapter will be able to both conduct efficient searches and generalize their information literacy skills.

References

American Psychological Association. (2001). *Publication manual of the American Psychological Association* (5th ed.). Washington, DC: American Psychological Association.

American Psychological Association. (2002). *Undergraduate psychology major learning goals and outcomes: A report.* Retrieved Aug. 10, 2004, from the American Psychological Association website: www.apa.org/ed/pcue/taskforcereport2.pdf

American Psychological Association. (2004). *Thesaurus of psychological index terms* (10th ed.). Washington, DC: Author.

Association of College & Research Libraries. (2000). *Information literacy competency standards for higher education.* Retrieved Aug. 10, 2004, from the Association of College & Research Libraries website: www.ala.org/ala/acrl/acrlstandards/informationliteracycompetency.htm

Joswick, K. E. (1994). Getting the most from PsycLIT: Recommendations for searching. *Teaching of Psychology, 21,* 49–53.

Kidd, S., Meyer, C. L., & Olesko, B. M. (2000). *An instructor's guide to electronic databases of indexed professional literature.* Available from the Office of Teaching Resources in Psychology website: www.lemoyne.edu/OTRP/teachingresources.html#edb

Merriam, J., LaBaugh, R. T., & Butterfield, N. E. (1992). Library instruction for psychology majors: Minimum training guidelines. *Teaching of Psychology, 19,* 34–6.

part IV

Ψ

Techniques of Teaching: Special Considerations

Part IV offers six chapters that further extend the discussion of strategies and tactics to include teaching large classes, using teaching assistants, teaching courses with laboratory components, teaching experiential and independent study courses, teaching through service learning, and distance learning.

19
Teaching Large Classes
Ψ

Katherine Kipp & Steffen Pope Wilson
University of Georgia & Eastern Kentucky University

Even a seasoned faculty member teaching a large class for the first time might be concerned about how to manage so many students and be an effective teacher to each one. Some of the obstacles in teaching large classes include making a personal connection with students, course preparation, student assessment, and course management. In this chapter we review several guidelines to help you teach large classes.

Teaching a Sea of Faces

Perhaps the most obvious challenge of teaching large classes is facing a sea of faces instead of unique individuals, as you might in a small class. However, you can make personal connections with the students in several ways. You could greet each student at the door on the first day of class, and follow up with that connection by arriving early to each class to interact with students as they arrive.

Another approach is to ask students to provide information about themselves on index cards on the first day of class. Examples of suitable information to request include hometowns, local jobs, hobbies, and special talents or interesting facts about themselves. You can review some of these on the second day. You should then tell students similar information about yourself (e.g., where you grew up, where you completed your education, part-time jobs that you held while you were in college, and your hobbies). This introduction should remain lighthearted and personal, without being an invasion of either the students' or your privacy. You can also collect and announce birthdays or special events in which students in the class are participating (Halgin & Overtree, 2002). Ask students to greet you if they see you on campus or in the community to increase opportunities for individual interactions with them (Porter & Stanley, 2002).

Preparing Teaching Materials
for a Large Class

The heavy emphasis on using lecture in large classes makes it important to use a variety of techniques to break up lecturing and make it more interesting. Some examples are using visual aids (such as graphs of research data), films, guest speakers, and demonstrations (Jenkins, 1991). Fortunately, most of the subfields in psychology lend themselves well to a variety of presentation methods. When you use technology to enhance your lectures, always have a back-up method of presentation ready in case your planned technology fails; you may be far from your office and unable to retrieve an alternative quickly (Porter & Stanley, 2002).

Because so much of the workload in a large class is class management, there is little time for new lecture preparation each semester. This limitation makes initial lecture preparation critical. Focus on developing a complete and working set of lecture notes that can be updated easily with the emergence of new information on a topic, but that do not require a complete reworking each semester.

Typically large classes are lower-level classes. Many of the students may be 18-year-olds just entering college and they may not know what to expect. Tailor your presentations and expectations to their abilities. As an example, students this age are usually still developing their note-taking skills. They may also be less willing to indicate verbally to you when they do not understand a point or an issue. Presenting well organized lectures and providing students with supplementary material may help them process lecture material more effectively.

It is also helpful to select a handful of themes that you want to convey in the course and to link topical information to those themes. One example is concentrating on critical thinking in large, lower-level classes because many of the students enter the course with preconceived ideas (and misconceptions) about psychology. Thus, focusing on critical thinking about psychology conveys the material for the course as well as helping students develop a skill for their education in general. Many resources exist for relating critical thinking to psychological topics, including texts by Smith (2002), Tavris (1995), and McBurney (2002). These texts relate critical-thinking essays and exercises to a variety of topics in psychology. You can use them to develop lecture material and in-class demonstrations, or you can assign them as supplemental texts for the course.

Incorporating techniques that allow students to interact during class promotes active learning and student engagement. For example, you can take the last 5 or 10 minutes of each class or time at the end of each topic area to allow students to compare and fill in notes. You can present problems and cases to generate discussion among small groups of students during class (Nilson, 2002). Asking students to turn to the person sitting next to them and share their thoughts on a topic is another way to encourage interaction. You can then ask several pairs of students to share their thoughts with the class.

Testing and Assignments

Exams are another component of teaching large classes that require careful preparation. Faculty most often use multiple-choice tests in large classes; it is unrealistic to assign a large number of meaningful writing exercises in this setting. Nevertheless, giving students a choice in assignments and testing can be a way to accommodate students with special interests and preferences. For example, a handful of students in a large class may prefer to take an essay instead of a multiple-choice exam. Because the number of these students is not likely to be large, it would be reasonable to accommodate them – students will appreciate that they were given the option. Similarly, you can give students the option of attending weekly discussion groups with a teaching assistant (TA) if you have one, writing a term paper, or making a class presentation. Again, most students will choose the discussion group. However, offering the term paper and class presentation will accommodate the small group of students who have special interests or experiences (Halgin & Overtree, 2002). For example, a student who is working for a childcare center might prefer to write a paper or make a class presentation on a topic in child development rather than attend discussion groups. Such class presentations by students especially interested in exploring a topic can also offer diversity in course instruction and learning opportunities for the students in the class.

Course Management

Attendance

Requiring attendance is a personal decision based on your teaching philosophy, although taking a class roll by reading everyone's name is certainly not an option in very large classes. To encourage attendance, you might select random days for short quizzes that could count towards the students' grades or be used for extra credit (Jenkins, 1991). You can use a seating chart system when attendance is required. For example, on the third day of class you might announce that each student's present seat is his or her seat for the semester. TAs can then create a seating chart. When attendance is required, TAs simply mark absent those individuals whose seats are empty.

Expectations

It is important to put all expectations for the course content and for classroom behavior in writing in your syllabus and explain these expectations to the students (Porter & Stanley, 2002). Because there are so many students, you cannot address your expectations to each student individually, so having those expectations in writing is imperative. It is important to stick to your stated policies, have contingency plans for yourself regarding the policies, and deal with problems immediately. If you don't attend to them, they tend to multiply very quickly among such a large student body.

Communication

It is most effective to use a course management system (CMS), such as Blackboard or WebCT, for communication with students. You can use these systems for grading, grade dissemination, handouts, assignments, lecture outlines, and making announcements. It is inevitable in all classes that some students will lose handouts and assignments. Because common problems in smaller classes are often multiplied in large classes, the 1 or 2 students in this situation in a smaller class can easily become 10 or 20 students (or more!) in a large class. Making course documents and grades available through CMS can be an efficient way to distribute this information.

You may also communicate with the entire class or small class groups via email with CMS. Students can be notified of changes in locations of meetings, extensions of dates of assignments, and so on. Students may communicate with each other as well, using the communication features of CMS to create study groups or request notes from missed classes.

Effective Use of TAs

In very large classes it is reasonable to have graduate or advanced undergraduate level TAs; they will be valuable additions to the course. It is critical that you train and communicate expectations to your TAs before the semester begins. Tell TAs of your responsibilities (e.g., present lecture material, create tests, put course materials on course management system, and meet individually with students as needed), and their responsibilities (e.g., take roll at each class meeting, lead discussion groups, and grade tests). Throughout the course, weekly meetings with TAs can address problems as they arise (e.g., how to deal with an abrasive student in a discussion group), so that quick and effective strategies for dealing with such problems are developed and implemented.

Because different TAs will have different talents, you can also distribute workloads among TAs accordingly. For example, some TAs may wish to lecture on topics within their area of expertise. Other TAs may be highly organized and computer literate and prefer to maintain the course website and course grading.

TAs can help make the class more personal and promote student understanding of course material. TAs can hold regular discussion groups and study sessions to promote smaller group interactions. You can assign groups of students to a specific TA, whom they can contact in addition to you, to discuss course material, assignments, or test questions (Nilson, 2002). TAs can also provide you with feedback on lectures, tests, and assignments to promote course improvement (Halgin & Overtree, 2002).

Students with Special Needs

You should identify students with documented special needs at the beginning of the course. TAs can help these students with such accommodations as recording tests, ensuring that an interpreter comes to class, or ensuring that tests are delivered to alternate testing locations (Halgin & Overtree, 2002).

 Conclusion

Large classes pose a number of challenges to instructors. However, we believe that with the right preparation, students can have effective and positive learning experiences in large classes (see Hilton, 1999). We hope that the suggestions made here will be useful to you in your large class teaching endeavors.

REFERENCES

Halgin, R. P., & Overtree, C. E. (2002). Personalizing the large class in psychology. In C. A. Stanley & M. E. Porter (eds.), *Engaging large classes: Strategies and techniques for college faculty* (pp. 290–8). Boston, MA: Anker.

Hilton, J. L. (1999). Teaching large classes. In B. Perlman, L. I. McCann, & S. H. McFadden (eds.), *Lessons learned: Practical advice for the teaching of psychology* (pp. 115–20). Washington, DC: American Psychological Society.

Jenkins, J. J. (1991). Teaching psychology in large classes: Research and personal experience. *Teaching of Psychology, 18*, 74–80.

McBurney, D. H. (2002). *How to think like a psychologist: Critical thinking in psychology* (2nd ed.). Upper Saddle River, NJ: Prentice Hall.

Nilson, L. B. (2002). Teaching social science to a small society. In C. A. Stanley & M. E. Porter (eds.), *Engaging large classes: Strategies and techniques for college faculty* (pp. 299–314). Boston, MA: Anker.

Porter, M. E., & Stanley, C. A. (2002). Summary of key concepts for teaching large classes. In C. A. Stanley & M. E. Porter (eds.), *Engaging large classes: Strategies and techniques for college faculty* (pp. 324–9). Boston, MA: Anker.

Smith, R. A. (2002). *Challenging your preconceptions: Thinking critically about psychology* (2nd ed.). Pacific Grove, CA: Brooks/Cole.

Tavris, C. (1995). *Psychobabble and biobunk: Using psychology to think critically about issues in the news*. New York: HarperCollins College Publishers.

20
Using Teaching Assistants Effectively

Ψ

Lauren Fruh VanSickle Scharff
Stephen F. Austin State University

When faculty use teaching assistants (TAs) effectively, everyone benefits: the instructor, the students enrolled in the course, and the TA. The instructor will have help with mechanical components of the course such as attendance, record-keeping, proctoring, grading, etc., and this support should give the instructor extra time to work on higher-level and more creative aspects of the course. The TA can also take on more active roles such as helping with class activities or leading discussion groups. The students benefit from the additional effort that goes into making the class successful and by having an additional resource person with whom to discuss questions and course content.

Other than receiving a paycheck and possible reduction in tuition and fees, how does the TA benefit? All of these efforts will take time away from the TA's own graduate studies. Part of the answer is that graduate students can learn many valuable lessons by working as TAs. Some positive outcomes are the development of reading and writing skills (gained by reading and grading papers), communication skills (gained by answering student questions and through discussions with students), organizational skills (gained through grade entry and spreadsheet management), and content information acquisition (gained by attending class, giving reviews, meeting with students, and explaining material). An additional major accomplishment will be the shift in perspective from student to teacher (although the direct teaching role initially may be limited[1]) and the development of pedagogical skills. Finally, the TA may acquire a faculty mentor.

In order for these positive outcomes to occur for everyone, there are several specific recommendations to keep in mind. For the most part, they fall within two general themes: good communication and the creation of an atmosphere of respect. Remember, TAs are not "slave labor" (despite being underpaid at many institutions).

Starting Out

Before the semester begins, schedule a meeting with your assigned TA. Make sure to set aside at least an hour so that you have plenty of time to get to know a little about your TA and to go over the expectations you have for the semester. Because they will be university employees, TAs should also go through general university and departmental orientations where they learn about relevant policies and procedures (see Davis & Huss, 2002, p. 143). In preparation for your meeting with the TA, have available a current syllabus for the course. (It may only be a nearly-finished draft, but it should at least include the course components and testing schedule.) If you do not put a detailed daily schedule on the syllabus itself for the students, give the TA a copy of the detailed calendar schedule from which you will be working.

To start your meeting, ask the TA about herself and her goals in the graduate program. Find out if the TA is also working another job or has any other responsibilities that the two of you might need to work around during the semester. Share a little bit about yourself and your background. In an effort to create an atmosphere of mutual respect and professionalism at the first meeting, share contact information with the TA. You will want her contact information for the syllabus as well as for general communication. Give her your email and personal phone numbers and tell her when it might not be okay to call. Discuss how she should address you. As part of the transition as colleagues-in-training, many faculty encourage graduate students to use faculty members' first names. (This step is often hard for them to take, but it makes a positive impression and they should ultimately feel comfortable doing it.) However, you may not want your undergraduate students doing the same, so ask the TA to address you more formally (e.g., "Dr. Scharff") when in the classroom or hallway. Starting off using a casual and personal approach will help set the framework for mutual respect and open communication.

The next things that you should discuss are the duties that you expect the TA to perform during the semester (e.g., attend class, grading, proctoring, etc.). When meeting with the TA, explicitly encourage that she communicate with you about her own schedule and deadlines. Stress that, although the position is one for which there will be professional expectations (e.g., punctuality, attention to detail, professional attire and attitude), you as the instructor also recognize that the TA's primary objective is to be successful in her own academic endeavors.

Point out the learning benefits of the assistantship work and discuss ways that the assistantship duties and the TA's own goals may both be achieved. For example, I have my TAs help me grade papers in my introductory psychology course. Although it is a lot of work, I point out that it is a great way to learn to appreciate fine aspects of good versus poor writing and to develop the TA's own writing ability. We also discuss the load and schedule for this task (often my classes have over 100 students). Generally, I make sure I return all papers to students no later than 1 week from the day on which they were submitted. The assignment and due dates for these papers are on my detailed course schedule. If my TA reviews her schedule and finds that she has major projects or exams that same week, we will talk about it ahead of time and do one of the following.

Either I will grade more of the papers for that assignment or we will return them to the students a few days later than usual.

In general, it is important to remember that in some cases you will be working with students just beginning the transition from undergraduate to graduate student. Unless they are explicitly welcomed as colleagues-in-training, they may feel hesitant to ask you to accommodate their academic or personal needs. If they do poorly on their own assignments due to what is viewed as a load of tedious assistantship work and an inflexible instructor, it will be difficult for everyone to recover. TAs may react by performing their duties poorly or even drop out of the program. (See Keith-Spiegel, Whitley, Balogh, Perkins, & Wittig, 2002, ch. 18, for a discussion regarding the ethics of the use of students as TAs.) Realistic expectations, communication ahead of time and a little bit of flexibility on the instructor's part can avoid most resentment-causing circumstances.

During the Semester

You can take several actions throughout the semester to build a positive relationship with your TA and promote the success of the assistantship. First, explicitly communicate your respect for the TA to the undergraduates in the class. Allow the TA to introduce herself on the first day. Remind the undergraduates throughout the semester that the TA is capable and available to help them.

If the TA is going to proctor exams for you, tell the class ahead of time and explicitly tell the class that the assistant has the authority to monitor for cheating and to collect exams if someone is caught cheating. This approach will empower the TA to act if necessary. Similarly, anytime a TA will be handling duties related to student grades (e.g., grading assignments, entering grades, recording attendance), make it clear to the students that you and the TA have informative, frequent communication (Keith-Spiegel, et al., 2002, chap. 20). This action will deter some students from trying to manipulate the TA, which may happen to TAs more often due to their typically younger ages and more similar status as students.

When a TA will be grading assignments, be sure to give detailed guidelines, and grade a few examples to review with her before she starts grading. Often new TAs will feel awkward about grading undergraduates' papers. Acknowledge this feeling and suggest that she may want to use a pencil at first when grading. Have her set aside any assignments that she is not sure how to handle and then review with her how you would handle them. Review a random selection of the graded papers prior to returning them to the students to make sure they are graded satisfactorily. Give feedback to the TA and be generous with your praise and support for work that is done well. Learning how to grade in a manner that is clear and gives useful feedback to the students is a major accomplishment, so use empathy and patience with the TA as she goes through the process.

Meet with the TA fairly regularly to make sure she knows what you're planning for upcoming classes and assignments. Such meetings are also good times to ask her how her own classes are coming along and to give some informal advising if appropriate. Ask the

TA for feedback regarding the class and your performance. She might have some insights about the class or your presentations that you have missed. Ask the TA for suggestions when preparing for upcoming activities. She might be able to share some activities that she experienced as an undergraduate or she might have ideas about how to improve what you plan to do. Instructors often forget to view the TA as a resource rather than simply as hired help.

Regular meetings with your TA can also facilitate the TA's transition from having only a student's perspective to including a teacher's perspective. Most students only consider what might make the course better for them personally. So, for example, students might think it would be reasonable to receive an extra credit opportunity that was not also given to the class at large. As the semester progresses, discuss with the TA your logic behind any extra credit assignments, make-up exams or assignments (who gets to take them and why), class management, lecture preparation, the testing and assignment schedule, and any other course issues that come up (other than those that require student confidentiality for some reason; see Keith-Spiegel et al., 2002, ch. 20). The amount of work and consideration that go into creating a successful course may come as a surprise to a TA because, before the assistantship experience, she only considered courses from the undergraduate perspective. Understanding a teacher's perspective will foster her development as a colleague-in-training, and it may also help her handle her own coursework because she can understand better her instructors' perspectives. Even if a TA has worked with another faculty member prior to you, sharing your logic about the course is still beneficial because an additional valuable lesson is that there is no one, correct way to handle different aspects of a course.

In conclusion, everyone can benefit when TAs are available if there is good communication and mutual respect between the instructor and TA. Some instructors hesitate to share any control with a TA and may believe they are doing TAs a favor by not asking them to assume many responsibilities. Other instructors may overburden TAs, leading to detrimental results for the TA and the course. However, if you share the responsibilities properly, the TAs will usually appreciate them, rise to the occasion, and learn from the experiences themselves.

NOTE

1 Although not specifically addressed in this chapter, some graduate assistantships place the graduate student as the instructor of record for a course. In such cases there should be more extensive training of the graduate assistant (e.g., Davis, Grover, & Burns, 2004; Davis & Huss, 2002). For a review of content in teaching of psychology courses, see Buskist, Tears, Davis, & Rodrigue (2002).

REFERENCES

Buskist, W., Tears, R., Davis, S., & Rodrigue, K. (2002). The teaching of psychology course: Prevalence and content. *Teaching of Psychology, 29*, 140–2.

Davis, S. F., Grover, C. A., & Burns, S. R. (2004). Training and evaluating Master's-level graduate teaching assistants. In W. Buskist, W. B. Beins, & V. S. Hevern, (eds.), *Preparing the new psychology professoriate: Helping graduate students become competent teachers.* (Retrievable at http://teachpsych.org/teachpsych/pnpp/)

Davis, S., & Huss, M. (2002). Training graduate teaching assistants. In S. F. Davis & W. Buskist (eds.), *The teaching of psychology: Essays in honor of Wilbert J. McKeachie and Charles L. Brewer* (pp. 141–50). Mahwah, NJ: Lawrence Erlbaum Associates.

Keith-Spiegel, P., Whitley, B., Balogh, D., Perkins, D., & Wittig, A. (2002). *The ethics of teaching: A casebook* (2nd ed.). Mahwah, NJ: Lawrence Erlbaum Associates.

21

Teaching Courses with Laboratories

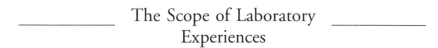

Dana S. Dunn
Moravian College

Laboratory courses in psychology involve "hands-on," active learning experiences for students, an opportunity for teachers to illustrate directly the power of the empirical method. Students take part in lab experiences by acting as participant or experimenter and, depending on a study's design, they occasionally fill both roles. In contrast to lectures or discussions, lab experiences bring abstract psychological concepts or theories alive for students. Arguably, actual demonstrations are sometimes more educationally involving than prepared descriptions of procedures and results conveyed by master teachers or well-written texts (e.g., Sutherland & Bonwell, 1996). Laboratory experiences are not a substitute for more traditional modes of learning; rather, they provide an additional and dynamic way of understanding behavior.

The Scope of Laboratory Experiences

Psychology courses that frequently use laboratory activities are research methods, statistics, tests and measurement, and some content courses, especially upper-level offerings (e.g., experimental psychology, cognitive psychology, physiological psychology, social psychology). Less commonly, some psychology departments also offer lab-based, advanced research methods courses in content areas (e.g., research methods in developmental psychology). Activities comprising a laboratory experience include experiments or quasi-experiments involving human participants or animal subjects, observational or qualitative research, computer-aided data analysis, scoring and interpreting psychological test results, and even in-class paper-and-pencil demonstrations. Some courses include laboratory work by adding an additional weekly meeting time (e.g., 3 lectures plus a lab), whereas other courses use class time for lab activities.

What constitutes a lab? Consider the *Stroop effect*, a staple of experimental psychology and a canonical laboratory experience (Stroop, 1935; see also Dunbar & MacLeod, 1984). In brief, participants see color names appearing in different shades (e.g., the word "green" appears in pink ink). They then try to list the words' colors out loud, a straight-forward but difficult task because reading the words (i.e., saying "green" instead of "pink") is all but unavoidable. Besides making such naming errors, longer latency times are associated with the *Stroop effect* (e.g., saying "green" when it appears in pink ink takes longer than when the same word appears in green ink). Reading about the *Stroop effect* is much less interesting than actually replicating – and thereby experiencing – this intriguing phenomenon of cognitive interference. To witness and understand verbal interference first hand, an instructor could supply students with ready-made materials for demonstrating the experiment during class. Alternatively, students could create their own stimuli, develop a research procedure, collect and analyze data drawn from classmates, and then present the findings in a subsequent class and submit a written lab report.

Emphasizing the Scientific Method and Research Practice

Any lab experience for students must emphasize the importance of the scientific method, the tools of inquiry psychologists use to pose and empirically address research questions. Where pedagogical demonstration is concerned, the essential elements of the scientific method include the need to make careful observations about behavior so that general conclusions can be drawn; the use of observations to formulate testable theories; reliance on experiments to tie observations and theory together in a controlled test; the careful evaluation of results with an eye to replication and independent verification by other researchers; and using reliable findings to develop new hypotheses to broaden theories about behavioral phenomena, thereby repeating the process cyclically in order to expand knowledge (for detailed discussion of and debate concerning empirical investigations and the "doing" of science, see e.g., Cacioppo, Semin, & Berntson, 2004; Driver-Linn, 2003; Kuhn, 1970; Platt, 1964; Popper, 1959; Watson, 1967).

This idealized description of the scientific method requires instructors to introduce students to the practical issues of conducting research as well. Discussions focused on observations and theory require that students develop *operational definitions* for variables – taking abstract ideas and identifying concrete representations that can be manipulated (*independent variables*) and measured (*dependent variables*) within an experiment. With instructor guidance, students decide whether dependent measures are behavioral or based on self-report. Students must learn basic experimental design, especially the minimal requirement of comparing the response of an *experimental group* with that of a *control group*. To create these groups, students must learn the significance of *randomly sampling* from representative populations to control for bias whenever possible (or relying on *random selection* to create experimental and control groups when only a haphazard sample of participants is available).

Lab courses in psychology often emphasize *quantitative research*, especially experiments, as the *sine qua non* of psychological investigation. *Qualitative research* is characterized by nonnumerical data and tends to involve verbal reports and subjective descriptions of behavior (e.g., Lincoln & Guba, 1985). Although experimentation is often the preferred approach to research in both the classroom and lab, instructors often introduce other research approaches while discussing research design. These approaches include *survey research* (e.g., Schwartz, Groves, & Schuman, 1998), *quasi-experiments* (e.g., Cook & Campbell, 1979), *case studies* (e.g., Stake, 1995), *naturalistic observation*, and *correlational methods*, among others. You can find brief overviews of most of these research approaches in basic research methods texts in psychology and specialized handbooks.

Planning Laboratories

Planning is everything where laboratory demonstrations are concerned. The key element of planning is *time*: How much is available – a class period, a few weeks, or an entire semester? Will there be multiple labs during a semester or only one or two? No lab will work well if it cannot be reasonably run in the time available, which must include the opportunity to discuss the findings, their interpretation and psychological meaning, as well as the more practical issues related to the demonstration (i.e., what worked well, what did not, and why?).

Planning also entails deciding on a specific lab experience, the nature of which is usually guided by the course topic. Will the lab be a replication of a published, possibly classic paradigm or a demonstration drawn from some other trustworthy source (e.g., a text's instructor's manual, an article from *Teaching of Psychology*)? Alternatively, an instructor can create lab exercises from scratch or ask the students (collectively, in groups, or individually) to develop research designs. Both of the latter options usually entail additional time and there is no guarantee that an untested lab will yield the hypothesized results (generally, the risk of obtaining null results is lower with "canned" demonstrations).

In either case, students should do *background reading* on the lab's topic. To save time, an instructor can provide readings or references – chiefly journal articles but sometimes books or book chapters – germane to the lab project. Ideally, however, students will conduct a search of the psychological literature themselves, which means they must learn to search a database (e.g., PsycINFO) to select appropriate references by topic or author, taking opportunity to familiarize themselves with a library's resources and possibly its interlibrary loan facilities. Reviewing relevant literature places a lab in context and prepares students for conducting a study, and interpreting and writing about its findings.

Once a research design is finalized, *materials* – stimuli, experimental apparatus, or any necessary props – are collected or created. Time will dictate whether an instructor should provide the materials or involve students in producing them in or outside of class. In fact, you might need to generate multiple sets of material, especially if students are collecting data individually rather than in pairs or groups. Whether the lab is done solo or by groups, I recommend *data sharing* – increasing statistical power by pooling a class's observations prior to beginning the analysis – unless there is a compelling reason not to do so. Such reasons include the strength of the effect involved (some labs, like the *Stroop effect*, do not require many observations) or because students introduced "pet" variables during data collection, precluding sharing due to design confounds across groups of experimenters.

Finally, instructors must determine the source of participants for the lab. This matter is simplified if a department maintains a *Human Participant Pool* and there is encouragement (i.e., extra credit), if not a formal requirement, for undergraduates to take part in research. Very often, of course, students running labs must recruit participants by relying on their family, friends, roommates, and classmates, which is not ideal from the perspective of experimental neutrality, control, and randomness, but does ensure that a lab experience actually occurs. Regardless of the participant source, the instructor must familiarize student researchers with the need to obtain *informed consent* and the ethics of experimentation, including the treatment guidelines and necessity for careful *debriefing* (APA, 1982, 1990, 1992; Sales & Folkman, 2000). Separate guidelines exist for research with animals (Akins, Panicker, & Cunningham, 2004; APA, 1993). You must set aside an appropriate amount of time to discuss the ethical aspects of psychological research, with special emphasis on the current lab.

Executing Laboratories

Although paper-and-pencil labs require little in the way of logistics, the same cannot be said of more complex labs. For a study to be run properly from start to finish, students must know their roles, which means that an instructor must help them create and learn the lab's *procedure*. Two excellent ways exist to accomplish this feat: Asking students to write (a) an APA style *Method* section (APA, 2001) for the lab before collecting any data and (b) a *script* outlining what they will say and do in the course of the lab (Dunn, 1999).

After studying these written directions, the next step is to *pilot* the study from beginning to end (including practicing *debriefing*) so that problems can be identified and resolved. Ideally, the instructor will serve as a participant during piloting, although classmates familiar with the study's purpose can also offer constructive comments.

Once piloting is complete, participants are recruited (in class or via a participant pool) and data collection begins. Ensuring the security and accuracy of participant data as students gather them is crucial. Use a coding system, typically a numerical one, to prepare responses for summary and preplanned statistical analyses. Instructors must decide whether students will perform calculations by hand, with a calculator, or using statistical software. Instructors are also responsible for insuring that students understand the rationale behind any analysis and how to interpret any results.

Evaluating Laboratories

Assessing what students learn in psychology is an important consideration for psychology educators (see Dunn, Mehrotra, & Halonen, 2004). One way to evaluate students' lab efforts is by having them write *research contracts* in advance, which stipulate their duties in concrete terms, as well as their responsibilities to any peer collaborators (e.g., Dunn, 1999). Instructors need only compare students' actual performance against the agreed-to contract. Alternatively, instructors can evaluate student conduct through traditional means, including written lab reports, in-class talks, or poster presentations.

Conclusion

Lab courses provide a microcosm for students to *do* psychology. Personal research experiences teach students how psychologists create, test, and revise theories, thereby expanding knowledge about behavior.

REFERENCES

Akins, C. K., Panicker, S., & Cunningham, C. L. (eds.) (2004). *Laboratory animals in research and teaching: Ethics, care, and methods.* Washington, DC: American Psychological Association.

American Psychological Association. (1982). *Ethical principles in the conduct of research with human participants.* Washington, DC: Author.

American Psychological Association. (1990). Ethical principles of psychologists. *American Psychologist, 45,* 390–5.

American Psychological Association. (1992). Ethical principles of psychologists and code of conduct. *American Psychologist, 47,* 1597–1611.

American Psychological Association. (1993). *Guidelines for ethical conduct in the care and use of animals.* Washington, DC: Author.

American Psychological Association. (2001). *Publication manual of the American Psychological Association* (5th ed.). Washington, DC: Author.

Cacioppo, J. T., Semin, G. R., & Berntson, G. G. (2004). Realism, instrumentalism, and scientific symbiosis: Psychological theory as a search for truth and the discovery of solutions. *American Psychologist, 59,* 214–23.

Cook, T. D., & Campbell, D. T. (1979). *Quasi-experimentation: Design & analysis issues for field settings.* Boston: Houghton Mifflin.

Driver-Linn, E. (2003). Where is psychology going? Structural fault lines revealed by psychologists' use of Kuhn. *American Psychologist, 58,* 269–78.

Dunbar, K., & MacLeod, C. M. (1984). A horse race of a different color: Stroop interference patterns with transformed words. *Journal of Experimental Psychology: Human Perception and Performance, 10,* 622–39.

Dunn, D. S. (1999). *The practical researcher: A student guide to conducting psychological research.* New York: McGraw-Hill.

Dunn, D. S., Mehrotra, C. M., & Halonen, J. S. (eds.) (2004). *Measuring up: Educational assessment challenges and practices for psychology.* Washington, DC: American Psychological Association.

Kuhn, T. S. (1970). *The structure of scientific revolutions* (rev. ed.). Chicago: University of Chicago Press.

Lincoln, Y. S., & Guba, E. G. (1985). *Naturalistic inquiry.* Newbury Park, CA: Sage.

Platt, J. R. (1964). Strong inference. *Science, 146,* 347–53.

Popper, K. R. (1959). *The logic of scientific discovery.* New York: Basic Books.

Sales, B. D., & Folkman, S. (eds.) (2000). *Ethics in research with human participants.* Washington, DC: American Psychological Association.

Schwartz, N., Groves, R. M., & Schuman, R. M. (1998). Survey methods. In D. T. Gilbert, S. T. Fiske, & G. Lindzey (eds.), *The handbook of social psychology* (vol. 1, pp. 143–79). New York: McGraw-Hill.

Stake, R. E. (1995). *The art of case study research.* Thousand Oaks, CA: Sage.

Stroop, J. R. (1935). Studies of interference on serial verbal reactions. *Journal of Experimental Psychology, 18,* 643–62.

Sutherland, T. E., & Bonwell, C. C. (eds.) (1996). Using active learning in college classes: A range of options for faculty [Special issue]. *New Directions for Teaching and Learning, 67.*

Watson, R. I. (1967). Psychology: A prescriptive science. *American Psychologist, 22,* 435–43.

22
Independent Study: A Conceptual Framework

Ψ

Jeffrey S. Katz, Bradley R. Sturz, Kent D. Bodily, & Michelle Hernandez
Auburn University

Teaching an independent study course is the ultimate service work. Departments typically do not require such a course, yet many faculty offer this experience for undergraduates. For example, our department does not require this course but an average of 15 percent of psychology majors register for it each year. Why then do we as teachers offer undergraduates this type of experience? Reasons vary from fostering enthusiasm for research, preparing students for graduate school, and interacting in an influential one-on-one style (Landrum & Nelson, 2002). So, if teachers choose to offer this experience, how should such they design it?

Unfortunately, there is no empirical consensus on what constitutes a high-quality independent study. However, it is not difficult to find informed opinions on the matter (e.g., Davis, 1999; Lamdin & Worby, 1976; McKeachie, 2002). In general, there is no perfect recipe, but certainly many ways to spoil the broth. Becoming a successful teacher (much like becoming a successful chef), requires developing a personalized style. This personalized style involves discovering what works well for an individual. Independent study is no exception. Given this caveat, this chapter offers a prescriptive opinion on what has worked well in our experience. We offer a conceptual framework in which to view independent thought that is general-process based (e.g., Bitterman, 2000) and hope that it will be effective in providing meaningful learning experiences for students who participate in independent study courses.

A Conceptual Framework

The main goal of any independent study course is to teach students how to think independently. We view independent thought similarly to Halpern's (2003) critical

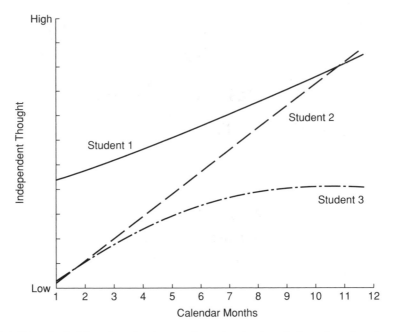

Figure 22.1: Hypothetical functions for three students showing how independent thought may develop as a function of time

thinking. Specifically, we view critical thinking as a problem-solving process that occurs through the utilization of cognitive skills. In general, the process is directed and leads to a desirable solution in a particular context. Analogously, independent thought develops as students acquire and fine-tune specific cognitive skills within the independent study context.

In our framework, all students have an ability to solve problems and develop independent thought (Richmond, 1998). Not all students, however, have developed this ability to the same level. Consequently, teachers must create and adopt teaching strategies that address such student variability. A useful aid in developing these strategies is a conceptual framework for independent thought. Specifically, independent thought can be placed on a continuum from low to high with unique student developmental time courses. Figure 22.1 shows hypothetical functions for development of independent thought for three students over the course of a year. From the onset, Student 1 is more advanced relative to the other students. However, the yearly progress of Student 1 is more gradual than Student 2 but slightly faster than Student 3. In this framework, we consider all students qualitatively the same in terms of abilities but quantitatively different with respect to development. Some students may never reach a particular level, which reflects a quantitative difference in independent thought. Thus, this framework stresses skill acquisition as contributing to the development of independent thought regardless of student developmental level.

Getting Started

Every semester teachers typically receive several requests from students regarding research opportunities. For instance, "I am interested in doing an independent study with a professor. Do you need any more assistance conducting your research this semester?" (anonymous student, personal communication, Aug. 18, 2004). Should teachers be selective with those undergraduate students with whom they collaborate? Absolutely. If teachers had time to conduct an independent study for each student request, selection would not be problematic. Unfortunately, time is an issue. A common pitfall for inexperienced teachers is the "someone wants to work with me" phenomenon. Although it might boost the ego, the last thing a teacher needs is a nonproductive student when launching a career.

Yet, the question remains, "What is the best way to select students?" In short, there is no best way, but we offer some useful suggestions. Each of the following examples provides a teacher with the opportunity to learn about potential students in some detail. First, require a minimum GPA (e.g., 3.0). Although there are exceptions to every rule, average students in the classroom tend to be average independent study students. Second, have a set of interview questions that addresses the student's seriousness and dedication. What are your career interests? Why do you want to conduct research? What do you want to get out of an independent study experience? Serious students have clear goals. The answers to the interview questions should reflect such goals. Third, if the student is unfamiliar to you, require a reference letter and/or suggest that he or she assist in the laboratory for a semester without earning independent study credit (some students may suggest this on their own). Fourth, remember that these factors might interact. For example, a teacher may prefer a dedicated personable student with a good work ethic and a GPA of 3.1 over an unpleasant 4.0 student with a poor work ethic. A good work ethic and personality can go a long way in creating pleasant experiences for you, the student, and other students who may work alongside you on any particular project.

Strategies

Our conceptual framework allows for the application of many teaching strategies. Several strategies for teaching independent study courses include discovery instruction, expository instruction, inquiry instruction, and problem-based learning (for reviews, see Coppola, 2002; Domin, 1999). Although teachers often utilize these strategies in large group laboratory settings, teachers may also apply these techniques to small groups. Importantly, teaching strategy choice is dependent largely on the desired level of structure (for tips on adding structure to an independent study course see Horner, Stetter, & McCann, 1998). Teachers may tailor the level of structure to suit a student's individual needs and developmental level.

We prefer a quasi-structured environment for students involved in empirical studies. This environment allows findings from projects on which students are working, as well as student progress, to alter the course of the independent study at any given moment.

Table 22.1: Skills that can be developed in an independent study course

Acquiring area-related vocabulary	Graphing
Asking research questions	Searching literature
Collaborating on projects	Presenting orally
Critically analyzing research	Reading primary literature
Collecting and analyzing data	Generalizing research findings
Practicing ethical conduct	Understanding contemporary concepts
Expressing complex ideas	Understanding research methods
Formulating hypotheses	Writing (APA format)

Source: Adapted from Kardash, 2000; Landrum & Nelson, 2002.

To foster independent thought, we prefer a discovery-based strategy in which students learn by working on various tasks. This teaching strategy allows students to develop at their own pace. Optimally, they learn how to learn. Students start with a task (or tasks) that they can complete quickly. We instruct them to inform us when they are ready for the next task or when they need assistance in solving a problem.

Task difficulty can (and should) increase sequentially. For example, students start as pilot participants in an experiment. They then learn to analyze and plot their own data. Next, we interactively discuss and interpret their results. The process typically leads to a literature search that helps students place these data and results into a larger research picture. To assist in this process we utilize two techniques that are known to improve conceptual learning across a variety of settings: (a) increase the number of exemplars (e.g., if data graphing is difficult, have the student create more graphs) and (b) increase the amount of time working with one exemplar (e.g., Kaminski, Call, & Fischer, 2004; Katz, Wright, & Bachevalier, 2002; Siegler, 1996; Wright 1997). These two principles are amenable to a multitude of skills (see table 22.1) that teachers may develop in an undergraduate independent study experience (Kardash, 2000; Landrum & Nelson, 2002).

One of the benefits of this strategy is that it prompts students to think and work independently on a topic that they find interesting. Additionally, it allows the teacher to provide guidance and support on technical and professional issues while continuing to tailor the independent study experience to developmental and individual needs of each student. Thus, many students thrive in this environment. They work at a pace that is often accelerated and at times pushes teachers to stay one step ahead of the students. Their independent thought clearly develops over the course of a semester (or semesters) as they begin to wrestle with challenging methodological and conceptual issues. These students often go on to complete honors theses and are ready for the academic challenges that await them in graduate school.

Teacher and Context

An important factor in advancing student independent thought is you, the teacher. If you are the type of teacher who welcomes any undergraduate into your laboratory and then pawns them off to a graduate or advanced undergraduate student with little (if any) further interaction, perhaps you are part of the problem. In a successful independent study nothing is truly independent. The experience depends on the quality of the teacher–student relationship. Such one-to-one relationships require frequently scheduled interactions (i.e., weekly or daily) to allow for careful and accurate evaluation of student progress.

This relationship does not suggest that graduate and undergraduate students should not be involved in the independent study process. To the contrary, we encourage their involvement. If graduate and advanced undergraduate students are available to contribute to the independent study process, then a hierarchical model of supervision is a viable option. In addition to the one-to-one interaction, a hierarchical model allows teachers to supervise students in directing other students. However, it is extremely important to monitor the progress of each student in the hierarchy. Laboratory meetings can provide one venue in which to monitor this progress.

Another factor that may seem to make a major difference is the type of institution in which you teach the independent study course. To explore this issue we collected undergraduate independent study descriptions from 10 top-tier teaching colleges and 10 top-tier research universities (i.e., universities with graduate programs; US News, 2004). Despite differences in categorical classification, all universities and colleges had relatively similar conceptions of independent study: individualized, self-directed, and self-paced learning focused on facilitating and promoting creative and independent thought. Despite this fact, the two environments are notably different (Freeman, 2002). At research universities students typically become involved in ongoing potentially publishable projects. These students play the role of research assistants. Independent projects often develop after a student has completed an independent study course and then moves to an honors project. In contrast, students at teaching colleges often have the opportunity to begin independent projects without first being a research assistant. However, regardless of student roles within the independent study experience and the context in which you teach, the conceptual framework presented in figure 22.1 remains applicable.

Conclusion

We hope that these comments will help you find the independent study teaching strategy appropriate for your personal style. Forming individual strategies through personal experience is the best way to accomplish this task. We believe these learning experiences are essential to becoming a master teacher. Perhaps William James (1890/1950) expressed it best when he said:

> If he keep faithfully busy each hour of the working-day, he may safely leave the final result to itself. He can with perfect certainty count on waking up some fine morning, to find himself one of the competent ones of his generation, in whatever pursuit he may have singled out. (p. 127)

Jeffrey S. Katz, Bradley R. Sturz, Kent D. Bodily, & Michelle Hernandez

ACKNOWLEDGMENTS

This article was supported by a National Science Foundation Grant IBN-0316113. Correspondence and reprints may be addressed to: Jeffrey S. Katz, Department of Psychology, 226 Thach Hall, Auburn University, Auburn, AL 36849. Email: katzjef@auburn.edu.

REFERENCES

Bitterman, M. E. (2000). Cognitive evolution: A psychological perspective. In C. Heyes, & L. Huber (eds.), *The evolution of cognition* (pp. 61–79). Cambridge, MA: MIT Press.

Coppola, B. (2002). Laboratory instruction: Ensuring an active learning experience. In W. J. McKeachie (ed.), *Teaching tips: Strategies, research, and theory for college and university teachers* (11th ed., pp. 235–44). Boston: Houghton Mifflin.

Davis, S. F. (1999). The valve of collaborative scholarship with undergraduates. In B. Perlman, L. McCann, & S. H. McFadden (eds.), *Lessons learned* (pp. 201–5). Washington DC: American Psychological Society.

Domin, D. S. (1999). A review of laboratory instruction styles. *Journal of Chemical Education, 76,* 543–7.

Freeman, J. E. (2002). Differences in teaching in liberal arts college versus research university. In S. F. Davis & W. Buskist (eds.), *The teaching of psychology: Essays in honor of Wilbert J. McKeachie and Charles L. Brewer* (pp. 247–57). Mahwah, NJ: Erlbaum.

Halpern, D. F. (2003). *Thought & knowledge: An introduction to critical thinking* (4th ed.). Mahwah, NJ: Erlbaum.

Horner, D. T., Stetter, K. R., & McCann, L. I. (1998). Adding structure to unstructured research courses. *Teaching of Psychology, 25,* 126–8.

James, W. (1950). *The principles of psychology* (vol. 1). New York: Dover Publications. (Original work published 1890.)

Kaminsi, J., Call, J., & Fischer, J. (2004). Word learning in a domestic dog: Evidence for "fast mapping." *Science, 304,* 1682–3.

Kardash, C. M. (2000). Evaluation of an undergraduate research experience: Perceptions of undergraduate interns and their faculty mentors. *Journal of Educational Psychology, 92,* 191–201.

Katz, J. S., Wright, A. A., & Bachevalier, J. (2002). Mechanisms of *same/different* abstract-concept learning by rhesus monkeys (*Macaca mulatta*). *Journal of Experimental Psychology: Animal Behavior Processes, 28,* 358–68.

Lamdin, L., & Worby, D. (1976). Across the desk: Teaching through independent study. *Alternative Higher Education, 1,* 61–7.

Landrum, R. E., & Nelson, L. R. (2002). The undergraduate research assistantship: An analysis of the benefits. *Teaching of Psychology, 29,* 15–19.

McKeachie, W. J. (2002). *Teaching Tips: Strategies, research, and theory for college and university teachers* (11th ed.). Boston: Houghton Mifflin.

Richmond, G. (1998). Scientific apprenticeship and the role of public schools: General education of a better kind. *Journal of Research in Science Teaching, 35,* 583–7.

Siegler, R. S. (1996). *Emerging minds: The process of change in children's thinking.* New York: Oxford University Press.

US News and World Reports (2004, June 8). America's Best Colleges 2005. Accessed from www.usnews.com.

Wright, A. A. (1997). Concept learning and learning strategies. *Psychological Science, 8,* 119–23.

23

Service-Learning

Ψ

Randall E. Osborne & Oren Renick
Texas State University, San Marcos

Service-learning is a process that can and needs to be revised constantly. As such, a prescriptive plan for how to engage in service-learning is more of articulating best practices. These practices will need to be refined by faculty members to: (a) fit the needs of a particular course, department, or program, (b) meet the needs of students, (c) provide the most beneficial service to the agency, organization, or individuals being served, (d) maximize student learning, and (e) generate a product that provides those being served and the students engaging in the service with a sense of closure.

Before attempting to delineate these "best practices," however, it is important to clarify what is meant by "service-learning." Bringle and Hatcher (1997) defined service-learning as a:

> type of experiential education in which students participate in service in the community and reflect on their involvement in such a way as to gain a further understanding of course content and of the discipline and of its relationship to social needs and an enhanced sense of civic responsibility. (p. 153)

For example, imagine that you want students in a course on emotional disorders in childhood to gain an applied understanding of these disorders. To accomplish this task, you might place students in a local community center and in a local mental health association with programming for children. The placement, itself, however, does not guarantee that students will gain the deeper understanding of course content, the broader appreciation for the discipline, or an enhanced sense of civic responsibility. Nor does the placement itself guarantee that the service they provide will meet an identified community need. One of the authors (RO) of this chapter taught such a course. He approached the two agencies, described the content of the course, culled from the agency supervisors the unmet needs of each agency, and discussed possible service projects students could complete that might address those needs.

The community center discussed a goal they had to improve youth perceptions of authority figures. One group from the course designed a project that placed community authority figures (police officers, judges, teachers, etc.) at the agency for evening activities with the youth. The authority figures led these activities in plain clothes. At the end of the semester, the authority figures came to the wrap-up session wearing their uniforms. The result was overwhelming: Many of the children could not believe that police officers or judges were real, everyday people who actually cared about them. This experience assisted students in seeing the concept of labeling and stigma from a very real perspective.

Another example from this same course involved the local mental health association that had purchased a videotape series on helping youth understand the implications of addiction. The association intended the videotapes to be used by local teachers, but the videotapes went unused. The student group interviewed local teachers and discovered that teachers did not use the videotapes because they did not come with prepackaged teaching materials; the teachers felt uncomfortable in teaching the material without guidelines. Students developed teaching packets and made handpuppets representing each character with which children could interact while the teacher discussed the video. The teaching materials became so popular that the local mental health association was given a grant by the state to develop similar materials for all other associations in the state.

Several national service-learning best practice documents are available including the Wingspread Principles (Honnet & Poulsen, 1989) and the work of Jeffrey Howard (1993). Simply put, the Wingspread Principles outline best practices for service-learning programs, and Howard's principles outline best practices for faculty to utilize in service-learning courses.

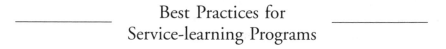

Best Practices for Service-learning Programs

The Wingspread Principles of Good Practice (Honnet & Poulsen, 1989) suggested that an effective service-learning program:

1. engages people in responsible and challenging actions for the common good;
2. provides structured opportunities for people to reflect critically on their service experience;
3. articulates clear service and learning goals for everyone involved;
4. allows for those with needs to define those needs,
5. clarifies the responsibilities of each person and organization involved;
6. matches service providers and service needs through a process that recognizes changing circumstances;
7. expects genuine, active, and sustained organizational commitment;
8. includes training, supervision, monitoring, support, recognition, and evaluation to meet service and learning goals;
9. ensures that the time commitment for service-learning is flexible, appropriate, and in the best interests of all involved; and
10. is committed to program participation by and with diverse populations.

Academic institutions assumed the responsibility for many of these components. Nonetheless, faculty wishing to incorporate service-learning into psychology courses should consider them as long-term goals allowing service-learning to become part of the campus culture. Several of these best practices, however, can and should be incorporated into the development of individual service-learning courses. Number 2 is an excellent example. Faculty must think about the course in which service-learning is to be included and develop assignments that provide students with multiple opportunities for guided reflection.

Best Practices for Service-learning Courses

Howard (1993) articulated best practices for service-learning courses. Some of these reflect the best practices for programs but are more easily applicable at the course level. Students' service experiences and course learning can be best integrated when faculty:

1. ensure that academic credit is for learning, not for service;
2. do not compromise academic rigor;
3. set learning goals for students;
4. establish criteria for the selection of community service-learning placements;
5. provide educationally sound mechanisms to harvest the community learning (methods for reflecting on what is being learned);
6. provide support for students to learn how to harvest the community learning (support for engaging in the necessary reflection on what is being learned);
7. minimize the distinction between the students' community learning role and the classroom learning role;
8. rethink the faculty instruction role (faculty do not always "lecture");
9. prepare for uncertainty and variation in student learning outcomes; and
10. maximize the community responsibility orientation of the course.

Several of these characteristics are more philosophical in nature. Most faculty set learning goals for students. The task with service-learning, then, is to think about developing service experiences that provide the greatest opportunity for students to focus on those goals. From our perspective, one of the most important of these "best practices" is reflection. Bringle and Hatcher (1995) noted that "reflection" must be (a) intentional, (b) related to the experience, and (c) connected to particular learning objectives. Faculty can reflect on the relationship between the service-learning projects and the development of their courses using the same principles.

Bringle and Hatcher (1995) summarized the criteria for the good practice of reflection. Effective reflection activities:

1. link experience to learning;
2. are guided;

3. occur regularly;
4. allow feedback and assessment; and
5. foster the exploration and clarification of values.

Assignments in service-learning-oriented courses that foster systematic and frequent reflection of the experiences as they relate to learning objectives will strengthen the very skills we value for our psychology majors. If we expect students, for example, to be able to understand a psychological issue from more than one perspective, our reflection assignments must require them to explore an issue arising from the service-learning experience and to explore it from multiple perspectives. One method might be to assign students a reading on the different perspectives in psychology (e.g., psychodynamic, humanistic, behavioral, cognitive, neurobiological, and sociocultural). You can follow this activity with an assignment that requires students to select some issue they are confronting in their service-learning experience and ask them to describe how someone operating from two or three of the perspectives would describe the nature of that issue.

Eyler, Giles, and Schmiede (1996) provided a useful rubric for developing reflection activities: faculty should remember the four Cs of reflection: (a) continuous, (b) connected, (c) contextualized, and (d) challenging. Reflection that is *continuous* requires students to reflect on the experience before, during, and after the experience. Reflection that is *connected* links the reflection to the course content and the course learning goals. Reflection that is *contextualized* is given a framework. Imagine, for example, that a faculty member is teaching abnormal psychology and has required students to do a service experience at a state hospital. Rather than just asking about the impact of labeling, she might ask students the following question: "Based on your service-learning experience and the individuals you met, why is it important to understand the impact of labeling on the individual being labeled?"

Finally, well-designed reflection activities are *challenging*. Such activities should push the student to consider difficult issues, to address those issues from multiple perspectives, and to explore contradictions and inconsistencies. Well-designed reflection activities move students beyond the simple cognitive levels of knowledge and comprehension and require them to integrate the experiences with their learning at the analysis and synthesis levels.

Summary

Although there are clearly many aspects of service-learning that we could address in this chapter, research suggests that two of the most important elements to the successful development, implementation, and outcome assessment of a service-learning experience in a course are: (a) setting clear learning goals that are linked to course content, and (b) developing continuous, connected, contextualized, and challenging reflection activities. Well-designed reflection allows students to demonstrate their competency with respect to learning goals and to maximize the benefits reaped from the service-learning experience.

In addition, well-designed reflection activities allow faculty to fulfill most of Howard's (1993) principles of good practice. Designing reflection activities also forces faculty to reflect on learning goals, to focus on the learning and not just the service, to provide methods by which students can maximize their learning, minimize the distinction between the community and learning roles, and to rethink the faculty instruction role. Designing reflection activities enhances the effectiveness of instruction and assists the faculty member in making students more active in their own learning.

REFERENCES

Bringle, R., & Hatcher, J. (1995). A service-learning curriculum for faculty. *Michigan Journal of Community Service Learning, 2,* 112–22.

Bringle, R., & Hatcher, J. (1997). Reflection. *College Teaching, 45,* 153–8.

Eyler, J., Giles, D., & Schmiede, A. (1996). *A practitioner's guide to reflection in service-learning: Student voices and reflections.* Nashville, TN: Vanderbilt University Press.

Honnet, E., & Poulsen, S. (1989). *Principles of good practice for combining service and learning.* A Wingspread Special Report. Racine, WI: The Johnson Foundation.

Howard, J. (1993). Community service learning in the curriculum. In J. P. F. Howard (ed.), *Praxis I: A faculty casebook on community service learning* (pp. 3–12). Ann Arbor, MI: OCSL Press.

24
Distance Learning: Psychology Online

Ψ

Mary N. Duell

University of Massachusetts at Lowell and Middlesex Community College

The internet plays a dominant role in our lives today. Technology provides information from across the globe at lightning speed. We get our mail, news, medical advice, and even gossip from Web-based sources. It is not surprising that delivering courses over the Web has become a major priority for many academic institutions. Although face-to-face interactions in a physical classroom between live students and an "expert" teacher will continue to be an important part of higher education, the internet truly opens the classroom to the world.

Is Web-Based Instruction Right for Me?

To answer this question adequately, you must consider several factors: your own personal and social characteristics, course selection, population(s) to be served, and time required for development and delivery. Many departments are pushing, even demanding, that faculty members offer Web courses. When department administrators make choices regarding distance-learning faculty, those choices often include faculty who are considered expert in a particular content area and who may be particularly entertaining in the classroom (Paloff & Pratt, 2001). However, research shows that the most popular faculty in the physical classroom may not always be the best in the virtual classroom (Brookfield, 1995, as cited in Paloff & Pratt, 2001). Simply put, entertainment skills may not easily translate to online environments. The willingness of faculty to empower students by giving up some control of the learning process and personal flexibility seem to be the best predictors of those faculty who are most likely to make a successful transition to the online environment (Paloff & Pratt, 2001).

Deciding which course(s) to engineer for the Web is another question that faculty must answer. Paloff and Pratt (2001) distinguished courses that are delivered entirely over the Web from those that use the Web to assist delivery. Some courses are well suited for exclusive delivery over the Web while others are not. According to these authors, courses that may not transfer well for exclusive Web delivery are laboratory courses and counseling courses. The extent to which Web technology is appropriate to meet the desired outcomes of the course must be evaluated.

Students who populate college and university courses are increasingly "nontraditional," and students who are attracted to distance learning are overwhelmingly nontraditional (Paloff & Pratt, 2001). Characteristics that confer nontraditional status are financial independence, part-time attendance, delayed enrollment, full-time work, dependents, single parenthood, and lack of a high-school diploma (Choy, 2002). The flexibility of the online classroom is often a major selling point for students enrolling in Web courses, and faculty must become comfortable with a more "elastic" teaching model.

Many faculty have the impression that online courses make fewer demands on a faculty member's time than traditional lecture courses. This perception is simply not true. Developing a course for Web delivery is time consuming, and delivering it to students requires that faculty are accessible 24 hours a day, 7 days a week. The design and delivery of course material over the Web is generally accomplished with specialized software, often referred to as a Course Management System, or CMS (Dabbagh & Bannan-Ritland, 2005). Online faculty must become thoroughly acquainted with the CMS used by their institution (see Hanna, Glowacki-Dudka, & Conceicao-Runlee, 2000, for a partial list of classroom software). Developing a new course or adapting an existing course for the online environment can be both time consuming and vexing.

Developing the Online Course

Once you have decided to deliver a Web course, you must adapt it for the Web. The actual engineering for the online environment depends on the software that is available. Be sure to check out the resources that are available to assist you; CMSs like Blackboard offer 24-hour support, 7 days a week. Seek out on-campus resources, such as faculty who have developed courses for online environments. Often, a department or entity within the university or college is available to offer software training and design help. Use it. Although the exact course materials and delivery methods are a matter of both taste and the CMS used, there are some basics: a syllabus, online notes and links to Web-based materials, communication strategies, assessment of student performance, and assignments.

Syllabus

A well-constructed syllabus is vital element of any course. However, when students do not come to a classroom, the syllabus becomes even more crucial because it is the principal means by which they come to understand the nature of the course and the instructor's expectations. A good online syllabus should contain the following information:

- Information about using the CMS, including access to technical support;
- Description of the course, including required and recommended materials and specific learning objectives;
- Summary of required readings, assignments, and exams;
- Schedule for release of online notes, assignments, and exams;
- Due dates for assignments and exams;
- Communication tools that you will use, how to use them, and etiquette for their use Grading criteria.

A major difference between online syllabi and standard course syllabi relate to the use of Web technology, such as communications tools and online notes. Although course content and objectives may be similar, the use of Web tools must be explained for online learners.

Online Notes and Web Links

Because Web students do not attend lectures in a traditional classroom, creating a set of online notes that students can readily access is an excellent way to assist learning. Depending on the CMS, you can add streaming video clips to "jazz" up the notes. You also can download graphics materials from the Web to include in online notes, provided that permission is obtained for copyrighted materials (see Dabbagh & Bannan-Ritland, 2005). Additionally, providing links to websites relevant to course topics is an easy way to add depth to the course. Such links may be included in the online notes or as a separate file(s) that students can access.

Communication

Communication in online courses may occur either asynchronously or synchronously. Asynchronous communication tools include discussion boards, email, and bulletin boards. Such tools do not allow for interaction with the instructor or other students in real time. Discussion boards help students focus on specific course content and expand their knowledge in specific content areas. They allow students to respond to questions posed by the instructor about a particular topic as well as postings made by members of the class about that topic. Well-crafted questions often elicit multiple postings by students (including new questions for consideration by the class) and result in a lively exchange of ideas among class members.

Email helps students stay connected and is perhaps the most important way for students to communicate concerns about the class to the instructor. Answer student emails promptly; 24-hour turn-around time during the week and 48-hour on the weekend is a good rule of thumb to follow.

Synchronous tools include live chat programs, video-conferencing, and electronic whiteboards, which enable live interaction with other students or the instructor (Dabbagh & Bannan-Ritland, 2005). Chats are popular synchronous tools, which allow students to access both the instructor and other students in a real-time environment. I typically schedule chats once a week for an hour. In large classes, chats may be difficult to manage. Palloff and Pratt (2001) suggested that chats work best if the number of participants is small (five or six students) and you create an agenda for the chat in advance. If classes are large or if students are required to attend a certain number of chats, you may need to consider scheduling more than a single chat session. You may also consider allowing students to read a recorded chat history to fulfill a chat requirement.

Assessing Student Performance

Assessing student performance in the online environment requires creativity and flexibility. Unless you require students to come to a testing center to complete exams, exam security is a concern. Objective online assessments that include only multiple-choice or true/false items may be useful, but you should use additional methods to evaluate students so that unsecure online tests are not the only measure of a student's mastery of course materials. Paloff and Pratt (2001) suggested that since participation is key to a successful online experience, assigning points for discussion board postings may be an effective evaluation tool. Likewise, papers concerned with important course topics may be effective evaluation instruments. You can post sample papers on the discussion boards as models for other students. Finally, you can assign points for chat participation. However, because some students may be unable to attend live chat sessions, you need to be flexible. Having those students read chat archives and respond via email to you may be a solution.

Assignments

You should determine specific reading and writing assignments prior to deploying the course. Assignments should be relevant to the learning objectives of the course as outlined in the course syllabus. You must also decide whether to use group (team) assignments. Team-based learning may serve as an excellent strategy for learning in the online environment (e.g., Hanna & Conceicao-Runley, 1999; Hanna et al., 2000). A team project that might be useful is a *WebQuest*, which allows groups of students to answer questions about a specific learning objectives using information exclusively derived from the Web (Dabbagh &Bannan-Ritland, 2005).

—————— Delivering the Course ——————

You must deliver the course in a manner that keeps students active and engaged in the learning process. My first discussion board is used for students to share information about themselves (see Hanna et al., 2000). Allowing students to post pictures of themselves on the first discussion board also helps build camaraderie.

As the course progresses, provide timely feedback to students about assignments, discussion boards, and exams. Important dates included in the syllabus should be reinforced with emails or announcements. Although online students must work independently, reminders help keep the course on track.

You also should explain etiquette for chats and discussion boards in the syllabus, and then purposely model these behaviors yourself. I believe that the most important guideline for online communication is respect for others. In a recent informal survey, my students reported that the major factor that spoils an online experience is being treated discourteously by other students or the instructor.

Seeking student feedback throughout the course is critical to the course's success. Providing thoughtful responses to students' suggestions may provoke additional discussion and improve the quality of the course for everyone. A willingness to make "mid-course" corrections when necessary demonstrates respect and flexibility for student opinions. Both are necessary ingredients for a successful online experience.

Finally, I have found that students who are close enough welcome a "face-to-face" meeting opportunity during the semester. I have typically scheduled a dinner meeting to bring students together to socialize at the end of the semester. In some cases, we used cellphones to call interested students who were unable to attend the meeting so they could feel connected. I have also had the opportunity to meet with several online students whose travels brought them to the area in which I live. Such experiences have been positive for both myself and the students. Although such meetings are certainly not a requirement for providing good instruction, they typically leave students with a good feeling about the online experience.

Conclusion

The internet affords a viable alternative to traditional classroom instruction. In fact, it has changed the way many faculty and students view teaching and learning. On the Web, students are global, classrooms are virtual, and learning is not framed by the traditional boundaries of time and space. Countless students will be the ultimate beneficiaries of faculty efforts to adapt instructional procedures and content to the Web.

REFERENCES

Choy, S. (2002). *Nontraditional undergraduates* (National Center for Education Statistics No. 2002-012). Washington, DC: National Center for Education Statistics.

Dabbagh, N., & Bannan-Ritland, B. (2005). *Online learning: Concepts, strategies, and application.* Upper Saddle River, NJ: Pearson Education.

Hanna, D. E., & Conceicao-Runlee, S. (1999). Building learning teams through computer-mediated conferencing. *Family Science Review, 12,* 183–92.

Hanna, D. E., Glowacki-Dudka, M., & Conceicao-Runlee, S. (2000). *147 practical tips for teaching online groups: Essentials of Web-based education.* Madison, WI: Atwood.

Palloff, R. M., & Pratt, K. (2001). *Lessons from the cyberspace classroom: The realities of online teaching.* San Francisco: Jossey-Bass.

part V

Ψ

Teaching and Mentoring Diverse Students

This section features six chapters that focus squarely on diversity issues: teaching and mentoring nontraditional students, students with disabilities, female students, racially and ethnically diverse students, academically at-risk students, and teaching across the entire diversity spectrum.

25
Teaching and Mentoring Nontraditional Students

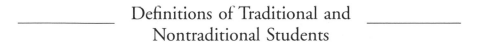

Cathy A. Grover
Emporia State University

The number of students over age 25 who attend college has been on the rise for several years (Bendixon-Noe, 1998). According to the US National Center for Education Statistics (NCES; 2002), only 27 percent of the undergraduates in 1999–2000 were "traditional students" with the other 73 percent being nontraditional in some way. Furthermore, an increasing number of graduates are entering graduate school later in life (Dittman, 2003).

Definitions of Traditional and Nontraditional Students

The NCES (2002) defined the "traditional" undergraduate as one who attends college full time immediately after earning a high-school diploma while relying on parents for financial support, and only working part time, if at all. According to the NCES, a "nontraditional" student meets any one or more of the following criteria: does not enter college immediately after completing high school, attends college only part time for at least part of the year, works 35 hours or more while attending college, is financially independent, has dependents other than a spouse, is a single parent, and did not earn a high-school diploma. However, not all institutions of higher education utilize the NCES definition of nontraditional student. For example, one small mid-western state university defines nontraditional students in the following ways: over age 24, married, parent, out of school for 2 or more years, and/or in the military or a veteran.

Researchers have reported several differences between traditional and nontraditional students. For example, nontraditional students value learning and faculty communication more than traditional students (Landrum, Hood, & McAdams, 2001), and nontraditional students rate faculty and advising more highly than traditional students (Bare, as cited in Landrum et al.). Unfortunately, attrition rates (leaving postsecondary education without a degree) are highest for nontraditional students (NCES, 2002).

Effects of Being Nontraditional _____
on Nontraditional Students

Nontraditional students frequently have nonacademic responsibilities and priorities influencing their academic schedules and decisions. Married students, for example, need to spend time with their spouse and children, and most likely have additional financial and household responsibilities. Despite the fact that students with children can be highly motivated to earn a college degree, child care and lack of support in the home can interfere with their educational efforts (Wagner, 2002). O'Laughlin (2004) has the following advice for faculty who are parents which also seems suitable for nontraditional students who are parents: volunteer to do fewer things, don't confuse working efficiently with working long hours, and seek multiple support systems (e.g., babysitters, after school programs, medical treatment options).

Military students must spend time fulfilling contractual obligations, such as weekend guard duty, using valuable time that might otherwise be available for academic needs like studying or conducting research. Fortunately, many of these added nonacademic responsibilities have provided these students with skills requisite for multitasking. As a teacher and mentor, you can encourage nontraditional students to adapt some of their parenting and work skills to their academic life (e.g., efficient scheduling and time management skills). However, older students or students who have been out of school for an extended period of time may be out of practice when it comes to allotting and spending time on academic endeavors, and may procrastinate seeking help from their professors or their younger, traditional counterparts. Prohaska, Morrill, Atiles, and Perez (2000) reported that academic procrastination of weekly reading assignments and academic work in general was higher for nontraditional (ethnically, economically, and culturally diverse) students than traditional students. However, older students had lower academic procrastination scores. They also found that academic procrastination scores were negatively correlated with cumulative grade point average. Clearly, having assignments due in such a manner that procrastination is minimized will benefit nontraditional students. For example, with written assignments, have the more manageable individual sections of an APA manuscript due weekly, return each section with feedback in a timely fashion, and collect the completed entire paper at the end of the semester.

Myers and Mobley (2004) suggested that the increased responsibilities of work and family may allow less time for nontraditional students to engage in leisure and exercise activities necessary for personal well-being. Decreased personal well-being could contribute to increased drop out rates of nontraditional students. Let your concern for their academic and personal well-being be evident. Landrum et al. (2001) found nontraditional students rated their professors' concern and care more positively, and appreciated their professors interacting with them more than traditional students did. As a teacher and mentor, encourage your nontraditional students to become involved in collegial opportunities that will provide physical activity, social interaction, and relaxation. For example, organize a departmental picnic, softball, bowling, or volleyball game for the students and include nontraditional students' dependants in the festivities. For those nontraditional students in need of more formal personal, financial, marital or family counseling, mentors should provide students with information about on-campus resources.

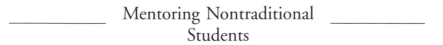

Teaching Nontraditional Students

Many nontraditional students may be first-generation college students with little or no exposure to the college environment. As such, you serve as a role model for students in and out of the classroom. Providing nontraditional students, as well as traditional students, with a model of collegiate behavior will help facilitate their transition into academia. For example, keep appointments and when you need to cancel give plenty of notice, answer questions promptly and clearly, be flexible but have limits that are clearly communicated, be supportive of all students and encourage them to be supportive of one another regardless of their differences, be respectful, be understanding and patient, and reward nontraditional students when they put forth their best efforts regardless of whether their accomplishments are perfect.

Allen (2002) provided a list of excellent teaching tips related to course planning, classroom teaching, communicating with students, and socializing students. She recommended clearly communicating your learning objectives, considering your students' perspectives when designing your course, encouraging community assignments, and providing opportunities for nontraditional students to refresh their academic skills. She also suggested requiring group activities that introduce students to varying backgrounds and perspectives, encouraging preclass reading assignments so that you engage students in active learning experiences and higher thought processing, using straight-forward language on tests and allowing different ways for students to demonstrate their knowledge, and allowing class time for group projects because it is often difficult for nontraditional students to meet classmates outside of class.

Mentoring Nontraditional Students

Effective mentoring of your nontraditional students will involve open and honest communication. Early on provide your mentees with tips as to their role in the relationship. These tips include, but may not be limited to, how to express clearly their professional and personal needs to you; assume responsibility for their own academic and professional development; become a good listener; determine their goals, and achieve them with their your assistance; reflect on their achievements as they strive to determine those goals; and respond to feedback (see American Psychological Association, 2004). Clear and concise communication of both parties' roles will enhance the mentor/mentee relationship. Convey to your nontraditional students and mentees that you will assist them in determining their academic and professional goals while taking into consideration their personal situations. Then, encourage them to determine early on what their priorities are, and then help them plan accordingly. Help them recognize what short- and long-term educational and professional opportunities are available. Be careful not tell them what path to travel, rather help them to determine what paths are available.

Knowing what resources your institution has available for nontraditional students will enable you to point them in the appropriate directions when they seek your advice on issues beyond your expertise. Some colleges have a student organization specifically for nontraditional students. Such organizations can be helpful in providing these students with both university (e.g., scholarship information) and community (e.g., babysitting and health related) resources, offering mentoring programs, and providing a facility with a study area, computer access, message board, and local telephone use. Additionally, many universities provide housing specifically for nontraditional students.

Conclusion

The majority of college students are no longer traditional; consequently, faculty in higher education must no longer teach and mentor using only traditional methods. Faculty need to provide both nontraditional and traditional students with greater educational experiences that enable them to be life-long learners. All college students, and particularly nontraditional students, will have a better educational experience if you Communicate with them, Appreciate them, Respect them, and Enjoy (CARE) them. Don't be surprised when they repay you in kind; role-modeling is a powerful teaching and mentoring tool!

References

Allen, M. J. (2000). Teaching non-traditional students. *APS Observer, 13*. Retrieved July 20, 2004, from www.psychologicalscience.org/teaching/tips/tips_0900.html

American Psychological Association. (2004). Developing a successful mentoring relationship. In Disability mentoring program. Retrieved July 20, 2004, from www.apa.org/pi/cdip/mentoring/tipsformentees.html

Bendixon-Noe, M. (1998) Nontraditional students in higher education: Meeting their needs as learners. *Mid-West Educational Researcher, 11*, 27–31.

Dittman, M. (2003). A changing student body: Today's psychology graduate students are more diverse and do more juggling. *Monitor on Psychology, 34*, 42.

Landrum, R. E., Hood, J. T., & McAdams, J. M. (2001). Satisfaction with college by traditional and nontraditional college students. *Psychological Reports, 89*, 740–6.

Myers, J. E., & Mobley, A. K. (2004). Wellness of undergraduates: Comparisons of traditional and nontraditional students. *Journal of Counseling, 7*, 40–9.

National Center for Educational Statistics. (2002). Nontraditional undergraduates: Findings from "The Condition of Education, 2002." Washington, DC: US Department of Education.

O'Laughlin, L. (2004). Parenting and academic careers. APA Graduate Students online. Retrieved July 20, 2004, from www.apaaa.org/apags/profdev/parenting.html

Prohaska, V., Morrill, P., Atiles, I., & Perez, A. (2000). Academic procrastination by nontraditional students. *Journal of Social Behavior and Personality, 15*, 125–34.

Wagner, J. G. (2002). Teaching the growing population of nontraditional students. *Keying In, 13*, 1–7.

26
Teaching and Mentoring Students with Disabilities

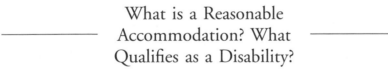

David E. Johnson
John Brown University

In 1990, President George H. W. Bush signed into law the Americans with Disabilities Act (ADA), paving the way for sweeping reforms in the treatment of persons with disabilities in the workplace and educational institutions. Prior to 1990, Section 504 of the Rehabilitation Act of 1973 provided legal protections. However, passage of the ADA received considerable media attention that focused on the potential impact of the law on business, industry, and education. The ADA mandated "reasonable accommodations" for individuals with disabilities. This vague term raised many questions.

What is a Reasonable Accommodation? What Qualifies as a Disability?

A disability is a "physical or mental impairment that substantially limits one or more of the major life activities of such an individual, a record of such an impairment, or being regarded as having such an impairment" (ADA, 1992, 12102-3, (2)). Reasonable accommodations make it possible for otherwise qualified persons to perform the duties or tasks required as part of their jobs or courses. There are limits to which an organization must go to accommodate a disability. Undue hardship for the organization based on financial and other considerations may obviate the requirement for an accommodation (Simon, 2001).

Likely as a direct result of Section 504 and the ADA, increasing numbers of students with disabilities now pursue postsecondary education (Lynch & Gussel, 1996; Vogel, Leyser, Wyland, & Brulle, 1999). Some of these students experience disabilities that are clearly obvious upon first meeting (e.g., total blindness or mobility difficulties). Other students present themselves with so-called "silent disabilities" that are less obvious (e.g., learning disabilities). Regardless of the type of disability, faculty today will likely teach and advise students with disabilities. Most faculty members do not possess specific training to deal with the potential requirements accommodations present. As a result, they may experience a variety of uncertainties and expectations.

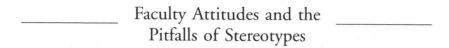

Faculty Attitudes and the Pitfalls of Stereotypes

Faculty should perform an attitude check before teaching students with disabilities. Several attitudinal pitfalls exist for faculty members. One pitfall involves the view of faculty as the gatekeepers of the academic integrity of the curriculum. Any deviation from normative teaching methodology calls into question the quality of the academic experience. When a student with a disability requests an accommodation, this perspective puts instructors in a dilemma. The fiduciary responsibility to the disabled student seems to conflict with the responsibilities to the common good of the entire class and academic integrity (Bento, 1996). Instructors may view students requesting the accommodation as asking for special favors that dilute the academic experience and put them at an advantage over the rest of the class.

This attitude is unwarranted. The ADA requires "reasonable accommodations" and does not mandate accommodations at all costs. The Department of Justice enforces regulations (28 C.F.R. 35.150) stating that reasonable accommodations do not include "fundamental alterations" of the educational program (Simon, 2001). Thus, accommodations do not equate to dilution of the academic standards.

A second attitudinal pitfall involves the reliance on stereotypes of persons with disabilities. These stereotypes can take many forms. Viewing students as possessing lower abilities may lead to interactions between faculty and students that interfere with the educational process. Even more corrosive to faculty–student relationships is the attitude that some students fake their disabilities to avoid unpopular or difficult course requirements (Beilke & Yssel, 1999). It is important to recognize that these attitudes parallel those encountered historically when other underrepresented groups gained greater access to higher education (e.g., women, racial minorities). Aside from the damage done to teacher–student communication, the attitude of lower ability on the part of the disabled student may affect students' attitudes toward their own abilities. Social psychologists refer to this attitude as stereotype threat, when stigmatized groups ultimately perform consistent with stereotypical expectations (Steele & Aronson, 1995). Clearly, instructors should not imply, even implicitly, that students with disabilities are "handicapped."

Faculty sometimes adopt another stereotype that involves students' unique abilities, rather than disabilities. For example, 20 years ago, a student who was blind informed me during the spring semester that she would be taking my statistics course in the fall semester. With all good intentions, over the summer, I had handouts, homework, statistical tables, and other course materials translated into Braille for this student. Why? How else would a blind person be able to read? My stereotype of blindness included the ability to read Braille. Fortunately, this student did, in fact, read Braille, rewarding my efforts. Subsequently, I discovered that Braille reading among the blind was quite low. In fact, due in part to mainstreaming of blind students over the last few decades, fewer learn Braille, which reduced the literacy rate of this group. My good intentions to accommodate this student and to be prepared well in advance of her enrollment was based on a stereotype and lack of information that could have resulted in considerable wasted time.

Are You Prepared?

Successful teaching and mentoring of students with disabilities occurs when both student and instructor are prepared for the learning experience. Now, most instructors cringe at the thought of additional preparation beyond what they already perceive as excessive. After all, who has the time to be an expert on the myriad disabilities that could be potentially encountered? Additionally, many instructors know from experience that students with disabilities sometimes request accommodations with short notice after the semester has started. There are several issues and practices that are relevant on this point.

First, virtually all postsecondary institutions operate an Office of Disability Services (ODS). These offices typically employ individuals who serve as advocates for students with disabilities. They also serve as clearinghouses for information about disabilities and may offer testing services, note-taking services, and a variety of other disability-specific aids. ODSs also serve as the official liaison between students and institutional personnel, that is, they collect the disability certifications provided by the students and inform faculty of the students' status and possible accommodations needed. A good working relationship between faculty and ODS personnel facilitates many aspects of the teaching and learning process.

Second, good preparation involves scheduling conferences with the students to discuss their learning history. Although the ODS provides invaluable information about disabilities in general, the students are probably in the best position to inform instructors of methodologies and techniques that proved to be effective in their past experience. Conferences with students are important in that they help instructors consider specific accommodations and how they might be implemented. They also serve an important function for the student. Beyond the personal contact between faculty and students, conferences serve as an important adjunct in students' development of self-advocacy skills. Disclosure of a disability poses a variety of threats and challenges for students that may influence future self-advocacy. Encountering an instructor who projects skepticism or insincerity may increase the reluctance of students with disabilities to request accommodations to which they are entitled (Beilke & Yssel, 1999; Lynch & Gussel, 1996; Nutter & Ringgenberg, 1993).

A final issue of importance related to preparation involves the use of technology. Instructors increasingly use the World Wide Web, including personally designed or commercial sites (e.g., BlackBoard) to distribute course materials and otherwise manage their courses. Using technology, in general, and the Web, specifically, provides many benefits for students with disabilities. However, as Banks and Coombs (1998) pointed out, a web can benefit a spider, but be a trap for a fly. The same is true for the Web. Computers and the Web provide students with disabilities with unprecedented access to information, but these advantages can easily disappear under certain circumstances. For example, websites may not meet accessibility standards for persons with low or no vision because the pages contain only image files with no accompanying textual description.

Tabular presentations may pose problems for students who use screen readers to retrieve information in an audio format because they may simply read text left to right, rendering the columns of the table virtually worthless (Banks & Coombs, 1998). Although there are many specific suggestions that could be made for specific disabilities (see Fichten et al., 2001 for technology recommendations and resources) there is one technology-related recommendation that covers many, if not most, disabilities. In addition to making Web materials accessible, post the materials as early as possible. Some students with disabilities require more time to acquire their textbooks in an alternate format. If the syllabus for the course listing the text(s) is posted before the semester begins, these students will be better able to be on the same schedule as students who picked up their texts at the campus bookstore the day before class begins (Fichten el al., 2001).

Use Your Resources

In addition to using the campus ODS and information from the student, the Web provides a huge amount of information on virtually all disabilities. This information is helpful to instructors in understanding the disabilities and may offer teaching strategies and methods. Many campus ODSs have excellent websites that are treasure troves of information for teaching students with disabilities.

Be Flexible and Expect the Unexpected

Some flexibility is obviously required at times when teaching students with disabilities, but it is not always on assignments or exams that instructors need to be flexible. Some accommodations will require changes in the classroom itself or the instructors' behavior during class. Instructors with a hearing-impaired student who uses a signer may initially find it disconcerting and distracting during class. If a hearing impaired student reads lips, the instructor must be aware of behaviors that prohibit lip-reading, such as talking while facing away from the students. Some blind students use guide dogs who make interesting additions to the classroom. Guide dogs "attended" my classes in two different semesters. One of them usually fell asleep and snored quite loudly whereas the other was flatulent. Both, obviously, created an interesting atmosphere that required a little tolerance on the part of the students and me. Fortunately, most disabilities will not produce such colorful situations in class.

Benefits of Teaching Students With Disabilities

So far, the focus of this essay has been on the preparation for teaching students with disabilities. Students with disabilities benefit from well-reasoned approaches to their instruction, but so do faculty (Johnson, 2002). Teaching disabled students gives faculty a new perspective on their teaching methods. Preparing accommodations requires instructors to rethink and reevaluate methods and strategies. Over time, faculty may develop practices in the classroom that are not helpful to students with disabilities. These same practices may also be counterproductive for students who do not have disabilities. Talking while facing the board or projection screen would be a hindrance to students who have hearing disabilities and rely on lip reading. Using a phrase like, "See how this graph illustrates an interaction" would be useless to a student who is blind. Crafting classroom practices that facilitate learning for students with disabilities will likely benefit all students.

A Word About Terminology

Instructors sometimes feel awkward when teaching students with disabilities because they have heard a host of terms being used to describe these students, such as "other-abled," or reference to a student who has no sight as "visually-challenged." In general, students appreciate using terminology that focuses on them as a student and does not attempt to "soften" their disability. The phrase "students who are blind" is much better than "blind students." The former acknowledges their role as a student, the latter focuses on their disability. Be sensitive to this issue and let the students be your guide. If they have a particular preference, use it.

Conclusion

The goal of the ADA was to provide "otherwise qualified" individuals the opportunity to succeed in the workplace and classroom. It appears to be well on its way to meeting this goal, and more. Passage of the ADA not only mandates that we consider practices that constitute fairness for students with disabilities, but also encourages us to be conscientious in evaluating our classroom practices. That cannot be a bad thing! (Johnson, 2002).

REFERENCES

Americans With Disabilities Act of 1990, Pub. L. No. 101-336, U.S.C. 12101 (1990).

Banks, R., & Coombs, N. (1998). World Wide Web: The spider and the fly. *CMC* (Computer-Mediated Communication Magazine). Retrieved July 15, 2004, at: www.december.com/cmc/mag/1998/feb/bankcoom.html.

Beilke, J. R., & Yssel, N. (1999). The chilly climate for students with disabilities in higher education. *College Student Journal, 33*, 364–71.

Bento, R. F. (1996). Faculty decision-making about "reasonable accommodations" for disabled college students: Information, ethical, and attitudinal issues. *College Student Journal, 30*, 494–501.

Fichten, C. S., Asuncion, J. V., Barile, M., Genereux, C., Fossey, M., Judd, D., Robillard, C., De Simone, C., & Wells, D. (2001). Technology integration for students with disabilities: Empirically based recommendations for faculty. *Educational Research and Evaluation, 7*, 185–221.

Johnson, D. E. (2002). Teaching students with disabilities. In W. Buskist, V. S. Hevern, & G. W. Hill IV (eds.), *Essays from e-xcellence in teaching, 2002* (ch. 4). Retrieved July 1, 2004, from the Society for the Teaching of Psychology Website: http://teachpsych.lemoyne.edu/teachpsych/eit/index.html.

Lynch, R. T., & Gussel, L. (1996). Disclosure and self-advocacy regarding disability-related needs: Strategies to maximize integration in postsecondary education. *Journal of Counseling & Development, 74*, 352–7.

Nutter, K. J., & Ringgenberg, L. J. (1993). Creating positive outcomes for students with disabilities. *New Directions for Student Services, 64*, 45–58.

Simon, J. A. (2001). Legal issues in serving postsecondary students with disabilities. *Topics in Language Disorders, 21*, 1–16.

Steele, C. M., & Aronson, J. (1995). Stereotype threat and the intellectual test performance of African Americans. *Journal of Personality & Social Psychology, 69*, 797–811.

Vogel, S. A., Leyser, Y., Wyland, S., & Brulle, A. (1999). Students with learning disabilities in higher education: Faculty attitude and practices. *Learning Disabilities Research & Practice, 14*, 173–86.

27
Mentoring Female Students

Ψ

Elizabeth Yost Hammer
Loyola University, New Orleans

I can honestly say that I would not be writing this chapter if it were not for the influence of my mentors. These mentors pushed me toward college, empowered me for graduate school, guided my graduate studies, and taught me to love my profession. What a difference strong mentors make in the professional lives of their students. Many writers have addressed the issues of advising and mentoring (e.g., Jacobi, 1991; Johnson & Huwe, 2003; Sikorski, 2004). In this chapter I focus on some issues that might be unique to teaching and advising female students.

As I considered this topic, I knew some qualities of a mentor that were important to me as a female student, but my ideas have become reconstructed as I am now on the other side of the desk. I contacted several female students whom I had mentored in some capacity at various points in my academic career, and I asked them the following questions: What did you need from your mentor? What was important to you in the mentoring relationship? What were the benefits of this relationship? How might these experiences be different for men? Eight students responded, and some interesting patterns emerged including the issues of empowerment, connection, and career advising. I address these patterns, and offer suggestions to maximize your success in mentoring female students. My experience has been exclusively with undergraduates, but you can alter many of these suggestions and apply them to graduate students as well.

Empowerment

The most commonly reported factor of importance was the notion of empowerment, an idea emphasized in research on mentoring (Liang, Tracy, Taylor, & Williams, 2002). One student explicitly stated, "Looking back at those people I would consider my mentors, I perceived from each of them a genuine belief that I could succeed. For me this was a very powerful, empowering, and affirming tool." Across the board, these women responded that their mentors promoted a sense of self-confidence and a belief in themselves that they could achieve their academic goals. There was a sense that their male peers had more confidence in their own abilities, especially in the areas related to science, which was nurtured and developed throughout high school. Female students often entered college with a shaky sense of confidence. Therefore, recognition, affirmation, support, and guidance from a mentor can go a long away in empowering female students to reach their potential and develop their interests. One student wrote, "I think for me the biggest benefits [of being mentored] were motivation, inspiration, and self confidence. My mentor always made me want to do well and strive to reach accomplishments that they thought I could make."

These women also described seeking a mentor with qualities, such as assertiveness, that they knew they needed to develop. As advisors, we know that this quality is important in the competitive workplace or graduate school, but Tannen (1990) found that women were less likely than men to use self-promotion and other assertive techniques in presenting themselves. One student stated:

> Qualities I look for and have found in previous mentors include independence, assertiveness, and a strong work ethic. Assertiveness is a personality trait that does not come naturally to me. I have noticed that I tend to seek mentors that display assertiveness so I can follow their example and become more assertive in my own life.

Hence, it seems that even if mentors are unaware of it, assertiveness training is a byproduct of mentoring female students that is very important to them.

Suggestions

To provide female students with a sense of empowerment, an effective mentor should look for opportunities to provide recognition and affirmation of their talents and abilities. When mentoring, look for strengths in the student that you can bolster and support. For example, if a student is weak in experimental design, point out how strong she is in psychological theory. This validation honors her ability and allows for a foundation on which to build. Many times empowerment happens with some small comment, such as, "I think you'd be a great grad student." Do not underestimate the power of a positive comment like this from a respected mentor. It may be the first time your student has heard this comment.

Find ways to publicize your female (and male for that matter) students' successes. Set up a bulletin board where you can post students' accomplishments, pictures from conferences, publications, etc. On this same board, post student opportunities such as nomination forms for campus awards, Psi Chi awards and grants information, and publication outlets. This simple activity demonstrates that you are proud of what the students accomplish and you support them stretching to the next level of academic engagement. Similarly, if you have regular group or lab meetings with your students, start with kudos to acknowledge their recent successes.

Provide female students with opportunities to learn skillful self-promotion. In lab meetings and class, I use a "self-promotion exercise." I talk to students about self-promotion as a self-presentation strategy and point out the gender differences in the use of this strategy. I then have them make strong self-promotional statements to the group. Typical of female responses to this exercise is to downplay the accomplishment with statements such as, "It's not that big a deal, but I won first in state for track at my high school." By pointing out these qualifiers, we can discuss appropriate ways to self-promote. Finally, I try to role-model appropriate self-promotion, making my mentees aware of my own academic accomplishments even if I am uncomfortable in doing so as well, and allow them to see their involvement in my own professional development.

Connection

Female students indicated that in order for mentoring to be influential, a trusting, respectful relationship must develop between the mentor and the mentee. One student expressed this point by saying, "I felt a personal attachment to my mentor that bordered on friendship. Although it was a friendship based on academic commonalities, I felt that my mentor cared about me not only as a scholar but also as a person." Without exception, students expressed a sentiment about connecting with the mentor in a meaningful, personal way. Such a connection is important in building a respectful relationship with the student so that she will value your opinion, advice, and modeling. Without this connection, a professor can still be influential, but the mentor/mentee relationship really does not exist. One student wrote:

> Looking back on my mentoring relationships, I feel I needed more than the occasional pat on the back or general advice. I needed a wise friend who didn't mind giving direction when needed, someone who made a conscious effort to know me well enough to give advice based on my individual circumstances.

Suggestions

This aspect of the mentoring relationship can be difficult for faculty who do not find it comfortable to interact with students. However, it is a quality on which all aspiring mentors should work. At a most basic level, be available for your students. By simply being available and letting students know they are not a bother to you, you are signaling that you care about them and are interested in their successes. Remember that you can be friendly without being familiar (Brewer, 2002).

Find a common bond with the student. This bond can be a common area of research interest (e.g., she is interested in pursuing her senior thesis in your research area), a common theoretical perspective (e.g., you both enjoy discussing attribution theory), or common academic experiences (e.g., you are both first-generation college students). This common ground provides a way to become comfortable talking with each other and may provide a foundation for a deeper professional relationship.

However, you should be continually aware of boundary issues. Although many students referenced a friendship aspect of their mentoring relationship, they stipulated that is was friendship based on academic interests. As mentors, it is up to us to monitor these relationships to ensure that they do not cross professional lines. For example, I find ways to bring conversations back to academics. If I am discussing summer travels, pets, or Mardi Gras with students, I eventually turn the conversation back to their academic experiences (e.g., What social-psychological phenomena did you see during Mardi Gras?). This approach helps me maintain comfortable boundaries while still connecting at a personal level. When students come to me with personal problems that go beyond my role as mentor, I send them to our university's counseling center (sometimes walking them there myself). I remind them that I am not a trained counselor, and I explain that the conversation transcends the boundaries of our relationship. I have never had a student who responded negatively to this comment.

Career Advising

A final theme that emerged was specialized career advising. Mentors, male and female alike, have the opportunity to be role models for female students in this important area. One student wrote, "My mentoring relationships were important to me because in the midst of making [career] decisions, I felt she was someone who had been where I was, and could give advice on where to go next." Students value mentors who can recognize the role strain that professional women experience and help teach, as one student puts it, "boundaries between personal and professional life." One student emphasized how much she valued seeing her mentor "balancing personal and professional lives and [seeing her] mentor placing priority on her own professional growth." Effective mentors should recognize that female students are likely to experience society's double standard that expects women to have both professional success and primary family responsibilities. Among others in their lives, they look to mentors as role models for professional life and activities.

Suggestions

Without compromising boundaries, allow students to know that you have a personal life outside of academics. Describe your hobbies on your website. Attend student activities (e.g., basketball games or concerts) so students may see you outside the typical classroom setting. Pepper your lectures with appropriate personal examples. By engaging in these activities while maintaining an active professional life, students can get an idea of the importance of balance.

Stay current on career options, especially as they relate to gender issues. There are regular sessions at regional and national conferences on this topic, and the American Psychological Association publishes statistics on various career issues on its website (www.apa.org). Be prepared to advise students on what careers might be more male-dominated and what that might mean to them as employees.

Train students (both through role-modeling and discussion) to say no. Mentors should arm their female students with skills to know when and how to say no in their professional lives, especially if they are in male-dominated professions. A student wrote, "I don't feel like I have anyone at work who understands my stress and what I'm going through when crises arise. Fortunately, I know several seasoned female [employees] who have given me job advice and things to do to relieve the stress and handle my job more effectively." Knowing how to say no can help a female student achieve an important balance in her own life.

Conclusion

In reflecting on this topic, I think much of what is important to students in a mentoring relationship is not achieved through direct verbal advice. Instead the intangible byproducts of mentoring (e.g., role-modeling, empowerment, connection) seem to make the biggest difference. As mentors, we need to be aware of these byproducts and reflect on ways, within our own mentoring styles, to increase these experiences for the enrichment of our female students' professional lives.

ACKNOWLEDGMENTS

I am grateful to the following students who so insightfully advised me on the main points in this chapter: Angelique Ganiaris (currently an undergraduate psychology major), Casey Gonzales (currently completing a master's in experimental psychology at Augusta State University), Angela Jacketti (currently a probation officer in New Orleans), Laura Moreau (currently working for Lutheran Social Services in Brooklyn New York), Leann R. Phillips (currently a Service Delivery Administrator in South Carolina), Kristina Anders (currently completing a master's in nonfiction writing in New York), Susan VanDyke (currently an attorney in Nashville, Tennessee), and Jacquie Wilson Watlington (currently a youth minister in Tennessee). I am proud of each of you. Keep up the good work.

REFERENCES

Brewer, C. (2002). Reflections on teaching. In W. Buskist, V. Hevern, & G. W. Hill IV (eds.), *Essays from e-xcellence in teaching, 2000–2001* (ch. 1). Retrieved Nov. 3, 2004, from the Society for the Teaching of Psychology website: http://teachpsych.lemoyne.edu/teachpsych/eit/eit2000/index.html

Jacobi, M. (1991). Mentoring and undergraduate academic success: A literature review. *Review of Education Research, 61,* 505–32.

Johnson, B. W., & Huwe, J. M. (2003). *Getting mentored in graduate school.* Washington, DC: American Psychological Association.

Liang, B., Tracy, A. J., Taylor, C. A., & Williams, L. M. (2002). Mentoring college-age women: A relational approach. *American Journal of Community Psychology, 30,* 271–88.

Sikorski, J. F. (2004). Teacher of teachers: An interview with James H. Korn. *Teaching of Psychology, 31,* 72–6.

Tannen, D. (1990). *You just don't understand: Women and men in conversation.* New York: Ballantine Books.

28

Teaching and Mentoring Racially and Ethnically Diverse Students

Ψ

Loretta Neal McGregor
Arkansas State University

Because the previous chapters have defined mentoring, I will move directly to discussing the special concerns associated with mentoring racially and ethnically diverse students. Because I was one of these students, I believe that I can adequately discuss the special needs involved in mentoring such students.

I began my academic training in higher education in the early 1980s. I was a first-generation college student attending a predominately Caucasian, private, liberal arts institution in the southwestern United States. College was a complete social and educational culture shock for me. However, I was very fortunate in that I had two wonderful individuals who played roles as primary mentors in my life. Additionally, I had many other secondary mentors who helped to shape and mold me through my academic training. Many of these relationships continue to this day.

The majority of the literature that discusses mentoring in education focuses on the mentor/graduate student protégé relationship (Atkinson, Nivelle, & Casas, 1991; Brown, Davis, & McClendon, 1999; Busch, 1985; Cronan-Hillix, Gensheimer, Cronan-Hillix, & Davidson, 1986; Tenenbaum, Crosby, & Gliner, 2001). However, many of the issues discussed and strategies designed to assist graduate students in developing a mentoring relationship also apply to undergraduates.

Many nonmajority students' first experience with higher educational training is similar to mine. These students are often first-generation students who find college and graduate school to be a strange, yet exciting, new place. Many of these students attend predominately Caucasian schools (Lee, 1999). Additionally, these same students often relocate miles away from a small, close-knit, extended family and community environment that has nurtured them (Landen, 1999). A large proportion of these students also experience financial burdens that are often associated with paying for college and meeting day-to-day expenses. However, these concerns are often more pronounced for many minority students (Lee, 1999). Any one of these changes or concerns often produces intense anxiety in many students. Nevertheless, the combination of events may seem overwhelming to many minority undergraduate and graduate students.

The vast majority of all full-time positions in postsecondary institutions (85 percent in 1998) are held by Caucasian, non-Hispanic faculty (US Department of Education, National Center for Education Statistics, 2002). With so few minorities among the ranks of faculty in predominately Caucasian schools, many nonmajority students feel that they have less access to mentors (Johnson & Huwe, 2003). Past research has suggested that protégés actively seek and often prefer to be mentored by someone who looks like them. Additionally, Blackwell (1989) suggested that many mentors seem to select protégés who are similar to them in sex, ethnicity, race, and social class. Johnson and Huwe (2003, p. 172) wrote:

> It is easy to understand why racial similarity is frequently a salient factor when seeking a mentor. Perceived similarity may foster deeper trust, mutual understanding, and bonding that may be difficult to achieve in a mentorship with a racially different mentor.

However, Lee (1999) reported that students in her study "felt that having an African American faculty member was less important than having a mentor" in one's career field (p. 7). She also noted, "Students reasoned that they could get the cultural connection they needed outside of the university" (p. 7). Eshner, Grant-Vallone, and Marelich (2002) reported the "racial similarity did not predict the amount of support that protégés received from their mentor nor protégé satisfaction with their mentors" (p. 1421).

How do you begin to address the myriad ethnic, cultural, and economic concerns of minority students? Much of the literature suggests that you must address successful mentoring on three levels: mentors, protégés, and academic institutions (Atkinson & Casas, 1994; Brinson & Kottler, 1993; Busch, 1985; Lee, 1999; Tenebaum et al., 2001). Here are a few suggestions on how mentors, protégés, and academic institutions can work together to form successful mentoring relationships.

Recommendations for Protégés

Students Must First Realize the Benefits of Having a Mentor

Mentors can provide students with both psychosocial and instrumental support (Tenebaum et al., 2001). Psychosocial support includes empathizing with students, providing both personal and career counseling, and serving as a role model. Instrumental support involves coaching and sponsoring protégés as well as providing exposure for networking opportunities. Students may find that multiple mentors are needed to gain adequate levels of both types of support.

Students Must Realize that They can Seek Support from a Variety of Individuals

Protégés should seek mentoring from both primary and secondary mentors. Primary mentors are typically individuals within the student's department or school. Secondary mentors can be individuals from other disciplines or areas outside the institution. Many protégés benefit from having a variety of mentors who can give them specific guidance. One person often cannot meet all of the special needs of a minority student.

Ethnic and Minority Students Must be Proactive in Seeking and Selecting a Mentor

Many minority students may be hesitant to initiate relationships outside of the classroom with nonminority faculty (Atkinson & Casas, 1994; Lee, 1999). However, Eshner et al. (2002) concluded that both protégés and mentors need to look beyond such characteristics as race and sex to consider the many ways in which they might benefit from forming a mentoring relationship. Therefore, students should actively identify potential mentors from among the faculty and then actively attempt to build a relationship with those individuals, regardless of race.

Protégés Must be Willing to Accept both Praise and Corrective Criticism in the Spirit in which it is Given

Protégés must also show appreciation for their mentor (Lee, 1999). Students should realize that their mentor has actively chosen to invest time and effort into their relationship. Most schools do not provide tangible rewards for individuals who volunteer to mentor. In fact, many mentoring relationships go unnoticed to everyone except the individuals involved in them. Mentoring takes time away from other scholarly activities. Thus, protégés should remember that mentoring is not a required activity but is often a labor of love. Additionally, any criticism the mentor offers should be viewed by the protégé as an opportunity for self-improvement and growth.

Recommendations for Mentors

Nonminority Faculty Should Actively Reach out to Minority Students

The small number of minority faculty should not be expected to mentor all of the minority students. Attempting to have only minority faculty members serve as mentors for ethnically and racially diverse students leads to reduced effectiveness of the minority faculty members in all areas and eventually causes burnout (Atkinson & Casas, 1994). If nonminority faculty members accept the responsibility of mentoring minority students, they must be sensitive to the ethnic and cultural differences that exist between them and their protégés (Lee, 1999). Nonminority mentors must allow their protégés to educate them about their ethnicity and culture. The mentor must demonstrate a willingness to learn about differences and to accept the information given by the protégé in a nonjudgmental or threatening manner. Learning about ethnic and racial differences from protégés also restores balance in the mentoring relationship because many minority students are well acquainted with European American culture.

Mentors Should Realize that They must Initially "Build an Air of Trust" with Protégés

Past cultural experiences may lead some protégés to feel threatened by nonminority faculty members, even those individuals who seek to assist them (Lee, 1999). Nonminority mentors should not be offended by the protégés need for self-preservation but they should simply accept it as it is and attempt to overcome it by building a trusting relationship with the protégé.

If Faculty Members Decide to Become Mentors, They Should Expect to Devote Time to Their Protégés

Mentors should not give the impression of being too busy to listen to their protégés (Lee, 1999). This type of behavior will lead protégés to feel neglected and undervalued, and the mentoring relationship will become strained. Faculty should not attempt to mentor more protégés than they can realistically support.

Recommendations for Academic Institutions

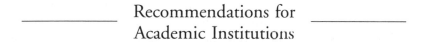

Institutions Should Provide Specific Training on the Special Needs and Cultural Behaviors of Minority Students

Ethnic and racial differences between mentors and protégés should be addressed not only by the mentors and protégés but also by the institution. The institution should provide support and special training for nonminority faculty members who desire to become mentors (Brinson & Kottler, 1993). Nonminority mentors may benefit from learning about the importance and significance of immediate and extended family in the life of the student, cultural traditions, and many other sociocultural concerns that may influence the student's performance and behaviors. Many mentors do not consider these factors as possible behavioral influences because of non-exposure to these factors in their own lives. Many minority mentors would gladly provide tips or special training for their colleagues who express an interest in learning more about cultural differences.

The Institution Should Support and Reward Effective Mentoring

Institutions should provide resources to assist mentors. Because mentoring is not in the official job description of most faculty members, institutions do not routinely provide support or compensations for mentors. Many mentors suggest that they do receive intangible rewards from mentoring (i.e., positive feelings of sharing their knowledge with others; the idea of contributing to the professional development of students; feelings of giving something back; Bush, 1985). Many faculty members feel the need to mentor because they were once the beneficiaries of a positive mentoring relationship (Atkinson & Casas, 1994). Although this is a noble position to take, institutions should encourage, recognize, and support faculty who engage in effective mentoring.

Institutions that Truly Value Mentoring have Developed Mentoring Strategies Specifically Designed to Target Ethnically and Racially Diverse Students

These institutions, in turn, have been rewarded for their efforts through increased retention rates and greater enrollment among minority students (Pardon, 1992; Redmond, 1990). Minority students may actively seek these types of institutions because of favorable recommendations given by current students about the mentoring that they received from faculty and administrators.

Conclusion

Although minority students face many concerns that are similar to those of their nonminority counterparts, they also encounter additional barriers and concerns that must be addressed. Issues regarding trust, cultural emphases on deference to authority figures, and the influence of extended family are only a few factors that often plague minority students. The effective mentoring of ethnically and racially diverse students requires commitment from the protégés, understanding and commitment from mentors, and support from academic institutions.

REFERENCES

Atkinson, D. R., & Casas, A. (1994). Ethnic minority psychologists: Whom they mentor and benefits they derive from the process. *Journal of Multicultural Counseling & Development, 22,* 37–50.

Atkinson, D. R., Neville, H., & Casas, A. (1991). The mentorship of ethnic minorities in professional psychology. *Professional Psychology: Research and Practice, 22,* 336–8.

Blackwell, J. E. (1989). Mentoring: An action strategy for increasing minority faculty. *Academe, 75,* 8–14.

Brinson, J., & Kottler, J. (1993). Cross-cultural mentoring in counselor education: A strategy for retaining minority faculty. *Counselor Education & Supervision, 32,* 1–10.

Brown II, M. C., Davis, G. L., & McClendon, S. A. (1999). Mentoring graduate students of color: Myths, models, and modes. *Peabody Journal of Education, 74,* 105–19.

Busch, J. W. (1985). Mentoring in graduate school of education: Mentors' perceptions. *American Educational Research Journal, 22,* 257–65.

Cronan-Hillix, T., Gensheimer, L. K., Cronan-Hillix, W. A., & Davidson, W. S. (1986). Students' views of mentoring in psychology graduate training. *Teaching of Psychology, 13*, 123–7.

Eshner, E. A., Grant-Vallone, E. J., & Marelich, W. D. (2002). Effects of perceived attitudinal and demographic similarity on proteges' support and satisfaction gained from their mentoring relationships. *Journal of Applied Social Psychology, 32*, 1407–30.

Johnson, W. B., & Huwe, J. M. (2003). *Getting mentored in graduate school.* Washington, DC: American Psychological Association.

Landen, B. V. (1999). Socializing and mentoring college students of color: The Puente project as an exemplary celebratory socialization model. *Peabody Journal of Education, 74*, 55–75.

Lee, W. Y. (1999). Striving toward effective retention: The effect of race on mentoring African American students. *Peabody Journal of Education, 74*, 1–11.

Padron, E. J. (1992). The challenges of first-generation college students: A Miami-Dade perspective. In L. S. Zwerling & H. B. London (eds.), *First-generation students: Confronting the cultural issue* (pp. 77–80). San Francisco: Jossey-Bass Publishers.

Redmond, S. P. (1990). Mentoring and cultural diversity in academic settings. *American Behavioral Scientist, 34*, 188–200.

Tenenbaum, H. R., Crosby, F. J., & Gliner, M. D. (2001). Mentoring relationships in graduate school. *Journal of Vocational Behavior, 59*, 326–41.

US Department of Education, National Center for Education Statistics. (2002). *The Gender and Racial/Ethnic Composition of Postsecondary Instructional Faculty and Staff, 1992–1998.* (NCES 2002-160). Washington, DC: Author.

29

Using Hope Theory to Teach and Mentor Academically At-Risk Students

Ψ

C. R. Snyder, Hal S. Shorey, & Kevin L. Rand

University of Kansas, Lawrence

Hopeful thinking allows young people to make commitments, to set goals, and to work effectively toward attaining those goals. This statement applies especially to the area of education. When lacking in hope, students lower their academic expectations and their subsequent performances suffer. Likewise, students' low hopes often become self-fulfilling prophecies in which they do not expend requisite energies for success. In this chapter, we describe how you can apply hope theory to foster academic successes in such students who would otherwise be at risk for academic failures.

Having hope means that students have well-defined goals, a belief in their ability to develop strategies for reaching those goals, and the requisite motivation to use those strategies. The combination of these three cognitive components of goals, pathways, and agency not only directly impacts academic achievements, but it also contributes to positive emotions. Abilities to retain high levels of positive affect enable high- relative to low-hope students to persevere longer and to expend more effort on challenging academic tasks (Shorey, Snyder, Feldman, & Little, 2004). Believing that they inevitably will succeed, high-hope students are not sidetracked by goal-blocking thoughts of failure. Accordingly, they experience less general anxiety and, more importantly, less anxiety in test-taking situations (Snyder, 1999).

High-relative to low-hope students obtain higher grades and achievement test scores throughout their elementary, junior high-school, high-school, and college years (Chang, 1998; Curry, Maniar, Sondag, & Sandstedt, 1999; Lopez, Bouwkamp, Edwards, & Teramoto Pediotti, 2000; Snyder, 2002). Furthermore, higher Hope Scale scores have predicted higher grade point averages, lower drop-out rates, and higher graduation rates across students' undergraduate careers even when controlling for entrance examination scores (Snyder, Shorey, Cheavens, Pulvers, Adams, & Wiklund, 2002). Clearly, it is advantageous to instill hope in academically at-risk students.

High-Hope Educational Systems

Both hope and performances are influenced by the academic systems within which students operate. Although hope theory (see Snyder, 1994; Snyder et al., 1991) has historical roots in individual differences, hope also can be conceptualized in organizational contexts (Luthans, Van Wyk, & Walumbwa, 2004; Shorey & Snyder, in press). There is, however, one key difference between individuals and organizations. For individuals, there is continual feedback among the three hope components as people appraise their goal-related progress in given environments. In this regard, positive and negative emotions inform individuals about the correctness of their selected pathways as they move toward desired objectives. Within organizations, on the other hand, emotions cannot be relied upon as feedback mechanisms because the goals, pathways, and agency hope components may not reside within the same unit.

In educational institutions, the goal-setting components fall under the purview of school or college administrators. In turn, instructors are responsible for (a) operationalizing the strategies (pathways) for reaching course goals (in their course syllabi), and (b) finding the necessary motivations (agency) to deliver the lessons with excitement and energy. Finally, students must find workable pathways and the necessary motivations to attain the instructors' educational objectives.

If any of the three hope components is not supported by the other components, students' hopes of achieving their educational goals will be diminished. Thus, goals set at one level must be supported by adequate pathways and motivations at the level below. For example, if instructors believe that administrators have dictated course objectives without their input and that those objectives seem out of touch with classroom realities, then instructors may have difficulty in implementing those objectives. The result is decreased instructor enthusiasm for teaching the material. So, the first step in fostering classroom hope is to make certain that the instructor believes in what is being taught. As such, teachers should have "a voice" in important decisions about course development and educational materials.

This dynamic between teachers and school administrations also applies to teachers and students. Teachers lay out the goals that students must pursue in order to succeed in the classroom. For this purpose, teachers can attend to the verbal reports and class evaluations of previous students. This feedback should facilitate the development of course objectives and materials relevant to students' real-world experiences. For example, authors of psychology texts often write with an eye toward examining other peoples' experiences rather than those of the students themselves (Snyder & Shorey, 2002). Anchoring the materials to students' experiences should facilitate deeper processing by allowing them to learn in the contexts of their personal objectives. Having taken such ownership, the students' goals are more likely to involve learning (see Dweck, 1999).

Once teachers and students share learning goals, teachers should not adhere too stringently to an emphasis on grades per se. We recommend against establishing grading schemes wherein some students must lose in order for others to win. For example, using grading curves in which only a certain proportion of students can attain high marks may transform the learning goals into performance goals, which are associated with lower levels of hope (Shorey et al., 2004). For those students who have performed poorly previously, such performance goals also may increase performance and test-taking anxieties and thereby portend actual failures (Dweck, 1999). Thus, over time, a self-fulfilling prophecy will lock academically at-risk students into patterns of discouragement and poor performances.

If students can pursue their learning goals and study without the implied threats of poor grades, they also should be more likely to enjoy the learning process and perform better. It should be understood, however, that we are not suggesting that instructors become lenient graders. On the contrary, having consistently high expectations encourages students to succeed. Students must sense, however, that there is a reasonable probability that they can attain course goals (see Rogers, 2002). To ascertain whether students perceive themselves as having reasonable chances of succeeding, you can ask them at the beginning of a course whether they see the criteria for successful classroom learning as being achievable and fair. Instructors do not always have to make changes based on such feedback, but we believe that teachers should remain open, flexible, and willing to listen because doing so demonstrates a caring and genuine commitment to students.

Hope for Teachers and Students

Assuming that you have established a high-hope environment and shared learning goals, you then can expect the best in learning and associated academic performances from your students. At this point, individual deficits in hope can be addressed. Before attempting to raise students' hopes, however, teachers must assess their own hopes. Teacher burnout is a significant problem (Snyder & Shorey, 2002). As an antidote, teachers must have goal pursuits that bring them joy in life domains outside of their work. These outside life areas often inspired them to teach in the first place. Deprived of such energizing and reinvigorating sources of joy and inspiration, however, teachers are similar to plants cut off from their roots. Teachers must stay connected to their hope-filled roots in order to remain models of hope for their students.

Assuming that teachers have hope, they then can focus on their students' hopes. In this regard, poor homework and test performances are clear indicators of problems. However, how can we know who is academically at risk, and the underlying reasons for such risk? Assessments of basic abilities and hope levels are needed (see Snyder, Feldman, Shorey, & Rand, 2002; Snyder, Lopez, Shorey, Rand, & Feldman, 2003). Even if students have low academic hopes and abilities, they may not be limited in other life arenas. In counseling and mentoring at-risk students, teachers should find out what is working in their students' lives and capitalize on those aspects. For example, a student's high social hope could sustain agency thinking until new learning strategies can be implanted to sustain academic hope. In contrast, lowered hope in life arenas outside of academics can reduce levels of academic motivation.

Teachers should consider students' lives outside of the classroom and remain aware of what is important to them. For example, peer and romantic relationship goals are particularly vital to high-school and college students. A loss of hope in these arenas can increase negative affect and lower agency for academic goals. As is the case for people in general, students always will attend to their basic goals (e.g., food, shelter, affiliation) before they pursue educational goals. To help in these life-management issues, teachers should be capable of giving referrals to their students about appropriate school and community resources.

Assuming that these basic needs are met, students then are more likely to apply themselves and expend energies on their studies. We caution against creating high levels of motivation, however, without first providing strategies to achieve the objectives. Encouraging students to push forward without the necessary routes or pathways will set them up for failure. Teaching strategies to obtain educational goals will create the cause-and-effect, "this leads to that," linkages that facilitate realistic goal setting. For example, students with understandings of such causality would not expect to earn high grades from studying a total of two hours the night before a midterm. Having set realistic goals (i.e., challenging yet achievable ones), however, students should know what to expect and be prepared for success experiences that will sustain their agency.

Finally, although teachers should not adopt parental roles in their interactions with students, being an instructor does mean being a coach or mentor. In such a role, instructors can have enormous impacts on their students' lives. Hopeful young people need adult role models who consistently are responsive, available, and caring. Such adult responsiveness, availability, and caring provide the secure base of hope that allows young people to find ways to achieve their own important academic and life goals (Shorey, Snyder, Yang, & Lewin, 2003).

Conclusion

Assuming that we have conveyed the importance and utility of hope theory for academically at-risk students, we encourage instructors to review the other sources that we have cited. Many of us (the authors included) who are high-hope instructors came from low-hope backgrounds where the future outlooks were rather stark. Most of us also can think of one person who took the time to care, to teach us the ways, and to light the spark of hope in our lives. Often, too, that hope-inducing adult was a teacher.

REFERENCES

Chang, E. C. (1998). Hope, problem-solving ability, and coping in a college student population: Some implications for theory and practice. *Journal of Clinical Psychology, 54*, 953–62.

Curry, L. A., Maniar, S. D., Sondag, K. A., & Sandstedt, S. (1999). *An optimal performance academic course for university students and student-athletes.* Unpublished MS, University of Montana, Missoula, Montana.

Dweck, C. S. (1999). *Self-theories: Their role in motivation, personality, and development.* Philadelphia: Psychology Press.

Lopez, S. J., Bouwkamp, J., Edwards, L. M., & Teramoto Pediotti, J. (2000, October). *Making hope happen via brief interventions.* Presented at the 2nd Positive Psychology Summit, Washington, DC.

Luthans, F., Van Wyk, R., & Walumbwa, F. O. (2004). Recognition and development of hope for South African organizational leaders. *The Leadership and Organizational Development Journal,* *25,* 512–27.

Rogers, C. (2002). Teacher expectations: Implications for school improvement. In C. Desforges & R. Fox (eds.), *Teaching and learning: The essential readings* (pp. 152–70). Malden, MA: Blackwell.

Shorey, H. S., Snyder, C. R., Feldman, D. B., & Little, T. (2004). *Theories of intelligence, academic hope, and effort exerted after a failure experience.* MS submitted for publication.

Shorey, H. S., Snyder, C. R., Yang, X., & Lewin, M. R. (2003). The role of hope as a mediator in recollected parenting, adult attachment, and mental health. *Journal of Social and Clinical Psychology,* *22,* 685–715.

Snyder, C. R. (1994). *The psychology of hope: You can get there from here.* New York: Free Press.

Snyder, C. R. (1999). Hope, goal blocking thoughts, and test-related anxieties. *Psychological Reports,* *84,* 206–8.

Snyder, C. R. (2002). Hope theory: Rainbows in the mind. *Psychological Inquiry,* *13,* 249–75.

Snyder, C. R., Feldman, D., Shorey, H. S., & Rand, K. L. (2002). Hopeful choices: A school counselor's guide to hope theory. *Professional School Counseling,* *5,* 298–307.

Snyder, C. R., Harris, C., Anderson, J. R., Holleran, S. A., Irving, L. M., Sigmon, S. T., et al. (1991). The will and the ways: Development and validation of an individual-differences measure of hope. *Journal of Personality and Social Psychology,* *60,* 570–85.

Snyder, C. R., Lopez, S., Shorey, H. S., Rand, K. L., & Feldman, D. B. (2003). Hope theory, measurements, and applications to school psychology. *School Psychology Quarterly,* *18,* 122–39.

Snyder, C. R., & Shorey, H. S. (2002). Hope in the classroom: The role of positive psychology in academic achievement and psychology curriculum. *Psychology Teacher Network,* *12,* 1–9.

Snyder, C. R., Shorey, H. S., Cheavens, J., Pulvers, K. M., Adams III, V. H., & Wiklund, C. (2002). Hope and academic success in college. *Journal of Educational Psychology,* *94,* 820–6.

30

Multiple Cultural Identities: Will the Real Student Please Stand Up?

Ψ

Loreto R. Prieto
University of Akron

The number of women entering doctoral level training in psychology has increased greatly within the past two decades; in fact, women represent the majority of the current graduate student body in psychology. This trend at the doctoral level is reflective of a sex-based shift in enrollment in psychology majors and graduate programs that has been occurring since the 1970s (American Psychological Association [APA], 2000; Pion et al., 1996). Because the majority of psychology students are now women, the professoriate in psychology will educate and train, as a continuing baseline, a diverse student body.

If the number of matriculating students of color and other diverse students in psychology continues to increase (e.g., Lesbian/Gay/Bisexual/Transexual [LGBT], nontraditionally aged, disabled, first-generation college; cf. Prieto et al., 2004) and are added into this equation, then it is safe to say that the professoriate in psychology will educate and train a diverse student body that routinely possesses multiple diverse identity axes. Moreover, such diversity includes not only students with multiple diverse axes, but also a mix of majority culture and diverse cultural axes (e.g., African American men, European American women, heterosexuals of color; gay men, etc.). This chapter will not even attempt to address the multitude of potential permutations possible (i.e., examining the biracial transexual); rather, I will principally discuss the implication of the intersection of polar, major, demographic characteristics (e.g., women/men, European Americans/ people of color, heterosexuals/LGBT). Thus, when it comes to dealing with diversity issues in the teaching of psychology, indeed, one size does not fit all.

Surprisingly, comparatively little has been written on the topic of multiple identity elements; almost all of the available identity development models pertaining to culturally diverse people treat humans as if they are diverse in only one demographic characteristic (e.g., are only LGBT, are only people of color, or are only women). Reynolds and Pope (1991) commented strongly on this fact, observing that many job ads contain the phrase "Minorities and women are encouraged to apply" as if these are two distinct classes of people and women of color do not exist. Some scholars have written about the nature of biculturality (cf. LaFromboise, Coleman, & Gerton, 1993), but this work has been largely only in the context of people of color adapting to both their own indigenous cultures as well as the European American majority culture.

The pressing question for psychology educators becomes "How does a teacher deal with the gestalt of a multiply identified student?" Should teachers relate to the lesbian, African American student primarily as a woman, a lesbian, or as an African American? The answer is: yes. This response is intended to relay the notion of the sheer inability of people to compartmentalize and dissect portions of their identities. Rather, it is more likely that persons who possess multiple, diverse, demographic axes (MDDA) experience and relate to both internal and social and environmental experiences with an amalgamation of their cultural perspectives. Such persons also are likely susceptible to having particular environments and situations draw more for particular elements of their MDDA so that their responses to such situations may emphasize a particular identity element more than another. For example, an African American man may espouse certain perspectives in the midst of a discussion of racism, and emphasize another perspective when considering the issue of sexism. Moreover, this man may do so differently than an Asian American man or Latino man, depending on how the interaction of their racial and male identities have been influenced by both the majority culture and their indigenous cultures. Finally, it is likely that individuals who possess MDDA but who also have a majority culture axis (e.g., a European American lesbian) can use their diverse axes and experience of oppression to help them come to an understanding on how they actually enjoy certain privileges because of their majority culture axis. For example, a European American lesbian may come to see that although she deals with a significant amount of oppression and strife from our male- and heterosexually-oriented society, she is still free from certain life difficulties and enjoys some privilege by virtue of being a European American and not having to deal with institutionalized racism in addition to everything else.

Implications for the Psychology Classroom

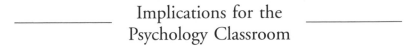

In teaching, advising, and mentoring situations dealing with students who possess MDDA, as with any personological characteristics, educators can: (a) nonthreateningly and nonintrusively consult the student as a source of her own self-definition; (b) recognize that the salience of any particular demographic axis and accompanying identity perspective for a student can be highly situation specific; and, (c) recognize the particular influence their own demographic characteristics exert, away from the general environmental press. These three heuristics can help to clarify issues and prevent confusion.

For example, with respect to the first point, it is very useful for educators, when and where safe, to ask students to relay (according to the their level of comfort) those aspects of their personal identity that form or inform their perspectives. Approaching students for this information may not always be possible (or advisable) in an open and public setting like the classroom but could be done in a more private, informal setting (e.g., chat after class in a professor's office). Not only does directly approaching students keep the instructor from guessing about students' identity axes, it also keeps instructors from presuming that because students possesses no "observable" diverse characteristics, students' identities do not contain diverse elements (e.g., European American men who are gay, very light skinned men who are biracial).

With respect to the second heuristic, keeping in mind the press of the environment and the specific situation pull for emphasizing particular identity elements can help instructors from becoming confused about seeming inconsistencies for MDDA students (or students who possess MDDA plus a majority culture axis). Not only may students vary in their development with respect to particular elements of their identities, but they may actually be unaware of the seemingly dichotomous positions they espouse concerning various aspects of their identity. For example, a European American woman may have developed a strong understanding of her womanhood and feminist lifestyle, but still be struggling with her White racial identity and questioning how these two axes fit in concert with each other within herself. To an instructor, this student might speak and act in a way that shows great commitment to social justice and equality for women, but at another time this instructor may also hear this same student espouse less than informed opinions on race relations or seem to have less of an awareness of her societal privilege as a European American. As another example, a gay African American man may have advanced his identity development as a person of color but still be strongly questioning his homosexuality – and may not even be aware of generally sexist notions he may hold as a man. His identity elements may even intersect, interfere, and confound one another – in this case, he may find less acceptance of himself internally and environmentally because his indigenous culture and the majority culture have strong dictates about masculinity and how a man should sexually orient himself.

Regarding the final heuristic, psychology educators should keep in mind the impact of their own stimulus value with respect to their personal demographic axes. Away from the general environmental press of, say, a classroom discussion, an instructor's demography can also be an incredibly strong, and sometimes superseding, influence on the degree to which students will emphasize or share their diverse perspectives. For example, discussions on race relations may be qualitatively different when held in a class instructed by a European American man versus an instructor who is a man of color. Objectively speaking, both of these instructors may establish a similarly "safe" environment for these students to share, yet the amount and type of sharing in which students engage may be different simply because of an instructor's demography.

For diverse students this differential openness is a function of survival and understandably moderating risk; for instructors it can be confusing and frustrating. When majority culture and culturally diverse identity elements mix within a particular instructor's demography, a "within-subject" effect may take place for an instructor. For example, women of color may feel quite able to share race-based perspectives with a man of color, but be a bit wary about discussing their feminist-based perspectives with this same man if they are unsure of his position on womanhood and male privilege. Finally, an instructor's consideration of her own demography and identity development allows an understanding of how instructor demographic characteristics, in concert with student demographic characteristics, can interact to reinforce the identity development of both parties (see Ponterotto, Fuertes, & Chen, 2000, for a full explication of Helms's racial identity and interactional models).

These three heuristics can serve as checkpoints for psychology educators to utilize so as to understand the dynamics of interactions with and among MDDA students. However, it is also necessary to point out that many other salient variables are present in such interactions, such as the heterogeneity of cultural identity within a group (i.e., not all Latinos have the same cultural perspective), the force and influence of acculturation (i.e., level of subscription to both the majority and indigenous cultures), and the force and influence of socioeconomic status variables (i.e., more matriculating students are from less wealthy backgrounds and are first-generation college goers).

Conclusion

The demography of students matriculating to the academy and into academic psychology has changed drastically over the last generation – no longer are European American, middle- to upper-class men the baseline of the psychology classroom or professoriate. This change in demography poses a tremendous challenge to all psychology educators to become skilled in teaching "nontraditional" students and also to recognize fully and welcome the fact that "traditional" students no longer exist. Although fully completing this transition to a new academic psychology will take time, psychology educators now have more resources than ever at their disposal to assist them in this endeavor (Prieto et al., 2004). As we move forward in adapting to the changing world of academic psychology, it is also a time to celebrate the strengths and richness of perspectives these new students bring to our discipline and our classrooms.

REFERENCES

American Psychological Association. (2000, April). *1998–1999 APA survey of undergraduate departments of psychology.* Washington, DC: Author.

LaFromboise, T., Coleman, H. L., & Gerton, J. (1993). Psychological impact of biculturalism: Evidence and theory. *Psychological Bulletin, 114*, 395–412.

Pion, G. M., Mednick, M. T., Astin, H. S., Hall, C. C. I., Kenkel, M. B., Keita, G. P., Kohout, J. L., & Kelleher, J. C. (1996). The shifting gender composition of psychology: Trends and implications for the discipline. *American Psychologist, 51*, 509–28.

Ponterotto, J. G., Fuertes, J. N., & Chen, E. C. (2000). Models of multicultural counseling. In S. D. Brown & R. W. Lent (eds.), *Handbook of counseling psychology* (3rd ed.) (pp. 639–69). New York: Wiley.

Prieto, L. R., Whittlesey, V., Herbert, D., Ocampo, C., Schomburg, A., & So, D. (2004). *Teaching about diversity: A follow-up survey of APA Division 2 Members.* MS submitted for publication.

Reynolds, A. L., & Pope, R. L. (1991). The complexities of diversity: Exploring multiple oppressions. *Journal of Counseling & Development, 70*, 174–80.

part VI

Ψ

Teaching Controversial Psychology Topics

The seven chapters in Part VI address teaching particularly sensitive topics, including evolution, sexuality, gender, race and ethnicity, religion, and drug use. This section also contains a chapter on teaching students who are "experts" on psychology.

31

Teaching Psychology When Everyone is an Expert

Ψ

David J. Pittenger
University of Tennessee, Chattanooga

With the possible exception of particle physics, abstract mathematics, and physical chemistry, few academic areas are free of the specter of contentious and controversial topics that arise when reviewing the contents of the discipline. Although most psychologists perceive psychology to be an objective science that attempts to address various topics with systematic empiricism, the simple fact is that many of the topics we examine and the conclusions we tentatively proffer are controversial. Consider the public reaction to Rind, Tromovitch, and Bauserman's (1998) literature review of the long-term effects of childhood sexual abuse. Their conclusions sparked considerable national indignation that culminated in a Congressional Joint Resolution condemning their findings (1999).

Although the controversy surrounding the Rind et al. (1998) article may represent an extreme case, it nevertheless illustrates an important matter that influences how we teach psychology and present our best ideas to our students. In essence, many students respond poorly to the dissonance created when what we teach contradicts what they believe.

As teachers of psychology, we suffer the fate that many students believe that they have a sound grasp of the causes of various behavioral phenomena. These beliefs may be sustained by anecdote and other personal experiences, and dubious sources of information presented through the popular media. Confronting these fallacies typically creates little more than general disappointment. In my experience, students are disenchanted to discover that they will not learn the secrets of dream analysis or that all psychologists are not like those they have seen on popular television talkshows. This reaction is typically replaced with an interest in the topics covered in the course.

The greater controversy arises, however, when what we teach challenges beliefs sustained by political ideology, religious doctrine, and other systems that drive a particular worldview. Many of the topics we cover have the potential to contradict strongly held beliefs that students have been taught to hold as unassailable. The question before us then is: "How do we attempt to teach controversial topics without becoming the center of controversy or allowing the controversy to overshadow the material presented in the course?"

The goal of teaching a course that is free of controversy is nearly impossible. Many of the essential topics in psychology are in one context or another controversial. Clearly, discussion of evolutionary theory is off-putting to students who are devout members of a religious faith that dismisses all components of classical and contemporary theories of evolution. Similarly, discussions of human sexuality, gender differences, race and intelligence, and other topics commonly reviewed in a general or advanced psychology course may well elicit strong reactions among one or more students. Consider, for example, the student who filed a sexual harassment complaint against his psychology professor who gave an hour-long lecture on masturbation (Wilson, 1995). According to the student's attorney, "[the instructor] is trying to argue that sexuality should not be guilt-ridden . . . and should be openly and freely discussed, and [the student] fundamentally disagrees" (p. A18).

As educators, we also have a responsibility to confront pernicious and ill-informed beliefs that unfairly harm others. Although we often teach students to be tolerant of ideals that are alien to them, we do not wish to endorse or remain sanguine regarding beliefs that have dubious moral, intellectual, or evidentiary foundations. Thus teaching, because it exposes students to novel concepts and perspectives, and often requires a clash of ideas, will create controversy.

Although it may well be impossible to prevent controversy from arising, you can adopt practices to contain the potential for controversy while maintaining an academic milieu that promotes the unfettered exchange of ideas. I presume that most controversy between individuals arises because of miscommunication or inability to appreciate the other perspectives. To that end, I believe that it is incumbent on the instructor to ensure candid communication and sensitivity to alternative perspectives. I offer my recommendations by examining the perspective of the student.

The advocacy group, Students for Academic Freedom, supports a website (www.studentsforacademicfreedom.org) that allows students to report anecdotes of unfair treatment they receive because of their political views. Understanding the types of events that affect students is helpful in reducing the tension created by a clash of ideas. The following is a distillation of the group's primary complaints against biased faculty.

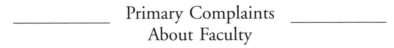

Primary Complaints About Faculty

Complaint 1: Requiring Readings or Texts That Cover Only One Side on an Issue

This complaint is relatively easy to avoid in psychology, where there is no shortage of debate regarding the merits of various perspectives. For example, when examining the status of repressed memories in an introductory psychology course, I had students read selective chapters from Terr (1994), and Loftus and Ketchm (1996) for the simple reason that the chapters presented diametrically opposite accounts of the phenomenon. The readings set the occasion for several lively discussions among students who believed strongly in the reality of repressed memories and students who did not. Students reported that they enjoyed the clash of perspectives and appreciated the opportunity to read viewpoints that were different than their own.

Having students read opposing points of view is often impractical, however. In these cases, I believe that it is essential for instructors to ensure that they present alternative perspectives. Admittedly, it is extremely difficult to present a perspective with which one disagrees. As these situations arise, I believe that the best policy is for instructors to announce their bias and describe how they attempt to reconcile the conflict between personal beliefs and the results of empirical research. Such self-declarations help defuse accusations that faculty engage in the surreptitious indoctrination of students and provide a useful model for students on how one attempts to reconcile matters of consciousness and evidence from research. Moreover, such moments afford the opportunity to model critical-thinking procedures during which a person sets aside personal biases and attempts to grapple with the merits of counterarguments and relevant data.

Complaint 2: Mocking Political or Religious Figures, and Introducing Material That is Unrelated to the Subject

Clearly, a personal attack against an individual, regardless of public standing, has no place in the classroom. However, many of the comments we faculty make in an off-the-cuff manner can become an unnecessary distraction. Hebel (2004) reported an example where a student asked an instructor, "Do you have any prejudices?" to which the instructor responded, "Yeah, Republicans." The student became incensed because he had meant to ask about the professor's preferences for writing styles, and, as a Republican, took offense to the quip. As another example, a former colleague of mine, who is a vegan, announced to the class that she tells her children that Ronald McDonald's lips are bright red with the blood of animal flesh. Several students complained to me that the comment was tangential to the material being presented in class and offensive to them in that it was an unnecessary interjection of personal beliefs into the lecture. In both cases, the quip seemed to overshadow whatever message the instructor wished to present.

By no means do I wish to imply that you remove all attempts to bring humor into the classroom and avoid the extemporaneous turn of phrase that captures the essence of point you wish to make. Rather, I recommend that you ensure that expressions of humor are not made at the expense of others. There is, of course, a distinction between *ad hominem* comments and criticism of an idea; this distinction may be difficult for some students to recognize. Therefore, the best tactic is to remind students of the distinction between the criticisms of ideas and the criticism of the person.

The latter point reiterates a theme that I hope emerges from this essay and the following chapters. A useful defense to classroom controversy is to adopt the role of a referee of ideas and to ensure that the discussion remains grounded in the discourse of the discipline. For psychology, the heart of the discourse is a rational review of the empirical evidence.

Complaint 3: Forcing Students to Express a Certain Point of View in Assignments

This complaint is most likely to arise from a student's misinterpretation. For example, in my advanced course on animal learning, I require students to read and write a reaction paper to Watson's APA presidential address (1913). On one occasion, a student complained to me that she rejected the central thesis of Watson's behaviorism given her Christian beliefs and was anxious that I would give her a bad grade if she argued against Watson. After a brief meeting wherein I outlined tactics she could use to frame her argument, she left content that she could present a counterargument without fear of retaliation. I have since revised the instructions for the assignment to ensure that students understand that I would evaluate the quality of their writing, not the position they took *per se.*

The lesson from this episode is that some students misinterpret the intention of an assignment. For example, a student may assume that writing an essay outlining evolutionary origins of a certain social behavior requires an endorsement of evolution. In these cases, I find it useful to remind students that a requirement to write about a topic is not a requirement that they adopt a particular perspective, only that they master the content of the material. In many cases, it is useful to reiterate this point throughout a course.

In some cases the instructor may wish to be more deliberate in warning students about the potential for controversy in a course. For example, those who teach human sexuality may include statements in the course syllabus outlining the potentially controversial content of the course and remind students of the school's stance on the free expression of ideas in the classroom. Much like the informed-consent contracts participants sign before beginning an experiment, course syllabi should offer students sufficient warning that portions of the course may be upsetting. Although these "boilerplate" disclaimers can be helpful, they are not effective by themselves. Therefore, it is helpful to remind students frequently of these goals, especially when introducing a new topic for discussion or as the class discussion becomes less focused on fact and more on tangential matters.

Conclusion

In general, much controversy can be avoided with a modicum of planning and discretion in the classroom. In many cases, preparing students for the potential of controversy avoids the development of the controversy. Similarly, providing students with the opportunity to review alternative perspectives alleviates much potential for problems. To the extent that the instructor demonstrates a respect for the students' perspective and facilitates a fair exchange of ideas, the risk for becoming the center of controversy is minimized.

REFERENCES

H. Con Res. 107, 106th Cong. (1999).
Hebel, S. (2004, Feb. 12). Patrolling professor's politics. *The Chronicle of Higher Education, 50 (23)*, A18.

Loftus, E., & Ketchm, K. (1996). *The myth of repressed memories: False memories and allegations of sexual abuse.* New York: St. Martins.

Rind, B., Tromovitch, P., & Bauserman, R. (1998). A meta-analytic examination of assumed properties of child sexual abuse using college samples. *Psychological Bulletin, 124,* 22–53.

Terr, L. (1994). *Unchained memories: True stories of traumatic memories, lost and found.* New York: Basic Books.

Watson, J. B. (1913). Psychology as the behaviorist views it. *Psychological Review, 20,* 158–77.

Wilson, R. (1995, March 17). Lecture on female masturbation harassed him, male student says. *The Chronicle of Higher Education, 41 (27),* A18.

32

Psychology of Race and Ethnicity

Ψ

James E. Freeman
University of Virginia

In order to help students appreciate the complexities of human behavior, it is important to discuss issues related to diversity. However, it is not easy to discuss issues of diversity, as race, ethnicity, and culture are often linked to sensitive feelings, or in some cases, strong prejudices. Some groups are associated with more negative stereotypes than others. Consequently the intentions or comments of a person of a different group can sometimes be misinterpreted or be perceived as insensitive.

However, it is important that teachers confront such controversial issues – if teachers do not take a stand, then the responsibility to shape students' attitudes is abrogated to others. Blanchard, Lily, and Vaughn (1991) showed that opinions of a confederate affected students' views on racism. When a student overheard a confederate express positive attitudes, the students later had more positive attitudes compared to students who did not hear a prior opinion. Likewise, students who overheard a previous negative opinion later had a more negative opinion. Students held these views even though the researchers measured their opinions anonymously. During a school term it is possible that a controversial racial event will happen. Thus, it is important that psychology teachers take a position on controversial issues because of the potential to influence the students' attitudes.

Defining Race and Ethnicity

Of the controversial issues related to race and ethnicity, one is the definition of race itself. Two editorials illustrate this point: One appeared in the *New York Times* (Malcomson, 2004), which precipitated a second piece published in the *Washington* Post (Williams, 2004). In the first column, Malcomson (2004) praised the keynote speech Barack Obama gave at the Democratic National Convention. Where Malcomson's praise went wrong, in Williams's (2004) opinion, was Malcomson's characterization of

Mr. Obama as "not black in the usual way." Although Mr. Obama self-identifies himself as African American, Malcomson points out that Mr. Obama's white mother raised him, and his Kenyan father returned to Africa when Mr. Obama was a baby. Malcomson suggested, "while [Mr. Obama] is black, he is not the direct product of generations of black life in America."

The question Williams (2004) posed to Malcomson (2004) is "Black like whom?" To be fair to Malcomson, he was speculating why Mr. Obama might appeal to white voters. Nonetheless, Williams raises an important point: what does it mean to be "stereotypically African-American?" Racial identity is a social construct and therefore is in some respects a personal one. Teachers and students must be careful about making assumptions about racial, ethnic, or cultural identity based on self-conceived notions of what race is. In Mr. Obama's case and others of mixed heritage, on what grounds should they identify themselves as belonging to one race versus another? It is important that students learn that everyone does not fit into neat categories. When relevant, it is best to have students self-identify their race rather than make assumptions based on how they look, their background, or the spelling of their last name.

Also teachers should be careful not confuse racial identity with ethnicity. For example, consider a student whose parents are from China but who was born and raised in Venezuela. The student speaks Chinese and Spanish, her home and native languages, respectively. Racially, she is Asian, but ethnically she could be considered Hispanic (defined as a person whose background is from a Spanish-speaking country). Confusing as this scenario may be, such cases are not uncommon and illustrate that race and ethnicity are slippery concepts. Gloria, Rieckmann, and Rush (2000) suggested that teachers should avoid asking students to speak as experts for their racial or ethnic group. First, it is not possible to be sure what group a student represents. Second, although personal case histories are valuable, their value is limited in that they are anecdotal and not systematic observations. One student's experience should not be taken as representative of a group. Finally, minority students may feel uncomfortable speaking for their groups because they may not want to stand out as being different. Confronting them about their minority status puts the spotlight on them personally. Gloria et al. made several suggestions how to teach about issues of race or ethnicity. Foremost they recommended teaching interactively. They suggested that using guest speakers, movies, student presentations, and group projects is more effective than using the traditional didactic approach.

Affirmative Action

Perhaps one of the most contentious issues related to race is affirmative action. It is unlikely to be raised as an issue in most psychology courses, but it does appear to be a perennial issue on college campuses. One approach is to present the position of the American Psychological Association (APA), which "resolved that the American Psychological Association reaffirms its commitment to affirmative action. American Psychological Association supports equality of opportunity for persons regardless of race, gender, age, religion, disability, sexual orientation and national origin" (APA, 2004a). This resolution and other APA publications on affirmative action and diversity are available online (see http://apa.org/pi). For example, an APA brochure answers frequently asked questions about affirmative action, such as: what it is, why it is still needed, what are the major criticisms, and whether recipients are less qualified (APA, 2004b). For a more scholarly review of the literature on affirmative action see Crosby, Iyer, Clayton, and Downing (2003). Another APA document (APA, 2004c) also addressed a related controversial question, "Can – Or Should – America Be Color-Blind?" This pamphlet presents findings that indicate that people respond differently, implicitly and explicitly, to other people based on race. Race cannot be ignored; therefore, color-blindness is unrealistic.

Another approach consistent with Gloria et al.'s recommendation to teaching interactively is to use in-class debates. However, take care if you use this approach because students who argue positions that are consistent with their beliefs tend to assimilate evidence consistent with their attitudes (Budesheim & Lundquist, 1999). Rather than allowing students to choose sides in a debate, Budesheim and Lundquist's research showed that students' attitudes on an issue change when they were required to argue a position in a debate that they originally oppose. They suggested that an effective approach is to have students prepare arguments for both sides of an issue and later tell them which side they will defend. Another suggestion is for students to defend one position in a debate and defend the other side in a written paper. The major point is to give students the ability to evaluate fairly both sides of a controversial issue. Sometimes, a little cognitive dissonance can be good, in that one way to reduce dissonance is through attitude change.

The Intelligence Controversy

Related to the issue of affirmative action is the controversy of whether there are racial differences in intelligence. There may not be a more emotionally charged racial issue. Specifically, there are significant and reliable differences between whites and blacks in IQ test scores and other standardized tests. The question itself is usually expressed in a biased light given that these data suggest that there are intellectual deficits in some racial groups. Instead, Wheeler et al. (1999) suggested reframing a new question, such as, "What accounts for the interpretations of differences in IQ between different racial groups?" Students need to understand how even the questions we ask can reflect hidden biases. Although one view suggests these differences exist primarily because of genetic factors, in my experience I have never had a student take the genetic position in a discussion (contrasted with many students who have an anti-affirmative action position). Instead, students become involved in a lively discussion about what is wrong with IQ tests. Although I discussed research methods earlier in my class, students often forget concepts such as reliability and validity, and instead regress to relying on anecdotal evidence.

Although standardized tests have limitations, they should provide students opportunities to evaluate empirical findings critically. For example, although researchers using twins and adopted children (e.g., MacKintosh, 1998) suggested a genetic influence, the question remains as to how much? A problem with such research is that the methods are inherently correlational or quasi-experimental in that race and environment of upbringing cannot be ethically manipulated. Thus, there is a possibility that other variables correlated with race may account for the differences. For example, race is correlated with socioeconomic status (MacKintosh, 1998). However, socioeconomic status does not account for all the differences. Variables other than genetics may account for the rest of the differences. For example Claude Steele and Joshua Aronson (Aronson, 2002; Steele, 1997; Steele & Aronson, 1995) suggested that a "stereotype threat" may be responsible for some of the differences. Stereotype threat occurs when a negative stereotype about a group affects the members of that group because they fear they will reflect the stereotype. Their research showed that African American students do less well on standardized tests when they identified themselves by race compared to African American students who did not. They proposed that the threat was activated for those students who identified their race, which produced anxiety and thereby impeded their performance. Likewise, women did more poorly on math tests under similar circumstances, presumably because of the threat of confirming the stereotype about women not being competent in math. When participants are aware of negative stereotypes related to their performance on a test, the threat of doing poorly impairs their performance.

The stereotype threat does not account for all the differences in IQ test scores, but again, a problem with correlational research is that there may be other important variables that are not considered. A strong genetic influence does not mean that environment has no effect. This point is often illustrated in introductory textbooks, which often use the example of plant seedlings that are genetically identical but which grow to different heights when planted in different-quality soils.

Conclusion

Students need to learn to not to judge other groups from their own cultural perspective. Controversial topics on race and ethnicity are effective mechanisms to get your students involved in discussions or debates where they can use and refine their critical thinking skills. After a critical examination of the empirical data, students may come to realize better the complexity of such controversial issues. Teachers should confront the controversial issues of race and ethnicity rather than being afraid to address them.

REFERENCES

American Psychological Association (2004a). Ethnic minority recruitment and retention. Retrieved Aug. 18, 2004, from ww.apa.org/pi/oema/oemares.html

American Psychological Association (2004b). Affirmative action: Who benefits? Retrieved Aug. 18, 2004, from www.apa.org/affirmaction.html

American Psychological Association (2004c). Can – or should – America be color-blind? Retrieved Aug. 18, 2004, from www,apa.org/ppo/issues/pfindings.html

Aronson, J. (2002). *Improving academic achievement: Impact of psychological factors on education.* San Diego: Academic Press.

Blanchard, F. A., Lilly, T., Vaughn, L. A. (1991). Reducing the expression of racial prejudice. *Psychological Science, 2,* 101–5.

Budesheim, T. L., & Lundquist, A. R. (1999). Consider the opposite: Opening minds through in-class debates on course-related controversies. *Teaching of Psychology, 26,* 106–10.

Crosby, F. J., Iyer, A., Clayton, S., & Downing, R. A. (2003). Affirmative action: Psychological data and the policy debates. *American Psychologist, 58,* 93–115.

Gloria, A. M., Rieckmann, T. R., & Rush, J. D. (2000). Issues and recommendations for teaching an ethnic/culture-based course. *Teaching of Psychology, 27,* 102–7.

MacKintosh, N. J. (1998). *IQ and human intelligence.* New York: Oxford University Press.

Malcomson, S. L. (2004, Aug. 1). An appeal beyond race. *The New York Times.* Retrieved Aug. 11, from www.nytimes.com.

Steele, C. M. (1997). A threat in the air: How stereotypes shape intellectual identity and performance. *American Psychologist, 52,* 613–29.

Steele, C. M., & Aronson, J. (1995). Stereotype threat and the intellectual test performance of African Americans. *Journal of Personality and Social Psychology, 69,* 797–811.

Wheeler, E. A., Ayers, J. F., Fracasso, M. P., Galupo, M. P., Rabin, J. S., & Slater, B. R. (1999). Approaches to modeling diversity in the college classroom: Challenges and strategies. *Journal on Excellence in College Teaching, 10,* 79–93.

Williams, V. (2004, Aug. 5). Black like whom? *Washington Post,* A19.

33

Evolutionary Psychology

Ψ

Lewis Barker
Auburn University

Two facts conspire to thwart psychology professors who teach evolution in American colleges and universities: of industrialized nations, Americans are among the *most* churchgoing and among the *least* scientifically educated. About 80 percent of Americans profess a belief in God (Taylor, 2003); of these, 35–45 percent believe in a Genesis account of human origins (Gallup, 1997). Should we be surprised that large numbers of American college students "don't believe in evolution"?

Having taught evolution-based psychology for 32 years in two universities in the Bible-belt, here I humbly offer what I've learned about the process. I teach a brain-based psychology, and remind students that brains emanate from genetic recipes that have changed through evolutionary time. Hence, incorporating perspectives that incorporate evolution, neuroscience, behavioral genetics, and comparative and environmental analyses provides an excellent foundation for understanding general psychology (consciousness, motivation and emotion, sensation and perception, learning and behavior analysis, and so forth) as well as evolutionary psychology (EP).

Openly Acknowledging the Science–Religion Rift

My approach to teaching EP in 1972 was straightforward: I lectured on evolutionary theory, and stated that most scientists agreed with Darwin that humans are biologically linked with other animals. I told students "We don't have time to explore alternative theories of human origins." Thirty years later, more students in my classroom seem both to be less well-read and to exhibit less critical thinking. In response, I am more circumspect, and spend more class time on what is meant by empiricism and scientific knowledge and alternative ways of gaining evidence and thinking about the world.

I begin by asking students about the differences in meaning when a person says "I feel that . . ."or "I believe that . . ." or "I know that . . ."? After some discussion, I quote Freud's (1930/1961) observation that scientific thinking tends to make us feel bad about ourselves – specifically, because Darwin's evolutionary theory relegated humans to a descent from the animal world. Despite how you may feel about this ignominy, or how it may conflict with your religious beliefs, is there evidence that supports Darwin's theory? Does the evidence lead to a better understanding of what is known about human origins and human behavior?

I then point out that the psychological sciences neither address the origins of life nor the proposition of a spiritual life after death – questions of great import to all thinking people. I believe that the combination of conflicting feelings, beliefs, and evidence-based thinking to address unanswered and often unanswerable questions produces cognitive dissonance. I suggest that one solution is a two-realm view that accommodates both scientific and religious belief systems (Anderson, 1999; Gould, 1999, 2002). Risking oversimplification, religious tracts do not inform our scientific understanding of the world, and science tells us very little about which values people should adopt. There is a way to practice religion each week and go to their psychology class on Monday, and not implode.

My focus remains, however, on teaching evolution as part of scientific psychology. However, a student persists, "evolution is only a theory – not a fact or a scientific law." This classroom challenge is on a list of the 15 questions students most frequently ask about evolution (see Rennie, 2002). Making Rennie's article required reading both challenges students to examine their arguments and relieves the professor from using limited class time to field *all* student concerns.

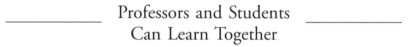

Professors and Students Can Learn Together

Professors lacking a good general science background (most of us?) are intimidated by not having all the answers for students' questions about evolution. However, we can model the search for knowledge: When asked a difficult question it is okay to say, "I am not sure about that, but let me see what I can find out. Want to help?" I use, and have given extra credit for students who visit, the NOVA website devoted to evolution (www.pbs.org/wgbh/nova/link/evolution.html) as well as the University of California, Santa Barbara, Center for Evolutionary Psychology website (www.psych.ucsb.edu/research/cep/).

Evolution Isn't What You Think It Is

Ernst Mayr's (1991) *One Long Argument* proposes that understanding (not to mention teaching) evolution is difficult. Contrary to anti-evolutionists' oversimplified vilifications, to understand evolutionary theory, both professor and student must first learn and then integrate several disciplines. In the early 1900s, for example, the addition of genetics provided a physical basis for Darwin's theory. A hundred years of genetic experiments clearly demonstrate that common gene sequences connect humans with all other life forms. Contemporary references to "the theory of evolution," then, imply genetic mechanisms and genomic science.

This modern synthesis incorporates other science specialties such as paleogeology (including theories of carbon dating, plate tectonics, climate change, and so forth) and paleobiology. For applications in psychology, add animal behavior, behavioral genetics, and all matters comparative (e.g., anatomy, physiology, psychology).

Many psychology professors may devote only a lecture or two "covering" evolution, and can address few of these related areas. However, you can point out that evolution is far more than the false allegation that humans descended from monkeys. Rather, the study of evolution is a comprehensive, integrative, scientific account of the origin of species featuring descent with modification.

Furthermore, few of the ideas that inform Darwin's theory of natural selection are in themselves controversial. Thus, for the student who doesn't believe in evolution, I ask, "do you not believe in geology? genetics? zoology? adaptation? ecological niches?" These sorts of questions prompt critical thinking – students examining their scientific understanding of the world as distinct from their religious beliefs.

Five Main Points of Evolutionary Psychology

I confess to my classes that after four decades of study, evolutionary theory is sufficiently difficult that I still don't understand all that it entails. I offer a simplified version consisting of five main points: Environment or "Nature," Life and Sex, Genetics, Natural Selection, and Sexual Selection.

Environment. To understand Darwin's theory of natural selection, I ask students to think about "nature" and "natural history." The best scientific evidence is that planet Earth has been in existence for about 4.5 billion years, and that life has been on it for about 3.5 billion years. What Darwin referred to as modification with descent is the history of how life forms changed over these 3.5 billion years. Unfortunately, I propose, humans evolved brains allowing us to understand time measured in minutes, hours, and a lifetime of years, but not the billions of years of natural history. Yet only this latter appreciation of time allows us to comprehend the changes in earth's history that preceded the present forms of life. (To make this point I use a visual figure of 450 dots, each representing ten million years – see figure 3.1 in Barker, 2004, p. 69).

Life and Sex. From a biological perspective, the "purpose" of all life, embodied in DNA, is to self-replicate, or reproduce (Dawkins, 1976). I ask my class which came first, the chicken or the egg? Occasionally a student will respond with the enigmatic answer attributed to Samuel Butler that "A chicken is an egg's way of making another egg." Other students may respond with the alternative, and a discussion ensues. DNA contains the genetic recipes for plants' and animals' biological structures, and I suggest that, for this reason, DNA is the physical basis for nature in nature/nurture questions. Because evolutionary scholars measure the survival and fitness of all organisms in terms of reproductive success, is humans' sexual nature any surprise? Is sexual desire rooted in DNA?

Genetics. I introduce genetics with a picture comparing a smiling human infant, a smiling chimpanzee, and a chick. The caption reads, "Why does my baby look more like an ape than a chicken?" A typical response is "because they are more closely related genetically." The point is made that different species are genetically related but cannot interbreed.

After introducing the human genome project, I remind students that gene sequencing of other species continues at a rapid rate. The genomes of humans and mice, for example, are separated by 70 million years of evolution, each has around 30,000 genes, and only about 300 of them are unique to each organism. Mice and humans share the same genes for blood pressure, temperature regulation, bone manufacture, cell division, tissue growth, and so on. Of genes linked to human disease, mice share 90 percent with humans, including those relevant to the development of HIV, obesity, osteoporosis, Down's syndrome, schizophrenia, diabetes, heart disease, Parkinson's disease, breast cancer, leukemia, malaria, and other maladies. As another example, genes coding for hemoglobin are identical in humans and chimpanzees, and that is why of all the animals in the world, only human hemoglobin is not rejected if infused into a chimpanzee, and vice versa.

Natural Selection. Natural selection is the means by which organisms better adapted to the environment produce more offspring than organisms less adapted. Hence, natural selection is about differential reproduction. Students typically confuse two different uses of the term *adaptation.* Darwin used the term to describe animals adapted through evolutionary processes – that is, animals adapted to the niche into which they are born (e.g., fish are adapted to water). In addition, humans and other animals also behave adaptively to better meet the local demands of the environment (e.g., Aleutians adaptively wear fur skins in arctic environments).

Darwin's "nature" is uncaring. During the earth's natural history, cataclysmic climate changes, including various huge asteroids periodically impacting the earth, have destroyed an estimated 95 percent of all life forms. Hence, natural selection entails environments providing selective pressures that organisms must overcome (or not), and exploit (or not), thereby increasing their fitness (or not). I suggest that this fact is at the heart of the science–religion controversy. Scientific understanding of the origin of life is at odds not only with creation accounts, but with a belief in a personal, caring, God. I remind students, however, many people have accommodated theistic beliefs and scientific accounts of life (see e.g., Anderson, 1999; Gould, 1999, 2002, as starting points).

Sexual Selection. Few people have read Darwin's (1859/1962) *Origin of Species*, in which he outlined natural selection. (I call natural selection Darwin's "red-in-tooth-and-claw" theory.) However, EP is also based on Darwin's "other" theory – that of sexual selection (see Darwin, 1871, 1872/1965). (I refer to sexual selection as his "dating and mating" theory.) Sexual selection is Darwin's theory that males and females compete for mates for reproductive purposes. Hence, sexual selection is about who reproduces with whom. EP also addresses specific issues in brain evolution (so-called cognitive modules that differ in males and females) as well as in social psychology, including sex differences in courting, attraction, mating, and parenting.

Many students respond with more interest to EP's accounts of sexual selection (addressing human relationships in the present) than to natural selection (addressing humans' relationship to other animals through evolution). However, students must have a basic understanding of the modern synthesis before jumping into dating and mating.

Conclusion

When teaching psychology from an evolutionary perspective, (a) acknowledge religious concerns, and provide resources that answer common questions about evolution and that address science–religion conflicts; (b) discriminate among believing, feeling, and knowing; (c) emphasize the complexity of the modern synthesis, and point out the difficulty of "not believing" in genetics; and (d) teach the components of evolution, such as Environment or "Nature," Life and Sex, Genetics, Natural Selection, and Sexual Selection. As is true in any classroom, humility, humor, and good-will go a long way in achieving educational goals.

References

Anderson, S. (1999). Science and religion: Two realms and their relationships. *Science, 286,* 907–8.

Barker, L. (2004). *Psychology* (2nd ed.). Upper Saddle River, NJ: Pearson Custom Publishing.

Darwin, C. (1859/1962). *On the origin of species by means of natural selection.* New York: Collier Books.

Darwin, C. (1871). *The descent of man, and selection in relation to sex* (2 vols.). London: Charles Murray.

Darwin, C. (1872/1965). *The expression of emotions in man and animals.* Chicago: University of Chicago Press.

Dawkins, R. (1976). *The selfish gene.* London: Oxford University Press.

Freud, S. (1930/1961). *Civilization and its discontents.* New York: Norton.

Mayr, E. (1991). *One long argument: Charles Darwin and the genesis of modern evolutionary theory.* Cambridge, MA: Harvard University Press.

Gallup, G. (1997). As cited in Religioustolerance.org. Retrieved Aug. 20, 2004, from www.religioustolerance.org/ev_publi.htm

Gould, S. J. (1999). *Rock of ages: Science and religion in the fullness of life.* New York: Ballantine.

Gould, S. J. (2002). *The structure of evolutionary theory.* Cambridge, MA: Belknap Press of Harvard University Press.

Rennie, J. (2002). Scientific American's *15 Answers to Creationist Nonsense,* www.angelfire.com/ok5/pearly/htmls/gop-evolution.html

Taylor, H. (2003). While most Americans believe in God, only 36% attend a religious service once a month or more often. *The Harris Poll #59.* Retrieved Aug. 20, 2004, from www.harrisinteractive.com/news/allnewsbydate.asp?NewsID=693

34

Teaching Human Sexuality

Ψ

Laura L. Finken
Creighton University

No issue creates a storm of controversy faster than the topic of sex; even the ivory towers of academia remain vulnerable to this tumult. For example, just within the last few years Nassau Community College in New York faced a lawsuit by taxpayers claiming that the sexually explicit materials presented in the Human Sexuality course violated students' rights because it conflicted with their religious beliefs (Garcia, 1997); the federal funding for a doctoral sexuality program at the University of Wisconsin-Madison was threatened by conservative legislators who disagreed with the would-be director's statement about abstinence-only programs ("Republicans Oppose Funds," 2002); and Dr. Dennis Dailey at the University of Kansas was forced to defend his Human Sexuality curriculum to the state legislature in a case that grabbed national attention ("KU Report Backs Dailey's Methods," 2003; Walker, 2003). Although the court eventually cleared Dr. Dailey and allowed him to continue offering the course, the Kansas state legislature subsequently passed an amendment to regulate the presentation of sexually explicit materials in classes (Rombeck, 2003). Ironically, the current sociopolitical climate makes it even more difficult to teach human sexuality courses today than it was decades ago when these courses were first conceived (Herold, 1997).

Despite these challenges, human sexuality courses continue to hold appeal because they have the potential to dispel misinformation, anxiety, and prejudice (e.g., Craig, 1985; Finken, 2002; Leiblum, 2001) and to impact students' personal beliefs as well as their attitudes about contemporary social issues (e.g., Cotten, 2003; Finken, 2003; Fischer, 1986; Galway, 1998). For the first time in many students' lives, a human sexuality course provides the opportunity to discuss sexuality factually, to consider the implications of this material to the world around them, and to find their own voices on these issues (Baber & Murray, 2001). Similarly, college is a time when many students step beyond their parents' supervision and face sexuality, as both a personal and societal issue, from a new vantage point. Although developmentally normal, this growth often results in changes that necessitate adjustments for both students and their parents, and human sexuality courses can accentuate these issues. By their very nature, then, human sexuality courses address fundamental existential concerns that will always generate controversy (Maddock, 1997), and typical course preparations will not suffice for a human sexuality course (Herold, 1997). In particular, Human Sexuality instructors need to be sensitive to the students in several critical ways.

Embracing Diversity

All students bring with them different experiences, religious backgrounds, cultural values, social attitudes, and coping abilities through which they will filter the class information (Baber & Murray, 2001; Dixon-Woods et al., 2002; Maddock, 1997; Petersen, 1997). Given such heterogeneity, it is unrealistic to expect that people will agree on the material presented, especially given that sexuality is so personal and value-laden. Thus, the design of course activities needs to accommodate this diversity: the goal should not be consensus, but rather perspective-taking and critical thinking within a respectful environment. In fact, a major advantage of using controversial topics in class assignments is the advancement of critical thinking by requiring students to consider multiple facets of an issue. In particular, debates can compel students to research and understand a position that challenges their own initial stance, thereby promoting perspective-taking (e.g., Budesheim & Lundquist, 1999; Finken, 2003). However, when course assignments require that students provide their own opinions about issues, the instructor should not prescribe specific beliefs that students must espouse to obtain a desired grade. Instructors should grade assignments on their comprehensiveness and depth of processing, not on which particular values students express (Brooke, 1999).

One potentially contentious topic that instructors will face in a Human Sexuality course is homosexuality. Although it is essential for all instructors to avoid marginalizing gay and lesbian students (Simoni, 1996), this concern becomes magnified within a Human Sexuality course. Students possess myriad strong opinions about this issue based upon their upbringing, experiences, and religious beliefs (Altemeyer, 1996). For some students, the research and presentation of material within the class will contradict their fundamental beliefs. For many students, the issue will seem abstract given that they have never had a homosexual friend or relative. For gay, lesbian, bisexual, and transgendered (GLBT) students, college might be their first opportunity to explore openly their sexual orientation. The combination of such diverse people with potentially intense feelings about homosexuality warrants caution and sensitivity on the instructor's part.

As a result, human sexuality instructors must be especially sensitive to issues of heterosexism. Instructors should be careful to use inclusive language when discussing relationships and sexual behaviors, as well as pointing out areas where there may be special considerations for GLBT people (e.g., the process of coming out, finding appropriate therapists for same-sex couples struggling with sexual dysfunctions). Human sexuality instructors can help decrease the prejudicial attitudes that many students have about gays and lesbians by presenting students with factual information, encouraging them to think critically, and creating a social norm of respect and acceptance within the classroom (Finken, 2002).

Handling Personal Issues

Students' personal experiences with sexual activities should not be a focus in a human sexuality course; however, at some level these experiences will clearly influence the students' interpretation of the material. Statistically, we know that the vast majority of college-age students are sexually active (Alan Guttmacher Institute, 1999). Ignoring this fact will make instructors appear as out of touch as the seventh-grade basketball coach discussing "change of life" euphemisms in a middle-school Health class. Nevertheless, how sexually experienced a student is should be irrelevant to the course. Experience does not necessarily generate accurate knowledge, and sexually naive students should be able to garner equivalent value from the course. The focus should be on the scientific knowledge of human sexuality, and it should be left to the students to apply this to their own lives rather than using their personal sexual choices and behaviors as a topic within the classroom.

Furthermore, the perception of how human sexuality courses address students' experiences through class activities has evolved over time. In previous decades, personalizing the course concepts through self-reflection and disclosure within safe discussion groups or journals was encouraged, and even considered to be an advantage of the course (e.g., Atwater, 1987; Barbour, 1989). However, more recently, heightened concern about confidentiality and even the ability to guarantee anonymity (e.g., within journals) questions the appropriateness of these activities. Indeed, course activities that require students to disclose personal information, such as their sexual behavior, "is ethically a dubious practice" at best (DeLamater, Hyde, & Allgeier, 1994, p. 314). Additionally, personal discussions of any kind within the context of a class place the instructor at risk of sexual harassment charges (Herold, 1997). Rather than forcing students to disclose their personal experiences, instructors can address topics by having students consider real-life cases from the media or hypothetical ethical dilemmas. Students may then identify which factors should be considered, integrate the course material with their values, and decide how they believe such situations should be resolved (DeLamater et al., 1994). This alternative provides a way for students to think critically about important issues and express their opinions without violating their privacy.

Finally, given the range of students' experiences, instructors must be aware of relevant statistics in a very concrete way. Estimates vary across studies, but approximately 22 percent of women and 1.3 percent of men have been raped (Laumann, Gagnon, Michael, & Michaels, 1994), with college women among the highest-risk age group (US Department of Justice, 2003). Moreover, 25 percent of women and nearly 18 percent of men report being sexually abused as children (Edwards, Hoden, Felitti, & Anda, 2003). These numbers translate into real students who come into the class with personal vulnerabilities, and by the nature of the course content will be forced to confront these potentially traumatic issues (Baber & Murray, 2001; Dixon-Woods et al., 2002). Because students typically view human sexuality instructors as knowledgeable and nonjudgmental, students often seek their help in dealing with sexual concerns (Brooke, 1999; Herold, 1997). Although personally counseling students would create a dual relationship, instructors need to be prepared to help students connect with appropriate support agencies (e.g., university counseling centers, YWCA).

Laying the Groundwork

Several steps can also be taken within the design of the course to ease the presentation of potentially sensitive issues. First, planning the order of the course material to progress gradually into more sensitive issues can desensitize students and minimize embarrassment and discomfort inherent with the material (Dixon-Woods et al., 2002). Second, forewarning students about potentially threatening material or activities is essential. A comprehensive syllabus will initiate the process of informed consent and may be viewed as a written contract for the course (DeLamater et al., 1994). However, instructors should provide additional advance notification about upcoming activities that may be difficult for some students (e.g., viewing sexually explicit material, watching an interview of a rape victim). For example, if a class activity will involve viewing pornographic materials, a week before the activity the instructor can take a few minutes at the beginning of class to describe what the activity entails and to encourage any students with concerns to see the instructor outside of class. After this initial description, a brief reminder at the beginning of additional classes for students who missed the initial warning will suffice. Simply announcing sensitive materials on the day of the activity is not enough warning because to express concerns or leave, students would have to identify themselves in front of the class, which could be uncomfortable and embarrassing (Brooke, 1999; Herold, 1997).

Although forewarning students about sensitive materials through a syllabus and class announcements provides basic course information, the other essential component of informed consent is choice. Students may have very legitimate and personal reasons for not wanting to complete certain assignments or participate in specific class activities; instructors need to be aware of such reluctance and to plan for it. Providing students with several assignment options about various topics and letting them select which (e.g., 4 out of the 6) assignments they would like to complete over the semester allows them to make decisions based on their interests, schedules, and potential areas of concern. Similarly, human sexuality instructors need to be reasonably flexible about their attendance policy on days involving sensitive in-class activities (Brooke, 1999). With advance notice, instructors may ask that students who have concerns talk to them outside of class. At that point, the instructor can differentiate between an excused and an unexcused absence, and even provide an alternative assignment that would not create undue stress for the student.

Finally, in designing course activities, human sexuality instructors should realize that at some point, they may have to defend these activities to their colleagues, the department chair, the administration, or potentially even students' parents. It is essentially impossible to teach human sexuality without offending someone at some point (Herold, 1997), and when students are offended, they may pursue higher channels for complaints. Human sexuality instructors, especially untenured ones, must consider the local political and academic climate (Ellingson, Tebbe, Van Haitsma, & Laumann, 2001; Rust, 1994). Consulting with colleagues prior to presenting sensitive material provides feedback and other perspectives regarding the appropriateness of the material. Moreover, even if not necessary, obtaining the chair's approval of sensitive materials provides protection for the instructor by giving the chair prior knowledge and creating a buffer zone of protection and accountability. Teaching human sexuality is both challenging and rewarding, but instructors need to take steps to protect both students and themselves.

REFERENCES

Alan Guttmacher Institute. (1999). Facts in brief: Teen sex and pregnancy. Retrieved July 22, 2004, from www.agi-usa.org/pubs/fb_teen_sex.html

Altemeyer, B. (1996). *The authoritarian specter*. Cambridge, MA: Havard University Press.

Atwater, L. (1987). The anonymous essay as symbolic interaction between sexuality professor and student. *Teaching Sociology, 15,* 250–6.

Baber, K. M., & Murray, C. I. (2001). A postmodern feminist approach to teaching human sexuality. *Family Relations, 50,* 23–33.

Barbour, J. R. (1989). Teaching a course in human relationships and sexuality: A model for personalizing large group instruction. *Family Relations, 38,* 142–8.

Brooke, C. P. (1999). Feelings from the back row: Negotiating sensitive issues in large classes. *New Directions for Teaching and Learning, 77,* 23–33.

Budesheim, T. L., & Lundquist, A. R. (1999). Consider the opposite: Opening minds through in-class debates on course-related controversies. *Teaching of Psychology, 26,* 106–10.

Cotten, A. A. (2003). The impact of a human sexuality college course according to gender: Comparisons of the 1970's and the 1990's. *Sex Education, 3 (3),* 271–80.

Craig, R. L. (1985). Human sexuality education: The long term effects of a college level human sexuality course on student sexual anxiety. Unpublished doctoral dissertation, University of South Dakota.

DeLamater, J., Hyde, J. S., & Allgeier, E. R. (1994). Teaching human sexuality: Personalizing the impersonal lecture. *Teaching Sociology, 22,* 309–18.

Dixon-Woods, M., Regan, J., Robertson, N., Young, B., Cordle, C., & Tobin, M. (2002). Teaching and learning about human sexuality in undergraduate medical education. *Medical Education, 36,* 432–41.

Edwards, V. J., Holden, G. W., Felitti, V. J., & Anda, R. F. (2003). Relationship between multiple form of childhood maltreatment and adult mental health in community respondents: Results from the Adverse Childhood Experiences survey. *American Journal of Psychiatry, 160,* 1453–60.

Ellingson, S., Tebbe, N., Van Haitsma, M., & Laumann, E. O. (2001). Religion and the politics of sexuality. *Journal of Contemporary Ethnography, 30,* 3–55.

Finken, L. L. (2002). The impact of a human sexuality course on anti-gay prejudice: The challenge of reaching male students. *Journal of Psychology and Human Sexuality, 14,* 37–46.

Finken, L. L. (2003). The complexity of student responses to in-class debates in a human sexuality course. *Teaching of Psychology, 30,* 263–5.

Fischer, G. J. (1986). College student attitudes toward forcible date rape: Changes after taking a human sexuality course. *Journal of Sex Education and Therapy, 12,* 42–6.

Galway, M. A. (1998). Attitudes and moral development during a college course on human sexuality (Doctoral dissertation, Virginia Polytechnic Institute and State University, 2003). *Dissertation Abstracts International, 63 (11-A),* 3837.

Garcia, K. (1997). Sex, tolerance and academic freedom. *Community College Week, 9 (20),* 2–3.

Herold, E. S. (1997). Controversies in sexual courses at colleges and universities in the 1990's. *Journal of Psychology and Human Sexuality, 9,* 71–86.

KU report backs Dailey's methods. (2003). *Contemporary Sexuality, 37 (6),* 7–8.

Laumann, E., Gagnon, J., Michael, R., & Michaels, S. (1994). *The social organization of sexuality: Sexual practices in the United States*. Chicago: University of Chicago Press.

Leiblum, S. R. (2001). An established medical school human sexuality curriculum: Description and evaluation. *Sexual Relationship Therapy, 16*, 59–70.

Maddock, J. W. (1997). Sexuality education: A history lesson. *The Journal of Psychology and Human Sexuality, 9*, 1–22.

Petersen, C. J. (1997). Developing objectives for an undergraduate human sexuality course. *The Journal of Psychology and Human Sexuality, 9*, 23–35.

Republicans oppose funds for U-Wisc. doctoral sexuality program. (2002). *Contemporary Sexuality, 36 (12)*, 8.

Rombeck, T. (2003, Dec. 19). Regents adopt policy on sex classes. *Lawrence Journal-World*. Retrieved Aug. 17, 2004, from www.ljworld.com/section/kusexclass/story/155533

Rust, P. C. (1994). Designing a course on sexuality: Issues, problems, and parameters. *Critical Sociology, 20*, 155–68.

Simoni, J. M. (1996). Confronting heterosexism in the teaching of psychology. *Teaching of Psychology, 23*, 220–6.

US Department of Justice. (2003, Dec. 18). Criminal victimization in the United States. Retrieved July 15, 2004, from Bureau of Justice Statistics: www.ojp.usdoj.gov/bjs/abstract/cvus/age775.htm

Walker, L. (2003, July 22). College classes on human sexuality face heightened scrutiny. *The Christian Science Monitor*. Retrieved June 16, 2004, from www.csmonitor.com

35

Psychology of Gender and Related Courses

Ψ

Margaret A. Lloyd
Georgia Southern University

This chapter will address issues relevant to the teaching of Psychology of Gender and related courses such as the Psychology of Women and the Psychology of Gender Roles. Although I have not taught the Psychology of Men course, my sense is that much of this discussion is also relevant to that course. My comments will center on instructional issues that cut across the different courses.

Opportunities Associated with Teaching Gender Courses

Developing Critical Thinking

Gender courses are particularly suited to teaching critical thinking. Becoming aware of the many forms of androcentrism (the assumption that the male is the norm) enables students to see their experiences and the world from a different perspective. Learning about gender practices in other cultures is another way that students can become aware of perspectives different from their own. Although it is important that students appreciate that there are different ways to view behavior and experience, the more important discovery is for them to appreciate that the cognitive "glasses" – assumptions and beliefs – everyone wears influence how they interpret their experiences and events in the world. This discovery is especially important when individuals are unaware that they are "wearing glasses."

Students also learn that psychological research is not value-neutral and that it is influenced by particular historical and social currents. They become familiar with the strengths and limitations of quantitative and qualitative research methods and understand that many issues are complex and do not lend themselves to clear-cut answers.

Developing Awareness of Gender in Everyday Life

Students enroll in gender courses because such courses address issues of practical and personal significance to them: relationships, sexuality, and work, among others. Because there is much ignorance and misinformation on these important topics, gender courses can play an important role in separating myths from realities. The discovery of personally relevant information and the exposure to nontraditional viewpoints can be liberating for students. These experiences can also be frustrating, especially when students are confronted with findings and viewpoints that contradict ego-involved attitudes.

Gender courses can sensitize students to the role of power and privilege in societies and to various social inequalities (sexism, classism, ethnocentrism, racism, heterosexism, etc.) and their effects. It is especially eye-opening when students discover that the values of dominant societal groups do not actually constitute values, but rather reflect "the way things are supposed to be."

What students learn about gender and its role in their lives can empower them to choose the kind of human beings they want to be rather than to accept, mindlessly, prescribed gender-role expectations. Some students may become involved in social justice activities as an extension of course-engendered insights.

Creating and Maintaining a Safe Classroom Environment

Certain issues discussed in gender classes can trigger strong negative emotions that can cause some students to disengage from the class. To prevent students' emotional withdrawal, instructors may want to set some ground rules for classroom discussion that support a safe classroom environment. I strongly suggest that instructors include such ground rules in their syllabi and discuss them on the first day of class. Introducing ground rules at the beginning of a course sets a positive tone early on and may prevent a discussion "fiasco" from occurring. It is also advisable that you state that you will abide by these rules and will try to model appropriate behavior.

In my gender courses, I use the following ground rules:

1. Refrain from sharing highly personal information.
2. If you have spoken once, let someone else speak before you talk again.
3. You have the right not to share your thoughts, feelings, or beliefs on a particular topic if you prefer.
4. Do not identify by name the personal experiences or beliefs revealed by other members of this class to anyone outside of class.
5. Although I hope this course will cause you to question your beliefs and will help you develop and articulate thoughtful rationales for them, there is no reward and no penalty for having particular beliefs.
6. Try to understand what individuals believe and why they think the way they do rather than automatically dismissing perspectives that are different from yours.

Margaret A. Lloyd

Some Challenges Associated
with Teaching Gender Courses

In addition to the usual pitfalls that confront teachers in any course (Lowman, 1995; McKeachie, 2002), some unique challenges arise in gender courses. In my experience, one stands out: dealing with the strong negative emotions that the course content can engender.

Erroneous Assumptions about Course Content and Format

Students come to gender courses with a great deal of misinformation, and they are usually unaware that much of what they know is unsupported personal opinion. Because they are typically unaware of the large body of empirical research on gender issues, students may assume that the course will consist of hashing out the "truth" through class debates. Others may be looking for an audience to validate their strongly held, but often ill-informed, views and emotions.

To correct these misimpressions, it is helpful to describe the content and format of the course on the first day of class. This tactic can head off students' frustrations grounded in false expectations about the course, and enlists their positive participation from the start. This information should also appear in the syllabus. It is helpful to let students know early on that there is an abundant research literature on gender and to stress that, as a science, psychology relies on research findings to understand issues (rather than on religious texts, for example).

Controversial Topics

Most gender courses include controversial topics such as sexual orientation and reproductive issues. Covering such issues may catch some students off-guard. It is helpful to forewarn students on the first day of class that you will cover these topics in case any students want to drop the course.

Over the course of the term, most students confront the realization that research contradicts a strongly held viewpoint. It is important that students have positive experiences in the classroom so that they will stay engaged with the material. Thus, you may want to tell them that you have also struggled with some of these issues, thereby "normalizing" confusion and uncertainty. For additional suggestions on facilitating effective discussions, see chapters 2, 3, and 6 in Lowman (1995). For a thoughtful exploration of the role of values in teaching, see chapter 25 in McKeachie (2002).

Maintaining Students' Interest in the Course

Students who enroll in gender courses are almost always interested in the material. Thus, initially, the instructor does not have to work hard to engage them in the course.

Unfortunately, students can also disengage from the course relatively easily if they perceive the instructor to be unfair, biased, or unsupportive. Because gender courses provide numerous opportunities for students to develop such perceptions, it is essential that instructors capture and maintain students' enthusiasm. One way to keep students involved is to design your course so that it includes graded components (papers, projects, classroom presentations) that harness their interests and get them actively involved in course material. Another way to keep students engaged is to use some informal opportunities for participation (for credit or not) throughout the course. These opportunities include in-class exercises and activities, class speakers, brief discussions of course-relevant current events, and outside events (relevant speakers and cultural events). Most gender textbooks or their ancillaries include a variety of interesting suggestions to involve students in the course material.

Instructors also need to address students' concerns about being graded down for expressing points of view that differ from the instructor's. I handle this issue by informing students early on that I am a feminist and that I teach the course from a feminist perspective. (Before I do that, I use an in-class exercise to help students understand the definition of the term and what it means and does not mean.) I explain that I am informing them of my perspective so that they will have a context from which to interpret my comments. I also assert that students need not become feminists, but that they need to be familiar with feminist perspectives and tools of analysis. To help them understand this idea, I make an analogy with a course in theories of personality. In that course, students need not embrace a particular theory of personality, but they should be knowledgeable about the key aspects of the different theories as well as their research methods. No doubt, students take my assurances of fairness with a grain of salt until they have the opportunity to observe my behavior in class and my grading of their work.

Displaced Anger

When students encounter information that is at odds with their own strongly held views, they understandably become upset. The upside of this reaction is that it means that students are engaged with the course. The downside is that when students get upset about course content, they may displace their anger onto the instructor (the "kill the messenger" phenomenon). Because controversial issues are most likely to trigger this phenomenon, it is helpful if the instructor does not introduce all such topics. Videotapes, readings, campus speakers, and community experts can be useful in this regard.

Another way to diffuse students' frustration and anger is to distribute feedback sheets after the first two (or more) exams. This strategy allows students to share, anonymously, their thoughts and feelings about the course. If students indicate that they are upset about something, you may be able to address this issue in class.

Some men who enroll in Psychology of Women and Psychology of Gender courses may become defensive when the class discusses discrimination against women. Over time, they can become resentful and may disengage from the course. To keep them involved, instructors can remind the class that they are not directing these statements at males as individuals and encourage the males in the class not to take them personally. It is important for men to feel that the instructor (especially if it is a woman) can empathize with them.

Course-Triggered Psychological Concerns

Some students in gender courses are gay or are struggling with their sexual orientation. Some are survivors of rape, sexual abuse, or sexual harassment, or have eating disorders. Many of these students enroll in a gender course to obtain information about these issues. Nonetheless, learning about them may trigger painful feelings and memories in some. Thus, it is helpful for instructors to announce that they are available to talk with students who have concerns about the course material or course-related personal issues (but not to provide counseling), and will be happy to make referrals to qualified professionals.

—————— Conclusion ——————

Teaching gender courses can be highly gratifying because instructors often observe that students improve their critical-thinking skills and discover important insights about gender. These courses also present unique challenges for instructors. Being aware of these challenges and knowing how to deal with them is essential to the effective teaching of gender courses.

REFERENCES

Lowman, J. (1995). *Mastering the techniques of teaching* (2nd ed.). San Francisco: Jossey-Bass.
McKeachie, W. J. (2002). *McKeachie's teaching tips: Strategies, research, and theory for college and university teachers* (11th ed.). Boston: Houghton Mifflin.

36

Teaching the Psychology of Religion: Teaching for Today's World

Ψ

Maureen P. Hester & Raymond F. Paloutzian

Holy Names University & Westmont College

Moving into the twenty-first century, the psychology of religion emerges as a strong scientific enterprise with a substantial base of theory and data that relate to all of the core topics in the parent discipline (Paloutzian & Park, 2005). Its development is evident by the vast array of books, journals, special issues of journals, and meetings devoted to it (Emmons & Paloutzian, 2003). Between the 1970s and the 1990s there was a 10 percent increase in departments offering the course (Hester & Lampert, 2000). Indeed, since the tragic events of 9/11 in which destruction and killing for political and cultural goals was justified on religious grounds, and in light of the myriad good deeds done in its name, the need for the psychology of religion as part of the menu of courses available to students is clear.

Several journals also have emerged that are rich resources for teaching psychology of religion: *The International Journal for the Psychology of Religion*; *Journal for the Scientific Study of Religion*; *Review of Religious Research*; *Journal of Psychology and Theology*; *Journal of Psychology and Christianity*; *Mental Health, Religion, and Culture*; and *Research in the Social Scientific Study of Religion*. In the last quarter century, the amount of published research has grown exponentially (Emmons & Paloutzian, 2003). In order to get a glimpse of this trend, we searched for the subject keywords *religion* and *spirituality* in the PsycINFO database for the 5-year periods 1979–83 and 1999–2003, a gap of 20 years. The number of hits for *religion* increased from 195 to 1,094 over this time period. The number of hits for *spirituality* increased from 0 to 1,796. These findings reflect a growing and expansive interest in these areas. Finally, in addition to many websites that reflect religiousness in one way or another, new websites are devoted specifically to the psychology of religion. Thus, with the number of resources available, the time is ripe for a psychology of religion course to be incorporated into a well-rounded psychology curriculum.

When preparing to teach a psychology of religion course, the essential points to consider include the orientation of the course, course design, and assignments and assessments. We briefly address each of these topics.

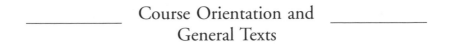

Course Orientation and General Texts

Major considerations that determine what orientation a course may take are the interests of the instructor and the nature of the institution and student population. If you teach a psychology of religion course, do it your way. Link it to your own interests. Whether they are social, developmental, personality, clinical, cognitive, or neuroscientific, research and reference material are available.

Examine the standard textbooks (Batson, Shoenrade, & Ventis, 1993; Beit-Hallahmi & Argyle, 1997; Paloutzian, 1996; Pargament, 1997; Spilka, Hood, Hunsberger, & Gorsuch, 2003; Wulff, 1997). Becoming familiar with them will enhance the resources you can bring to the classroom. Other compilations of research are invaluable, such as Paloutzian and Park's comprehensive *Handbook of the Psychology of Religion and Spirituality* (2005), which includes an in-depth treatment of all major topics in the field.

Comparing and contrasting the two chapters on the psychology of religion published in the *Annual Review of Psychology* will also be helpful in gaining a sense of history as well as learning what is new in the field. Gorsuch (1988) reviewed the years shortly following the establishment of APA Division 36, Psychology of Religion (Jan. 1, 1976), whereas Emmons and Paloutzian (2003) captured the field at the beginning of the twenty-first century.

Course Resources and Design

The orientation of your psychology of religion course is integrally related to the way you design it. You can aim for a course with a basic science flavor, a focus on the development of religion, a clinical orientation to help students examine both the pathological and healthy sides of religion, a course based in personality theory and research to help students understand how various theories interpret religion, and an approach centered around the problem of how to measure aspects of religion and spirituality.

Scientific

Essential to a basic science course are the topics of history and measurement. Good summaries of the field's history can be found in Hester (2002), Paloutzian (1996), and Wulff (1997). Teachers still assign parts of James (1902) and Freud (1927). Hill and

Hood (1999) provide a landmark compendium of measures of religiousness and spirituality, each with a helpful review, key citations, and a presentation of the instrument. The newest findings in neuropsychological explorations of religion and religious experience can be found in Newberg and Newberg (2005). Kirkpatrick's (2005a, 2005b) evolutionary approach promises to put psychology of religion firmly in the orbit of the other life sciences.

Religious Experience

One of the major topics in the field is religious experience, for example, mysticism, meditation, and spiritual consciousness. Several sources provide ample coverage of religious experience. Spilka et al. (2003) devote two chapters to religious experience and mysticism. Hood, Hill, and Williamson (2005) present new material on mystical, spiritual, and religious experience, and Spilka (in press) covers the research on religious practice and prayer. Research on forgiveness (McCullough, Bono, & Root, in press; McCullough & Worthington, 1999) enriches these topics by relating them to other facets of behavior, such as interpersonal relations.

Developmental

Designing a course with a strong developmental theme is useful both for its relation to students' lives and having comprehensive resources available. For example, Spilka et al. (2003) devote three chapters to the developmental process that are inclusive and helpful. The Paloutzian and Park (2005) *Handbook* contains four chapters that comprehensively examine research on religion and spirituality in children, adolescents, and adults through old age and dying. Sinnott (2001–2) summarizes current research on religion and adult development. Kirkpatrick (2005) presents a landmark contribution employing attachment processes at the root of relationships to God. Combined, these materials provide a rich knowledge-base that students find applicable to their own development.

Personality

Two items are particularly valuable if you wish to design a course with an emphasis on personality. Wulff (1997) explained classical and contemporary theories of psychology of religion, and a special issue of the *Journal of Personality* (Emmons & McCullough, 1999) contains articles by leading experts on topics such as whether spirituality is a sixth factor of personality (extending the 5-factor model), virtues and self-control, conversion and personality change, attachment theory, genetics and religiousness, etc. Classics by James (1902) and Freud (1927) stimulate uninhibited discussion that is enhanced by Rizzuto's (1979) object-relations theory and Corveleyn and Luyten's (2005) summary of international empirical psychodynamic research.

Social

Designing a course for a social-psychological orientation includes an emphasis on attitudes, behaviors, and social-cognitive processes inherent in religiousness. For example, you can teach students about the relation between religion and prejudice by having them study how intrinsic and extrinsic religious motivations affect people's attitudes and behavior toward people of other races and ethnic groups (Allport & Ross, 1967; see e.g., Paloutzian, 1996; Spilka et al., 2003). Altemeyer and Hunsberger (in press) present important research on fundamentalism and right-wing authoritarianism that brings attitude research to a new level of sophistication. Fundamentalism receives an even fuller treatment by Hood et al. (2005), who provide vivid accounts of snake-handling, Amish, Islamic, and Pentecostal fundamentalist groups. Synthesizing ideas from clinical and social psychology, the concept of religion as a meaning system (Paloutzian & Park, 2005; Park, 2005; Silberman, in press a) provides an integrative language and framework for discussing topics that range from basic processes to terrorism (Silberman, 2005).

Clinical

A course designed with a clinical theme can be almost magnetically interesting by careful use of classical writings such as James's (1902) descriptions of the depressive behavior of St. Augustine and John Bunyan. Textbook summaries of the recent work on the relation between religion and clinical and health variables are readily available in textbooks on relgion. In addition, Shafranske (1996) edited a comprehensive book linking religion and clinical practice. Pargament's (1997) landmark integration of research on religion and coping updated by his recent chapter (Pargament, Ano, & Wachholtz, 2005), are "musts" for any psychology of religion course designed with a clinical emphasis. Other topics also offer promise: forgiveness (McCullough & Worthington Jr., 1999; McCullough et al., 2005), emotions (Emmons, 1999; 2005) and health (Koenig, 1998; Mills, 2002; Oman & Thoresen, 2005). After designing the course, we turn to assignments and assessments.

———— Assignments and Assessments ————

Assignments can include journals, research options, visiting another religious tradition, and exams. Students can take a series of religious measures (Hill & Hood, 1999) and assess their own scores. They can also reflect on their own religious development or answer questions about change over the lifespan or the role of crisis in religious development. Learning interviewing techniques provides opportunities for students to question people of all ages on their religious experience or development. Pargament (1997), whose interest is in religion and coping, prepares students carefully, giving detailed instructions for interviewing people in sensitive situations (e.g., in a hospital waiting room).

When students are asked to visit a religious tradition other than their own, two possible assignments emerge. Using the terms of Glock and Stark's (1965) five dimensions of religion (belief, knowledge, practice, feeling, and effects), students can write a short reflection page. For the same assignment, you can offer a two-part group project. After deciding which religious groups to visit (students must visit three or four different communities per group), students each write a paper focusing on the comparative analysis of the function of the two religious groups with questions provided (leadership, objectives of the service, religious education program, etc.). Their team project is to share their varied experiences and to develop a possible research design to investigate specific differences among different religions.

Many research challenges are possible. For example, B. Spilka (personal communication, 2004) stated the following research idea to his students: "I would like to propose a question that was asked around 1910 but never researched. Does the way one prays imply certain god images held by the prayers?" Then he explains that in order to answer this question, they need the following resources: (a) a theory – what kind of God images ought to lead to what kinds of prayers?; (b) a method – it is necessary to measure God images and forms of prayer; (c) a tool – for example, they should devise a questionnaire; (d) data – collect it, analyze it, and write a report. If the project yields positive findings, the students who conducted it may submit this research for presentation at a professional psychological convention. Students who conduct a research project such as this one report that it integrates their learning of theory, methods, and published findings around a new idea.

Final Thoughts

Because the psychology of religion is not a traditional course in the curriculum, it offers great possibilities for both orientation and assignments. In these times of intense international conflict, much of it based on religious differences, the psychology of religion offers a place to become informed, and to discuss and widen people's perception of the influence of religion. If there ever was a time when this course was needed in the psychology curriculum, it is now.

REFERENCES

Allport, G. W., & Ross, J. M. (1967). Personal religious orientation and prejudice. *Journal of Personality and Social Psychology, 5*, 432–43.

Altemeyer, B., & Hunsberger, B. (2005). Fundamentalism and authoritarianism. In R. F. Paloutzian & C. L. Park (eds.), *Handbook of the psychology of religion and spirituality.* New York: Guilford Press.

Batson, C. D., Scheonrade, P., & Ventis, W. L. (1993). *Religion and the individual: A social psychological perspective.* Oxford: Oxford University Press.

Beit-Hallahmi, B., & Argyle, M. (1997). *The psychology of religious behaviour, belief and experience.* London/New York: Routledge.

Corveleyn, J., & Luyten, P. (in press). Psychodynamic psychologies and religion: Past, present, and future. In R. F. Paloutzian & C. L. Park (eds.), *Handbook of the psychology of religion and spirituality.* New York: Guilford Press.

Emmons, R. A. (1999). *The psychology of ultimate concerns.* New York: Guilford.

Emmons, R. A. (2005). Emotion and religion. In R. F. Paloutzian & C. L. Park (eds.), *Handbook of the psychology of religion and spirituality.* New York: Guilford Press.

Emmons, R. A., & McCullough, M. E. (1999). Religion in the psychology of personality. *Journal of Personality, 67* (Special issue.)

Emmons, R. A., & Paloutzian, R. (2003). The psychology of religion. *Annual Review of Psychology, 54,* 377–402.

Freud, S. (1927/1961). *The future of an illusion* (J. Strachey, trans.). New York: Norton. (Originally published, 1927.)

Glock, C. Y., & Stark, R. (1965). *Religion and society in tension.* Chicago: Rand McNally.

Gorsuch, R. L. (1988). Psychology of religion. *Annual Review of Psychology, 39,* 201–21.

Hester, M. P. (2002). Psychology of religion: Then and now. In S. F. Davis & W. Buskist (eds.), *The teaching of psychology: Essays in honor of Wilbert J. McKeachie and Charles L. Brewer* (pp. 459–70). Mahwah, NJ: Erlbaum.

Hester, M. P., & Lampert, M. D. (2000, May). *Psychology of religion in the academic curriculum: Current status.* Poster session presented at the annual meeting of the Western Psychological Association, Portland, OR.

Hill, P. C., & Hood Jr., R. W. (1999). *Measures of religiosity.* Birmingham, AL: Religious Education Press.

Hood Jr., R. W., Hill. P. C., & Williamson, W. P. (2005). *The psychology of religious fundamentalism: An intratextual model.* New York: Guilford Press.

James, W. (1902/1958). *The varieties of religious experience.* New York: Longmans. (Mentor ed., New American Library, 1958.)

Kirkpatrick, L. A. (2005a). *Attachment, evolution, and the psychology of religion.* New York: Guilford Press.

Kirkpatrick, L. A. (2005b). Evolutionary psychology: An emerging new foundation for the psychology of religion. In R. F. Paloutzian & C. L. Park (eds.), *Handbook of the psychology of religion and spirituality.* New York: Guilford Press.

Koenig, H. G. (ed.) (1998). *Handbook of religion and mental health.* New York: Academic Press.

McCullough, M. E., Bono, G., & Root, L. M. (2005). Religion and forgiveness. In R. F. Paloutzian & C. L. Park (eds.), *Handbook of the psychology of religion and spirituality.* New York: Guilford Press.

McCullough, M. E., & Worthington Jr., E. L. (1999). Religion and the forgiving personality. *Journal of Personality, 67,* 1141–64.

Mills, P. J. (2002). Spirituality, religiousness, and health [Special issue]. *Annals of behavioral medicine, 24 (1).*

Newberg, A. B., & Newberg, S. K. (2005). The neuropsychology of religious and spiritual experience. In R. F. Paloutzian & C. L. Park (eds.), *Handbook of the psychology of religion and spirituality.* New York: Guilford Press.

Oman, D., & Thoresen, C. E. (2005). Religion and spirituality: Do they influence health? In R. F. Paloutzian & C. L. Park (eds.), *Handbook of the psychology of religion and spirituality.* New York: Guilford Press.

Paloutzian, R. F. (1996). *Invitation to the psychology of religion* (2nd ed.). Boston: Allyn and Bacon.

Paloutzian, R. F., & Park, C. L. (eds.) (2005). *Handbook of the psychology of religion and spirituality.* New York: Guilford Press.

Pargament, K. I. (1997). *The psychology of religion and coping.* New York: Guilford Press.

Pargament, K. I., Ano, G. G., & Wachholtz, A. B. (2005). The religious dimension of coping: Advances in theory, research, and practice. In R. F. Paloutzian & C. L. Park (eds.), *Handbook of the psychology of religion and spirituality.* New York: Guilford Press.

Park, C. L. (2005). Religion and meaning. In R. F. Paloutzian & C. L. Park (eds.), *Handbook of the psychology of religion and spirituality*. New York: Guilford Press.

Rizzuto, A.-M. (1979). *The birth of the living God: A psychoanalytic study*. Chicago: University of Chicago Press.

Shafranske, E. P. (ed.) (1996). *Religion and the clinical practice of psychology*. Washington, DC: American Psychological Association.

Silberman, I. (in press a). Religion as a meaning system: Implications for the new millennium. *Journal of Social Issues* (Special issue), *61 (4)*.

Silberman, I. (2005). Religious violence, terrorism, and peace: A meaning system analysis. In R. F. Paloutzian & C. L. Park (eds.), *Handbook of the psychology of religion and spirituality*. New York: Guilford Press.

Sinnott, J. D. (ed.) (2001–2). Spirituality and adult development, Parts I, II, and III. *Journal of Adult Development, 8 (4), 9 (1), & 9 (2)* (Special issues).

Spilka, B. (2005). Religious practice, ritual and prayer. In R. F. Paloutzian & C. L. Park (eds.), *Handbook of the psychology of religion and spirituality*. New York: Guilford Press.

Spilka, B., Hood Jr., R. W., Hunsberger, B., & Gorsuch, R. (2003). *The psychology of religion. An empirical approach* (3rd ed.). New York/London: The Guilford Press.

Wulff, D. M. (1997). *Psychology of religion: Classic and contemporary* (2nd ed.). New York: Wiley.

37

Drugs and Behavior

Ψ

Scott A. Bailey
Texas Lutheran University

Recreational and therapeutic drugs are familiar to many students either as a result of direct personal experience or through people they know. Students enroll in the drugs and behavior (D&B) course because the material is relevant in their lives. Having the genuine interest of students affords the professor real advantages.

The D&B course provides numerous opportunities for critical thinking. Indeed, there is so much misinformation about drugs in the popular press and on the internet that I sometimes assign students to collect it to contrast with that presented in the textbook. This activity leads to engaging questions and discussions concerning the origins of misleading and inaccurate information.

An interesting feature of the content of the D&B course is that it is ever-changing, lending the professor opportunities to develop perspective and understanding with the students on topics such as drug laws, research findings, and the development of new therapeutic agents. The downside to such rapid growth in course material is that you can easily feel daunted. Developing class presentations from the variety of textbooks available for the course, each of which has significant strengths and weaknesses, is one way to minimize these concerns. Being armed with the *Physician's Desk Reference*, or access to online resources such as the one provided by RxList Inc. (2004) is helpful when students query about drugs unfamiliar to the professor.

At the Outset of the Course

I find it useful to get the students' attention with a couple of statements. My opening statement to them is often akin to:

Greetings, and welcome to the first day of what promises to be an outstanding semester. Before we review the course syllabus and discuss the nuts and bolts of this course, I need to

announce that for budgetary reasons, it has become necessary to combine our lab component with that for the human sexuality course.

After breaking the ice with this type of statement, I make a much more serious statement
about the course:

> Okay. Although there is not a laboratory for it, my experience with this course suggests that
> we will likely engage in some lively conversations. Let me be clear from the outset that what
> is said in this room must remain here. Students in this class sometimes share personal
> experiences, including those that might cause them to be viewed negatively by some
> members of the campus community or elsewhere. If people do not feel they can share their
> experiences and perspectives without risking judgment by others, we have failed. In short,
> we stand to benefit a tremendous amount from an atmosphere of openness in this class,
> and I implore each of you to be both open to and protective of the comments your
> colleagues share. Mutual respect is perhaps more important in this class than in any other
> we offer.

In my experience, this set of comments contributes to the success of the course. The
first comment usually draws laughter. By observing students' reactions to this comment,
you can begin to determine who in the class may be disturbed by comments that are
likely to be shared in the class. I prefer strongly that I learn about student sensitivity as
a result of a joke from me versus when a student shares something real. It is important
that the students are aware of the disparate views and life experiences that are repre-
sented in the room, and that such variety creates the need for open-mindedness.

The humor in the first comment lends to rapport that is particularly important when
teaching the D&B course. The second comment shows that my sense of humor is
balanced by my very serious view on mutual respect.

The range of student experiences with and perspectives on drugs and related issues is
surprisingly wide. It sometimes amazes me that students arrive at college without having
been exposed in some fashion to the drugs and concepts that we discuss in the class. On
the other hand, some students have experienced or witnessed drug use of such a nature
and extent that it is remarkable they are in college. By creating an atmosphere of respect
and promoting open-mindedness, it becomes possible for students across this range to
benefit from one another.

I have taught the D&B course at large, state institutions and at a small, church-related
institution, and found each to have students from all ranges of experience and perspective. You must work to ensure that everyone considers everyone else's view, no matter
how naive or reflecting of experience it may be.

Finally, at the outset of the course I make it clear that the purpose of the course is not
to persuade, but to inform. The course content includes substances that are illegal for
some or all of the population in some or all countries, and some students develop their
perspectives as a function of the legal status of drugs. I describe the law as a set of rules,
formed through political processes, that is subject to change over time. The course, then,
need not dwell on legal matters. Instead, we can consider legal issues occasionally, while
lending most of our attention to the issues more central to psychology.

———————— Favorite Assignments ————————

Students report on their use of information from the course in conversations with family and friends, when considering reports in the news, and in various other facets of their lives. Indeed, students have told me that their roommates sometimes borrow their textbooks merely because they want to learn about the topic. Apparently merely owning the course textbook is sufficient to catalyze discussions of course-relevant material.

It is easy to capitalize on the fact that the course is relevant in so many facets of students' lives. One way to accomplish this objective is through assignments, some of which students appreciate long after the course is over. Some of my favorites include:

Abstinence Project

This assignment always shows up in course evaluations as one of the students' favorites. On the first day of class I trick them into telling me what their favorite drug is when they are providing their contact information and some demographic data. Note that if the favorite drug is therapeutic in nature, it is not the target for this assignment (I actually had a student ask me once whether she needed to give up insulin for the assignment).

The assignment is to abstain from use of one's favorite recreational drug for 28 days – the length of many compulsory and intensive treatment programs. For many students, caffeine and nicotine are the drugs of choice. Other students, of course, identify alcohol. Some students, however, indicate illicit substances, which might potentially create a dilemma for the professor and anyone with whom these students speak. Having established that any information shared in the class is to be held in confidence obliges the faculty member and all members of the class to act accordingly.

During the 28 days, each student is to refrain from telling anyone else why he or she has determined not to use the drug. In order that the shift in drug use appears attributable to the students' choices rather than an assignment, everyone in the class is asked not to share with anyone that an assignment calls for the discontinued use of a drug. Throughout the abstinence period, the students monitor and record their awareness of thoughts about the drug, comments from others about their cessation of use of the drug, exposure to various forms of news and media that address the drug, and so on, in a journal. The journal, in turn, is used as a springboard for writing a summary report of the experience.

Grades on this assignment are not based on whether students are successful at abstaining from their favorite drug for the designated period, but on how well students attend to and describe their experiences. Interestingly, some students choose to start over if they "fall off of the wagon."

Some students will expect the professor to have "walked the walk" prior to requiring them to discontinue use of a substance. It may be advisable to do the assignment yourself either in advance of requiring it, or along with your students.

Book Assignment

I ask students to choose any fiction or nonfiction book that they have not read that contains at least some material related to drugs – recreational or therapeutic, licit or illicit. The assignment is to critique the book's representation of the drug or a related issue. The students are to treat the course textbook as accurate in order to have information with which to compare drug and related information as portrayed in the book.

Having a class full of students with the same charge may create a situation in which students are tempted to borrow from one another. Notwithstanding the ease with which students can cheat on this assignment, comments from students about it suggest that it is worth administering. Indeed, many students have expressed appreciation for the opportunity to read a book of their choosing, and indicate that this assignment is the closest thing to reading for pleasure that they did during the semester.

Commercial

Virtually all students have seen television commercials for therapeutic drugs. Given the laws that require indicating potential side-effects of such drugs, it is striking that many such commercials have more cautionary information than information to recommend using the substance at hand.

Following this model, I have students develop one-minute commercials for recreational substances. They are to portray use of the drug as desirable, and the warning portion of the message is to represent all relevant side-effects, counterindications, and so forth. These "commercials" are often amusing ways to introduce each given family of drugs during the course.

—— Conclusion ——

The D&B course is my favorite course to teach. It offers enormous possibilities for fostering critical thinking. It is relevant to the lives of everyone in ways that are hard to determine – could convenience stores, newspapers, magazines, and the like exist without the revenue that comes from drug marketing and sales?

For psychologists, the downside to teaching this class is that it is hard to find an appropriate textbook. The available books for this course include sociocultural (e.g., Ray & Ksir, 2004) and biosystems-based (e.g., Julien, 2005) approaches. Although behavioral factors are addressed in some books (e.g., Maisto, Galizo, & Connors, 2004; McKim, 2003), it is difficult to find books that address this material as well as they cover, say, drug pharmacodynamics. By drawing on several resources, however, you can offer a course that is appropriate for psychology students. Doing so is to offer a course that is stimulating for the students and professor alike.

REFERENCES

Drug information, health information and monographs provided by RxList Inc. (2004). Retrieved Nov. 14, 2004, from www.rxlist.com

Julien, R. M. (2005). *A primer of drug action: A concise, nontechnical guide to the actions, uses, and side effects of psychoactive drugs* (10th ed.). New York: Worth.

Maisto, S. A., Galizo, M., & Connors, G. J. (2004). *Drug use and abuse* (4th ed.). Ft. Worth, TX: Harcourt Brace.

McKim, W. A. (2003). *Drugs and behavior: An introduction to behavioral pharmacology* (5th ed.). Upper Saddle River, NJ: Prentice Hall.

Physician's Desk Reference. (2003). Montvale, NJ: Thomson Healthcare.

Ray, O., & Ksir, C. (2006). *Drugs, society, and human behavior* (10th ed.). Boston: McGraw Hill.

part VII

Ψ

Classroom Management Issues

This section features four chapters dealing with the delicate issue of teacher and student comportment. These chapters cover ethical issues in teaching, general rules of student classroom conduct, dealing with problem students, and academic honesty.

38
Ethical Teaching

Ψ

William Douglas Woody
University of Northern Colorado

Questions regarding the nature of ethical thought and behavior drive scholarly research programs in philosophy departments around the globe. Teachers of psychology face the daunting task of applying millennia of ethical inquiry to the practical daily questions that arise in the challenging environment of a college or university classroom. To aid psychologists in this endeavor, the American Psychological Association (APA) addresses teaching concerns in the most current ethics code (APA, 2002). This chapter follows current APA guidelines to clarify the ethical responsibilities of teachers and concludes with a discussion addressing the importance of explicitly teaching ethics during graduate education and an appeal for teachers of psychology to see their work in a larger ethical context.

Ethical Principles of Psychologists and Code of Conduct

The Ethical Principles of Psychologists and Code of Conduct (APA, 2002) begins with five ethical principles. The principles are not in themselves enforceable, but their role is to present the rationale for the code of conduct and to aid psychologists in resolving disputes that may fall outside those directly addressed in the code. These "aspirational" (APA, 2002, p. 1062) principles include (a) beneficence and nonmaleficence, (b) fidelity and responsibility, (c) integrity, (d) justice, and (e) respect for people's rights and dignity. The spirit of the principles drives the 10 sections of enforceable ethical standards. Only section 7 is devoted exclusively to "Education and Training" (APA, 2002, pp. 1068–9), but ideals related to activities of teaching exist throughout. These ideals embody teachers' ethical responsibilities for competence, fairness, appropriate relationships, informed consent, and confidentiality in the light of the principles and the standards.

Competence

For teachers, competence implies several criteria. Competence involves thorough, accurate, and current knowledge of the subject matter as well as adequate preparation for each day's class. In a national survey, more than 90 percent of instructors reported struggling with this requirement (Tabachnick, Keith-Spiegel, & Pope, 1991). Teachers face numerous daily obstacles to study and preparation, but despite these pressures, they must recognize their responsibilities to students and to the field, and must model appropriate scholarly behavior (Svinicki, 2002).

Competence in teaching goes beyond familiarity with the material and preparation for each day's class. Competence also involves teaching skill. Teachers must know and use teaching methods appropriate for class size, students' sophistication, demographic composition of the students, and department, university, and national requirements for the course. Teachers must include appropriate material and provide students with the skills necessary to complete the course and prepare for future courses (e.g., skills for literature searches, statistical analyses, or critical thinking). Beyond the codified elements of a course, teachers must present balanced perspectives, willingly state their own biases, and be aware of the inherently persuasive nature of teaching (Friedrich & Douglass, 1998). Concerns of ideological balance have recently moved to the forefront of popular discussions of the professoriate (e.g., American Association of University Professors, 2004; Klein, 2004; Martinez, 2004). Competence also involves fairly rewarding classroom assistants at the graduate or undergraduate level and not excessively delegating tasks to persons who do not have primary responsibility for the course. Finally, competence may include additional requirements for people who teach in certain areas. For example, applied teachers may need to have experience with the skills they teach, and those who teach ideologically challenging courses face particularly difficult tasks in avoiding bias (see chapters 31–7 in this volume).

Fairness

Fairness is paramount in teaching contexts, and teachers must maintain fairness in several ways. The APA code of conduct states that "psychologists do not engage in unfair discrimination based on age, gender, gender identity, race, ethnicity, culture, national origin, religion, sexual orientation, disability, socioeconomic status, or any basis proscribed by law" (APA, 2002, p. 1064). Instructors must avoid bias against or in favor of particular students, regardless of whether their biases reflect any of the factors listed above, a student's athletic or social affiliation, or the degree to which they like or dislike a particular student. Although non-academic evaluations of students likely remain unavoidable, teachers must separate academic evaluations from personal evaluations. For example, some professors grade students' work anonymously so that personal biases remain separate from students' identities and group memberships. Students (Keith-Spiegel, Tabachnick, & Allen, 1993) and teachers (Tabachnick et al., 1991) recognize fairness as central to the credibility of departments, universities, and the field.

Maintaining fairness presents additional challenges. For example, not all students speak academic English as a native language. Additionally, approximately 6 to 8 percent of freshmen at 4-year colleges and universities report disabilities, and increasing numbers of students come to the university with learning disabilities that may not be readily apparent (Henderson, 2001). Instructors must provide all students with fair opportunities to demonstrate their knowledge, and teachers often struggle to balance the testing or classroom needs of a student with a disability with the needs to be fair and rigorous to all students in a given course. Blindly equal treatment of all students does not guarantee a level playing field (Wittig, Perkins, Balogh, Whitley, & Keith-Spiegel, 1999). A student-centered approach may be necessary to fit course requirements and activities to the unique needs of individual students (Van Note Chism, 2001).

Fairness includes other considerations. For example, extra credit, if available, must appropriately fit the class material and be equally available to all students (Palladino, Hill, & Norcross, 1999). Similar issues emerge when teachers offer credit for participation in research. Psychology classes tempt researchers seeking access to large numbers of participants, and if instructors offer rewards for participation, they must arrange alternative means of earning credit. Additionally, professors must protect fairness by taking reasonable steps to prevent cheating (see chapter 41 this volume). Group projects may require methods to monitor individual effort so that each group member earns a grade that reflects his or her contributions. Fairness must extend to the teaching aspects of research as well. In a significant departure from earlier codes (see Smith, 2003), the new code (APA, 2002) mandates that "faculty advisers discuss publication credit with students as early as feasible and throughout the research and publication process" (APA, 2002, p. 1069) to maintain fairness in teacher–student collaborative research. Fundamentally, professors must strive to reward students' efforts, contributions, successes, and failures as evenly as possible.

Relationships

The code of conduct addresses numerous concerns in human relationships. The central idea, listed in the code of conduct as both a principle and as part of the code, is to do no harm (APA, 2002). First, the code of conduct forbids *quid pro quo* sexual harassment (i.e., when an individual's response to sexual advances affects his or her evaluation) as well as hostile environment sexual harassment (see US Equal Opportunity Employment Commission, 2004). Second, teachers and students have professional relationships. The power differential between professors and students or advisees precludes sexual relationships across these lines. Despite the obvious costs, such behavior remains too common historically (e.g., Buckley, 1994) as well as in contemporary academia (Cahn, 1986). Such behavior often severely impacts lives and destroys careers.

Nonsexual relationships can also pose problems (Keith-Spiegel, 1999). Dual relationships can be just as destructive for academics as for therapists. Dual relationships exist if an instructor is "at the same time in another role with the [student]," if an instructor is "at the same time in a relationship with a person closely associated with or related to [the student]," or if an instructor "promises to enter into another relationship in the future with [the student] or a person closely associated with or related to [the student]" (APA, 2002, p. 1065). Dual relationships pose special difficulties in small communities, where an instructor may be likely to see students outside of the classroom. Such relationships compromise teachers' abilities to maintain fairness and threaten the critical perception of fairness that must be maintained in academia.

Informed Consent

Students, like research participants, must be fully informed in classes and throughout their academic careers. Students must receive information about their programs including requirements for such milestones as graduation, completion of a thesis or dissertation, or licensing. More specifically, teachers must provide accurate information to each class regarding the subject matter, means of evaluation, and the nature of the course. A thorough syllabus (McKeachie, 2002) is a practical and legal necessity.

Confidentiality

Teachers must respect students' confidentiality in several ways. First, teachers must not place undue pressure on students to self-disclose in class or in written projects. Although the code of conduct (APA, 2002) allows some exceptions to this rule, I discourage teachers from pushing students, particularly undergraduates, to disclose in class. Second, teachers must protect students' academic information from other students. Instructors may not publicly post grades, and instructors must conceal students' scores while returning papers and examinations. Third, teachers must protect students' information from other outside parties. According to the Family Education Rights and Privacy Act (National Education Association, n.d.), instructors may share students' academic information only with legitimately interested parties within the university, and instructors may not share a student's information with any outside party, even the student's parents, unless the student has signed a written agreement to do so. Fourth, instructors must securely and confidentially store all records from courses for a period of time as dictated by university regulations. Any breaches of confidentiality may result in legal consequences in addition to academic consequences. Some exceptions exist. For example, an instructor should break confidentiality only in cases in which a student may harm himself or herself or others or in cases of child or elder abuse.

———— Teaching Ethical Teaching ————

Explicit graduate education in ethical teaching remains rare, and even if graduate students take an ethics course, the course may not focus significantly on teaching. Only 6 percent of graduate students surveyed in one study had to complete an ethics course before teaching a class (Branstetter & Handelsman, 2000). Students who do not have an ethics class available must rely on traditional mentoring and modeling. Relying on mentors to model ethical behavior, which Handelsman (1986, p. 371) called "ethics training by 'osmosis'," presents numerous problems. Additionally, 47 percent of the graduate students in this study reported that they were not required to consult with a faculty mentor regarding teaching (Branstetter & Handelsmann, 2000). Teachers of psychology must address the lack of formal ethics training for future professors. Although some graduate classes explicitly address ethical issues in college teaching (Vattano, personal communication), these remain too rare, and ethical teaching is too important to leave untouched.

The Larger Ethical Context

Teachers of psychology should see university teaching within the larger historical context. University professors participate in an administrated system of teaching. The modern university system emerged in part to provide structure to the mentoring process (Viney & King, 2003), and today's university system continues numerous ancient traditions of students who endure mental, physical, or financial hardships for the sake of an opportunity to sit at the feet of a teacher and learn. Such traditions are exemplified by the young men who sit at the feet of Socrates (Plato, 1961) as well as by Martha's sister Mary as she sits at the feet of Jesus of Nazareth (Luke 10:39, the Bible) and by those seeking knowledge in Eastern traditions (see Ratti & Westbrook, 1999; Yang, 1996). Whether the teacher answers to Professor, Doctor, Sifu (Yang, 1996), Sensei (Ratti & Westbrook, 1999), Rabbi, Elder, Paq'O (Gordon, Mace & Berg, 2000), Shaman (Gordon et al., 2000), or any other title, the relationship involves the student's trust, faith, and hope and the teacher's responsibility to help the student learn. Many teaching models exist, and all rest upon the student's trust in the teacher (Woody & Thomas, 2002). Teachers in any context must recognize this trust and the immense responsibilities it confers.

Conclusion

In all contexts, the first responsibility of the teacher, regardless of title, is to the student. Historically, teachers act as the *speculum mundi* (mirror of the world) for their students. The focus on learners as individuals worthy of respect, dignity, and integrity reinforces learners despite the hardships they accepted to find the teacher and helps teachers grow by seeing beyond their personal strengths and weaknesses. Ethical respect for the integrity of the student is central; students are sacred – they justify the existence of the teachers. Modern university regulations can obscure this idea, but they cannot lessen its importance. The success of students is the success of the teachers. Foundationally, teachers provide students with the tools to take the field further. Herein lies the hope of psychology and society. Teachers succeed only when their students go beyond them.

ACKNOWLEDGMENTS

I thank Dr. Blaine Peden for helpful comments on a draft of the chapter.

REFERENCES

American Association of University Professors (March 3, 2004). Controversy in the classroom: A statement issued by the AAUP's Committee A on Academic Freedom and Tenure. Retrieved August 1, 2004 from www.aaup.org/statements/SpchState/comaclass.htm

American Psychological Association. (2002). Ethical principles of psychologists and code of conduct. *American Psychologist, 57*, 1060–74.

Branstetter, S. A., & Handelsman, M. M. (2000). Graduate teaching assistants: Ethical training, beliefs, and practices. *Ethics and Behavior, 10*, 27–50.

Buckley, K. W. (1994). Misbehaviorism. In J. T. Todd & E. K. Morris (eds.), *Modern perspectives on John B. Watson and classical behaviorism*, (pp. 19–36). Westport, CT: Greenwood Press.

Cahn, S. M. (1986). *Saints and scamps: Ethics in academia.* Totowa, NJ: Rowman & Littlefield.

Friedrich, J., & Douglass, D. (1998). Ethics and the persuasive enterprise of teaching psychology. *American Psychologist, 53*, 549–62.

Gordon, O., Mace, B., & Berg, L. (April, 2000). *Environmental epistemology of the Andean people of Peru.* Paper presented at the annual meeting of the Rocky Mountain Psychological Association, Tuscon, Arizona.

Handelsman, M. M. (1986). Problems with ethics training by "osmosis." *Professional Psychology: Research and Practice, 17*, 371–2.

Henderson, C. (2001). College freshmen with disabilities: A biennial statistical profile. Washington, DC: Heath Resource Center. Retrieved Sept. 20, 2004, from www.heath.gwu.edu/PDFs/collegefreshmen.pdf

The Holy Bible: New international version. (1985). Grand Rapids, MI: Zondervan.

Keith-Spiegel, P. (1999). Ethically risky situations between students and professors outside of the classroom. In B. Perlman, L. I. McCann, & S. H. McFadden (eds.), *Lessons learned: Practical advice for the teaching of psychology* (pp. 225–31). Washington, DC: American Psychological Society.

Keith-Spiegel, P. C., Tabachnick, B. G., & Allen, M. (1993). Ethics in academia: Students' views of professors' actions. *Ethics and Behavior, 3*, 149–62.

Klein, A. (2004, July 9). Worried on the right and the left. *Chronicle of Higher Education.* Retrieved Aug. 1, 2004 from http://chronicle.com/weekly/v50/i44/44a02101.htm

Martinez, J. C. (2004, Jan. 27). Bill aims to curb profs' classroom politicizing. *Denver Post.* Retrieved Aug. 1, 2004 from www.denverpost.com/Stories/0,1413,36%257E53%257E1917039,00.html

McKeachie, W. J. (2002). *McKeachie's teaching tips: Strategies, research, and theory for college and university teachers* (11th ed.). Boston: Houghton Mifflin.

National Education Association (n.d.) Family Education Rights and Privacy Act. Retrieved Aug. 1, 2004, from www.ed.gov/policy/gen/guid/fpco/ferpa/index.html

Palladino, J. J., Hill IV, G. W., & Norcross, J. C. (1999). Using extra credit. In B. Perlman, L. I. McCann, & S. H. McFadden (eds.), *Lessons learned: Practical advice for the teaching of psychology* (pp. 57–60). Washington, DC: American Psychological Society.

Plato (1961). *The collected dialogues of Plato including the letters.* E. Hamilton & H. Cairns (eds.). Princeton, NJ: Princeton University Press.

Ratti, O., & Westbrook, A. (1999). *Secrets of the samurai: Martial arts of feudal Japan.* Edison, NJ: Castle Books.

Smith, D. (2003). What you need to know about the new code: The chair of APA's Ethics Code Task Force highlights changes to the 2002 Ethics Code. *Monitor on Psychology, 34*, 62–5.

Svinicki, M. D. (2002). Ethics in college teaching. In *McKeachie's teaching tips: Strategies, research, and theory for college and university teachers* (11th ed., pp. 306–18). Boston: Houghton Mifflin.

Tabachnick, B. G., Keith-Spiegel, P., Pope, K. S. (1991). Ethics of teaching: Beliefs and behaviors of psychologists as educators. *American Psychologist, 46,* 506–15.

US Equal Opportunity Employment Commission (2004). Sexual Harassment. Retrieved Aug. 1, 2004, from www.eeoc.gov/types/sexual_harassment.html

Van Note Chism, N. (2002). Valuing student differences. In *McKeachie's teaching tips: Strategies, research, and theory for college and university teachers* (11th ed., pp. 128–47). Boston: Houghton Mifflin.

Viney, W., & King, D. B. 2003. *A history of psychology: Ideas and context* (3rd ed.). Boston, MA: Allyn & Bacon.

Wittig, A. F., Perkins, D. V., Balogh, D. W., Whitley Jr., B. E., & Keith-Spiegel, P. (1999). Treating students differentially: Ethics in shades of grey. In B. Perlman, L. I. McCann, & S. H. McFadden (eds.), *Lessons learned: Practical advice for the teaching of psychology* (pp. 219–24). Washington, DC: American Psychological Society.

Woody, W. D., & Thomas, P. A. (2002). *Heterogony of models, goals, and means in teaching.* Paper presented at the annual meeting of the American Psychological Association Convention, Chicago, IL.

Yang, J. M. (1996). *The essence of Shaolin White Crane: Martial power and qigong.* Roslindale, MA: Yang Martial Arts Association.

39
Establishing Classroom Etiquette: General Rules of Classroom Conduct

Ψ

Lisa Damour
John Carroll University

Classroom instructors have two main duties with regard to their students: to teach course-related material and skills, and to maintain a classroom environment that allows every student to learn. Although a large literature exists on how to teach course materials (e.g., Davis, 1993; Leamnson, 1999; Lowman, 1995), much less support exists on how to make the classroom a place where the students treat each other, and the instructor, with respect.

Although most students come to class ready to learn, many instructors find that they have a few students each semester whose behavior disrupts the classroom environment. For the sake of the other students in the class, instructors cannot allow disruptive behavior to go unaddressed. When it comes to establishing classroom etiquette, instructors should set a considerate tone, clarify classroom policies at the beginning of the semester, and then trouble-shoot problems as they arise.

What follows is a brief overview of how to establish and maintain a respectful learning environment. Interested readers may learn more about classroom etiquette in one of the many excellent books on working with college students (e.g., Brinkley, Dessants, Flamm, & Fleming, 1999; Curzan & Damour, 2000; McKeachie, 2002).

Setting a Respectful Tone and Laying Ground Rules

The most effective way for instructors to create a respectful environment within their classrooms is to treat students respectfully. At minimum, instructors should come to class prepared, start class on time, use class time effectively, end class on time, and address students as mature young adults. In addition to using their own actions to communicate an air of respect, instructors can use the course syllabus to provide students with ground rules for classroom etiquette. Some instructors include in the syllabus policies about a variety of classroom behaviors such as bringing cellphones to class, arriving to class late, or falling asleep during class.

Although it is certainly the instructor's right to provide an extensive list of rules about disruptive behaviors that might occur during the semester, doing so communicates that the instructor does not expect the students to act maturely, and students may feel compelled to live down to the instructor's expectations. Unduly rigid rules may come back to haunt the instructor. For example, the instructor who gets a flat tire on the way to class will soon regret his or her practice of forbidding students to enter the classroom if they arrive more than 10 minutes late.

Instead, many instructors use their syllabus to clarify where they stand on issues that vary from one instructor to another, such as whether students may eat and drink during class. All policies should be guided by the nature of the course (e.g., how does class attendance factor into the course in general?), the nature of the classroom (e.g., is it a large classroom where students probably would not disrupt their peers if they bring coffee to class?), and the instructor's personal preferences (e.g., students who eat during class distract some instructors).

When articulating classroom etiquette policies, instructors should feel free to remind students that they provide such policies to promote the learning of all of the students in the course. In designing policies, instructors should be mindful that it is always easy to relax the rules as the semester proceeds, and virtually impossible to "toughen up" over time. For example, instituting a lateness penalty midway through the semester is awkward at best.

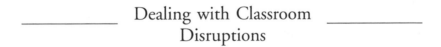

Dealing with Classroom Disruptions

Even instructors who treat students respectfully and include basic rules of etiquette in the course syllabus may find that classroom disruptions occur. Disruptive classroom behavior can be active or passive and intentional or accidental. Some students whisper to each other during class, others do crossword puzzles; some students make no effort to arrive at class on time, others are late for reasons beyond their control.

At times, instructors may feel personally offended when their students misbehave. This reaction is understandable given that most instructors are devoted to their discipline and their teaching. Yet instructors must not allow themselves to react to their own hurt feelings by humiliating an offending student. Doing so abuses the power differential between instructor and student and may likely contribute to further classroom problems. Students who faculty treat disrespectfully will find ways, however subtle, to reciprocate. The innocent students who witness such behavior may lose respect for the instructor whose behavior is no better than that of the offending student. Classroom management techniques serve everyone's interests when they effectively address disruptions without shaming students. Here is some advice on how to address, respectfully and effectively, some of the most common breaches of classroom etiquette.

Arriving to Class Late

Instructors may prevent most late arrivals to class by making a point of starting class on time. To delay the beginning of class until a quorum of students has arrived encourages students to come late and wastes the time of students who are prompt. If a student consistently arrives to class late, instructors should catch the student after class and ask, kindly, what is going on and point out that late arrivals unfairly distract other students. Few students will continue to come late once an instructor has pointed out the problem; instructors should remind students who arrive late of any course lateness policies. Unavoidable situations, such as a childcare problem or an unusual traffic jam, can make students late. For this reason, instructors should wait for a pattern to emerge and then ask the student about his or her lateness before reacting to the problem. In all cases, identify the nature of the problem before deciding on a solution.

Talking During Class

Students occasionally carry on private conversations during class. Some instructors prefer to ignore such behavior and reason that interrupting class activities to address the chatting students only further disrupts the class. Yet, to ignore such behavior sends the message that the instructor does not notice or care about what individual students are doing.

Instructors who tend to walk around the room while lecturing can continue to lecture while strolling nearby the talking students; doing so almost unfailingly stops in-class chatting. Alternatively, the instructor can assume that the students are talking about course material (which may be the case), and respectfully ask them to share their ideas with the class as a whole, or ask if they have a question. If the students were talking about the class, everyone benefits, and if they were not, these students will likely stop their private conversations. A gentle sense of humor can also be put to good use when managing classroom disruptions. For example, an instructor might alert whispering students that the classroom acoustics are such their conversation can be heard by all and that, to preserve their own privacy, they should save their conversation for after class.

Extracurricular Activities During Class

Some students read the newspaper, do homework, or even play games on their cellphones during class. Such behavior may not actively disrupt the activity of the classroom, but it distracts the instructor and nearby students from the task at hand and, consequently, disrupts the learning environment. Instructors should not tolerate these open signs of disrespect; tacitly allowing extracurricular activity during class damages the morale of students who do the work of paying attention.

To check extracurricular activity when it occurs at the beginning of class, instructors should assume that the student does not realize that class is underway. Directing a simple "We've started" at a newspaper-reading student will usually do the job. When extracurricular activity emerges mid-way through class, the instructor should feel free to direct the student to "Please save that for after class."

Laptop computers present a special problem in that instructors cannot always tell whether students are using them for legitimate purposes, such as note taking. Students using computers for nonclass purposes often distract those around them. Instructors who suspect that a student is misusing a laptop during class should catch the student after class, point out that his or her computer use appears to be distracting other students, and make clear the expectation that if he or she must bring the computer to class, it is used only for course purposes. Students respect instructors who notice and address these kinds of classroom details.

Addressing Widespread Breaches of Classroom Etiquette

The foregoing advice applies to situations where disruptive behavior is limited to one or two students. If several students arrive to class late, talk during class, or do crossword puzzles, their behavior indicates a broader problem. Students usually engage in group demonstrations of disrespect when they feel that the instructor has somehow been disrespectful toward them. To set the class back on track the instructor must figure out what has gone wrong.

As soon as group misbehavior begins, instructors should try to determine if their students are justified in feeling that their time is being wasted. Instructors who cannot identify problems in their course design or approach should consult with a trusted colleague, or if available, professionals at a teaching and learning center. Colleagues may be able to help identify the problem by looking over the course materials, or quietly sitting in on a class. Instructors who figure out what has gone wrong should inform their class that they are aware that a particular approach to the class has not been working, that they will implement a new approach immediately, and that they look forward to the students' cooperation and feedback regarding the change.

In cases in which instructors cannot identify the problem, they should take time to talk with the students about their obvious concerns about the course, to solicit their feedback on what aspects of the class are not working well, and to recruit their help in making a plan to conduct class in a new, more useful, way. If such a discussion feels uncomfortable, a written feedback form can solicit helpful information anonymously from students. After reviewing the comments and suggestions on these forms, instructors should share with students any patterns reflected in the commentary and inform students of plans to address their concerns.

Conclusion

Once instructors establish classroom etiquette, students are able to make the most of the process of teaching and learning. A respectful classroom environment allows students to do the real work of meeting together as a class: to engage difficult and delicate topics, to take on intellectual risks, and to challenge themselves and each other.

ACKNOWLEDGMENTS

Much of the thinking in this chapter has grown out of the collaborative efforts that are an essential part of all good teaching. Special thanks go to my colleague Anne Curzan of the Department of English at the University of Michigan.

REFERENCES

Brinkley, A., Dessants, B., Flamm, M., & Fleming, C. (1999). *The Chicago handbook for teachers: A practical guide to the college classroom.* Chicago: University of Chicago Press.

Curzan, A. L., & Damour, L. K. (2000). *First day to final grade: A graduate student's guide to teaching.* Ann Arbor: University of Michigan Press.

Davis, B. G. (1993). *Tools for teaching.* San Francisco: Jossey-Bass.

Leamnson, R. (1999). *Thinking about teaching and learning: Developing habits of learning with first year college and university students.* Sterling, VA: Stylus; Oakhill, UK: Trentham Books.

Lowman, J. (1995). *Mastering the techniques of teaching* (2nd ed.). San Francisco: Jossey-Bass.

McKeachie, W. J. (2002). *McKeachie's teaching tips: Strategies, research, and theory for college and university teachers* (11th ed.). Boston: Houghton Mifflin.

40

Problematic College Students: Preparing and Repairing

Ψ

Janie H. Wilson & Amy A. Hackney
Georgia Southern University

This chapter focuses on rapport-building as a way to reduce the likelihood that students will interpret our intentions as negative. We also address interpersonal problems that might occur and how we might best deal with them. Finally, we explore our interpretations of students' problematic behaviors and how we might best avoid having negative perceptions of students who emit them.

The Classroom Environment

Classroom rapport centers on warmth and liking between an instructor and students, a bond nurtured by a positive attitude toward students. Instructors can achieve this type of classroom environment through instructor immediacy behaviors such as smiling at students, learning students' names, and sharing personal stories, when relevant (e.g., Gorham, 1988; Gorham & Christophel, 1990). In short, showing respect for students, or letting them know that we actually like them and want them to do well in the course, builds a positive atmosphere. If students know we respect and like them, they report more motivation to perform well (Christensen & Menzel, 1988; Frymier, 1994; Wilson & Taylor, 2001), enjoy the subject matter more (Christensen & Menzel, 1988; McCroskey, Fayer, Richmond, Sallinen, & Barraclough, 1996), learn more (Christensen & Menzel, 1988; Frymier, 1994), and project higher grades in the course (Wilson & Taylor, 2001). Although most of the existent data are correlational, a positive classroom at least has the potential to enhance learning and reduce problematic behaviors.

By communicating our respect for students, we combat misperceptions students might have regarding our behaviors. Social psychology has taught us that misperceptions may stem from at least three errors in person perception: stereotyping (Allport, 1954; Swim

& Sanna, 1996), the fundamental attribution error (Heider, 1958; Knowles, Morris, Chiu, & Hong, 2001; Ross & Nisbett, 1991), and self-fulfilling prophecy (Rosenthal & Jacobson, 1968; Smith, Jussim, & Eccles, 1999). If we reprimand a student for reading the newspaper during class, the student may recall stereotypical traits of authoritarian professors and attribute the cause of the reprimand to an overly controlling personality. If, however, we communicate to our students that we like them and respect them, they will be more likely to correct their automatic stereotypical perceptions. When a student earns a poor grade on a paper, it might be tempting to assume that the professor is a cold and unreasonably demanding teacher. However, if the professor has communicated liking and respect to the student, the student is more likely to correct a dispositional attribution and recognize the role of incomplete work in the grading of the paper. Finally, if students expect a professor to be demeaning, they may set in motion a self-fulfilling expectation. Fearful students may avoid participating in class discussions. This lack of class participation may frustrate the professor, causing the professor to make demeaning comments and fulfill students' original expectation. We can avoid or at least minimize the initial negative expectations by building rapport in the classroom.

When Problems Arise

Sorcinelli (2002) offered excellent suggestions on how to deal with problems in large classes, but any-size class could suffer from the same problems. For our purpose, we consider two types of problems: personal and interpersonal. Many of us believe that personal issues, those that affect only the individual, are lesser problems than interpersonal issues, which we must deal with to maintain a positive classroom atmosphere. Being unprepared, missing deadlines, missing class, working on unrelated material, and cheating are students' problems. Certainly their grades will be lower as a result, and many students may fail the course. Although we regret that some students do not perform well, and we try to be supportive, at least personal issues affect only individual students. Ultimately, students are responsible for their own performance. Interpersonal issues, however, necessitate quick and effective intervention to protect others and maintain a positive learning environment. Interpersonal problems may occur when students talk during lecture, use cellphones, arrive late or leave early, communicate boredom, and challenge authority.

Students talking during lecture can interrupt the instructor and impair others' ability to hear it. It seems simple to ask students to stop talking; however, it is not so simple to ask students to stop talking and model respect at the same time. As an alternative, we could ask students if they have any questions, perhaps looking at the disruptive student; call on the talking student by name to answer the next question; or casually walk over to the talking student and lecture beside him or her for a minute. For any of these approaches, a smile will soften the implied reprimand and may even build rapport by sharing the reprimand only with the talkers.

Talking may not be restricted to students within the class; a student may answer a cellphone call. In our experience, a glance from the professor will shorten the call, and it is unlikely to happen again. As for students who merely forget to turn off their cellphones, it only takes a second to turn it off when it rings, and the class can have a laugh together in the knowledge that we've all made the same mistake at least once.

Arriving late and leaving early are common problems in the classroom, with arriving late the most likely behavior to happen. To address this problem, instructors might have homework due at the beginning of class, with late homework accepted for feedback but not graded. A related option is to have an oral quiz in the first 5 minutes of class. This approach works best if the instructor does not repeat items, so students who come in late cannot answer earlier items. When students need to leave early, you can ask them to sit near the door.

A student may communicate boredom by yawning loudly, reading the newspaper, or clipping fingernails. Behaviors such as these are clearly disrespectful and will erode the fabric of a positive classroom. The most obvious response is for us to be more engaging, perhaps by using interesting examples, allowing students to interact more, and teaching enthusiastically. Students can focus on lectures for approximately 20 minutes (Fulford, 2001); therefore, we should consider varying our teaching methods: lecture, classroom exercise, group discussion, demonstration, and so on (Simplicio, 2001).

Continuous loud yawning or rude comments might actually reflect challenges to authority, with the offensive student seeking a confrontation. Unfortunately, any public confrontation is likely to place the instructor in a negative light. Challenges to the instructor's authority must be handled privately. If a student challenges an idea that has been presented, you should be able to offer research to support the claim or at least offer to locate specific evidence and share it with the class. Similarly, students should be encouraged to find research in support of their view and share the information. If a student challenges a grade, a written rationale from the student should accompany the request for reevaluation. This tactic circumvents a mutiny, allows the student to think through the argument, and allows the professor to give full attention to the request without classroom pressures. Written requests also keep the class on task rather than waste class time with individual arguments.

Occasionally, you may have a student who insists on challenging your authority on a regular basis. In this situation, some instructors might ask the student to come by the office and discuss the problem; open communication is useful as long as the instructor remains supportive. Tantleff-Dunn, Dunn, and Gokee (2002) found that three-quarters of a sample of college students reported that they tried to resolve a conflict by speaking directly with their professors. Unfortunately, an alarming number of students also reported that the professor either denied a problem or did nothing at all about it. It is not surprising that students were dissatisfied with their instructor's attitude. In fact, students reported that the outcome (e.g., grade change) was less important to them than the professor's interpersonal style. Thus, we should not be tempted to believe that being lenient is the answer; students were not looking for, nor did they appreciate, a lenient professor.

In the same study, most students reported that problems are associated with what they consider to be unfair grading practices, and this perspective leads them to label the situation as an interpersonal conflict. A syllabus that clearly states grading policies is a good beginning, but you must be careful to follow your policies and not put yourself in the position of making judgments about students' excuses. One approach is to drop two homework or quiz grades, explaining to students that you have built in some room for unusual circumstances that might come up. Instructors can also allow students to make up any and all missed tests in the hour following the final exam, with the understanding that the format of each test may be more difficult than the original. For other large assignments, instructors can deduct 5 percent of the assignment grade for each day it is late. This focus on building in a safety net for grades allows students to continue to function through personal problems and prevents the instructor from having to decide which excuses are legitimate.

Continued patience and respect toward rude students often helps them to reevaluate their perceptions. Similarly, you might regularly want to reexamine your perceptions of students, particularly those who cause problems for you. Just as students may misperceive teacher behaviors, teachers often misperceive student behaviors. First, whether conscious or not, we might stereotype our students based on age, gender, and physical attractiveness, to name a few characteristics. Second, we should try to assume situational rather than dispositional reasons for students' behaviors. For example, rather than think students leave class because they are lazy or don't care about learning, it might be worthwhile to assume that students leave class when they feel ill. Third, negative expectations may lead us to "ask for" negative student behaviors, whereas positive expectations may help students to excel (Rosenthal & Jacobson, 1968).

Conclusion

We hope this chapter has communicated our belief that prevention of classroom problems is preferable to repairing damage after problems arise. Prevention is based primarily on a positive social milieu in the classroom, over which we have much control. The first step toward a peaceful environment is liking our students and modeling the respect we hope to foster in others. Creating a classroom community based on rapport reduces the potential for students to interpret our course requirements, grading practices, and classroom behaviors negatively. When problems do arise, we can address them in myriad ways, but the key to effective management remains becoming accurate in our perceptions of students' behaviors. As we know from the social-psychological literature, the best way to avoid making negative attributions is to get to know our students as individuals.

REFERENCES

Allport, G. W. (1954). *The nature of prejudice.* Reading, MA: Addison-Wesley.

Christensen, L. J., & Menzel, K. E. (1998). The linear relationship between student reports of teacher immediacy behaviors and perceptions of state motivation, and of cognitive, affective, and behavioral learning. *Communication Education, 47,* 82–90.

Frymier, A. B. (1994). A model of immediacy in the classroom. *Communication Quarterly, 42,* 133–44.

Fulford, C. P. (2001). A model of cognitive speed. *International Journal of Instructional Media, 28,* 31–40.

Gorham, J. (1988). The relationship between verbal teacher immediacy behaviors and student learning. *Communication Education, 37,* 40–53.

Gorham, J., & Christophel, D. M. (1990). The relationship of teachers' use of humor in the classroom to immediacy and student learning. *Communication Education, 39,* 46–62.

Heider, F. (1958). *The psychology of interpersonal relations.* New York: John Wiley.

Knowles, E. D., Morris, M. W., Chiu, C., & Hong, Y. (2001). Culture and the process of person perception: Evidence for automaticity among East Asians in correcting for situational influences on behavior. *Personality and Social Psychology Bulletin, 10,* 1344–56.

McCroskey, J. C., Fayer, J. M., Richmond, V. P., Sallinen, A., & Barraclough, R. A. (1996). A multi-cultural examination of the relationship between nonverbal immediacy and affective learning. *Communication Quarterly, 44,* 297–307.

Rosenthal, R., & Jacobson, L. (1968). *Pygmalion in the classroom: Teacher expectations and student intellectual development.* New York: Holt, Rinehart, and Winston.

Ross, L., & Nisbett, R. E. (1991). *The person and the situation: Perspectives of social psychology.* New York: McGraw-Hill.

Simplicio, J. S. (2001). How to recognize and counteract student inattentiveness in the classroom. *Journal of Instructional Psychology, 28,* 199–201.

Sorcinelli, M. D. (2002). Promoting civility in large classes. In C. A. Stanley & M. E. Porter (eds.), *Engaging large classes* (pp. 44–57). Bolton, MA: Anker Publishing.

Smith, A. E., Jussim, L., & Eccles, J. S. (1999). Do self-fulfilling prophesies accumulate, dissipate, or remain stable over time? *Journal of Personality and Social Psychology, 77,* 548–65.

Swim, J. K., & Sanna, L. (1996). He's skilled, she's lucky: A meta-analysis of observers' attributions for women's and men's successes and failures. *Personality and Social Psychology Bulletin, 22,* 507–19.

Tantleff-Dunn, S., Dunn, M. E., & Gokee, J. L. (2002). Understanding faculty–student conflict: Student perceptions of precipitating events and faculty responses. *Teaching of Psychology, 29,* 197–202.

Wilson, J. H., & Taylor, K. W. (2001). Professor immediacy as behaviors associated with liking students. *Teaching of Psychology, 28,* 136–8.

41

Preventing, Detecting, and Addressing Academic Dishonesty

Ψ

Gregory J. Cizek

University of North Carolina, Chapel Hill

An essential expectation in the academy is that of academic integrity. One of the most difficult issues facing any instructor arises when that expectation is violated. Nonetheless, as competition, grade, and time pressures for students increase, and as the cultural approbation toward various forms of cheating decreases, the challenge for instructors becomes greater.

This chapter focuses on academic dishonesty – or, colloquially, cheating. I provide a definition of the concept and suggestions for preventing cheating, for detecting its occurrence, and for dealing with the behavior and its aftermath.

What is Academic Dishonesty?

Academic dishonesty is any intentional action or behavior that: (a) violates the established rules governing the completion of a test or assignment, (b) gives one student an unfair advantage over other students on a test or assignment, or (c) decreases the accuracy of the intended inferences arising from a student's performance (Cizek, 2003). Studies of cheating indicate that its incidence increases across the grade levels, with greatest frequency at the high-school and college levels. Approximately 90 percent of students admit to having cheated on a test or assignment; it is estimated that 3–5 percent of students cheat on any given test or assignment.

The possible ways in which cheating can occur are nearly limitless and described in detail elsewhere (Cizek, 1999). Cheating occurs on tests, such as when one student copies answers from another (willing or unwilling) test-taker. A student may use unauthorized materials such as a cheat sheet or another prohibited source of information or assistance. A student might bring the material into the testing environment, or take a "break" to consult materials outside the classroom. A test-taker can transmit images of test pages to another student via a cellphone and receive text messages with answers almost instantaneously. In large classes, one (presumably more able) student might take a test for another. It would be cheating if a student obtains a test accommodation, such as extra time, that is unwarranted.

Cheating occurs on assignments, too. The most common form of cheating on papers, projects, or other assignments occurs when a student inappropriately uses material taken from another source. This form of cheating, called plagiarism, is defined as using the original words, thoughts, or ideas of another person without appropriate citation or referencing, usually for the purpose of intentionally misrepresenting such words, thoughts, or ideas as one's own (Cizek, 2003). Technological advances have also facilitated the ease with which students can engage in plagiarism (although it has also facilitated detection of the behavior). Cheating on assignments also occurs when, contrary to the instructor's directions for an out-of-class assignment, a student uses impermissible books, notes, time, or the assistance of another person. The practice of razoring – removing of material from a journal, book, or other document for the purpose of preventing others from gaining access to the source – also constitutes academic dishonesty.

Obviously, instructors need accurate information about students' knowledge and skills in order to plan instruction, assign grades, determine eligibility for awards, and so on. However, academic dishonesty can undermine an instructor's efforts to create high-quality tests or assignments. Any form of cheating that results in inaccurate information about a student impairs the instructor's ability to perform his or her job, introduces unfairness to other students who have not cheated, and undermines the foundations of intellectual life of the academy.

Preventing Academic Dishonesty

The adage about an ounce of prevention being worth a pound of cure applies to cheating. Because cheating can be difficult to detect, because the costs involved in responding to cheating are often high, and because relatively simple steps can be taken to deter cheating, prevention is the first and most important step that instructors can take.

Prevention of academic dishonesty comprises two aspects. One aspect involves informing students about and promoting a high level of academic integrity generally. The second aspect involves implementing specific strategies related to the particular type of cheating to be deterred.

Table 41.1 provides a list of general strategies for preventing cheating and promoting academic integrity. A key strategy is the need for instructors to inform students – explicitly and preferably at the beginning of a semester – about the meaning and value of academic integrity, and about the specific actions that constitute appropriate behavior on tests and assignments. Instructors can also help students understand academic integrity by providing counterexamples (i.e., illustrations of actions that would violate the expectations or rules established by the instructor for the course).

Table 41.2 provides eight specific strategies for preventing cheating on examinations; table 41.3 contains strategies for preventing cheating on written assignments.

Table 41.1: General strategies for promoting academic integrity and preventing cheating

1. At the beginning of the semester, inform students of the type, frequency, and value of tests, assignments, and other components that will count toward their grade.
2. Be fair and open about student evaluation. Provide students with adequate notice and concrete description of the content, length, format, timing, guidelines or other requirements for completing tests or assignments and information about the grading scale that will be used. Avoid scheduling examinations or due dates for major papers concurrently with other important assignments or examinations.
3. Explicitly introduce students to the requirements of academic integrity at the beginning of the course and give reminders as needed. Provide concrete illustrations of inappropriate actions and specific examples of appropriate actions. Inform students of penalties for academic dishonesty.
4. Limit the number of tests and assignments that count toward a grade.
5. Use grades only as indicators of achievement. Avoid "grading on the curve."
6. Promote an assessment climate in which students see grades not only as indicators of achievement, but also as valuable indicators of their strengths and weaknesses.
7. Become familiar with common methods of cheating on tests, and methods used to plagiarize.
8. Institute an honor code.

Table 41.2: Strategies for preventing cheating on tests

1. Avoid test formats that make cheating easier (e.g., reduce reliance on multiple-choice items in favor of constructed-response formats). Use alternate forms of tests in which item positions are scrambled. Avoid "take-home" tests. Avoid repeating test questions or reusing test forms from semester to semester.
2. Keep test materials secure.
3. Keep track of all test materials distributed and returned.
4. Know the identity of each test-taker.
5. Prohibit the use of cellphones, CD players, pagers, calculators with communication capabilities, and similar devices.
6. Remain vigilant while proctoring a test. Keep a record of the seating location of each test-taker.
7. Inform students that statistical methods for detecting answer copying may be used.

Detecting Academic Dishonesty

An entry in table 41.1 suggests that instructors should become familiar with the cheating methods used by students. Any list of cheating methods would be infinitely long, but a sampling of the variety of methods can assist instructors in detecting academic dishonesty. Tables 41.4 and 41.5 provide samples of the actions or indicators that cheating may have occurred on a test or assignment.

Table 41.3: Strategies for preventing plagiarism

1. Explicitly teach students about plagiarism. Use specific examples of plagiarized text or an unacceptable paraphrase and an explanation regarding what makes it so.
2. Structure writing assignments to be less susceptible to plagiarism. Avoid reusing topics from semester to semester. Consider assigning topics instead of permitting students to choose their own. Design written assignments that are focused, unique, or locally relevant. Require longer assignments to be completed in stages.
3. Provide, in advance, a scoring rubric or evaluation framework that details requirements for the written assignment such as topic to be covered, order of required elements, style, resources to be used, specific subheadings, etc.
4. Inform students that methods may be used to detect plagiarism. Several software programs and internet sites exist to help instructors detect plagiarism (see Cizek, 2003).
5. Become familiar with students and their writing styles. Avoid the use of teaching assistants (TAs) to grade assignments or provide training for TAs to help them recognize plagiarism.
6. Incorporate assessment of written project content or student presentations into course examinations.

Table 41.4: Examples of potential indications of cheating on a test

Before a test, an instructor . . .

1. discovers that there are missing copies of a test or answer key.
2. observes that one or more students seem unconcerned about the upcoming test.
3. receives a request from a student for a special test accommodation.
4. notices that one or more students take seats that differ from their usual locations.
5. sees information written on desk surfaces, chalkboards, etc.

During a test, a student . . .

1. is absent.
2. wears a baseball cap, uses headphones, etc.
3. avoids eye contact with the instructor.
4. seems unusually nervous, anxious.
5. frequently drops pen, sharpens pencil, etc.
6. uses restroom frequently or for an unusually long time.
7. fidgets with materials in desk, bookbag, clothing, etc.
8. exchanges materials with any other student.
9. appears to be looking at another student's test.
10. completes the test in an unexpectedly short period of time.

After a test, an instructor . . .

1. observes that a student's performance is dramatically better than his or her previous work.
2. notices unusual similarities in two or more students' responses.
3. notices unusual similarities between a student's responses and material in a textbook, etc.
4. finds cheat sheets on the floor, etc.

Source: Adapted from Cizek, 2003.

Table 41.5: Potential indications of plagiarism in written work

1. The writing style, language, vocabulary, tone, grammar, or other features of assignment are not commensurate with written work the student usually produces.
2. There are awkward changes in verb tense, pronouns, structure, or organization of the paper.
3. Portions of the composition seem out of place or do not relate to the overall content of the paper; after a relevant introduction, the student's paper changes to become less obviously relevant to the assignment.
4. Strange text or characters, such as a date or URL, appear in the footer or header of a paper.
5. The work contains changes in font, pitch, color, shading, formatting, page layout, line spacing, margins, pagination, etc.
6. The paper contains references to graphs, charts, accompanying material, citations, chapters, footnotes, or additional text that are missing.
7. The writing mentions ideas, persons, settings, etc., with which the student is not likely to be familiar.
8. The work contains citations or references to sources or materials to which the student is not likely to have access.
9. When asked, the student has difficulty responding to simple questions about what he or she wrote.

Source: Adapted from Bates & Fain, 2002.

Table 41.6: Steps to consider when responding to possible cheating

1. Assess the likely impact of confronting a student during a test. Consider the impact that a (perceived) allegation of cheating would have on an innocent student's test performance. Avoid confrontations that may distract or impair other students' performances.
2. Document all evidence, observations, etc., including dates, times, and corroborating witnesses to potential cheating. Also document any conversations with a student suspected of cheating.
3. Do not accuse a student of cheating. Instead, describe the student's actions or work samples that are the source of concern. As a first step, ask to meet with the student to discuss the concern and ask the student to provide any information that might explain the apparent plagiarism, copying, etc. If appropriate, have a third party present at the meeting.
4. Remind the student of policies concerning academic honesty provided in the syllabus for a course, the directions for an assignment, the college Handbook, or other source.
5. Follow through on stated penalties for academic dishonesty.
6. Know and follow institutional guidelines or policies for reporting or substantiating potential cheating.
7. Encourage and support other faculty members who promote academic integrity.

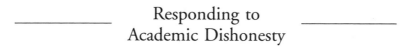

Responding to
Academic Dishonesty

Responding to cheating is perhaps one of the most difficult tasks that instructors face. Confronting a student about possible cheating can be uncomfortable for both parties, and the disincentives for doing so are strong. Nonetheless, responding to potential breaches is essential for maintaining a culture of academic integrity. Any responses must be implemented with both care and fairness to protect all involved, particularly if the suspicion about cheating turns out to be unfounded. Table 41.6 provides a list of steps to consider when responding to a potential instance of cheating.

Conclusion

Like any other aspect of teaching, dealing with the potential for cheating is an important dimension of an instructor's role and responsibility, and a key element in the intellectual life of the academy. With adequate awareness and understanding, an instructor can be prepared to prevent, detect, and respond to potential cheating and to ensuring fairness in assessment and grading.

REFERENCES

Bates, P., & Fain, M. (2002). Detecting plagiarized papers. Available at: www.coastal.edu/library/plagiarz.htm

Cizek, G. J. (1999). *Cheating on tests: How to do it, detect it, and prevent it.* Mahwah, NJ: Erlbaum.

Cizek, G. J. (2003). *Detecting and preventing classroom cheating: Promoting integrity in schools.* Thousand Oaks, CA: Corwin.

part VIII

Ψ

Evaluating Student Learning

Part VIII includes five chapters covering test construction, written and oral assignments, group work, effective grading, and writing letters of recommendation.

42

Test Construction

Ψ

John A. Juve
University of Missouri, Columbia

Measuring academic achievement can be a daunting and challenging task that requires constructing test items that accurately measure student learning objectives. The process of constructing good test items is a hybrid of both art and science.

The purpose of this chapter is to offer prescriptive suggestions for developing selected-response (e.g., multiple-choice) and supply-response (e.g., essay) test items. Although these suggestions are not exhaustive, they represent some of the most commonly cited suggestions in test development literature.

Relation of Instruction and Assessment

Before introducing the suggested guidelines for constructing test items, I discuss the important relation between instruction and assessment. A necessary condition for effective and meaningful instruction involves the coexistence and continuous development of the instructional, learning, and assessment processes.

The relation of instruction and assessment becomes evident when instructors closely examine the roles of each process. For example, Gronlund (2003) emphasized this relation when he stated that, "instruction is most effective when directed toward a clearly defined set of intended learning outcomes and assessment is most effective when designed to assess a clearly defined set of intended learning outcomes" (p. 4). Essentially, the roles of instruction and assessment are inseparable.

Pedagogic research (e.g., Ory & Ryan, 1993) has encouraged faculty members to use Bloom's Taxonomy to analyze the compatibility of their instructional process, their desired student outcomes or objectives, and their test items. As an instructor, you will use test scores to make inferences about student content mastery. Consequently, it is essential that these inferences are valid. Your inferences are more likely to be valid when the test items are comprised of a representative sample of course content, objectives, and difficulty. Therefore, as you begin to develop your test items, remember the relation between course objectives, instruction, and testing.

Table 42.1: Suggestions for developing multiple-choice items

1. Stems should present clearly formulated problems.
2. Make the reading and vocabulary difficulty of items as simple as possible.
3. Correct answers should clearly represent the best choice.
4. Distracters should be plausible, but distinguishably less correct.
5. Avoid absolute terms (e.g., never) frequently associated with false statements.
6. Items should measure important learning objectives.
7. State item stems in a positive form.
8. Make response choices grammatically consistent with the item stem.
9. Include repetitive words in the item stem instead of the choices.
10. Make response choices approximately the same word length.
11. Each item should be independent.
12. Use familiar or content appropriate terms to reduce unnecessary item difficulty.
13. Present response choices in a logical order (e.g., random).
14. Avoid using verbatim statements copied from lecture notes or books.
15. Use 3 to 5 response choices for each item.
16. Avoid using response choices with similar interpretations or meanings.
17. Use efficient item response formats for reading and selecting response choices.
18. Create distracters based on common student misconceptions or errors.

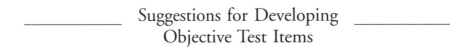

Suggestions for Developing Objective Test Items

Multiple-Choice Items

Multiple-choice items represent the most frequently used selected-response format in college classrooms; instructors should become adept at creating and revising them (Jacobs & Chase, 1992). The benefits of using multiple-choice items include accurate and efficient scoring, improved score reliability, a wide sampling of learning objectives, and the ability to obtain diagnostic information from incorrect answers. The limitations include the increased time necessary for creating items that accurately discriminate mastery from nonmastery performance, the difficulty of creating items that measure complex learning objectives (e.g., items that measure the ability to synthesize information), the difficulty and time-consuming nature of creating plausible distracters (i.e., incorrect response alternatives), the increased potential for students to benefit from guessing, and the difficulty of the items can easily become a function of reading ability, even though reading ability may not be the purpose of the assessment. Table 42.1 (above) provides suggestions for developing multiple-choice items. Here is a poor multiple-choice item:

_____ 1. Extraneous variables
  a. invalidate univariate experimental outcomes.
  b. may operate to influence the dependent variable and thus invalidate the experimental outcome.
  c. are always unwanted.
  d. change the results of your experiment.

The item stem is poorly constructed because it does not provide a clearly formulated problem, primarily due to its brevity. Response choice "a" unnecessarily introduces reading difficulty by using complicated vocabulary. Response choice "b" is problematic given that it is visibly longer than the other response choices and reflects a verbatim statement copied directly from a textbook. The length and the verbatim language of response choice "b" provide examinees with clues for selecting the correct answer. Together, response choices "a" and "b" are problematic because they use similar language, making it more difficult for examinees to select a correct answer based on their content knowledge. Response choice "c" is problematic because it uses an absolute term (i.e., always) frequently associated with false statements. In general, it is difficult to identify the correct response choice because the item stem is ambiguous and the distracters are not distinguishably less correct. Here is an improved multiple-choice item.

_____ 1. An extraneous variable is described as
  a. a factor that is manipulated by the experimenter.
  b. the effect side of a cause-and-effect relationship.
  c. an unwanted factor that can influence an experimenter.
  d. the cause side of a cause-and-effect relationship.

True–False Items

True–false item formats typically measure the ability to determine whether declarative statements are correct. True–false judgments are difficult to construct because they usually reflect isolated statements with no frame of reference (e.g., Thorndike, 1997). The benefits of using true–false items include ease of construction, accurate and efficient scoring, flexibility in measuring learning objectives, and the usefulness for measuring outcomes or objectives with two possible alternatives. The limitations include an increased guessing potential, the difficulty of creating unequivocally true or false items, the items typically measure trivial knowledge, and the items do not provide diagnostic information from incorrect answers unless students are required to change false statements into true statements. Table 42.2 presents suggestions for developing true–false items. Here is a poor true–false item.

_____ 1. Unfortunately, plagiarism is not uncommon in colleges and universities for established professionals and students.

This item is problematic because it is presented in a negative format. True–false items are more effective when they reflect simple, positive declarative statements. Avoid negatively worded statements because your items should assess student content knowledge and not the ability to read and interpret complex sentences. Here is an improved true and false item.

_____ 1. Plagiarism is a common problem for colleges and universities.

Table 42.2: Suggestions for developing true and false items

---

1. Present items clearly, briefly, and in a positive format.
2. Items should be defensibly true or false.
3. Avoid absolute terms (e.g., always).
4. Items should measure a single, important concept.
5. Avoid verbatim statements from lectures or books.
6. Avoid terms that unnecessarily increase item difficulty.
7. Use slightly more (15%) false items because they discriminate more effectively.
8. Avoid ambiguous or indefinite terms.
9. Use items that measure more complex learning objectives.
10. Items should be approximately equal in word length.
11. Avoid terms that may be offensive.
12. Provide adequate information so students can respond accurately.
13. Attribute statements of opinion to a reliable source.
14. When measuring cause-and-effect relations use only true statements.

Matching Items

Matching items measure associative learning or simple recall, but they can assess more complex learning objectives (Jacobs & Chase, 1992). The benefits of using matching items include ease of construction, accurate and efficient scoring, and short reading and response times. The limitations include measurement of simple recall or associations, difficulty in selecting homogeneous or similar sets of stimuli and response choices, and provision of unintended clues for response choices. Table 42.3 presents suggestions for developing matching exercises. Here is a poor matching exercise.

Directions: Match the following:

_____ 1. B. F. Skinner	A.	$r = +1.00$
_____ 2. Sigmund Freud	B.	measure of variability
_____ 3. Perfect positive correlation	C.	operant conditioning
_____ 4. Standard deviation	D.	psychoanalysis

This matching exercise is poorly constructed because the directions are vague and brief. Matching exercises should include directions that clearly state the basis for matching and explain if a response choice can be used more than once. This exercise also uses hetero-geneous content. Here is an improved matching exercise.

Directions: Match the response choices (right) with the stimuli (left). Each response
choice should only be used once.

____ 1. presents statistical findings	A. Title page
____ 2. a short summary of the article	B. Abstract
____ 3. includes the full address of the author(s)	C. Introduction
____ 4. reports the bottom line of the experiment	D. Method
____ 5. bibliographic information	E. Results
____ 6. tells how the experiment was conducted	F. Discussion
____ 7. reviews previous research	

Table 42.3: Suggestions for developing matching items

1. Provide clear directions and expectations.
2. Use homogeneous or similar matching content.
3. Arrange stimuli and response choices in random order.
4. Use more response choices and fewer stimuli to prevent students from relying on elimination.
5. Include 5 to 15 matching items.
6. The item stimuli should be longer than the response choices.
7. Each section should appear on the same page.
8. Group stimuli on the left and response choices on the right.
9. Each item should present a single idea or problem.
10. Use capital letters for responses.
11. Items should measure specified learning objectives.
12. Provide designated spaces for students to write their responses.
13. Present items in a positive format.
14. Avoid verbatim statements copied from lectures or books.
15. Avoid grammatical clues.
16. Avoid terms that may be offensive.

Suggestions for Developing Essay Test Items

Essay questions are more useful than selection-type items when measuring the ability to organize, integrate, and express ideas (Gronlund, 2003). The benefits of using essay items include ease of construction; the items typically measure more complex learning objectives; and the items effectively measure the ability to organize, compose, and logically express relations or ideas. The limitations include the fact that essays are time consuming to grade, decreased score reliability when compared with objective items, the time required to answer each item limits the ability to sample several learning objectives, and language dependence. Table 42.4 presents suggestions for developing essay items. Here are examples of poor and improved essay items.

Table 42.4: Suggestions for developing essay items

1. Items should clearly explain the required task.
2. Items should measure a specific, typically complex learning objective.
3. Provide scoring criteria for each item (i.e., assign point values).
4. All students should respond to the same items.
5. Provide a suggested time limit for each item to facilitate time management.
6. Items should have a clearly defensible correct answer.
7. Pretest items by writing exemplar or sample answers.
8. Avoid terms that may be offensive.

Learning Objective: The student should be able to explain how the normal curve serves as a statistical model for describing data.

Problematic item:
  Directions: describe the normal distribution.

Improved item:
  Directions: explain the relation between the mean and the variance in a normal distribution (10 points). Briefly describe how the standard normal distribution serves as a statistical model for estimation and hypothesis testing (10 points).

 The first item is problematic because the focus is too broad. Examinees can take a wide variety of approaches to answering the item, but will likely not know the instructor's intent. Also the item does not specifically measure the intended learning objective. Lastly, the first item does not identify the possible point values. Assigning point values will help examinees to organize their responses and manage their testing time more efficiently.

Conclusion

This chapter provided instructors with prescriptive suggestions for constructing or revising test items. The assessment process involves more than merely constructing test items. Instructors should also become adept at administering, scoring, and interpreting tests. If you are interested in learning more about assessment, I recommend the works previously cited and Adkins (1974), Airasian (1997), Ebel and Frisbie (1986), and Frye (1989).

REFERENCES

Adkins, D. C. (1974). *Test construction: Development and interpretation of achievement tests.* Columbus, OH: Charles E. Merril.
Airasian, P. W. (1997). *Classroom assessment* (3rd ed.). New York: McGraw-Hill.

Bloom, B. S., Engelhart, M. D., Furst, E. J., Hill, W. H., & Krathwohl, D. R. (1956). *Taxonomy of educational objectives: The classification of educational goals.* New York: David McKay.

Ebel, R. L., & Frisbie, D. A. (1986). *Essentials of educational measurement* (4th ed.). Englewood Cliffs, NJ: Prentice-Hall.

Frye, B. J. (1989). Planning student evaluation, constructing tests and grading. In D. Greive (ed.), *Teaching in college* (pp. 169–201). Cleveland, OH: INFO-TEC.

Gronlund, N. E. (2003). *Assessment of student achievement* (7th ed.). Boston: Allyn & Bacon.

Jacobs, L. C., & Chase, C. I. (1992). *Developing and using tests effectively: A guide for faculty.* San Francisco, CA: Josey-Bass.

Ory, J. C., & Ryan, K. E. (1993). *Tips for improving testing and grading* (4th ed.). Newbury Park, CA: Sage.

Thorndike, R. M. (1997). *Measurement and evaluation in psychology and education* (6th ed.). Upper Saddle River, NJ: Prentice-Hall.

43
Principles of Effective Grading

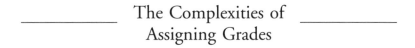

Ψ

Peter J. Giordano
Belmont University

If you ask most faculty why they became college professors, they are not likely to say, "Grading! It's because I love grading student work and talking to students about their grades!" Nevertheless, evaluating coursework and assigning grades is a very important teaching activity. If handled with care, grading can be beneficial both to students and faculty.

The Complexities of Assigning Grades

Before discussing principles of effective grading, consider some of the complexities of the grading landscape. First, although grading is a separate activity from assessment, the two are closely connected and often the line between them is blurred. Assessment is the process of gathering information about student learning, whereas grading involves evaluating and judging this information (Brookhart, 1999). Assessment may be used to help gauge student learning outside of the formal evaluation process in the course (Angelo & Cross, 1993). For example, near the end of a class an instructor might ask students to explain in writing a particularly difficult concept as a way to assess their understanding, without assigning grades to their responses. A similar question might be asked on a formal evaluation such as a test. In this latter case, grades are then used to evaluate learning.

Second, grades mean different things to different constituencies in the academic enterprise (Milton, Pollio, & Eison, 1986). Students, faculty, parents, employers, academic administrators, or graduate-school admissions committees all bring their own perspectives to the meaning of grades. Consider the example of a grade dispute. Any faculty member who has observed the unfolding drama of a grade challenge or, worse, been directly involved in one, can attest to the truth of this observation.

A third issue is the difference between grades as a summative versus a formative measure of learning (Angelo & Cross, 1993). Perhaps too often faculty view grades as a numeric indicator that captures how students performed on a specific assignment or on an entire body of work throughout the course. This understanding of grading is accurate but incomplete. Faculty can also use grades in a formative sense to help students ascertain where they are academically strong and where they need improvement. This formative understanding of assigning grades, particularly grades that students earn during the term rather than at its conclusion, can help students improve their performance while the semester is still underway. Milton et al. (1986) argued persuasively that grades should be used formatively, not just to rank students. In a related sense, faculty can also use the process of grading to become more effective teachers (Bain, 2004).

Finally, faculty must grapple with the psychometric issues embedded in constructing evaluation instruments and assigning grades. If evaluation instruments such as tests are not psychometrically sound, then it follows that grades lose their meaning. A sample of relevant questions include (a) Are the evaluations I use reliable and valid measures of student learning?; (b) What is the best way to aggregate grades at the end of the semester, especially when grades might be based on different scales of measurement (e.g., a percentage score on a test vs. a rubric score on a course project); and (c) Should I use a contract grading system instead of a points-for-performance system? Addressing these questions is beyond the scope of this chapter, but I raise them to highlight some of the inherent complexities of grading. Chapter 42 of this book deals with issues of test construction.

Principles of Effective Grading

As the discussion thus far makes clear, assigning grades is a complex teaching activity with important implications for individual and social dynamics in the classroom. In the remainder of this chapter, I offer some principles of effective grading.

Always Recognize the Complex Nature of Assigning Grades

I have clearly made this point already, but I believe it is a central, organizing principle to keep at the forefront of your thinking about grades. As soon as you forget it, you are in danger of becoming a "number cruncher" rather than a facilitator of learning. Paradoxically, although faculty should pay careful attention to the complexity of grading, faculty should simultaneously deemphasize grades with students, as studies suggest too much emphasis on grades undermines student performance (e.g., Sheldon, 2004).

In a phrase, assigning grades is more than computing a number and connecting it to a corresponding letter, especially to students. Here is one, all too common, example. If a student approaches you after an assignment and is upset that he or she received a 90 rather than a 95, it is important to treat the concern respectfully. In your mind, the student might be splitting hairs and attaching far too much value to the 5-point difference. What matters most, however, is the student's perspective. Arguing with a student in this situation is typically fruitless and likely will fuel the flame of disappointment. A better approach is to empathize with the student's frustration, while explaining how you arrived at the grade you did. Paying attention to the student's specific concerns will help you understand the unique personality and needs of this student, so that you can help him or her be even more successful in the future. Lowman (1995) and Milton et al. (1986) provided excellent discussions of different types of students and their impact on classroom dynamics.

Be Sure Your Grades Reflect What You Want Students to Learn

This principle may seem self-evident, but it is deceptively tricky. For example, a central goal for your Introductory Psychology course may be for students to learn to think scientifically about behavior and mental events (Halonen, Bosack, Clay, & McCarthy, 2003). If a student can earn an A in your course, however, by correctly answering only factual multiple-choice questions without showing evidence of scientific reasoning about psychological phenomena, then grades do not reflect an important learning goal in the course. It is important, therefore, to be intentional in aligning course goals, assessments, and grades. In this way, grades become a meaningful measure of student learning, rather than a necessary evil not clearly connected to relevant learning outcomes (Bain, 2004).

Assign Frequent Grades and Assess a Variety of Skills or Domains

Students generally have some anxiety about their evaluation. By having frequent evaluations and grades and by measuring a variety of cognitive skills (e.g., factual recall, thinking, writing) you provide a greater chance for students to develop intellectually (Brookhart, 1999; Davis, 1993). If you currently use primarily tests to assess and grade students, experiment with other approaches such as essays, problem sets, take-home exams, oral exams, group exams, or portfolios (Davis, 1993). In general, by sampling student performance with a variety of methods and across cognitive skills you obtain a more complete understanding of their progress.

Be Explicit About Your Grading Policies and Procedures

Performance expectations and methods of calculating grades should be crystal clear to students. The syllabus should carefully describe assignments, clearly indicate the relative weight of each assignment, and outline how you will compute and assign grades. If you have a complex system of assignments and grades, I suggest you let a colleague unfamiliar with your course examine your syllabus to make sure you have adequately explained things.

Treat Students Fairly and with Equality

I have included fairness and equality in one principle, although these issues are not identical. The former relates to being consistent with your stated policies for the course.

For example, if your syllabus indicates that the final exam in your course counts 30 percent toward the final grade, then it is imperative that it does so. The fairness dictum relates to the principle of being explicit with students about grading policies and procedures. It is not fair to students if you are unclear about this important dimension of the course. I believe it is better to have too much information in your syllabus about these issues rather than too little. Certainly some flexibility in your syllabus can be useful (Davis, 1993). However, reserve this flexibility for issues of course pacing and scheduling. I strongly recommend against altering your grading policies once the course starts.

Regarding equality, never play favorites or give one student an opportunity that is not available to all students in the class. For instance, at the end of the semester if a student approaches you asking about extra credit opportunities to improve a poor course grade, never allow such extra credit unless you make this opportunity available to other students in the class. Even if a student is in a precarious academic situation (e.g., risk of withdrawal from the university) because of his or her performance in your class, you should stay with the stated policies for your course. Students typically respect the explanation that it would not be fair to others in the class if one student had the opportunity when other students did not. Additionally, your position in this type of situation is strengthened if all semester you have encouraged students who are struggling to come speak to you soon after a poor grade, rather than waiting until the end of the term. Some students might need special encouragement, especially if they are shy or intimidated by college professors (see Lowman, 1995).

Avoid Grading on a Curve

I agree with McKeachie (2002), Walvoord and Anderson (1998), and Davis (1993) that grading on a curve can interfere with student learning and should be avoided. Announcing to a class of 30 students at the outset of a semester that "Three of you will receive As, three will receive Fs, and the remainder will be somewhere in between" is anathema to a hospitable learning environment. This approach to grading, which I have admittedly described in the extreme, may intimidate students and encourage them to see you as arbitrary and cold-hearted in your approach to assigning grades. Grading on a curve also suggests that grades are a limited resource, something that students must compete for in an academic environment of survival of the fittest.

Given these potential problems, it is best to utilize a clearly articulated criterion-referenced grading system. In this type of system, grades are based on mastery or competence in specific content or behavioral domains. In theory, therefore, all students have the potential to earn an "A" in the class, although properly constructed evaluation devices that are sensitive to individual differences in learning would not yield such a distribution of scores.

One caveat is important to note. It is vital to be sensitive to your institutional climate regarding grade distributions. If a criterion-referenced grading system leads to too many high grades in the view of a department chair or dean, for example, it will be useful to review your criteria for assigning grades. Revised criteria should then be clearly communicated to students at the start of the next term.

Conclusion

Good teachers, even experienced ones, spend lots of time talking to other teachers about their craft (Bain, 2004). They exchange ideas on teaching philosophy and practices they employ. Talking about issues related to principles of effective grading should also be a part of the ongoing conversation among teachers. With proper care and attention, grading can be an effective tool in the teacher's array of pedagogical techniques.

REFERENCES

Angelo, T. A., & Cross, K. P. (1993). *Classroom assessment techniques: A handbook for college teachers* (2nd ed.). San Francisco: Jossey-Bass.

Bain, K. (2004). *What the best college teachers do.* Cambridge, MA: Harvard University Press.

Brookhart, S. M. (1999). *The art and science of classroom assessment: The missing part of pedagogy.* ASHE-ERIC Higher Education Report (vol. 27, no. 1). Washington, DC: The George Washington University, Graduate School of Education and Human Development.

Davis, B. G. (1993). *Tools for teaching.* San Francisco: Jossey-Bass.

Halonen, J. S., Bosack, T., Clay, S., & McCarthy, M. (2003). A rubric for learning, teaching, and assessing scientific inquiry in psychology. *Teaching of Psychology, 30,* 196–208.

Lowman, J. (1995). *Mastering the techniques of teaching* (2nd ed.). San Francisco: Jossey-Bass.

McKeachie, W. J. (2002). *Teaching tips: Strategies, research, and theory for college and university teachers* (11th ed.). Boston: Houghton Mifflin.

Milton, O., Pollio, H. R., & Eison, J. A. (1986). *Making sense of college grades.* San Francisco: Jossey-Bass.

Sheldon, J. (2004). Evaluation: Grading students without degrading learning. *National Teaching and Learning Forum, 13 (3).* Retrieved May 6, 2004, from www.ntlf.com/restricted/v13n3.htm

Walvoord, B. E., & Anderson, V. J. (1998). *Effective grading: A tool for learning and assessment.* San Francisco: Jossey-Bass.

44
Written and Oral Assignments

Ψ

Harold L. Miller, Jr. & Casey L. Lance
Brigham Young University

Initially we sought methods of written and oral assignments that were identifiably unique to the psychology curriculum. Our search was unsuccessful, however, and we turned instead to articulating the desiderata for written and oral assignments that effectively enhance students' understanding of the subject matter of the psychology curriculum, and to documenting exemplars. We assert that, in addition to the advance of understanding, the well-crafted assignment simultaneously informs the teacher of the status of students' understanding.

That students write to demonstrate and improve their understanding of the subject matter is age-old. To be successful, written and oral assignments should meet three criteria. First is the assurance that the assignment coheres with the teacher's objectives for the course in which the assignment is embedded, and that it links to what both precedes and follows in the course design (cf. Morgan & Morgan, ch. 9 this volume). Pointing up the relevance of the assignment to course objectives and fitting it meaningfully into the student's experience within the course underscore its credibility for students and teacher alike. The second criterion is that the details of the assignment, including its due date, and its grading rubric (if indeed it is to be graded) be stated clearly (again, cf. Morgan & Morgan this volume). You should give students adequate opportunity to seek further clarification if needed. Last, the grading rubric applied to the assignment should inform students of correctible deficiencies, should any exist, as well as pointing them in productive directions for future improvement.

Writing and speaking, both formally and informally, about assigned material can provide students with an invaluable index of the extent of their understanding of the material and promote further learning (Nodine, 1999, 2002). The acts of writing and speaking are self-revealing (students discover in the moment whether their understanding is what they had assumed) and may also be publicly revealing (to peers or the teacher or both as the occasion dictates). As such they can be of real, even irreplaceable value to the teacher's assessment of student performance in the course – a persuasive premise for the inclusion of writing and oral assignments in course requirements (McKeachie, 2002).

Informal and Formal Assignments

A wide range of options is available to the teacher for both informal and formal written and oral assignments. Informal assignments typically require less preparation on the part of both student and teacher. They can be introduced and completed within the same class meeting and can be used strategically to steer the remainder of the meeting or subsequent meetings (see Angelo & Cross, 1993, for a now-classic compilation of such assignments). In a simple illustration, during a class meeting students gather in small groups to discuss a question presented to all. After a brief period of discussion, each group provides a short answer in writing or an oral presentation. The teacher then utilizes the answers, or a sample of the answers, to orient the remainder of the class meeting or future meetings. Among recent variations on this simple protocol are Problem-Based Learning (www.udel.edu/pbl/) and Case Study Teaching (http://ublib.buffalo.edu/libraries/projects/cases/ubcase.htm), which now publishes case-based assignments for undergraduate psychology courses.

More formal assignments may require the students' time either in class or outside of class. In either case, careful prescription of the assignment (unless it is meant to be unstructuredly creative) usually will enhance its effectiveness. Among other things, the teacher should specify the genre of assignment (for example, essay, report, review, poster, PowerPoint show, etc.), the required stylistic and format conventions, and the due date. At the same time, the specification of the grading rubric for the assignment will alert students to the relative importance of its components and the expectations to which their work will be accountable. Ideally, formal assignments will include provision for one or more revisions prior to the final product, with each revision receiving the benefit of written commentary, including suggestions for improvement (Handelsman & Krest, 1999).

The Trade-off between an Assignment's Depth and Divided Authorship

Much can be said in favor of written and oral assignments with sole authorship, particularly if the assignment requires the student to engage in extensive work outside of class meetings – for example, in library or laboratory or field research. Coming up against the demands of such an assignment is at once sobering and enthusing, especially if it represents the opportunity to add understanding of a topic of personal interest. It has the further advantage of preparing students who may pursue an academic or research career with first-hand experience in the inevitable aloneness of rigorous scholarship.

On the other hand, it is worth pointing out that academic work, both intra- and inter-disciplinary, is increasingly a team effort. Even in the more general marketplace of post-baccalaureate employment that awaits many students, teamwork is an asset that makes a virtue of written and oral assignments requiring cooperative completion in a small group. However, team assignments, even if well specified and well intended, should carry this caveat to the teacher: The likelihood of the assignment's success is inversely related to the amount of work it will require outside of class. Generally, the teacher is best advised to implement team assignments that can be pursued and completed during class meetings. This strategy optimizes the extent to which students in a team promote each other's understanding of the subject matter while defusing the perceived inequities (and attendant animosities) that invariably result when the team is required to do work outside of class.

TBL: An Instructive and Potentially Productive Model

Models of teaching that make a place for written and oral assignments often do so by situating those assignments in the traditional context of lectures and examinations while minimizing the amount of work on the assignments that is actually performed during class meetings. Nor is it unusual for such assignments to be due toward the end of the course. An alternative model, known as Team-Based Learning (TBL; see Michaelsen, Knight, & Fink, 2004; also http://atlasservices.ou.edu/idp/teamlearning/index.htm), is a radical departure from tradition and casts the use of written and oral assignments in new light.

At the heart of TBL is the readiness assessment, administered at the outset of a topical unit to assess students' understanding of the assigned reading for the unit; that is, their readiness to consider the conceptual content of the unit. Following the readiness assessment is a judicious mix of (a) instruction that focuses on the concepts diagnosed by the assessment as problematic for students and (b) application activities designed to promote further understanding of selected concepts. These activities consist of written and oral assignments with the proviso that student teams complete them during the class meeting rather than outside of class. The out-of-class work that students perform is exclusively the assigned reading and preparation for the readiness assessments.

Used properly, TBL readily conduces to teamwork: a ready exchange among team members about the task at hand, the conceptual material it invokes, and the completion of the product the assignment specified. Students teach each other as the occasion requires and draw from each other's strengths in formulating a production plan and the product itself – all within the confines of the time allotted within the regular class meeting. Although inequity is not necessarily dissolved in this process, it is possible to negotiate it on the spot in the service of the team's product and thus practice skills that are likely to be valuable in later workplaces. TBL assignments favor tasks with alternative solution paths and multiple correct answers while requiring teams to provide rigorous justification (*vis-à-vis* the grading rubric) of their particular solutions in written or oral statements or both.

An Outline of Prospective Assignments

The outline that appears below lists sample findings in the published intersection between the design and implementation of written and oral assignments and the teaching of psychology. The references in the outline are representative of informal and formal assignments that, when used in a manner consistent with the three criteria offered earlier, promise to enhance students' understanding.

I. Written Assignments
    A. Progressive papers (Finken & Cooney, 2003; Hemenover, Caster, & Mizumoto, 1999)
    B. Multiperspectival papers (Carlson, 1992)
    C. Group papers and projects (Dunn, 1994; Herringer, 2000; Millis, 2001)
    D. Reflective writing
       1. Logs (Ferrari & Scher, 2000)
       2. Diaries (Mayo, 2003)
       3. Journals (Connor-Greene, 2000; Langer, 2002;)
       4. Letters home (Keith, 1999)
    E. Portfolios (Rickabaugh, 1993)
    F. Interpretive writing (Beins, 1993)
    G. Short writing (Butler, Phillmann, & Smart, 2001; Wade, 1995)
    H. Literature reviews (Froese, Gantz, & Henry, 1998; Henderson, 2000; Poe, 1990)
    I. Written feedback (Willingham, 1990)
    J. Reaction papers (Mio & Barker-Hackett, 2003)
    K. Knowledge maps (Czuchry & Dansereau, 1996)
    L. Student newspapers (Bryant & Benjamin, 1999)
II. Oral Assignments
    A. The use of presentation software (Downing & Garmon, 2001; Marek, Christopher, & Koenig, 2002)
    B. Multimedia presentations (Giuliano, 2001)
    C. Workshop presentations (Goldstein, 1993)
    D. Debates (O'Kon & Sutz, 2004)
    E. Minilectures (Goodwin, 1994)
III. The Combination of Written and Oral Assignments
    A. Multimedia presentations (Hansen & Williams, 2003)
    B. In-class poster sessions (Baird, 1991)

Conclusion

To the extent that the teacher's objectives for a course include the advancement of students' understanding of its factual and conceptual material, the inclusion of written and oral assignments as part of the course requirements is strongly indicated. These assignments, formal and informal, can serve the student and teacher as assays of the depth and quality of the student's understanding. They can be particularly effective when demonstrably connected to antecedent and subsequent events in the course schedule. Coupling a clear and comprehensive prescription of the assignment with a grading rubric (when the assignment is to be graded) may further enhance its efficacy.

Teachers should carefully weigh the relative merits of individual versus small-group assignments, as well as those of assignments that can be completed during class meetings – as advocated by TBL – rather than requiring work outside of class. When assignments are properly designed, their results inform students of the status of their understanding and point them in productive directions for further understanding. The sample assignments included in the chapter's culminating outline exemplify promising means by which you may achieve this estimable outcome.

REFERENCES

Angelo, T. A., & Cross, K. P. (1993). *Classroom assessment techniques: A handbook for college faculty* (2nd ed.). San Francisco: Jossey-Bass.

Baird, B. N. (1991). In-class poster session. *Teaching of Psychology, 18*, 27–30.

Beins, B. C. (1993). Writing assignments in statistics classes encourage students to learn interpretation. *Teaching of Psychology, 20*, 161–4.

Bryant, W. H. M., & Benjamin Jr., L. T. (1999). Read all about it! Wundt opens psychology lab: A newspaper assignment for history of psychology. In L. T. Benjamin, B. F. Nodine, R. M. Ernst, & C. Blair-Broeker (eds.), *Activities handbook for the teaching of psychology* (vol. 4, pp. 47–9). Washington, DC: American Psychological Association.

Butler, A., Phillmann, K.-B., & Smart, L. (2001). Active learning within a lecture: Assessing the impact of short, in-class writing exercises. *Teaching of Psychology, 28*, 257–9.

Carlson, J. F. (1992). From Metropolis to Never-neverland: Analyzing fictional characters in a personality theory course. *Teaching of Psychology, 19*, 153–5.

Connor-Greene, P. A. (2000). Making connections: Evaluating the effectiveness of journal writing in enhancing student learning. *Teaching of Psychology, 27*, 44–6.

Czuchry, M., & Dansereau, D. F. (1996). Node-link mapping as an alternative to traditional writing assignments in undergraduate psychology courses. *Teaching of Psychology, 23*, 91–6.

Downing, J., & Garmon, C. (2001). Teaching students in the basic course how to use presentation software. *Communication Education, 50*, 218–29.

Dunn, D. S. (1994). Lessons learned from an interdisciplinary writing course: Implications for student writing in psychology. *Teaching of Psychology, 21*, 223–7.

Ferrari, J. R., & Scher, S. J. (2000). Toward an understanding of academic and nonacademic tasks procrastinated by students: The use of daily logs. *Teaching of Psychology, 37*, 359–66.

Finken, L. L., & Cooney, R. R. (2003). A comparison of progressive and two-draft writing assignments in introductory psychology courses. *Teaching of Psychology, 30*, 246–8.

Froese, A. D., Gantz, B. S., & Henry, A. L. (1998). Teaching students to write literature reviews: A meta-analytic model. *Teaching of Psychology, 25*, 102–5.

Giuliano, T. A. (2001). Student presentations of the life and work of prominent social psychologists. *Teaching of Psychology, 28*, 269–71.

Goldstein, G. S. (1993). Using a group workshop to encourage collaborative learning in an undergraduate counseling course. *Teaching of Psychology, 20*, 108–10.

Goodwin, C. J. (1994). Toward *eloquentia perfecta* in the history and systems course. *Teaching of Psychology, 21*, 91–3.

Handelsman, M. M., & Crest, M. (1999). Improving your students' writing: Arts and drafts. In B. Perlman, L. I. McCann, & S. H. Mcfadden (eds.), *Lessons learned: Practical advice for the teaching of psychology* (pp. 179–84). Washington, DC: American Psychological Society.

Hansen, C. E., & Williams, M. R. (2003). Comparison of cross-cultural changes: From traditional lecture course to contemporary course with biblio-learning, video-learning, and experiential exercises. *Journal of Instructional Psychology, 30*, 197–206.

Hemenover, S. H., Caster, J. B., & Mizumoto, A. (1999). Combining the use of progressive writing techniques and popular movies in introductory psychology. *Teaching of Psychology, 26*, 196–8.

Henderson, B. B. (2000). The reader's guide as an integrative writing experience. *Teaching of Psychology, 27*, 130–2.

Herringer, L. G. (2000). The two captains: A research exercise using Star Trek. *Teaching of Psychology, 27*, 50–1.

Keith, K. D. (1999). Letters home: Writing for understanding in introductory psychology. In L. T. Benjamin, B. F. Nodine, R. M. Ernst, & C. Blair-Broeker (eds.), *Activities handbook for the teaching of psychology* (vol. 4, pp. 30–2). Washington, DC: American Psychological Association.

Langer, A. M. (2002). Reflecting on practice: Using learning journals in higher and continuing education. *Teaching in Higher Education, 7*, 337–51.

Marek, P., Christopher, A. N., & Koenig, C. S. (2002). Applying technology to facilitate poster presentations. *Teaching of Psychology, 29*, 70–2.

Mayo, J. A. (2003). Observational diary: The merits of journal writing as case-based instruction in introductory psychology. *Journal of Constructivist Psychology, 16*, 233–47.

McKeachie, W. J. (2002). *Teaching tips: Strategies, research, and theory for college and university teachers* (11th ed.). Boston: Houghton Mifflin.

Michaelsen, L. K., Knight, A. B., & Fink. L. D. (2004). *Team-based learning: A transformative use of small groups in college teaching.* Sterling, VA: Stylus Publishing.

Millis, K. K. (2001). Comparing two collaborative projects in a cognitive psychology course. *Teaching of Psychology, 28*, 263–5.

Mio, J. S., & Barker-Hackett, L. B. (2003). Reaction papers and journal writing as techniques for assessing resistance in multicultural courses. *Journal of Multicultural Counseling and Development, 31*, 12–19.

Nodine, B. F. (1999). Why not make writing assignments? In B. Perlman, L. I. McCann, & S. H. McFadden (eds.), *Lessons learned: Practical advice for the teaching of psychology* (pp. 167–72). Washington, DC: American Psychological Society.

Nodine, B. F. (2002). Writing: Models, examples, teaching advice, and a heartfelt plea. In S. Davis & W. Buskist (eds.), *The teaching of psychology: Essays in honor of Wilbert J. McKeachie and Charles L. Brewer* (pp. 107–20). Mahwah, NJ: Erlbaum.

O'Kon, J., & Sutz, R. (2004, Aug. 4). Using in-class debates to teach gender issues in psychology. Article posted to PSYCHTEACHER@list.kennesaw.edu.

Poe, R. E. (1990). A strategy for improving literature reviews in psychology courses. *Teaching of Psychology, 17*, 54–5.

Rickabaugh, C. A. (1993). The psychology portfolio: Promoting writing and critical thinking about psychology. *Teaching of Psychology, 20*, 170–2.

Wade, C. (1995). Using writing to develop and assess critical thinking. *Teaching of Psychology, 22*, 24–8.

Willingham, D. B. (1990). Effective feedback on written assignments. *Teaching of Psychology, 17*, 10–13.

45
Group Work
Ψ

Patti Price
Wingate University

In preparing students for life beyond college, skills in working effectively with others must be taught. Group work enables students to learn skills they will need to communicate with others, to solve problems, to engage in critical thinking, to prepare for employment, and to take on complex tasks (Johnson & Smith, 1997; Mello, 1993). Regardless of area of study, students must be able to show future employers they have the ability to work successfully with others (Forman, 1994, as cited in Livingstone & Lynch, 2002). Additionally, these experiences are also effective teachers of time-management skills (Garvin & Butcher, 1995).

---------------- Student Attitudes ----------------

With the obvious benefits to group work, it would seem that students would welcome the opportunity for it. Indeed, according to Huxham and Land (2000) students' initial attitudes toward group work are at least partially positive. Students reported a sense of excitement at getting to know and to interact with other students and at obtaining new knowledge. Students also reported some anxiety as well as hesitancy. Unfortunately, after several experiences with group work, students lost their initial excitement and enthusiasm, leaving only the anxiety and ambivalence.

The anxiety and ambivalence may be due to the phenomenon of social loafing (Bourner, Hughes, & Bourner, 2001). Although students reported the group experience was beneficial in terms of the learning involved, they also reported a great deal of frustration when others did not contribute equally to the final product.

For group work to be a positive experience, it is essential that the instructor carefully plan the assignment, which must be sufficiently complex (Meyers, 1997). Additionally, decreases in student loafing may occur when the task is more difficult and requires input from all group members. Livingstone and Lynch (2002) noted that faculty must have open and frank conversations with students regarding ground rules, including the amount of work that will be involved and how it will be evaluated. Teachers should also state the benefits of working as a group.

Group Assignment

Included in the planning process is the assignment of students to groups. Keep the number of groups to a manageable number so you can easily monitor both the project's progress and group dynamics (Duemer et al., 2004). Additionally, do not assign more than five students to any single group because increases in social loafing may occur with increases in group size (Bourner et al., 2001).

Traditionally, instructors assign students to groups in one of three ways: student choice, random assignment, or criteria-based (Huxham & Land, 2000). Of these methods, most instructors use student choice or random assignment (Halstead & Martin, 2002). Student-selected groups tend to be ineffective as some students may feel left out of the process (i.e., shy students) or may be left out intentionally (Mitchell, Reilly, Bramwell, Solnosky, & Lilly, 2004). Student-selected groups are also less likely to be diverse and to engage in critical thinking because new ideas may not be introduced. Additionally, time is often not managed effectively because it is spent talking about topics off-task. Student-selected groups emphasize the individualistic learning approach.

When instructors assign groups, a sociocultural focus takes center stage. With the sociocultural approach, group members are more likely to work together for the benefit of the team and are less likely to focus on personality conflicts. Instructor-assigned groups also benefit from the opportunity to get to know class members with whom they might not otherwise interact (Mills, 2003).

Task Division

To increase the likelihood that groups will function as teams, tasks should be dividable and assigned so that each individual has a responsibility in contributing to the group's success (Livingstone & Lynch, 2002). This tactic gives the individual a feeling of empowerment and decreases anxiety and social loafing. Groups can also gain a sense of empowerment if you allow them to select their own topic rather than randomly assigning one (Mills, 2003).

Delegate specific responsibilities with each group member's job. Roles that you can assign include group leader, mediator in times of conflict, time-management director, and others as called for by the task. In assigning students to groups with one individual as the group leader, it is important that this individual keep a sense of humor in times of group conflict and be assertive and confident in his or her abilities to guide others. The individual should have some skill as recognized by classmates (e.g., knowledge related to the project, seniority, previous knowledge about the instructor's expectations; Duemer et al., 2004). The group mediator should be someone who can openly discuss the group's shortcomings including issues of social loafing. Students' frustration with group experience often results when they fail to discuss group interaction problems such as one student failing to contribute or one student trying to complete the group work individually. The time-management director should have the ability to keep the group on task by providing specific deadlines and communicating completion of each individual's assigned task to the group as a whole (Duemer et al., 2004). Setting deadlines helps keep the group on-task and helps to avoid tension due to one or more individuals not completing an assigned task.

Encouragement of Teamwork

After the instructor assigns groups and the roles within groups, teach your students how to work together as a team (Johnson & Johnson, 1989/1990). The instructor must assist students in getting to know one another, possibly through icebreaker activities; coach them in honestly communicating with one another; educate them in behaviors supportive of the other group members; and train them in conflict resolution skills. It may also be necessary to assist students in communicating with each other when both traditional and nontraditional students are grouped together (Huxham & Land, 2000). Because it is likely that nontraditional students will have work and family obligations, which make it difficult to meet outside of class time, instructors may consider setting aside class time for group work. This tactic also allows the instructor to observe group dynamics. Groups that work together as a cohesive unit generally experience increased group performance (Meyers, 1997).

Peer Evaluations

Another essential component in increasing collaboration is the use of peer evaluations (Duemer et al., 2004). Barfield (2003) found that students who had the least experience with group work were significantly more likely to support a single group grade for all members. More experienced students had likely experienced a social loafer in the past and were more supportive of individual evaluations. Supporting this notion, Meyers (1997) noted that there was less social loafing when all members were required to contribute because each person had a specific assigned role peers evaluated them based on their performance in that role. Most students' experiences in the past have involved a single group grade, which likely contributed to their negative views of group work (Huxham & Land, 2000). Individual assessments not only produced decreased social loafing, but also increased the instructor's ability to evaluate group dynamics as they relate to the individual as well.

In establishing peer evaluations, instructors should develop a rubric to ensure that all students use the same criteria when assessing their peers (Johnson & Smith, 1997). Setting criteria decreases the likelihood of grade inflation, which occurs when all members are assigned a high score regardless of effort. Lejk and Wyvill (2001) found that assessments conducted in private resulted in better score distinctions between low and high performers. However, in using private assessments, self-evaluations should be excluded. Individuals who contributed significantly tended to underrate their performance; and individuals who contributed less tended to overrate their performance.

One rubric that you can use for peer evaluations includes assigning individuals a score ranging from −1 to 3 (Goldfinch, 1994, as cited in Lejk & Wyvill, 2001) for performance in six different categories including motivation/responsibility/time management, adaptability, creativity/originality, communication skills, general team skills, and technical skills. Webb (1997) suggested an alternative list of performance categories that included the ability to work together and generate new ideas, open handling of conflict and controversy, the ability to give and receive help, equality of participation, social loafing, and division of labor. Johnson and Johnson (1989/1990) also suggested awarding bonus points for actions of support for other team members. This technique has been successful in assisting shy students in contributing to the group.

Another method that can be used for individual assessment is the Complex Peer Evaluation Instrument (Smith, Berry, & Eastman, 1995, as cited in Johnson & Smith, 1997). Members of the group assess each other in five areas: effort, cooperation, initiative, technical knowledge/expertise, and overall contribution. For each category, group members score each other on the basis of 100 points for a possible total of 500 points. The person with the top score in the group is given the 100 and the others are given a score based on the ratio of their score to the top score. Additionally, a paired comparison is used in which each possible combination of pairs is listed under each of the five categories. The scorer must choose which student of each pair rated highest in each category. Although this method of assessment has worked well to discriminate among high and low performers, the instructor must be aware that discrimination based on gender and ethnicity may occur and may require a score adjustment.

Conclusion

Group work requires a great deal of work on the instructor's part to ensure a positive learning experience for all students. Instructors must assign students to groups, ensure that tasks are assigned to each group member, instruct students in proper teamwork, and ensure fair peer assessment. However, the end result will be a positive and overall less stressful outcome for instructors because students learn that group work can be a constructive experience.

Group work allows students to learn the essential skills of working effectively with each other: they learn communication and interpersonal skills, creative problem-solving, and time-management skills that are directly transferable to the workplace (Livingston & Lynch, 2002). Thus, group work prepares students to enter the workforce and to work effectively within their communities.

REFERENCES

Barfield, R. L. (2003). Students' perceptions of and satisfaction with group grades and the group experience in the college classroom. *Assessment & Evaluation in Higher Education, 28,* 355–69.

Bourner, J., Hughes, M., & Bourner, T. (2001). First-year undergraduate experiences of group project work. *Assessment & Evaluation in Higher Education, 26*, 19–39.

Duemer, L. S., Christopher, M., Hardin, F., Olibas, L., Rodgers, T., & Spiller, K. (2004). Case study of characteristics of effective leadership in graduate student collaborative work. *Education, 124*, 721–6.

Garvin, J. W., & Butcher, A. C. (1995). Group projects for first-year university students: An evaluation. *Assessment & Evaluation in Higher Education, 20*, 273–88.

Halstead, A., & Martin, L. (2002). Learning styles: A tool for selecting students for group work. *International Journal of Electrical Engineering Education, 39*, 245–52.

Huxham, M., & Land, R. (2000). Assessing students in group work projects: Can we do better than random? *Innovations in Education and Teaching International, 30*, 17–22.

Johnson, C. B., & Smith, F. I. (1997). Assessment of a complex peer evaluation instrument for team learning and group processes. *Accounting Education, 2*, 21–41.

Johnson, D. W., & Johnson, R. T. (1989/1990). Social skills for successful group work. *Educational Leadership, 47*, 29–33.

Lejk, M., & Wyvill, M. (2001). The effect of the inclusion of self-assessment with peer assessment of contributions to a group project: A quantitative study of secret and agreed assessments. *Assessment & Evaluation in Higher Education, 26*, 551–61.

Livingstone, D., & Lynch, K. (2002). Group project work and student-centred active learning: Two different experiences. *Journal of Geography in Higher Education, 26*, 217–37.

Mello, J. A. (1993). Improving individual member accountability in small group settings. *Journal of Management Education, 17*, 253–9.

Meyers, S. A. (1997). Increasing student participation and productivity in small-group activities for psychology classes. *Teaching of Psychology, 24*, 105–15.

Mills, P. (2003). Group project work with undergraduate veterinary science students. *Assessment & Evaluation in Higher Education, 28*, 527–38.

Mitchell, S. N., Reilly, R., Bramwell, F. G., Lilly, F., & Solnosky, A. (2004). Friendship and choosing groupmates: Preferences for teacher-selected vs. student-selected groupings in high school science classes. *Journal of Instructional Psychology, 31*, 20–32.

Webb, N. M. (1997). Assessing students in small collaborative groups. *Theory into Practice, 36*, 205–13.

46

Writing Letters of Recommendation

Ψ

R. Eric Landrum
Boise State University

Writing letters of recommendation (LoR) may qualify as one of the most time-consuming and critical tasks performed by faculty, yet faculty rarely receive training or guidance as to how to craft a successful LoR (Range et al., 1991). The scholarship concerning LoR deals mostly with how letters are perceived and evaluated, and indirectly addresses writing LoR.

General Concerns

Many letters are so positive about the student that they provide little discriminatory power. Moreover, there appears to be greater reliability between two letters written by the same letter-writer for two different students compared to two separate letters written for the same student (Aamodt, Bryan, & Whitcomb, 1993). The letters may say more about the letter-writer than the applicant! Keep these concerns in mind as you prepare letters of recommendation for your students.

Confidentiality

The Family Education Rights and Privacy Act of 1974 (FERPA, or the Buckley Amendment) permits students access to their educational records (Binder & Gotkin, 2001). When students opt for an open file (i.e., open to the student), under certain circumstances they would have access to the LoR. However, the Buckley Amendment also allows students to waive their right to access to the LoR (called a closed file – unavailable to the applicant); many graduate schools provide this option. Ault (1993) found that students who selected the open-file option believed they could see their letter of recommendation if they are not accepted (only enrolled students can have access to their application files). When the letter-writer knows that the applicant might see the letter (e.g., open file), the letter-writer tends to say nicer things (Aamodt et al., 1993). Faculty need to be aware of this potential bias when writing LoRs.

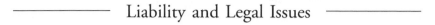

Liability and Legal Issues

Truthfulness is essential when writing a LoR – it is important to provide details that justify your conclusions, whether they are positive or negative (Swenson & Keith-Spiegel, 1991). Writing an unfavorable letter may place you at risk for defamation without the supporting factual basis for your claims. How can you defend yourself from such a claim? Generally, if the statement is factual, truthful, and made in good faith, it is not actionable as libel (Binder & Gotkin, 2001). Faculty should also keep the written request for an LoR from the student (Council of Undergraduate Research [CUR], 2002). Bell (1984) suggested the use of phrases such as "providing the information that was requested" or "providing information to be used for professional purposes only" in the opening paragraph of your LoRs. Inclusion of such phrases may help to imply that the information was not intended to hurt or damage anyone's reputation.

A potential letter-writer has three choices: refuse to write, write a truthful letter, or write a "no comment" letter that supplies objective, non-evaluative details (Sendor, 1997). Faculty are not required to write LoRs (Swenson & Keith-Spiegel, 1991); if the letter can only be negative, it may be best to avoid writing a letter altogether. Swenson and Keith-Spiegel (1991) suggested that if you decline to write a letter for a student, inform the student privately to protect yourself from allegations of slander.

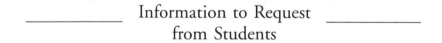

Information to Request from Students

The arduousness of writing a truthful letter can be reduced by having students provide you with the specific information. What type of information might you request from your students? I compiled the following lists from various sources (Keith-Spiegel, 1991; Keith-Spiegel & Wiederman, 2000; Landrum, 1996; Lloyd & Dewey, 1997; Meyer, 2002; Range et al., 1991; University of Wisconsin at Stevens Point, 1999; Zimbardo, 1976). Faculty members should customize these informational requirements for their particular needs.

Information Provided on a Student's Résumé/Curriculum Vitae

Whether LoRs are for a job or graduate school, you may want the student to provide you with a résumé or curriculum vitae (CV). Below are items that would normally be included in these documents:

- Complete name (maiden name, if applicable), including nicknames
- Current contact information: mailing address, telephone numbers, email address
- All higher education institutions attended, locations and dates, including degree status: completed (month, date) or anticipated completion (month, date)
- Major(s), and minor(s) (if any)
- Grade-point average, overall and in the major
- A statement of career interests and professional goals, perhaps with emphasis on strengths and interests as they relate to these goals
- A brief listing of work experience
- A listing of any conference presentations and publications
- Honors and awards received, membership in honor societies, departmental assistant-ships, independent research, specialized computer skills, foreign language skills
- A listing of references/referees, with accurate contact information.

Encourage your students to customize these materials to fit each situation – a résumé for a job application may contain different information and be formatted differently compared to a CV for a graduate school application.

Information Requested from a Student Applying for a Job

Requesting the following additional information from students should facilitate writing LoRs for students applying for a job:

- A résumé, focusing on work experiences and preparation
- A list of relevant, completed courses
- Unofficial copy of transcripts with any courses from the faculty member writing the letter highlighted
- Information from any class assignments on which the student did well
- A summary of the types of contacts (i.e., interactions) with the student, with dates
- A copy of the job advertisement.

Information Requested from a Student Applying to Graduate School

The informational needs for writing an LoR for a graduate school applicant differ from those of a job applicant. These are potential sources of information are helpful when writing LoRs for students with graduate school aspirations:

- A CV focusing on the student's academic accomplishments (e.g., conference presenta-tions, publications)
- The student's personal statement
- GRE scores (verbal, quantitative, analytical)
- An unofficial copy of the student's transcripts, with any courses taken with the faculty member writing the letter highlighted

- Reference/Referee Forms. If the student is requesting a closed file, the student needs to sign the waiver. If there is no form, be sure that students forward to you any instructions provided by the graduate programs
- Some faculty want students to provide pre-addressed and stamped envelopes for letters sent directly to graduate schools. Others prefer to use departmental stationery and postage. Let students know your preference
- The student needs to provide each letter-writer with a master-list of schools with the following information presented for each application: (a) name and mailing address of graduate program, (b) type and level of program to which the student is applying, (c) any additional forms to fill out, (d) letter due dates, and (e) whether materials are returned to student or sent directly by the faculty member. Address letters to specific individuals if possible.

Encourage students to give you at least 3–4 weeks' notice before the first LoR due date; the more time, the better. Faculty need to teach students to ask "would you be willing to write a strong letter of recommendation?" Strong letters can be a pleasure to write; moderate or weak letters can be a struggle at best, and a liability at worst. Some students may not ask you for a LoR if they realize that you cannot write a strong LoR.

Suggestions for Writing the Letter of Recommendation

I close with some suggestions for letter writing, as well as an outline for the structure of a typical LoR (see also Bates College, 1998). I find that using an outline facilitates letter-writing. There is no evidence that this approach is superior, but for me, having a set format makes letter-writing efficient, helping with the momentum of starting and completing letters.

Opening/First Paragraph

State the student's full name, with an indication that he or she has specifically requested the LoR in support of a job application or graduate-school application. For graduate-school applicants, try to customize the letter with the name of the graduate program or department and the name of the university. For job applicants, use the specific job title and the name of the company.

Second Paragraph

Provide a brief overview of the nature of the relationship between you and the student. You might recall classes that the student has taken from you. If the student was a teaching assistant (TA) or research assistant (RA), mention that here, with dates. Close this paragraph with a statement of how well you feel you know the student.

Third (and Successive) Paragraphs

Offer details about the performance of the student in your classes, as an RA or TA, and any other interactions (e.g., research student, internship, officer of Psi Chi, etc.). This information naturally segues into an analysis and evaluation of the skills, abilities, and potential for future success. If possible, relate how the student came through at the right time and completed an important task; such details add clarity and credibility to your letter (Baxter et al., 1981; Knouse, 1983). Favorable anecdotes about the student offer a richness that helps put their accomplishments in perspective (Brown, 1999). Numerous approaches exist for describing the student applicant: the University of California-Berkeley (2003) offers some possibilities: (a) intellectual characteristics, (b) knowledge of field of study, (c) ability to communicate, (d) industry and self-discipline, (e) personal effectiveness, and (f) potential for graduate study/career.

Last Paragraph

Present a brief summary of the students' accomplishments and qualifications in the last paragraph. You might offer to provide more information if necessary, and close with a global recommendation. For my most qualified students, I usually close like this: "I support Chris Smith's application to your graduate program in psychology with my highest recommendation and without reservation."

───── Other Considerations ─────

Letter-writers should strive for complete truthfulness and to provide as much detail as possible, using specific statements about student performance, enhancing the credibility of the LoR and the letter-writer (Knouse, 1983). Hence, "strong" letters tend to be longer. When writing letters, any reference to race, national origin, religion, sex, physical disability, marital status, or age may raise discrimination issues. Avoid such references, except for the appropriate use of gender pronouns (CUR, 2002). Writing a letter of recommendation does not have to be the "agony" that Zimbardo (1976) described: When students are properly prepared and faculty are aware of the relevant issues, writing a strong letter of recommendation can actually be a pleasure.

REFERENCES

Aamodt, M. G., Bryan, D. A., & Whitcomb, A. J. (1993). Predicting performance with letters of recommendation. *Public Personnel Management, 22*, 81–90.

Ault, R. L. (1993). To waive or not to waive? Students' misconceptions about the confidentiality choice for letters of recommendation. *Teaching of Psychology, 20*, 44–5.

Bates College. (1998). *Letter of recommendation worksheet.* Retrieved Feb. 9, 2000, from www.bates.edu/career/glance/reference/recletter.html

Baxter, J. C., Brock, B., Hill, P. C., & Rozelle, R. M. (1981). Letters of recommendation: A question of value. *Journal of Applied Psychology, 66,* 296–301.

Bell, J. D. (1984). Letters of recommendation/verbal references should not become endangered communications: An analysis of rights, responsibilities, and duties of references. San Antonio, TX: Southwest American Business Communication Association. (ERIC Document Reproduction Service No. ED260175.)

Binder, L., & Gotkin, V. (2001). *Legal and confidentiality issues encountered in writing letters of recommendation.* Retrieved from the Council of Emergency Medicine Residency Directors on April 27, 2004, at www.cordem.org/news/2001/legaliss.htm

Brown, L. L. (1999). Fourteen ways to write a better letter of recommendation. *Professional School Counseling, 3,* 141–5.

Council on Undergraduate Research. (2002). *Legal implications of letters of recommendation.* Retrieved April 27, 2004, from www.uah.edu/legal/pdf_files/legal_implications_of_lltrs_of_rec.pdf

Keith-Spiegel, P. (1991). *The complete guide to graduate school admission: Psychology and related fields.* Hillsdale, NJ: Erlbaum.

Keith-Spiegel, P., & Wiederman, M. W. (2000). *The complete guide to graduate school admission: Psychology, counseling, and related professions.* Mahwah, NJ: Erlbaum.

Knouse, S. B. (1983). The letter of recommendation: Specificity and favorability of information. *Personnel Psychology, 36,* 331–41.

Landrum, R. E. (1996, May). *Faculty writing letters of recommendation.* Paper presented at the Midwestern Psychological Association meeting, Chicago.

Lloyd, M. A., & Dewey, R. A. (1997). *How to get good letters of recommendation.* Retrieved April 27, 2004, from www.psywww.com/careers/lettrec.htm

Meyer, J. F. (2002). *Recommendation letter guidelines.* Retrieved April 27, 2004, from http://sociology.camden.rutgers.edu/jfm/rec-ltr.htm

Range, L. M., Menyhert, A., Walsh, M. L., Hardin, K. N., Ellis, J. B., & Craddick, R. (1991). Letters of recommendation: Perspectives, recommendations, and ethics. *Professional Psychology: Research and Practice, 22,* 389–92.

Sendor, B. (1997). Liability and letters of recommendation. *The American School Board Journal, 184,* 14–15.

Swenson, E. V., & Keith-Spiegel, P. (1991). *Writing letters of recommendation for students: How to protect yourself from liability.* Retrieved on April 27, 2004, from www.lemoyne.edu/OTRP/otrpresources/otrp_lor.html

University of California, Berkeley. (2003). *Guidelines for writing letters of recommendation.* Retrieved April 27, 2004, from http://career.berkeley.edu/Letter/LetterGuidelines.stm

University of Wisconsin at Stevens Point. (1999). *Letters of recommendation.* Retrieved April 27, 2004, from www.uwsp.edu/psych.reco.htm

Zimbardo, P. G. (1976). Reducing the agony of writing letters of recommendation. *Teaching of Psychology, 3,* 187–8.

part IX

Ψ

Assessment of Teaching

This section contains five chapters. These essays cover in-class assessment strategies, traditional forms of faculty evaluation, peer review, video feedback, and teaching portfolios.

47
Using Student Evaluations to Improve Teaching

Ψ

Victor A. Benassi & Lee F. Seidel
University of New Hampshire

The practice of college students evaluating their teachers at the end of an academic term is ubiquitous in the United States and has increased in other countries as well (Lewis, 2001b; McKeachie, 2002). Students' ratings and written comments are collected, analyzed, and reported to individual faculty, department chairs and university administrators, and sometimes students and the general public. Results of students' evaluations can and often do have significant impact on faculty in terms of annual reviews, retention, tenure and promotion decisions, and salary raises. This chapter focuses on a different use of student evaluation results – faculty self-improvement. It describes how faculty can use student evaluations of teaching to identify their relative strengths and weaknesses as teachers and position them to develop interventions aimed at improving their teaching.

Many surveys of faculty report that students are not able to provide reliable or valid information concerning teachers' performance. Although there has been much debate about the extent to which student evaluations are reliable and valid, our view is that there is considerable research showing that students can provide reliable and valid evaluations (cf. d'Apollonia & Abrami, 1997; Greenwald, 1997; Greenwald & Gilmore, 1997; Marsh, 1984; Marsh & Roache, 1997; McKeachie, 1997; Theall & Franklin, 1990). Researchers agree that results from student evaluation surveys can be used for self-improvement if faculty interpret properly (e.g., McKeachie, 1997; 2002). The good news is that teachers can easily acquire the skills needed to evaluate many aspects of their performance.

Before proceeding, we mention two caveats. First, students often prefer teaching that "enables them to listen passively – teaching that organizes the subject matter for them and that prepares them well for tests" (McKeachie, 1997, p. 1219). However, students perform better (e.g., retention, higher-order thinking) when they are actively engaged in the classroom (McKeachie, 1997). Teachers may thus be rewarded by students for engaging in classroom behavior that is not conducive to their course objectives. Second, teachers who receive poor evaluations from students may become anxious, defensive, and discouraged (McKeachie, 1997). These teachers may find it difficult to develop a self-improvement plan. However, a consultant from a teaching and learning center or a trusted colleague may be able to help them develop a viable self-improvement plan.

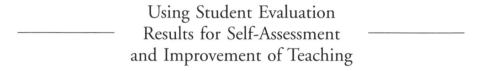

Using Student Evaluation Results for Self-Assessment and Improvement of Teaching

This section discusses several ways that student evaluation data may be used by teachers. Space does not permit us to discuss additional approaches such as student focus groups (Tiberius, 2001) and student quality teams (Spence & Lenze, 2001).

Preparing Your Own Questions

One benefit of standardized student evaluation forms is that they tap dimensions that are generally applicable to college courses – for example, course organization, presentation of material, answering students' questions, and grading practices. However, these forms may not capture information about dimensions relevant to a particular course or instructor. It is precisely course- and instructor-specific information provided by students that will be most informative when a teacher develops a self-improvement plan. In addition to administering a standard teaching evaluation form, we recommend that instructors prepare additional items tailored specifically to the course being evaluated. Some institutions make available a large pool of items, from which instructors select those appropriate for their courses.

Rando (2001) provided useful tips on writing teaching assessment questions. He recommended that faculty craft questions to elicit student responses that faculty can use to make specific teaching improvements. Asking students to "rate the quality of this class" will give the teacher a general reading of students' impression, but specific items usually prompt more useful responses. It is good practice also to ask open-ended questions that provide students with the opportunity to reflect on the course. If you ask superficial questions, you will receive superficial responses.

Interpreting Students' Written Comments

Many evaluation forms include items that students rate on some type of scale (e.g., poor to excellent; weak to strong). These forms also ideally include opportunities for students to write comments on the same form that has rating items. (Specific instructions to students can increase the likelihood that they actually write comments on the form.) You can examine written comments in relation to students' ratings of the scale items (Lewis, 2001a). Most rating forms include a summary item such as "Overall, how would you rate this instructor? (1 = *Poor*; 5 = *Excellent*)." The individual rating forms may be sorted according to the rating each student assigned to this item. You should read comments associated with each item with several questions in mind:

1. Are there any emergent themes in the comments?
2. Do students who rate the course more positively comment on different aspects of the course than students who provided a lower rating?
3. Do students who provided a low rating offer any common concerns or criticisms (e.g., poor organization; confusing exam items)?
4. Do students' comments agree with the instructor's self-assessment?

Lewis (2001a) suggested the addition of a second dimension after an initial examination of student comments using the approach described above. Construct a grid in which one dimension is made up of the ratings given to the summary item (or some other item of interest) and the second dimension consists of certain key aspects of a course (e.g., subject matter; organization/clarity; interactions with students [see Lewis, 2001a, table 3.2]). Assign each written comment to one of the quadrants of the 5 × 5 grid. Review of comments usually prompts certain insights about students' reactions to the course. For example, if students who provided an overall rating of 4 or 5 were as likely to indicate that tests were not aligned with the subject matter emphasized in course objectives, the teacher may want to examine this criticism in depth (cf. Benassi, Jordan, & Harrison, 1994).

Obtaining Mid-semester (or Earlier) Student Input

Do not wait until the end of the term to obtain input from students. Experts recommend that teachers secure student evaluation data by midsemester, preferably earlier (Lewis, 2001c). Review the comments as soon as possible and then discuss any important themes (positive and negative) with the class. Tell the students if there are any issues related to the course that you are prepared to address and provide your rationale for doing so. Also, if you choose not to address certain student concerns, tell your students why.

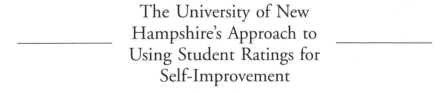

The University of New Hampshire's Approach to Using Student Ratings for Self-Improvement

At the University of New Hampshire, faculty receive a summary of all evaluation questions as well as the individual rating forms for each of their courses during a term. The summary provides descriptive statistics (means, standard deviations, frequency distributions) for each of 14 standard questions and additional questions a faculty member has included on the survey. Students write narrative comments on the back of the forms.

The questionnaire also taps basic demographic information (e.g. class standing) as well as an estimate of "expected grade" and the "average number of hours devoted each week to the course outside of class."

The Center for Teaching Excellence (CTE) publishes annually the means and standard deviations for the 14 questions by course prefix (department or program) and academic unit (college), as well as for the overall university. The CTE also provides faculty members a recommended methodology for examining students' ratings and written comments. We ask faculty to compare their specific item scores for each of the 14 questions with a logical comparator group (e.g., their department or other sections of the same course) and to record their observations. How much an item score is above or below the comparator mean – given the standard deviation – is the first conclusion that faculty draw from these data. We introduce caveats about the plusses and minuses of comparing an individual's mean ratings against those of a normative group (cf. McKeachie, 1997; Cashin, 1990) and instruct them to rank order the mean scores they have received for each of the 14 questions. We then advise faculty to identify the three highest and lowest item scores. The high and low items and their associated written comments identified using this approach are often the same across courses that individual faculty teach.

Having compared specific results with appropriate norms and identified high and low items, the faculty member is then able to use these data to reconsider teaching practices. CTE staff recommends that faculty develop a plan to address the three lowest-ranked items whether they are above or below the norm presented by an appropriate comparator group. CTE staff also offer to assist faculty as they develop this intervention plan. This plan may involve significant course redesign, providing significantly more detail in the course syllabus, and possibly changing behavior in the classroom. In other instances, the plan may involve simple modifications.

Another dimension of our recommended method asks faculty to sort students' ratings and comments by demographic and descriptive variables. We advise faculty to sort the original questionnaires by factors such as expected grade and class level. This sorting method helps faculty discern students' concerns that often remain hidden until the results are stratified and examined.

Making Changes

Obtaining, organizing, and interpreting student evaluation results are necessary but insufficient steps if you want to improve your teaching. You must also develop a viable intervention plan. Minor corrections often will be all that are needed, whereas in other cases you may need to invest significant time and energy into redesigning your course and working on improving your in-class teaching behavior. What follows are recommendations based on Marincovich's (1999) excellent advice.

First, be sure to obtain concrete, behaviorally oriented information from students so that you can make concrete changes in your teaching (cf. Murray, 1997). Second, consult with a colleague, a staff member from your teaching and learning center, or perhaps students (e.g., Spence & Lenze, 2001) about ideas and suggestions for interventions that may be appropriate given your student evaluation profile. Third, start with small changes and review how well they are working with your students. If a larger change plan is needed, implement components of the plan over a period of time. Fourth, although the evaluation of even a single student may be important and insightful, be careful not to make large changes simply because one or a few students provide negative input. Again, seek advice before making changes. Finally, there is a large and growing literature on college teaching that you will no doubt find informative and useful (e.g., McKeachie, 2002).

Conclusion

Better teaching promotes better student learning. Your students can be one source of useful information as you strive to move along a path toward teaching excellence. The approaches described in this chapter will assist you in making the best use of this source of input. Most important, the time and effort required to develop and implement a self-improvement plan will pay off down the line.

REFERENCES

Benassi, V. A., Jordan, E. A., & Harrison, L. M. (1994). Using teaching modules to train and supervise graduate TAs. In K. G. Lewis (ed.), *The TA experience: Preparing for multiple roles* (pp. 183–8). Stillwater, OK: New Forums Press.

Cashin, W. E. (1990). Students do rate different academic fields differently. In M. Theall & J. Franklin (eds.), *Student ratings of instruction: Issues for improving practice* (pp. 113–21). San Francisco: Jossey-Bass.

d'Apollonia, S., & Abrami, P. C. (1997). Navigating student ratings of instruction. *American Psychologist, 52,* 1198–1208.

Greenwald, A. G. (1997). Validity concerns and usefulness of student ratings of instruction. *American Psychologist, 52,* 1182–6.

Greenwald, A. G., & Gilmore, G. M. (1997). Grading leniency is a removable contaminant of student ratings. *American Psychologist, 52,* 1209–17.

Lewis, K. G. (2001a). Making sense of student written comments. In K. G. Lewis (ed.), *Techniques and strategies for interpreting student evaluations* (pp. 25–33). San Francisco: Jossey-Bass.

Lewis, K. G. (2001b). *Techniques and strategies for interpreting student evaluations.* San Francisco: Jossey-Bass.

Lewis, K. G. (2001c). Using midsemester student feedback and responding to it. In K. G. Lewis (ed.), *Techniques and strategies for interpreting student evaluations* (pp. 33–44). San Francisco: Jossey-Bass.

Marincovich, M. (1999). Using student feedback to improve teaching. In P. Seldin (ed.), *Changing practices in evaluating teaching: A practical guide to improved faculty performance and promotion/tenure decisions* (pp. 45–69). Bolton, MA: Anker.

Marsh, H. W. (1984). Students' evaluations of university teaching: Dimensionality, reliability, validity, potential biases, and utility. *Journal of Educational Psychology, 76,* 707–54.

Marsh, H. W., & Roache, L. A. (1997). Making students' evaluations of teaching effectiveness effective: the critical issues of validity, bias, and utility. *American Psychologist, 52,* 1187–97.

McKeachie, W. J. (1997). The validity of use. *American Psychologist, 52,* 1218–25.

McKeachie, W. J. (2002). *McKeachie's teaching tips: Strategies, research, and theory for college and university teachers* (11th ed.). Boston: Houghton Mifflin.

Murray, H. G. (1997). Effective teaching behaviors in the college classroom. In R. P. Perry and J. C. Smart (eds.), *Effective teaching in higher education: Research and practice* (pp. 171–204). New York: Agathon Press.

Rando, W. L. (2001). Writing teaching assessment questions for precision and reflection. In K. G. Lewis (ed.), *Techniques and strategies for interpreting student evaluations* (pp. 77–84). San Francisco: Jossey-Bass.

Spence, L., & Lenze, L. F. (2001). Taking student criticism seriously: Using student quality teams to guide critical reflection. In K. G. Lewis (ed.), *Techniques and strategies for interpreting student evaluations* (pp. 55–62). San Francisco: Jossey-Bass.

Theall, M., & Franklin, J. (1990). *Student ratings of instruction: Issues for improving practice.* San Francisco: Jossey-Bass.

Tiberius, R. (2001). Making sense and making use of feedback from focus groups. In K. G. Lewis (ed.), *Techniques and strategies for interpreting student evaluations* (pp. 55–62). San Francisco: Jossey-Bass.

48

In-Class Learning
Assessment Strategies

Ψ

Regan A. R. Gurung
University of Wisconsin, Green Bay

Assessing ongoing student learning provides a wealth of opportunities to optimize both teaching and learning. Every class period can be used to tap student learning. A multitude of in-class assessment techniques exist: Angelo and Cross (1993) described 50 different techniques, articles in the *Teaching of Psychology* document the creation of others, and various pedagogical books discuss still more (e.g., Davis, 1993; McKeachie, 2002). This chapter suggests a variety of different ways you can successfully assess in-class learning.

Why should you care about classroom assessment? Angelo and Cross (1993) highlighted several key assumptions about classroom assessment. For example, the quality of student learning is strongly tied to teaching, and one of the first steps of effective teaching consists of making class goals and objectives explicit and then getting clear feedback on whether students are meeting those goals. In-class assessment allows for such feedback. Assessment also provides faculty with ways to answer questions about their own teaching, thereby improving what they are doing. Even more important, classroom assessment enables instructors to provide students with useful feedback early and often, which improves learning.

Common Techniques

Student Nonverbal Behavior

The first set of techniques entails learning to recognize your students' nonverbal behavior. Student's facial expressions provide a guide to their level of engagement and understanding. Take the time to look at how your students are reacting to class material. Watch for frowns or blank stares. If blank stares abound, provide time for students to register the material you present. Allowing time for students to think about the material you present is important to their understanding of it.

Ask Questions

The most basic in-class assessment technique is just to ask specific questions. Replace the vague "Any questions?" query with a specific application question that tests whether students understand your main point. For example, after discussing different research designs, describe a research study taken from a current newspaper or news magazine and ask students to identify the method used. Work on methods to learn students' names so they will feel comfortable responding to your questions.

Comment and Criticism Cards

Sometimes it is difficult to get students to talk in class. One way to promote class discussion is to use Comment and Criticism Cards (CCCs). Hand out an index card and have students write down 2–3 main questions about each reading they should have done by class time, their summary of the main points of the class period, or their main criticisms of the assigned readings. Then call on individual students and have them read aloud what they have written on their cards. By having the card in front of them everyone should have something to say. Students feel less anxiety and pressure and are more likely to be active processors of the material when they are prepared to speak. Collect the cards at the end of class so you get a clearer sense of what all of your students learned from the readings and class. You can address issues, problems, and criticisms that were not covered on any particular day in the next class period.

Student Generated Test Items

Another way to assess students' level of understanding is to have them generate sample test questions: Have your students write either multiple-choice or essay questions during class. This activity provides a break from periods of direct lecturing and allows students to see if they really know the material well enough to write a good question on it. Take 2–3 minutes to have each student individually write one question. Then have students pair up and evaluate and edit each other's questions. Finally, randomly call on students to read their questions aloud and have other students answer them. At the end of class collect all the questions. Using some of these questions on later exams further reinforces active participation in this exercise.

Group Engagement Exercises

Whereas writing questions allows students to focus on what they are learning, a different form of assessment involves the use of applying theory to practical situations. Use Group Engagement Exercises (GEEs) in which in groups of 3–5 students work on applied problems relating to topics discussed in class. In my introductory psychology classes (120 students), I organize students into groups of five and provide them with a weekly group exercise. They have 10 minutes to work on it, after which I collect answer sheets (one per group), and then have different groups discuss their answers aloud before the entire class. I then go over the answers and clarify any misconceptions. This immediate application of the day's learning ensures that they know if they understood the lecture or not. Some examples include: (a) describing a sequence of behaviors (you are reading, you hear a voice, you recognize the person, jump up, and hug them) and having the groups describe the brain parts involved in the action, (b) reading a magazine report of a study and having the groups identify the research method used and extraneous variables involved, (c) providing various behavior changes and having the groups identify what form of classical or operant conditioning produced those changes, and (d) providing abnormal psychology case studies and have the group identify the psychological disorder.

The Minute Paper

The Minute Paper is a quick way to encourage students to reflect on what they learned during the class session or during a portion of class. At the end of class (e.g., in about the last minute) ask students to list the most important thing that they learned that day and any lingering questions that they might have about the day's material. There are many variations on this theme (e.g., Wilson, 1986). In one variation, students evaluate one of the topics covered that day. Specifically, ask your students to analyze the strengths and weaknesses of a theory discussed in class. In another variation, the Reflection Sheet, give your students 5 minutes to list what they already knew regarding the day's topic and something new they learned that day.

The Muddiest Point

The Muddiest Point is a variation on the minute paper theme focusing on areas of confusion in class. At the end of the class ask your students to list the most confusing aspect from the lecture. Another variation is the Half-Sheet Response (McKeachie, 2002; Weaver & Cotrell, 1985). Have your students tear off a half sheet of note-book paper and respond to direct questions about the day's lecture. For example, "Evaluate the ____ theory/concept," "Apply the ____ theory/concept to your everyday life," "Put the ____ theory or concept into your own words," "To what other parts of this course does this theory or concept relate?"

The Sentence Summary

The Sentence Summary is an effective way both to assess if students can synthesize material and correspondingly assess their thinking and writing skills. In one sentence ask your students to summarize the gist of a theory or area of study. For example, "What are the main approaches to studying psychology? Name one important theorist for each approach and summarize the main contribution of each."

The Pretest/Post-test Method

The Pre/Post Test Method involves basic research methodology to test learning. At the start of class, ask the class a set of questions that relate to the material you will be covering. Have students put the sheets away and then conduct class. At the end of the session have students take the same test again (either print it on the back of the pretest or collect the first set and hand out a second sheet). Have students exchange sheets, grade the answers, and then discuss the questions producing the largest pre/post differences. You can score the tests and have either count towards the students' grade. The pre-tests, in particular, provide an assessment of how well the students prepared for class.

Technology-Aided In-Class Assessment

The newest in-class assessment technique relies heavily on technology. Textbook publishers now offer classroom feedback systems in which each student has a handheld electronic keypad that they may use to respond to a question you pose. Using software provided by the company, you may take attendance, and calculate class responses and averages to multiple-choice and true–false questions. Given the anonymous and aggregated nature of the feedback (the accuracy of any specific student's response is not illustrated), students may be more likely to participate (versus raising their hands or speaking), thus providing a quick assessment of their knowledge of material discussed in class. Based on the responses you can decide whether to spend more time on a topic or move on.

Implementing
In-Class Assessments

Here are some important points to keep in mind about conducting any of the above assessments:

1. If you have not used any form of in-class assessment before, start small. Select one or two assessment methods.
2. Good assessment requires time, energy, and good planning.
3. Provide students with feedback on the assessment as soon as possible. The delay between the behavior and the consequence should be minimal to maximize learning. The sooner students know whether they understand the material correctly, the sooner can they adjust their learning strategies to enhance their academic performance.
4. Immediate, explicit use of in-class assessment data also shows the students that you take learning seriously and that their feedback is important.
5. Review difficulties from a previous class in the very next class or provide online or in-class handouts explaining difficult issues.

6. Take the time to develop your assessment questions and pick the method that is best for your teaching style and your classroom. Be prepared to jettison methods that do not fit your pedagogical style or your students learning patterns.

7. Remember to tell students exactly how your assessment works and why you are using it. Even in-class group work, a key active learning exercise, is something many students do not enjoy.

8. Take the time to explain all the benefits of assessments.

9. Inform students in advance that you will be using certain assessments.

10. Always allow extra time the first time you use an assessment.

Final Thoughts

In-class assessments can make teaching and learning more effective. You can even make in-class assessments count for credit and serve as an measure of attendance (e.g., if students do not turn in the Minute Paper they were not in class and get no credit for it). Alternatively, you can make in-class assessments anonymous if you fear that students will not accurately report on their learning (e.g., social desirability to look like they understand). For some assessments (e.g., Muddiest Point), anonymity is critical, as students may not otherwise want to admit that they did not understand a point (and imply that the instructor was unclear). Finally, experimenting with new assessments may energize both you and your courses.

REFERENCES

Angelo, T. A., & Cross, P. K. (1993). *Classroom assessment techniques: A handbook for college teachers.* San Francisco: Jossey-Bass.

Davis, B. G. (1993). *Tools for Teaching.* San Francisco: Jossey-Bass.

McKeachie, W. J. (2002). *Teaching tips: Strategies, research, and theory for college and university teachers* (11th ed.). Lexington, MA: Houghton Mifflin.

Weaver, R. L., & Cotrell, H. W. (1985). Mental aerobics: The half-sheet response. *Innovative Higher Education, 10,* 23–31.

Wilson, R. C. (1986). Improving faculty teaching: Effective use of student evaluations and consultation. *Journal of Higher Education, 57,* 196–211.

49

Lesser Discussed Aspects of Peer Review: Context, Out-of-Classroom Work, and Communication

Ψ

Baron Perlman & Lee I. McCann
University of Wisconsin, Oshkosh

Peer review of teaching is a cornerstone of the scholarship of teaching and is part of many colleges' and universities' personnel practices. Faculty invested in more public discussions of teaching and more professional approaches to its assessment and improvement have detailed the major components of peer review (e.g., Chism, 1999; Perlman & McCann, 2002). In this chapter we will present some lesser discussed aspects of peer review – the context within which it occurs, out-of-classroom activities such as peer review of syllabi and student course opinions, and communication.

─────── Context Issues ───────

Peer review of teaching is by definition transactional. However, having faculty in the same department, college, or university working together has its perils, especially if they have prior relationships.

Personal and Cultural Factors

Often faculty choose or know well the person with whom they will be working on a peer review. They typically have impressions of these colleagues, including how well they teach. Despite prior relationships that may be social and relaxed, reviewers need to impress on their peer review colleagues what their expectations are, how seriously they take the process, and what the anticipated outcomes will be. Working with a colleague known in other settings can be unsettling, and reviewers need to be sensitive to changing tones and roles.

Summative reviews are done for some type of evaluative, personnel purpose and often convey the expectations of the department or organization. The person being reviewed may expect a perfunctory approach because the institution values scholarship, or because teaching is seldom discussed within the department in any formal way. Regardless of such expectations, reviewers should undertake peer review as a serious professional obligation with the goal of helping the person being reviewed to become a better teacher.

Faculty should not accept department or institutional cultures that dismiss or minimize peer review. Teaching must be prized and nurtured. At the end of the day or career it is the work with our students that matters most. All teachers, no matter how accomplished in the classroom, can benefit from carefully thinking about, and attending to, their teaching – exactly what a peer review process is supposed to accomplish. Going through the motions may be easy, but it is duplicitous, and contributes little to excellence in teaching.

The Syllabus and Student Opinion Surveys

Attending to teaching does not follow any one set formula. For example, a great deal of pedagogical review can be done prior to attending a colleague's class, or in addition to classroom visits and the meetings that precede and follow the visit (Perlman & McCann, 2002).

Syllabi

A course syllabus is often the first material teachers give students. Faculty may assess syllabi on the clarity of writing, completeness, and content (nature of assignments, timing during the course, instructor accessibility, grading standards, and so forth). Additionally, faculty doing a classroom visit are interested in how the particular class meeting they will attend fits into the overall goals of the course, where it falls in the rhythm of the semester, and what to expect – all theoretically communicated in the syllabus.

Much substantive mentoring and productive discussion can follow review of a colleague's syllabus. How boring is it? By the end of the semester has it proven to be accurate or deceptive advertising? What would make it better? Suggesting that a colleague read other colleagues' syllabi is a simple step toward improving this facet of teaching.

Using the syllabus as a sounding board can reflect back to its author both synchronous and discordant echoes. Shulman (2004) emphasized the serious intellectual discussion that may take place. For example:

- What is the thesis of the syllabus?
- What decisions were made about what was included and excluded in the course?
- With what does the course begin and with what does it end? Why? What do these beginnings and endings say about the teacher's vision and understanding of the discipline?
- Does the syllabus attempt to persuade students about something, and if so, what? Did the teacher deliberately leave out passionate or intellectual arguments?
- What would we conclude about the teacher's depth, quality, and conception of the discipline; concern about student learning; what it means to teach; and how quality education is defined if we only read the syllabus? Would these conclusions be accurate?
- If we expect students to be fascinated with parts of the course or the course as a whole, is the syllabus presentation of the content interesting?

Student Opinions of Teaching

A second domain where productive discussion may be elicited is in looking at student opinion surveys of colleagues' teaching. Some colleagues make light of student evaluations, argue vociferously that they are invalid, or dismiss them out of hand. Valid or not, our experience is that such colleagues often are anxious about what student opinion data tell others and themselves about their teaching, and that a study of course evaluations can be useful.

Colleagues engaged in peer review need to know that student evaluations will be looked at with an eye toward teaching improvement. Reviewers should always let colleagues with whom they are working speak first, pointing out strengths or weaknesses in the opinion data and their interpretation of specific points. The goal is to make sense of the student opinions and find suggestions for improvement. We do not recommend attending to differences in numerical evaluations of two or three decimal points, but instead trying to understand broad and important themes that students are highlighting. Of course, such evaluations have to be framed in a context themselves: size of the course, required or elective, or inherently exciting material.

In essence, the desired outcome of a focus on student opinion data is to structure and deepen the peer review interaction and conversation about teaching, using numerical data and simple interpretations as a springboard for more substantive pedagogical discussion. However, never let particularly positive or negative evaluative data go unnoticed. Sometimes peer review means feeling good about successes in one's teaching, and sometimes it means admitting we have not yet totally mastered the art and craft of teaching. Just as peer review is transactional, the process of becoming a good teacher is developmental. Both take time.

———— Listening ————

Listening is a critical and underdiscussed component of the peer review process. To listen and be heard can be rare occurrences in academe. Reviewers need to:

- *Get colleagues' stories.* People who teach need to talk about what they do. Reviewers need to assist colleagues in identifying what is going wrong and what is going right in their teaching lives. In our experience, good listening helps colleagues feel comfortable in talking about their teaching in terms of specific experiences, behaviors, and feelings.
- *Help colleagues focus* on meaningful issues. Good listening helps colleagues (a) identify their most important concerns, especially if they have a number of them, and (b) work on "high-leverage" issues, those that will make a difference in their teaching. Some issues that make a difference are successes – maintaining what produced them, understanding them, and transforming their form to other areas of our colleagues' teaching.

Ways of Listening

Listening is an *active* process involving:

- Listening to the speaker's words. An important rule of thumb is never to assume you know what a colleague means. If teachers use phrases such as "the class was bored," "I felt disorganized," or "That portion of class was an important teaching moment," always ask them to tell you more. It is in the telling that the important content and understanding lies.
- "Listening" to the speaker's body language. Many times we say one thing but communicate another with our foot tapping, tense body posture, or facial expression.
- Listening with silence. We cannot overemphasize the place of silence when meeting with a colleague during peer review. Silence allows others to think, deepen their appreciation for their teaching, and not be rushed. In this case, silence is a mark of respect.

Quiet listening encourages others to speak freely and verbalize their ideas, but a lack of attention discourages conversation, and is open to a wide variety of interpretations (e.g., lack of interest). Good listening practices include:

- Looking at people's eyes as they speak.
- A relaxed posture, often leaning slightly forward.
- Minimizing gestures such as fidgeting and yawning (boredom), arms crossed on one's chest (power, disapproval), or foot tapping (impatience).

The Power of Paraphrasing and Clarifying

Reviewers need to restate colleague's messages to ensure that they have accurately understood what was said. To paraphrase accurately, as we listen we need to ask ourselves constantly what the person's basic content and emotional messages are. If you paraphrase, colleagues know you are "really" listening to them, and you and your colleague will be on the "same page" during peer review. Clarifying brings vague material into sharper focus. You can look at someone and say:

"I don't quite understand, can you restate that?"

"I'm confused, let me try to tell you what I hear you saying."

"I lost you there. Are you saying . . . ?"

"I'm not sure I understand, can you tell me more?"

Good listening also involves summarizing what you heard across several ideas or minutes and asking for feedback. For example:

"I was wondering if the teaching methodologies you want to use in the course we have been discussing are really the right ones for you? You expressed some doubt. Did I hear you correctly?"

"I want to make sure I understand you. You said your students' performance is not up to your standards and you are not planning any course changes but you want them to do better. Is that right?"

The effect may be that someone feels truly heard and understood.

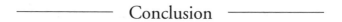

Conclusion

We have attempted to focus on some less-frequently discussed elements of peer review. Yet we feel we have only scratched the surface of relationships, hearing what others really mean and communicating in ways that we are understood. Peer review and teaching are both processes of exploration. Teachers teach and they also talk with others about what it is they do. We hope these ideas will help you to have more meaningful discussions about teaching.

REFERENCES

Chism, N. V. N. (1999). *Peer review of teaching: A sourcebook*. Bolton, MA: Anker Publishing.

Perlman, B., & McCann, L. I. (2002). Peer review for meaningful teaching enhancement. In S. F. Davis and W. Buskist (eds.), *The teaching of psychology: Essays in honor of Wilbert J. McKeachie and Charles L. Brewer* (pp. 189–201). Mahwah, NJ: Erlbaum.

Shulman, L. S. (2004). *Teaching as community property: Essays on higher education*. San Francisco: Jossey-Bass.

50
Improving Teaching Through Video Feedback and Consultation

Ψ

Steven Prentice-Dunn, Kristen L. Payne, & Judy M. Ledbetter
University of Alabama

New instructors often harbor doubts about their performance in an unfamiliar role. At most universities, they only receive feedback at the end of a course and from one source (students). However, such information is not sufficiently timely or broad in scope to be helpful. We suggest that more useful feedback for beginning faculty and graduate teaching assistants can come from the use of video.

Video can validate other sources of feedback (e.g., students, peer observers), without the need to rely on the memory of others for an accurate account (Prentice-Dunn & Pitts, 2001). Videotapes also give the instructor a student's perspective of the class and help establish the mindset necessary to change an ineffective style (Plotnik, 1997). Reviewing tapes with a practiced instructor redirects the novice instructor's attention away from personal mannerisms to student learning (McElroy & Prentice-Dunn, 2004; Meyers & Prieto, 2000).

One of the most robust findings in the educational research literature is the effectiveness of videotape feedback (Paulsen & Feldman, 1995; Weimer & Lenze, 1991). Several studies reveal that viewing oneself is associated with improved instruction (e.g., Abbott, Wulff, & Szego, 1989). Indeed, Meyers and Prieto (2000) described dramatic changes that often occur following self-observation. However, consultation with an experienced instructor may be a crucial component of improvement (Dalgaard, 1982). For example, in one meta-analysis, instructors who received both student rating results and consultation improved to the 74th percentile of instructor ratings at the end of the term (Cohen, 1980), compared to the 58th percentile received by those receiving ratings alone. Thus, it appears that video and consultation can be a potent combination for fostering improvement.

Preparing the New Instructor

Krupnick (1987) noted that although videotape can be an invaluable asset, it has the potential to do harm unless preparatory steps have been taken. Foremost among these steps is to convince instructors to record representative teaching and not a class specifically planned for the benefit of the camera. Teachers who almost exclusively lecture may spend the entire session conducting a group discussion. Instructors who favor a variety of techniques may revert to a lecture because they assume that the consultant wants to see "traditional" teaching. Thus, establishing that the video is intended as a snapshot of one's daily teaching and not a command performance is a necessary first step.

Another aspect of setting the stage for fruitful interaction is to counter the frequently held belief that teaching is not amenable to substantive changes. New instructors often fail to see that the excellence of their favorite professors came with considerable effort and some failures. Sviniki (1994) offered a concise rebuttal to the enduring myths about teaching that may block motivation to improve. Instructors should read such articles to establish the mindset that effective teaching can be developed.

Before viewing the tape, the recorded instructor should be warned of the tendency to become focused excessively on appearance. Most of us implicitly carry the image of videos as the highly polished products seen on commercial television. Thus, we are ill-prepared for the cosmetic distortions that come with even the most advanced portable equipment available for college classrooms. One look at the video often reveals a voice that is higher pitched than previously thought, hair that is askew, or eyes that appear to have dark shadows beneath them. Thankfully, such "video-induced despair" (Krupnick, 1987) can be minimized with forewarning, repeated viewing, and from seeing that the consultant focuses instead on organization, explanations, and the reactions of students to the material.

Timely viewing of the video is important so that thoughts and feelings about the class are fresh in the memory (Davis, 1993). Although Krupnick (1987) recommended watching the video with the instructor, we have found that new teachers appreciate the privacy of first viewing the tape alone.

Checklists focus the instructor's analysis of the video. For example, Davis (1993) offered 4–10 questions in each of the following areas: (a) organization and preparation (e.g., Do you state the purpose of the class and its relation to the previous class?), (b) style of presentation (e.g., Do you talk to the class, not to the board or windows?), (c) clarity of presentation (e.g., Do you give examples, illustrations, or applications to clarify abstract concepts?), (d) questioning skills (e.g., Do you ask questions to determine what students know about the topic?), (e) student interest and participation (e.g., Do you provide opportunities for students to practice what they are learning?), (f) classroom climate (e.g., Do you address students by name?), and (g) discussion (e.g., Do you draw out quiet students and prevent dominating students from monopolizing the discussion?). Other checklists focus on lectures (Diamond, Sharp, & Ory, 1978) or specific teacher behaviors (Weimer, Parrett, & Kerns, 1988).

Conducting the
Consultation Session

The meeting between the new instructor and the consultant should always begin with a reminder of the collaborative nature of the session. We also find it useful to review briefly the instructor's course goals and the topic and objectives of the recorded class. Prentice-Dunn and Pitts (2001) provided several guidelines for the session:

Focus on the Positive First

Questions such as "What did you see on the tape that worked well?" or "What did you observe that you liked?" force the recorded instructor to think of strengths and counteract the tendency to be inappropriately self-critical. Although new instructors sometimes appear surprised by this line of inquiry (and may even need assistance initially), a balanced approach makes it likely that any problems discussed later will not be met with defensiveness.

Allow the Instructor to Take the Conversational Lead

Krupnick (1987) and Geis (1991) advised that the recorded instructor take the conversational lead during the meeting. Such a strategy works best after setting the positive tone for the session. Although the consultant will always have a list of issues to discuss, it is common to have most of these matters first raised by the instructor.

Give Positive Feedback in the Grammatical Second Person

Brinko (1993) stated that compliments given as "you" statements will enhance self-esteem. For example, feedback phrased as "You really encouraged several of the quieter students to speak" is preferable to "I noticed that several of the quieter students participated in the discussion." The former statement attributes the behavior to the teacher's effort rather than leaving the cause ambiguous.

Frame Negative Aspects of the Performance in Terms of Improvement

Negative information can be especially aversive when the feedback is about complex skills that are practiced in public. To the novice instructor, evaluative audiences appear at every turn. Thus, handling negative feedback requires particular care.

The initial period of the consultation session devoted to successes prepares the instructor for a question such as "What would you like to improve?" Such phrasing avoids the sting to self-esteem that comes from using terms such as "wrong" and "incorrect." In addition, having the instructor supply the answer reduces the tendency to react defensively when a problem is identified by someone else.

Just as a compliment is more powerful when couched as a "you" statement, so too is information critical of one's presentation (Brinko, 1993). Instructors receive feedback better when it is presented in the first person or third person. Examples of appropriate comments include "I followed much of the summary, but then expected more coverage of the final topic" and "The students may have had difficulty following the final part of the summary."

Given the tendency for beginning instructors to be self-critical, the consultant should present negative comments without resorting to strong terms. In addition, the consultant should explicitly distinguish between minor and major issues for the instructor's attention. For example, the instructor may judge "remembering to scan the entire classroom" as equal in importance to "providing an organizational scheme for a lecture," unless the consultant makes the distinction.

Combine Your Reactions with Those of Students, if Available

Geis (1991) observed that "a particular message gains credibility when it is one of a series of similar messages, from a variety of sources" (p. 11). The consistency between the student's and consultant's lists of strengths and weaknesses is often remarkable and impresses novice instructors that evaluation is not a haphazard process.

When inconsistencies do arise, the consultant can provide a welcome perspective for the teacher. For example, it is common for our introductory psychology students to complain about the difficulty of the exams, due to the tremendous amount of material covered in the beginning course. New instructors are comforted to hear that such responses are normative and do not necessarily reflect shortcomings on their part.

Identify Short-Term Goals and End the Session on a Positive Note

Every meeting should end with the instructor identifying a few specific areas to target for improvement. These areas will then provide the focus for the next meeting. We also recommend reiterating the instructor's strengths and expressing appreciation for his or her efforts to provide a high-quality experience for the students in the course. Virtually all new instructors work extraordinarily hard and yet receive little acknowledgment. A simple expression of appreciation can go far in establishing a relationship that motivates instructors to offer their best effort.

Listen More Than You Speak

Carroll and Goldberg (1989) noted that consultation works best for instructors who can identify discrepancies between expected and actual performances. Fortunately, it is rare to find a first-time teacher who has no idea about what can be improved. Indeed, the problem more frequently encountered is getting instructors to realize that they already have several strengths. Much of the consultant's time will be devoted to drawing out the instructor's concerns and encouraging reflection on the advantages and disadvantages of a particular teaching technique or proposed course of action.

Suggesting that consultants practice restraint does not mean that they have little to offer. Although new teachers may know what needs modifying, they usually need help with how to enact those changes. Providing concrete recommendations for how to increase student participation is but one example of how to use your expertise to facilitate improvement. New instructors also appreciate hearing about similar obstacles that consultants have encountered and their attempts to overcome them. Such disclosure not only creates rapport, it also illustrates that beginning instructors face common adjustments and that challenges occur throughout one's career.

Conclusion

The initial teaching experience establishes strategies and attitudes that can follow the new instructor for years. When video is combined with consultation, beginning instructors get invaluable information about translating assumptions about teaching into practice (Buskist, Tears, Davis, & Rodrigue, 2002). Such feedback can set the tone for a teaching style that is effective and enriching to students and instructors alike.

REFERENCES

Abbott, R. D., Wulff, D. H., & Szego, C. K. (1989). Review of research on TA training. In J. D. Nyquist, R. D. Abbott, & D. H. Wulff (eds.), *Teaching assistant training in the 1990s* (pp. 111–23). San Francisco: Jossey-Bass.

Brinko, K. T. (1993). The practice of giving feedback to improve teaching: What is effective? *Journal of Higher Education, 64*, 574–93.

Buskist, W., Tears, R. S., Davis, S. F., & Rodrigue, K. M. (2002). The teaching of psychology course: Prevalence and content. *Teaching of Psychology, 29*, 140–2.

Carroll, J. G., & Goldberg, S. R. (1989). Teaching consultants: A collegial approach to better teaching. *College Teaching, 37*, 143–54.

Cohen, P. A. (1980). Effectiveness of student-rating feedback for improving college instruction: A meta-analysis of findings. *Research in Higher Education, 13*, 321–41.

Dalgaard, K. A. (1982). Some effects of training on teaching effectiveness of untrained university teaching assistants. *Research in Higher Education, 17*, 39–50.

Davis, B. G. (1993). *Tools for teaching.* San Francisco: Jossey-Bass.

Diamond, J., Sharp, G., & Ory, J. C. (1978). *Improving your lecturing.* Urbana, IL: University of Illinois Office of Instructional Resources.

Geis, G. L. (1991). The moment of truth: Feeding back information about teaching. In M. Theall & J. Franklin (eds.), *Effective practices for improving teaching* (pp. 7–19). San Francisco: Jossey-Bass.

Krupnick, C. G. (1987). The uses of videotape replay. In C. R. Christensen & A. J. Hansen (eds.), *Teaching and the case method: Text, cases, and readings* (pp. 256–63). Boston: Harvard Business School.

McElroy, H. K., & Prentice-Dunn, S. (in press). *Graduate students' perceptions of a teaching of psychology course.*

Meyers, S. A., & Prieto, L. R. (2000). Training in the teaching of psychology: What is done and examining the differences. *Teaching of Psychology, 27,* 258–61.

Paulsen, M. B., & Feldman, K. A. (1995). *Taking teaching seriously: Meeting the challenge of instructional improvement.* ASHE-ERIC Report No. 2. Washington, DC: George Washington University.

Plotnik, R. (1997). Model for being an effective instructor. In R. Sternberg (ed.), *Teaching introductory psychology: Survival tips from the experts* (pp. 119–36). Washington, DC: American Psychological Association.

Prentice-Dunn, S., & Pitts, G. S. (2001). The use of videotape feedback in the training of instructors. In S. Meyers & L. Prieto (eds.), *The teaching assistant training handbook: How to prepare TAs for their responsibilities* (pp. 89–102). Stillwater, OK: New Forums Press.

Sviniki, M. (1994). Seven deadly comments . . . that block learning about teaching. *National Teaching and Learning Forum, 3,* 4–6.

Weimer, M., & Lenze, L. F. (1991). Instructional interventions: A review of the literature on efforts to improve instruction. In K. A. Feldman & M. B. Paulsen (eds.), *Teaching and learning in the college clasroom* (pp. 653–82). Needham Heights, MA: Ginn Press.

Weimer, M., Parrett, J. L., & Kerns, M. (1988). *How am I teaching?: Forms and activities for acquiring instructional input.* Madison, WI: Magna Publications.

51

Creating Teaching Portfolios

Ψ

Erin B. Rasmussen
Idaho State University

Since Boyer's (1990) call to obscure the line between teacher and scholar, the teaching portfolio has become the standard for documenting teaching excellence at many institutions of higher learning (Minter & Goodburn, 2002; Murray, 1997). Institutions emphasizing teaching (e.g., liberal arts and community colleges) have historically required portfolios for tenure, promotion, and post-tenure review; however, administrators at more research-focused universities are increasingly insisting on them (Minter & Goodburn, 2002).

Contingencies for tenure and promotion aside, the teaching portfolio can be a powerful tool that requires teachers to contemplate their views on teaching and to reflect on whether their design of a course is consonant with their perspectives on teaching – what might be considered a formative evaluation. It is this process of consideration and self-evaluation that might be the most compelling use for teaching portfolios.

The teaching portfolio contains two main parts – the statement of teaching philosophy and evidence of one's teaching behavior and efficacy. The statement of teaching philosophy shapes the rest of the portfolio and provides a foundation for how teaching is conceptualized, implemented, and assessed. Evidence of a faculty member's teaching behavior and efficacy includes the provision of various teaching artifacts (e.g., copies of tests, assignments, descriptions of demonstrations, etc.) and narratives of how the artifacts reflect the teaching philosophy. This structure allows teachers to assess whether they are fulfilling their teaching objectives and whether there is consistency between their teaching philosophy and their actual teaching behavior.

Many approaches to constructing a teaching portfolio exist, and the following recommendations represent a culmination of suggestions from several authors (see Constantino & DeLorenzo, 2002; Edgerton, Hutchings, & Quinlan, 1993; Forsyth, 2003; McKeachie, 2002; Minter & Goodburn, 2002; Murray, 1997; Seldin, 1991, 1993, 1995, 2004). Bear in mind that the teaching portfolio should be an individual creative process and product. Hence, you should regard these suggestions as guidelines, not as strict requirements.

——————— Planning the Portfolio ———————

Before constructing the portfolio, consider the purpose of the portfolio and the audience for whom it is prepared. The structure of the portfolio may vary as a function of the specific reasons for constructing it. For example, you might construct a teaching portfolio that a tenure and promotion committee will read differently than one developed for personal improvement in teaching or one intended for a nomination packet for a teaching award. The audience and purpose will determine what gets placed in the portfolio and possibly what is said in the statement of teaching philosophy.

Practical issues include cost and time. The cost of a complete portfolio may vary between $30 and $50 for materials (includes 5-inch binder[s], paper, acetate sleeves, dividers, printing and copying costs, possible video or audio tapes; Wyatt & Looper, 1999). The portfolio often takes 12–15 hours across several days to complete (Wyatt & Looper, 1999), although the timeframe can be much larger, depending on the range of content to be included in the portfolio. Clearly, the creation of a teaching portfolio should not be a last-minute endeavor.

One helpful way to initiate a teaching portfolio is to consult, if your school has one, your college or university's center for teaching and learning; many centers have developed materials for on-campus workshops for creating portfolios. Alternatively, it might be beneficial to examine a few exemplary teaching portfolios by other faculty members in your department or institution. Some examples can be found in Seldin (2004; pp. 52–233).

——————— Text ———————

The average portfolio contains between 8 and 12 pages of text (Seldin, 2004), with the rest of the portfolio used as artifacts (in appendix form) that illustrate points made in the statement of teaching philosophy. A table of contents (not included as text) listed at the beginning of the portfolio may serve as a reference for the portfolio's organization.

Begin the portfolio proper with a paragraph or two that describes courses taught. This description should include the titles of the courses, how often they are taught, and descriptions of each course (e.g., undergraduate vs. graduate course, core or elective, the number of students enrolled, etc.).

The statement of teaching philosophy may be placed after the course descriptions. The statement of teaching philosophy is most likely the longest section of the text and requires the most thought. Your statement of teaching philosophy should address your philosophical perspective regarding teaching, including what the ideal teaching environment might entail and articulation of personal beliefs about how students learn best in a classroom. Moreover, the teaching philosophy should express your views and values of how teaching best occurs (e.g., what the ideal characteristics of a good teacher might be, the goals of good teaching, and how to achieve those goals) (Korn, 2002). It should include aims, objectives, competencies, and expectations of student performance in the classroom. It may also be beneficial to emphasize places in which the statement reflects the mission of the department and college or university (Seldin, 2004). Another topic to discuss may include mentoring of students, including reflection on whether your approach for mentoring undergraduates differs from graduate students or how you use teaching assistants (e.g., as grade keepers or teachers in training). Also consider enclosing a short paragraph about your philosophy on grading and the procedures you use for grading.

Once your teaching philosophy is stated, the rest of the text may be used to describe classroom activities and professional teaching-related activities that reflect your teaching philosophy. For example, a teacher may articulate in her statement that frequent feedback facilitates learning. She might provide examples that reflect how this philosophy informs her teaching (e.g., daily quizzes that are offered on specific material from the textbook). Include detailed descriptions of, and purposes for, the assignments that are given.

Selecting and Organizing Artifacts

Include teaching artifacts to provide evidence of teaching behavior that is consistent with your statement of teaching philosophy. I have constructed the following list of artifacts from several sources as a guideline, but it is in no way exhaustive (see Constantino & DeLorenzo, 2002; Forsyth, 2003; Edgarton et al., 1993; Minter & Goodburn, 2002; Murray, 1997; Seldin, 2004):

Artifacts from Yourself:
1. Course materials. These include, but are not limited to: syllabi, handouts, overheads, copies of PowerPoint slides, quizzes, exams, paper assignments, study guides, etc.
2. Representative student samples of graded assignments and exams.
3. An ongoing record of your students' career choices and postgraduation placements.
4. A record of the number of students advised and time spent advising.
5. Information on your availability to students (e.g., the number of visits from students during office hours).
6. A video of teaching a class (see chapter 50 in this volume).
7. A description or evidence of technological aids used in the classroom (e.g., overheads, webpages, WebCT)

Artifacts from Others:
1. Teaching evaluations (see chapters 47 and 48 in this volume).
2. Evidence of supervision of internships, honors or Master's theses, and dissertations. (Perhaps a copy of the abstract or penultimate draft of the final product may be included, although these items may take up substantial space.)
3. Written review of teaching by a peer.
4. Copies of letters related to teaching awards given by the college or university, professional organizations, and undergraduate and graduate student organizations.
5. Test scores from courses taught.
6. Notes, cards, or testimonials from students.

Products:
1. Copies of presentations or publications of research on teaching, including collaborations with students.
2. Copies of preparation of textbooks, workbooks, or other pedagogical aids.
3. Editorial board membership of a teaching journal or newsletter.
4. Evidence of participation in or presentation of teaching workshops at professional conferences or on campus.
5. Evidence of subscribing to and reading journals on teaching.
6. Evidence of membership in teaching organizations.
7. Evidence of participation in course/curriculum development committees.
8. Summary of curricular revisions.

With the exception of Items 7 and 8, these items can be highlighted on your curriculum vitae.

Deciding what artifacts to include in a portfolio is not easy. A "more is better" approach may dilute the quality of the portfolio, although the sheer amount of paper may make the portfolio look ostensibly impressive. Again, it is best to consider the purpose of the portfolio and begin there. You should also determine whether it is best to include representative work or your best work (Murray, 1997). When it comes to including student samples, for example, you may want to show the best students' work because doing so might reflect higher-quality teaching. However, an average student's work may be a more honest (and believable) approach. Murray (1997) stated that it might be useful to include both best and average work, and possibly a sample of poor-quality work, although this approach might lead to a larger portfolio. Perhaps the most compelling questions that will determine what you should place in the portfolio are those items that address its function (Murray, 1997): Does the material placed in the portfolio support your philosophy of teaching, and does the material support a pattern of growth in your teaching ability?

Compile Supporting Data

Although artifacts are excellent sources of qualitative data for the corroboration of statements made in your teaching philosophy, compiling numbers on quantitative aspects of teaching from semester to semester is also beneficial. For example, using your institution's standard teaching evaluation, you may create a table that shows your average ratings for each item on that instrument over time. Another table or graph that might be useful is one that shows, on an annual basis, the number of students advised who were accepted into graduate school or accepted positions in various fields.

Electronic Portfolios

The electronic age allows for the presentation of information with less paper. Many faculty who submit teaching portfolios as job résumés (e.g., elementary and secondary educators) present them electronically, and this trend is slowly creeping into higher education (Wyatt & Looper, 1999). Creating an electronic portfolio entails scanning artifacts and materials onto a CD or other data-storing archive. Narratives can be created into a word-processing file and then archives and appendices can be hyperlinked through the text document. You may also purchase software that creates portfolios (see Wyatt & Looper, 1999, p. 73). In addition to using less paper, electronic portfolios allow the inclusion of graphics and video or audiotaped presentations and are easily publishable on the internet, easily duplicated, and easily accessed (Constantino & DeLorenzo, 2002).

Conclusion

A teaching portfolio is a valuable tool that showcases a faculty member's teaching interests, products, and efficacy. Although creating a portfolio may be an arduous task, the process can be enlightening, as it provides a structure for organization of thoughts and ideas on teaching, and articulation on your views of teaching. Moreover, the final product provides a foundation of ideas and perspectives that can be refined and extended for years to come.

ACKNOWLEDGMENTS

I thank Dr. Steven Lawyer and Ms. Ann Ward for helpful comments and suggestions on an earlier draft.

REFERENCES

Boyer, E. L. (1990). *Scholarship reconsidered: Priorities of the professoriate.* Princeton, NJ: Carnegie Foundation for the Advancement of Teaching.

Constantino, P. M., & DeLorenzo, M. N. (2002). *Developing a professional teaching portfolio: A guide for success.* Boston: Allyn & Bacon.

Edgerton, R., Hutchings, P., & Quinlan, K. (1993). *The teaching portfolio: Capturing the scholarship in teaching.* Washington, DC: American Association for Higher Education.

Forsyth, D. R. (2003). *The Professor's guide* to *teaching: Psychological principles and practices.* Washington, DC: American Psychological Association.

Korn, J. H. (2002). Beyond tenure: The teaching portfolio for reflection and change. In S. F. Davis & W. Buskist (eds.), *The teaching of psychology: Essays in honor of Wilbert J. McKeachie and Charles L. Brewer* (pp. 203–13). Mahwah, NJ: Erlbaum.

McKeachie, W. (2002). *Teaching tips: Strategies, research, and theory for college and university teachers* (11th ed.). Boston: Houghton Mifflin.

Minter, D., & Goodburn, A. M. (2002.) *Composition, pedagogy, and the scholarship of teaching.* Portsmouth, NH: Boynton/Cook Publishers.

Murray, J. P. (1997). *Successful faculty development and evaluation: The complete teaching portfolio.* ASHE-ERIC Higher Education Report no. 8. Washington, DC: The George Washington University, Graduate School of Education and Human Development.

Seldin, P. (1991). *The teaching portfolio.* Bolton, MA: Anker.

Seldin, P. (1993). *Successful use of teaching portfolios.* Bolton, MA: Anker.

Seldin, P. (1995). Answers to common questions about the teaching portfolio. *Journal on Excellence in College Teaching, 6,* 57–64.

Seldin, P. (2004). *The teaching portfolio: A practical guide to improved performance and promotion/tenure decisions* (3rd ed.) Bolton, MA: Anker.

Wyatt, R. L., & Looper, S. (1999). *So you have to have a portfolio: A teacher's guide to preparation and presentation.* Thousand Oaks, CA: Corwin Press.

part X

Ψ

Teaching Within the Larger Context of Academic Life

The final section features six chapters that address a diverse range of issues related to being a college or university teacher. These issues include helping students with their personal problems, inviting students to become research collaborators, student and faculty professional development, the department chair as mentor, and political considerations.

52

Helping College Students with Personal Problems: Should I Help and How?

Ψ

Marcia Rossi
Tuskegee University

Most faculty members who teach at the university level recognize that students are vulnerable to a host of personal and academic problems. Psychology faculty may be even more aware of such problems, because students may be more willing to approach psychology faculty than faculty from another discipline. However, talking with students and assisting them with personal problems can consume significant amounts of time. For instance, a survey of full-time faculty members in US medical schools found that participants discuss personal problems with students on average 48 minutes per week (Brown & Barnett, 1984). Problems most often cited by these faculty involved financial concerns, emotional health, and relationships with other faculty members.

If you are a new faculty, or are anticipating becoming one, you may wonder whether and how you might offer assistance should a student come to you with a personal problem. Some faculty may warn you not to get involved. Others may recommend you refer the student for professional help. Still others feel it is their duty to help students in any way possible. So what should you do? In this chapter, I offer some guidelines for deciding how and when they should offer assistance to students seeking help with personal problems.

Before attempting to resolve a problem, it is helpful first to understand the nature and seriousness of the problem. Student personal problems come in all forms and degrees. Some are so severe that they require professional assistance, such as suicidal impulses. Others are simply temporary setbacks, such as an argument with a room-mate. In attempting to assist students, personal problems may be broken conveniently into four basic categories. View these categories as heuristic in nature; many problems overlap categories.

Types of Personal Problems

First, students often encounter academic problems. Problems such as poor grades, requesting accommodations for learning disabilities, asking assistance in preparing for careers, and needing assistance with study skills fall into this category.

Second, students experience relationship problems. Such problems include homesickness, difficulty finding a romantic partner, breaking up with a romantic partner, problems with roommates or friends, problems with parents, and problems with other faculty. In addition, nontraditional students in particular may have families who need their assistance, such as tending to small children who are sick and cannot attend day care, or helping an ill relative.

Third, students face financial problems. Financial problems are often related to and exacerbate many other problems. For instance, students who have limited resources may not have a car, which prevents them from getting transportation to the library, which in turn may affect academic success. Students who must work two jobs to stay in school may be called into work and miss class unexpectedly.

Finally, increasingly students suffer health-related problems, both physical and mental. For instance, students may suffer from depression and have suicidal thoughts. Other students may have chronic health issues such as asthma, sickle-cell anemia, diabetes, and the like. I have had students with all of the above, including one with a chronic and severe seizure disorder. Recently, I had a student with a heart condition, whose medication requires that he rest in the afternoon. His condition required him to take classes only in the morning and limited his study time. Still other students have unplanned pregnancies and must contend with the pregnancy, numerous doctor visits that may interfere with classes, health complications during pregnancy, childbirth and caring for the child, or miss classes due to abortions.

The problems of college students today are often so complex that it could well consume your entire day trying to help students sort out the best course of action in attempting to solve their problems. How should you proceed, then, to help provide meaningful assistance when and if it is warranted?

Guidelines for When to Help and How

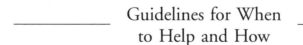

*Guideline No. 1: Be open, nonjudgmental,
and listen to determine the nature of the problem*

When a student approaches you to discuss a problem, it is often with great trepidation. The student may fear rejection or be embarrassed to talk about the situation. The fact that the student has selected you to talk to suggests that he or she trusts you. Remember that you have been asked for help from someone in a difficult position. How you respond to that person may make a critical difference in whether the problem gets solved and how the person feels about you and possibly other faculty members in general. By listening carefully with an open, nonjudgmental attitude, you will be more likely to determine the nature of the problem. Keeping these points in mind, you must consider how to respond: what to say, what not to say, and how you may be able to help.

The American Psychological Association Ethics Code (2002), Standard 2.01a, states that psychologists should provide services and teach only within the realm of their competence, based on their education, training, and professional experience. Thus, if the student relates to you a problem that is of a serious personal nature, you should not attempt to counsel him or her unless you are a licensed clinical psychologist or counselor. Rather, you should listen empathically and attempt to understand the core of his or her concerns.

At times, the student may talk about one problem that in reality is masking a more serious concern, or one that is more embarrassing about which to talk. Considerate questioning will help reveal the true nature of the problem and understanding the true nature of the problem will help to determine how to help the student.

Some problems will be of such a nature that you may readily provide assistance. For instance, if it is an issue of low GPA and you are the student's academic advisor, your responsibility is to help the student take appropriate courses and course load to improve his or her GPA, and direct the student to the appropriate source for finding tutorials or to improve study skills. Many campuses offer tutoring services in a variety of disciplines. Some campuses may have an office designed to teach students better study and testing skills. Finally, in some cases, the student may have an undiagnosed learning disability and may need to be referred for professional evaluation or to institutional support services to provide accommodations.

If a student has an identified learning disability, federal law requires that the student receive accommodations to assist him or her. However, in some cases, the student may be unaware of having a disability, but is struggling with coursework and is frustrated and perhaps depressed. Sending the student to a psychotherapist may help to some degree, but if the cause of the depression is the learning disability, then the sooner the student is evaluated, the more likely his or her academic performance will improve and the depression lessen. Indications of a disability include a discrepancy between aptitude and performance, and reports by the student or professors that the student has difficulty understanding test material or reading, but seems to understand the course material in class. Pastorino (1999) and Foushe'e and Sleigh (2004) both offer excellent additional suggestions on how to help students who are struggling academically.

Guideline No. 2: Know appropriate campus and community resources to make referrals

Knowing the nature of the problem will facilitate making the appropriate referral. Thus, you should become familiar with the resources in your institution and community so you may make appropriate referrals. Knowing where to direct students for the appropriate type of help is important. If you are unable to suggest a source of help, the student's problem may worsen, or he or she may feel that you do not care.

If you feel that the student needs professional therapy or counseling, you should consider referring him or her to your campus counseling center. If your institution has no onsite counseling center, it may have an arrangement with a community counseling center that may offer reduced rates for students or for individuals with lower incomes.

Recognizing that a student needs professional counseling may take several discussions with the student. Your ability to recognize such situations may improve as your level of experience as a faculty member grows. Warning signs of adolescent suicide are published by the American Academy of Child and Adolescent Psychiatry (2004).

If you feel that a student needs professional help immediately, it can be helpful to make the contact for the student with his or her permission. If a student is suicidal or seriously depressed, he or she may not have sufficient energy to follow through with the contact. Asking the student if you may escort him or her to the counselor or call to see if he or she arrived at the counselor may be beneficial in showing the student you care, an essential first ingredient in helping the student. Although this may be considered going beyond the call of duty, I believe that by doing so, you will know you are doing all you can, especially if the student is, in fact, suicidal.

Guideline No. 3: Recognize that there are limits on how much you can help

Unfortunately, some problems are so severe or complex that they require either an enormous time commitment from you or they are unsolvable. You should recognize that there are limits on how much you can help some students with their personal problems. At some point, you may have to say to the student that you have done all you can. You may not be competent to deal with the situation if it is a complex psychological problem requiring professional assistance. You may have spent numerous hours attempting to assist the student, with no end in sight. For instance, if a student has emotional difficulties over the break-up of a romance and you have listened and made referrals as needed, but the student still persists in contacting you to discuss the situation, your only recourse may be to tell the student gently that the appropriate person with whom to discuss his or her problem is a campus counselor. Faculty members must decide for themselves where this point is, but the important thing to remember is that everyone has a limit. If you have shown genuine care and concern, and have made the necessary referrals to appropriate resources, you should feel confident that you have done all that reasonably can be expected.

Conclusion

Student personal problems are increasingly complex and difficult. Listening openly will help you understand the nature of the problem. Being aware of potential resources will assist you in making appropriate referrals and will help prevent you from feeling over-whelmed with your students' problems. Avoid offering personal advice for nonacademic issues; doing so may be considered unethical (Keith-Spiegel, 2004.) Finally, being able to recognize when you have reached your capacity to help a student will protect both your emotional well-being and time, and will best serve the student.

REFERENCES

American Academy of Child and Adolescent Psychiatry. (2004). *Facts for families No. 10: Teen suicide.* Retrieved Oct. 31, 2004, from www.aacap.org/publications/factsfam/suicide.htm.

American Psychological Association (2002). Ethical principles of psychologists and code of conduct. *American Psychologist, December.* Retrieved Oct. 31, 2004, from www.apa.org/ethics/code2002html.

Brown, J. C., & Barnett, J. M. (1984). Response of faculty members to medical students' personal problems. *Journal of Medical Education, 59*, 180–7.

Foushe'e, R. D., & Sleigh M. J. (2004). Going the extra mile: Identifying and assisting struggling students. In B. Perlman, L. I. McCann, & S. H. McFadden (eds.), *Lessons learned: Practical advice for the teaching of psychology* (vol. 2, pp. 303–11). Washington, DC: The American Psychological Society.

Keith-Spiegel, P. (1999). Ethically risky situations between students and professors outside the classroom. In B. Perlman, L. I. McCann, & S. H. McFadden (eds.), *Lessons learned: Practical advice for the teaching of psychology* (pp. 225–30). Washington, DC: The American Psychological Society.

Pastorino, E. (1999). Students with academic difficulty: Prevention and assistance. In B. Perlman, L. I. McCann, & S. H. McFadden (eds.), *Lessons learned: practical advice for the teaching of psychology* (pp. 193–9). Washington, DC: The American Psychological Society.

53

Inviting Students to Become Research Collaborators

Ψ

Susan R. Burns
Morningside College

What role does student research play in the teaching of psychology? Beyond students learning the basics of psychological research including experimental design, data coding, and analysis (Bendersky & Chiang, 2004), the opportunity for professional development and mentoring of the next generation of psychologists using hands-on discovery is outstanding. Chapman (2003, B5) clearly noted that "student research is a way of celebrating what we value most in academe . . . [research] highlights the accomplishments of our students and the efforts of everyone who has helped them along the way." From a student's perspective, LaRoche (2004, p. 20) acknowledged that "research opens an arena for the development of crucial educational goals such as fine-tuning critical thought and the carrying out discovery." This chapter highlights proactive measures that faculty can use to involve students in the research experience (i.e., the "how") and reflects on the benefits of such inclusions (i.e., the "why").

Identifying Potential Students

You have made the decision to begin a research program, but are not sure which students to invite as collaborators. Ossoff (1998, p. 19) noted that although faculty "would like to believe it is so, students are not necessarily going to be drawn to the glow of our intellects like moths to a flame, no matter how brightly we may radiate." How then do we attain viable, reliable students?

There are some very obvious and practical measures you can take to identify quality students. For example, in most departments, it is reasonably easy to identify "visible" students. Students who are involved with Psi Chi, psychology clubs, or who are actively engaged in the classroom, typically are students looking for opportunities to further their learning in psychology. Regardless of the level of visibility, if you do not know the student(s) well, speak with your colleagues to assess their attitude toward prospective undergraduate collaborators. They likely have had contact with these students, either in their classes or in other capacities, and have formed valuable opinions. It is also important to mention that quality research collaborators do not always have to be the best students academically. Although a strong academic background is beneficial, more important is a student's desire to grow professionally.

Ossoff (1998) offered two additional approaches for identifying potential undergraduate collaborators: a programmatic approach and an informal one. With the programmatic approach, she recommended using the classroom to spark student interest in research. This style ranges from utilizing in-class projects for integration of students into the research experience to the incorporation of service learning as a way to pique students' interest in hands-on learning. A programmatic approach also can simply involve conveying excitement and enthusiasm for "doing science" (Ossoff, 1998, p. 18). With an informal approach, the professor makes an additional effort to "show interest in the student" (ibid.), for example, by scheduling informal meetings with a student after class to discuss research possibilities.

When looking to increase the number of students in your research group, it may prove useful to expand the role of existing student collaborators, allowing current research students to recommend their peers. It is not critical for your research assistants to "get along"; however, it can make your life a lot easier! Student input in the selection process may help prevent potential personality conflicts that might arise. Students often have a unique insight into their peers' efforts in group situations because of previous classroom experiences.

Communicating Expectations and Selection of Research Topics

Once you have selected the student(s) to invite as research collaborator(s), communicate your expectations for their contributions to your research team. Although you can clearly delineate the research *process*, students may lack clarity concerning their role in the process. Thus, it is important to know the level of involvement you expect. Obviously, there are various levels at which you can engage students: from simply having them collect data to participation in every level of the process. Because my experience has been with the latter, I have a very clearly outlined set of expectations, comparable to a syllabus with objectives and outcomes, that I give to the student researchers at the beginning of each semester.

Another consideration is that many psychology departments have the option for students to take "research hours" or some type of independent study which allows them to receive academic credit for their involvement in research. It is possible your department has an established contract or syllabus associated with these course-like options. Because involvement of students in research often consists of time spent *outside* of a typical classroom setting, it is important to inform students about the necessary commitments and contributions.

In my experience, your selection of research topic has largely to do with the type of institution at which you teach. For example, if you teach at a research institution, you likely have a predesigned research agenda that students can "walk into" without much consideration of searching for a research topic. However, if you are at a smaller, private, or liberal arts college, you may need to take a more flexible approach in the selection of research topics. For example, you can look for student-guided ideas for research, perhaps in the context of senior theses and group or individual-designed projects. Research collaboration, either across disciplines on your campus or across campuses also is a good source for research topics.

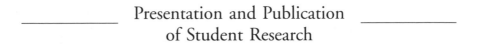

Presentation and Publication of Student Research

The research process is not complete until it is made public. There are an ever-increasing number of venues for student presentation and publication. For example, there are regional student conventions (e.g., Great Plains Student Psychology Convention). Most regional conferences (e.g., MPA, SWPA, etc.) and national conferences (e.g., APA and APS) have Psi Chi sessions exclusively for student presentations. There also are journals designed specifically for the publication of student research (e.g., *Psi Chi Journal of Undergraduate Research, Journal of Psychological Inquiry, Modern Psychological Studies*). Another possibility to consider is creating your own student presentation outlet. This venue can be a simple as an afternoon designated for departmental presentation of students' research or as large and complex as a weekend conference with invitations sent to other schools and guest speaker(s).

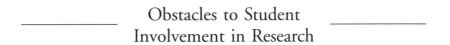

Obstacles to Student Involvement in Research

Obviously, the involvement of students in research does not come without costs. There are potential barriers that may discourage you from involving students in research (e.g., teaching load, no departmental or administrative support, or the belief that focusing on students' research may move you away from your interests). However, the rewards of involving students in research can be far greater than any of these obstacles. Seeing your students making connections between what they have learned in class and what they experience via their own research is phenomenal. For example, a student of mine had difficulty identifying appropriate statistical analyses for various research designs in her experimental psychology course, but after conducting her own research, she has a much better understanding of the logic behind research design and statistical analysis. Additionally, knowing that you are helping students on the path to personal and professional success also is highly rewarding. Nevertheless, finding a healthy balance between encouraging student involvement in research and your other faculty responsibilities is a must, especially if you are untenured.

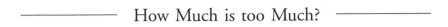

How Much is too Much?

At some point in the process of involving students in research, you may begin to feel a bit overwhelmed by the number of students wanting to be involved, especially if you are at a small college or in a small department. It is important that you find a workable number of students that you can include effectively in research. Because of the extra effort on your part, and the needs of each of the students involved, you may ultimately have to turn students away. Although turning students away may be difficult, it may be the perfect opportunity for you to encourage your colleagues to invite students to become research collaborators.

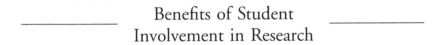

Benefits of Student Involvement in Research

From the student's perspective, the involvement in research has great potential for payoff. Landrum (2002, p. 15) nicely outlined several benefits for students to become involved in research:

- "Acquisition of skills and knowledge not easily gained in the classroom
- Opportunity to work one-on-one with a faculty member
- Opportunity to contribute to the advancements of the science of psychology
- Exposure to general research techniques helpful for pursing later graduate work
- Opportunity to practice written and oral communication skills by preparing for and attending professional conferences and preparing and submitting manuscripts for publication
- Cultivation of mentoring relationships with a faculty member that will be helpful for acquiring letters of recommendation."

Lapatto (2003) also noted that investigation on the benefits of student involvement in research supports "the view that faculty mentors provide the essential structure and consideration that fosters competence, independence, and maturity in the student" (p. 142). These are qualities that faculty may not be able to foster in a class setting, but when working one-on-one or in a small research group situation, students are allowed to take a more active role in their education and thus become more autonomous in their learning.

For faculty, the typical tenure-decision criteria consist of elements such as teaching, scholarship, and service (in varying orders depending upon the institution). The involvement of students in research allows for faculty professional development in each of these areas. Research allows for unique teaching experiences that are irreplicable in the classroom setting, thus introducing another important consideration: evaluation of the collaboration process. If your institution does not require students to complete teaching evaluation forms for their involvement in research (regardless of whether they are enrolled in research hours or not), I strongly recommend that you conduct such an evaluation. If you do not feel the typical course evaluation form is appropriate, then design your own. There are two primary benefits for having your students evaluate their research involvement: documentation of your efforts to involve students in research and appropriate student feedback on how you can improve this process.

From a professional stance, an inclusion of the presentations and publications made by your students in your vita (e.g., a section entitled *Faculty Supervision of Student Research*) is appropriate to demonstrate an aspect of your own scholarly development. Chapman (2003, B5) recognized that undergraduate research "enhances faculty members' professional lives. Particularly at a college that emphasizes good teaching, undergraduate research often helps keep faculty members abreast of disciplinary trends and developments." Mathie et al. (2004) noted that when faculty teach undergraduates about the research process, those students gain insight on the scholarship of discovery. Finally, many institutions are pleased to recognize faculty's support of student research at conferences and in publications as a service to the college and may use these activities as a recruiting device for prospective students.

Conclusion

Your desire to invite students to become research collaborators indicates a commendable desire to mentor students through the process of becoming professionals and instilling passion for learning. Such activities are evidence of quality teaching in psychology and a recognition that learning can extend beyond the classroom.

REFERENCES

Bendersky, K., & Chiang, T. M. (2004). Creating time for undergraduate research in psychology at a liberal arts institution. *Council on Undergraduate Research Quarterly, 24,* 160.

Chapman, D. W. (2003, Sept.). Undergraduate research: Showcasing young scholars. *The Chronicle of Higher Education,* B5.

Landrum, R. E. (2002). Maximizing undergraduate opportunities: The value of research and other experiences. *Eye on Psi Chi, 6,* 15–18.

Lapatto, D. (2003). The essential features of undergraduate research. *Council on Undergraduate Research Quarterly, 20,* 139–42.

LaRoche, K. (2004). Advantages of undergraduate research: A student's perspective. *Eye on Psi Chi, 8,* 20–1.

Mathie, V., Buskist, W., Carlson, J. F., Davis, S. F., Johnson, D. E., & Smith, R. A. (2004). Expanding the boundaries of scholarship in psychology through teaching, research, service, and administration. *Teaching of Psychology, 31,* 233–41.

Ossoff, E. P. (1998). Involving the undergraduate in faculty research. *Eye on Psi Chi, 2,* 18–20.

54
Fostering Student Professional Development

Ψ

R. Eric Landrum

Boise State University

Students receiving an undergraduate education in psychology are prepared for many future endeavors, but do not receive training sufficient to qualify for licensure as a psychologist. Some pursue graduate education, but many students use their bachelor's degree to seek good jobs. This chapter highlights the strategies that students can use while an undergraduate that will promote professional development and provide a competitive edge in whatever career path they pursue. Professional development includes activities such as research assistantships, teaching assistantships, internships, a senior thesis, and organizational involvement.

The Role of Grades

There is no doubt that grades intertwine with the teaching and learning process – grades are a necessary component. The use of grades began in America at Yale University in 1783, using the descriptive terms Optime, Second Optime, Inferiores, and Pejores (Milton, Pollio, & Eison, 1986). These descriptions were used for a 4-point grading scale just after 1800, and in 1813 the first grade-point averages (GPA) were calculated.

Whereas grades can be useful in assessing student learning, high grades should not be the sole objective for students. "Grades, rather than learning, become the primary objective of many students; the appearance of achievement becomes more important than the achievement itself" (Pollio & Beck, 2000, p. 84). I have told students many times that if I were an employer or a member of a graduate admissions committee, I would rather see an applicant with a 3.5 GPA who had been a research assistant, completed an internship, and served as a Psi Chi officer compared to someone with a 4.0 GPA who had done nothing outside the classroom. Grades, along with Graduate Record Examination (GRE) scores and letters of recommendation, remain the "big three" primary selection factors for graduate admissions (Keith-Spiegel, 1991; Keith-Spiegel & Wiederman, 2000). Good grades are necessary, but not sufficient for student success.

Competition of Post-Baccalaureate Opportunities

Every year since 1995, over 70,000 students have graduated with their psychology bachelor's degree in the United States – in 2001–2 (the latest year available) there were 73,534 psychology graduates (National Center for Education Statistics, 2003). Competition in the workforce is usually fierce for the best jobs, and in difficult economic times, competition for any job can sometimes be fierce. Chen (2004) noted that, on average, college graduates will have 8 different jobs during their lifetimes; over this span, they will be required to work in 3 different professions or occupations. With so many new psychology graduates each year, students need a competitive edge.

Graduate education continues to be a popular option, and the competitiveness for some graduate degrees and specialty areas is high. Landrum (2004) presented data made available from the American Psychological Association (APA) (2003) that highlighted both the popularity and competitiveness of graduate school admissions. Based on these data, for example, clinical Ph.D. programs received 18,392 applications during 2001–2. From this pool, only 10.5 percent of these applicants were accepted. Clinical Psy.D. programs had 4,982 applications and 40.8 percent were accepted, and for master's degree clinical programs, 4,218 applications and 49.4 percent were accepted. Clinical psychology remains the most popular degree for Ph.D. and Psy.D. applications, and clinical is second only to counseling psychology in master's degree applications. By the way, students interested in the clinical Ph.D. usually have to do better than the 3.5 GPA alluded to earlier – because of competitiveness, GPA cutoffs as high as 3.8 or 3.9 are not uncommon.

Professional Development Opportunities for Students

Many different professional development opportunities exist for students outside of the standard curriculum and the classroom. What are these professional development opportunities, and how can we maximize student benefits?

Research Assistant (RA)

Research assistantships provide students with opportunities to assist faculty in a research program. There are many advantages to serving as an RA, such as (a) acquiring skills and knowledge not easily gained in the classroom, (b) contributing to the advancement of psychology, (c) using general research techniques helpful for pursuing later graduate work, (d) practicing written and oral communication skills by preparing for and attending professional conferences and preparing and submitting manuscripts for publication, and (e) cultivating a mentoring relationship with a faculty member that will be helpful for acquiring strong letters of recommendation.

Davis (1995) highlighted the advantages for faculty members in their research collaboration with students: (a) witnessing student professional growth and development, (b) keeping current in the literature, (c) keeping analytic skills fine-tuned and active through the design and completion of research, (d) generating meaningful empirical data, (e) maintaining and expanding professional networks through attending conventions, especially for students, and (f) enhancing effectiveness as a teacher through active involvement in research.

Although the RA–faculty collaboration is often a positive experience, problems can arise. Slattery and Park (2002) described strategies to help faculty avoid problems in research collaboration: meet students regularly, mentor student researchers in whatever way possible, train students carefully for tasks given to them, and choose student researchers carefully. Research collaboration is a serious commitment by both student and faculty – you should carefully nurture this relationship and monitor progress toward research and learning goals.

Teaching Assistant (TA)

Serving as a TA is usually much less involved and time-consuming than being an RA. Usually, a TA helps a faculty member for one semester in the administration of a specific course, such as Introduction to Psychology. Responsibilities of teaching assistants differ depending on the instructor and course – these duties might include attending class, holding office hours, and assisting the faculty member in grading. The teaching assistantship is an excellent way for students to build a mentoring relationship with a faculty member, and it is a fairly low-risk activity. Sometimes working with an instructor as a TA can lead to other opportunities such as a research assistantship.

Internship

The internship experience provides a realistic job tryout. Students learn about the type of environment they would work in and the type of economic support they might receive. Although many students have a positive internship experience, some students come back from an internship with the conclusion, "I do not want to do that for a career." That is valuable information! Although it is unfortunate that the student did not have a more positive experience, it is better to have an unsatisfying 16-week internship experience than pursue a career that leads to miserable employment.

Internships have many benefits – I have culled descriptions of these benefits from various sources (Jessen, 1988; Mount Saint Vincent University, 1998; University of Michigan at Dearborn, 1998): (a) practical, on-the-job experience; (b) development of professional and personal confidence, responsibility, and maturity; (c) understanding the realities of the work world and the acquisition of human-relations skills; (d) the opportunity to examine a career choice closely and make professional contacts; (e) the chance to test the ideas learned in the classroom out in the field; and (f) learning what careers not to pursue. Internships can be a strong complement to classroom learning, and provide a chance for students to explore potential career avenues.

Senior Thesis

At many colleges and universities, undergraduates have the opportunity to complete a senior thesis project (sometimes it is required). What is the difference between an RA position and a senior thesis? Generally speaking, as RAs, students assist in faculty research. Students might make some suggestions and put their own "spin" on the research, but the research program essentially belongs to the faculty member. For a senior thesis project, students are the principle investigators, and own the research; the faculty member serves as advisor. Often, in a senior thesis project the student gets to test his or her own research ideas. With careful planning and the proper supervision, students can make this project into something that will help them stand out from the crowd, perhaps leading to a conference presentation (or publication or both), and help build rapport with a faculty member.

Psi Chi

Psi Chi, the National Honor Society in Psychology (www.psichi.org), was founded in 1929 for the purpose of encouraging, stimulating, and maintaining excellence in scholarship in psychology students, and for the advancement of psychology. Psi Chi membership is conferred on students who have met minimum qualifications at institutions where there is a chapter (not all students can be members). Involvement in your local chapter can lead to opportunities to develop leadership skills. At major regional and national conferences held each year, Psi Chi has an important presence in promoting the scholarly achievements of students. Psi Chi has a long tradition of providing student-friendly programming at these conferences. Even if your institution does not have a Psi Chi chapter, there may be a psychology club available (or think about helping students start one). Usually, these clubs are open to anyone with an interest in psychology, and members do not have to be psychology majors. Often, students who are unable to join Psi Chi (e.g., low GPA) can be active and involved as members of a local psychology club. Becoming active in student organizations such as Psi Chi can help students to network and make connections that lead to additional professional development opportunities, such as working with faculty members.

Conclusion

With over 70,000 new psychology graduates each year, competition for the best jobs in the workforce, as well as the competition for graduate-school admissions, is powerful.

For long-term success, students must be more than good "book" students earning high grades; these students need to develop a well-rounded set of skills and abilities that provides the best chances of success. Faculty members can promote student professional development by providing meaningful outside-of-class activities such as those highlighted in this chapter. There are clear benefits to the faculty member in working with students in a variety of areas. Thus, both faculty and students benefit when teaching and learning continue outside the classroom.

REFERENCES

American Psychological Association. (2003). Applications, acceptances, and new enrollments in Graduate Departments of Psychology, by degree and subfield area, 2001–2002 [Table]. *Graduate study in psychology 2003*. Washington, DC: Author.

Chen, E. K. Y. (2004). *What price liberal arts education?* In Siena College (ed.), *Liberal education and the new economy*. Loudonville, NY: Siena College.

Davis, S. F. (1995). The value of collaborative scholarship with undergraduates. *Psi Chi Newsletter, 21 (1)*, 12–13.

Jessen, B. C. (1988). Field experience for undergraduate psychology students. In P. J. Wood (ed.), *Is psychology for them? A guide to undergraduate advising* (pp. 79–84). Washington, DC: American Psychological Association.

Keith-Spiegel, P. (1991). *The complete guide to graduate school admission: Psychology and related fields*. Hillsdale, NJ: Erlbaum.

Keith-Spiegel, P., & Wiederman, M. W. (2000). *The complete guide to graduate school admission: Psychology, counseling, and related professions* (2nd ed.). Mahwah, NJ: Erlbaum.

Landrum, R. E. (2004). New odds for graduate admissions in psychology. *Eye on Psi Chi, 8*, 20–1, 32.

Milton, O., Pollio, H. R., & Eison, J. A. (1986). *Making sense of college grades*. San Francisco: Jossey-Bass.

Mount Saint Vincent University. (1998). Benefits to the co-op student. Retrieved on Dec. 1, 1998, at http://serf.msvu.ca/coop/st_ben.htm

National Center for Education Statistics. (2003). *Digest of education statistics 2002* (Publication NCES 2003-060). Washington, DC: US Department of Education.

Pollio, H. R., & Beck, H. P. (2000). When the tail wags the dog: Perceptions of learning and grade orientation in, and by, contemporary college students and faculty. *The Journal of Higher Education, 71*, 84–102.

Slattery, J. M., & Park, C. L. (2002, Spring). Predictors of successful supervision of undergraduate researchers by faculty. *Eye on Psi Chi, 6*, 29–33.

University of Michigan at Dearborn. (1998). Benefits to the student. Retrieved Dec. 1, 1998, at http://casl.umd.umich.edu/casl_stubenefits.html

55

Professional Development Through the Integration of Teaching, Scholarship, and Service: If It's Not Fun, I'm Not Doing It

Ψ

Matthew T. Huss
Creighton University

Although the focus of this handbook is on the teaching of psychology, we rarely teach in an academic vacuum (Fretz et al., 1993). The reality is that teaching is only a third of the tenure, promotion, and merit-based compensation process for the bulk of colleges and universities. If you want to continue to teach, you must adhere to the explicit and implicit encouragement by academia to engage in scholarship and service. However, that does not mean we should treat each of these areas separately. In fact, I argue that scholarship and service should be integrated with teaching; faculty should pursue activities in areas that match their personal and professional expertise, and look to always have fun when they are doing it.

We continually hear that graduate education focuses on professional development as a researcher, at the exclusion of teaching (e.g., Jarvis, 1992). In graduate school we conduct research, write manuscripts, and apply for grants to continue our research. Although this process is often instructive, it does not have the evaluative component that we experience as full-fledged professionals. Rarely do graduate students prove themselves for 5 years, ask a group of peers across academic disciplines to evaluate them, and then look for another graduate program if they fail to meet unspecified standards of professional worth. Furthermore, graduate students may teach a class or even several classes during their graduate education, but they will rarely teach two, three, or four classes at a time while simultaneously being a productive scholar and engaging in professional service.

Despite the failure of graduate education to mimic precisely the multiple demands of professional academia, a *teacher* can do several things to also become an effective scholar. First, identify and access the resources you need to produce scholarship. Identifying resources could mean negotiating for startup costs and looking for appropriate maintenance of existing facilities (e.g., physiological and animal labs are regularly restocked with supplies), requesting specific time to be set aside for research, identifying administrative support for scholarship (e.g., course reductions, research centers), applying for internal or external funding sources, and trying to attract good undergraduate and graduate research assistants. You may have all the abilities in the world but lack the resources and opportunities to demonstrate those abilities, so make sure you first place yourself in a position to be successful. Part of the reason you put yourself in this position is to develop successful work habits early. Professionals who start slowly rarely become productive (see Bland & Schmitz, 1986). For example, don't plan on being the first to arrive and the last to leave the office in a couple of years, after you get your teaching under control and you are settled in a new community. Do so immediately.

Network with other professionals in your department, in the university, in the community, nationally, and internationally. Most people do not think about networking in their own department, yet your own department may be the best source for professional socialization and the best place for junior faculty to develop a mentoring relationship. Newer faculty should approach experienced faculty for advice and support; some institutions even have formal mentoring programs. Faculty also should extend their professional network beyond the department by sitting on local community boards, continuing to keep in touch with past students and colleagues, and attending professional conferences. By networking with other professionals, you increase your exposure to the newest innovations in your field as well as improving your access to potential collaborators. This practice is true whether you are contacting a fellow academic at a national conference or the director of a local psychiatric hospital whose son participates in Little League with yours. Personally, I would produce almost no scholarship if my presentations and publications with former colleagues and community contacts were eliminated.

Look for readily accessible sources of data. The most obvious place to start is your dissertation. For many of us, it may be painful to return to the bane of our existence but if you want an easy source for at least one, if not multiple, publication opportunities, the dissertation is the best place to start. For those researchers with applied interests, watch for existing real-world data sets that are screaming for someone to come along and mine them. For example, a professional from a local mental health clinic contacted me several years ago about some clinical data they had sitting around and wondered if I would be interested in examining them. After about a year of heavy labor from a student and constant complaining about the lack of experimental rigor in collecting the data, we crafted a publishable manuscript and had it accepted by a very good journal. Today that manuscript is one of my most oft-cited publications.

Most importantly, scholarship does not have to be separate from teaching! Effective scholarship and effective teaching should go hand-in-hand. You can integrate research and scholarship by giving students the option of completing an independent research project as an alternative way to fulfill a paper requirement for a course, require independent research projects in research methods or experimental psychology, or conduct pedagogical scholarship that may specifically focus on your classroom activity. Many of the same skills we try to teach our students are the skills necessary to complete quality scholarship. It only makes sense that good teaching goes along with good scholarship.

Also realize that students themselves can be one of the best sources for new ideas and vitality. On more than one occasion, class discussion has sparked a research idea that I eventually turned into publishable project.

Few people pursue a Ph.D. or academia because of the attraction of service; most faculty see it as a necessary evil for tenure. However, service can be *and should be* a desirable task. I had a professor who once said that, "If it's not fun, I am not doing it." This statement was by a man who many people did not automatically identify as a *seeker of fun*; he was right nonetheless. In academia, we often have the professional flexibility, expertise, and intellectual interests to pursue things that we think are fun. I don't plan on sitting on our college's Committee on Committees anytime soon (oh yes, we have one). However, I am an active member of our Pre-Law Advising Committee because of my interest and experience in the law, and have been a member of committees related to campus construction because I worked for my father's construction company while I was going through school. These activities were interesting to me; they were fun.

You will find your service responsibilities more rewarding if you get involved in service that allows you to use your professional expertise. I have provided my expertise as a clinical psychologist to design a treatment protocol for a domestic violence program, select appropriate risk assessment instruments for a forensic hospital, and evaluate the effectiveness of a substance abuse program. These activities all counted as service and also allowed me later to collect data and generate additional scholarship as well as obtain internships and employment for students. As a psychologist, you could use your expertise to evaluate assessment processes at your university or sit on the board of local daycare if you are a developmental psychologist. Furthermore, my own university looks more favorable on community service that utilizes my expertise rather than sitting on a church board or assisting with a local charity. Pursue service that overlaps with your scholarship and teaching (Mathie, 2002). Try to communicate to outside agencies that you can help with outcome assessment of their program or training of employees in a way that produces meaningful results for them and publishable manuscripts for you. Also realize that your service can be of great help to your teaching by giving you real-world examples to bring back to the classroom. Every professional task should affect every other professional task, and hopefully improve all of them.

Finally, realize that professional development should be just that, developmental in nature. During your first year, do not expect to be president of the faculty senate or publish a four-volume book series. Identify realistic goals that are in keeping with your abilities, interests, and the scholarly and service expectations of your university as your career progresses. Realize that there will be ebb and flow to your teaching, scholarship, and service. You will have personal demands that have an impact on your professional productivity and your interests will change over time. You may not have any desire to be an administrator now and maybe you cannot imagine ever leaving the classroom, but 20 years from now you may need a break and be ready for the demands of being a department chair or college administrator. Teaching, scholarship, and service must not and should not be mutually exclusive of one another. Rather, they should be interdependent so that success in one can lead to success in the other areas. Above all else, they should be fun.

REFERENCES

Bland, C. J., & Schmitz, C. C. (1986). Characteristics of the successful researcher and implications for faculty development. *Journal of Medical Education, 61*, 22–31.

Fretz, B. R., Garibaldi, A. M., Glidden, L. M., McKeachie, W. J., Moritaugu, J. N., Quina, K., et al. (1993). The complete scholar: Faculty development for those who teach psychology. In T. V. McGovern (ed.), *The handbook for enhancing undergraduate education* (pp. 93–121). Washington, DC: American Psychological Association.

Jarvis, D. K. (1992). Improving junior faculty scholarship. In M. D. Sorcinelli & A. E. Austin (eds.), *Developing new and junior faculty* (pp. 63–72). San Francisco: Jossey-Bass.

Mathie, V. A. (2002). Integrating teaching and service to enhance learning. In S. F. Davis & W. Buskist (eds.), *The teaching of psychology: Essays in honor of Wilbert J. McKeachie and Charles L. Brewer* (pp. 163–78). Mahwah, NJ: Erlbaum.

56
Mentoring From Your Department Chair: Building a Valuable Relationship

Ψ

Linda M. Noble
Kennesaw State University

Many resources exist to help you succeed as a new faculty member. Some focus on effective teaching (e.g., McKeachie, 2002), whereas others deal with scholarly productivity (e.g., Magnuson et al., 2003). Some address faculty life more broadly and give advice about preparing for the different stages of an academic career (e.g., Darley, Zanna, & Roediger, 2004). Many books exist on the challenges facing new faculty (Boice, 1992; Menges & Associates, 1999). The ultimate goal of these materials is to help you become a successful and productive faculty member. Although it is difficult to find time to read these resources when you are struggling with the demands of a new job, I encourage you to do just that. These authors discuss the actual experiences of many new faculty and offer excellent advice about avoiding some of the pitfalls they have seen.

You may also have the benefit of having one or more colleagues serve as mentors in your professional life. Some of you may find that your hiring institution expects you to participate in a formal mentoring program in which a more experienced faculty member becomes your assigned mentor. Although these kinds of formal programs are becoming more common (Cavanaugh, 2002), you may find it awkward to develop a mentoring relationship with someone who has been assigned to you. Other faculty may develop less formal mentoring relationships that grow spontaneously. Both types of mentoring relationships, especially the less formal ones, can have a powerful and positive impact on your career. However, for many faculty, these informal relationships do not develop easily. Boice (1992) interviewed several cohorts of new faculty and found many new faculty sat in their office waiting for senior faculty to approach them, and senior faculty stayed in their offices assuming the new faculty would come to them if they needed something. Of course, in that situation, very little mentoring took place. I encourage you to reach out to your new colleagues and respond to their attempts to reach out to you. Some of these connections may be the most important ones in your professional career.

Department Chairs and _____
_____ Deans as Mentors

Another source of mentoring for you will be your department chair, and at times, your dean. Chairs' and deans' roles in mentoring new faculty is widely recognized as part of their jobs, and resources are available to assist them in this role (e.g., Bensimon, Ward, & Sanders, 2000; Leaming, 2003; Wergin, 2003).

I believe your chair is often the best person to help you deal with both the day-to-day problems you face and longer-term issues, like tenure and promotion. Of course, your chair is also your supervisor and some authors have suggested that this dual role is a serious problem for effective faculty and administrator mentoring (Mark, 1982). As a new faculty member you do not know your chair well, and you may hesitate to approach your chair when you have a problem. However, it is in your best interest to attempt to develop a trusting and positive relationship with your chair. At the very least, you should begin your new position assuming you can informally ask your chair to help you when you need it.

If you find your chair is unsupportive when you seek advice, you can always search for mentoring from other sources. My guess is that your colleagues know how your chair has responded to these kinds of situations in the past, and you should consult them if you have concerns. If, however, your chair is helpful when approached, you have laid the groundwork for your chair to be an important source of day-to-day advice. Being able to consult your chair regularly could be very helpful to you. The mentoring your chair provides during a formal performance evaluation takes on a different "tone" than mentoring outside of this process. In this context, it may seem that the chair's feedback is more formal and evaluative than the informal and developmental advice you receive during a spontaneous talk with him or her.

Circumstances Requiring _____
_____ Mentoring from your Chair

Having spent 10 years as a chair and a dean, I would argue that some instances require you to consult your chair instead of other mentoring resources. Unfortunately, in spite of all the published resources, the good advice of your colleagues, and your good intentions, you are likely to find yourself facing some situations as a new faculty member that leave you uncertain about what to do. Let me share with you some examples of such instances, and suggest that, especially in these situations, you turn to your administrators for guidance and mentoring.

One of the leading sources on the challenges faculty may experience is *The Ethics of Teaching: A Casebook* (Keith-Spiegel, Whitley, Balogh, Perkins, & Wittig, 2002). Keith-Spiegel et al. (2002) provided some concrete examples of complex issues you may face and illustrated how things can go wrong both in and outside the classroom. They also suggested younger and less-experienced faculty members may be at greater risk than senior colleagues when confronted with these situations.

For example, they talked about the challenges of dealing with difficult students in the classroom, handling instances of academic dishonesty, and issues that can develop as you form relationships with your students and your colleagues. In many of these cases, especially those that typically fall under some institutional policy, your best resource should be your department chair.

Although your faculty colleagues may offer you well-intentioned advice, it is typically your chair and your dean who are most familiar with the policies and procedures at your institution and are in the best position to help you deal with the situation. Your administrators also are the persons who will likely be involved if a student makes a formal complaint about something you have done. If that situation arises, it is in your best interest to have discussed the situation with your chair early on and worked with him or her on an action plan. Administrators like faculty to keep them informed, so they are not blind-sided by problems. If you have previously discussed a situation with your chair, it will help your chair explain your decisions to an upset student or parent who drops by his or her office unannounced.

Instances of academic dishonesty easily illustrate my point. According to Keith-Spiegel et al. (2002), this issue is one of the more challenging problems for faculty. In my experience, it is often the way faculty members handle a situation in which a student is suspected of cheating, and not their judgment of whether cheating has occurred, that may cause problems. Faculty are accustomed to a good deal of autonomy in how they organize their courses, and they typically establish their own course policies and procedures in their syllabus.

Real problems may occur, however, when a faculty member establishes course policies or handles a situation in a way that contradicts university policies. For example, if your institution has an established process for confronting a student about academic dishonesty and you do not follow the process, you may have violated the student's due process. Suppose you believe a student has cheated and unilaterally decide to fail the student in your course, or alternatively, tell the student he or she must drop your course. In this case, you may have taken action against the student, violating established procedure at your institution and setting yourself up for some serious problems. Students in this situation may not take your decision lightly and could file a formal complaint, or worse, take legal action against you. At the very least, they are likely to visit your chair, especially if they believe they are innocent. This situation is a good example of why it is so important to know the policies at your institution and to consult your chair before you take any action against students suspected of academic dishonesty. If your chair supports the decisions you make, he or she will be able to explain to the student that you have followed institutional policy appropriately, and will likely be more effective in resolving the matter. Alternatively, if you have taken action without involving your chair, he or she will feel blind-sided by the student, and may be unable to explain or support what you have done. This outcome is not a good one for you, the student, or your chair.

Another example of a situation in which you should involve your chair is if you want to change your course in the middle of the semester. Most syllabi are considered a "contract" with students (Keith-Spiegel et al., 2002), and major changes to a course currently underway could create hardship for students. If you decide to add an extra assignment or eliminate an exam, you should discuss these changes with your chair. Together, you should be able to determine how to best handle the changes. Many institutions have policies related to syllabi and grading. Your chair will be most familiar with these policies and can help you implement what you want to do within these guidelines. Again, if you unilaterally make such sweeping changes without consulting your chair, he or she may have to deal with one or more of your students without understanding what you have done and why. Again, this situation is also not a good one for you, your students, or your chair.

One more example should convince you to seek out your chair for mentoring. It is not uncommon for new faculty to teach courses that a senior faculty member has taught for a long time. You might find yourself in this situation and discover you may have different goals for the course than your more senior colleague. You may wish to use different grading standards or different course assignments. It won't be long before students notice these differences and begin to ask questions about why you require this or that aspect of the course when your senior colleague does not. Under these circumstances, especially if your senior colleague is not offering to work with you regarding the course, you should consult your chair about how to implement your changes while maintaining a positive working relationship with your colleague. Some of the more common conflict between junior and senior faculty occurs over curriculum matters. Again, consult your chair.

Conclusion

When all is said and done, I hope you find yourself surrounded by a good support system throughout your career. Consulting the resources reviewed above, the published literature, your colleagues, and your administrators can make a real difference in your effectiveness as a faculty member. You should not hesitate to use them all.

REFERENCES

Bensimon, E. M., Ward, K., & Sanders, K. (2000). *The department chair's role in developing new faculty into teachers and scholars.* Bolton, MA: Anker.

Boice, R. (1992). *The new faculty member.* San Francisco, CA: Jossey-Bass.

Cavanaugh, J. C. (2002, Winter). Broadening faculty mentoring programs. *The Department Chair, 12,* 26–7.

Darley, J. M., Zanna, M. P., & Roediger III, H. L. (eds.) (2004). *The compleat academic: A career guide* (2nd ed.). Washington, DC: American Psychological Association.

Keith-Spiegel, P., Whitley Jr., E. B., Balogh, D. W., Perkins, D. V., & Wittig, A. F. (2002). *The ethics of teaching: A casebook* (2nd ed.). Mahwah, NJ: Erlbaum.

Leaming, D. R. (ed.) (2003). *Managing people: A guide for department chairs and deans.* Bolton, MA: Anker.

Magnuson, S., Davis, K. M., Christensen, T. M., Duys, D. K., Glass, J. S., Patman, T., Schmidt, E. A., & Veach, L. J. (2003). How entry-level assistant professors master the art and science of successful scholarship. *Journal of Humanistic Counseling, Education and Development, 42,* 209–22.

Mark, S. (1982). Faculty evaluation in community colleges. *Community/Junior College Quarterly, 6*, 167–8.

McKeachie, W. J. (2002). *McKeachie's teaching tips: Strategies, research, and theory for college and university teachers* (11th ed.). Boston: Houghton Mifflin.

Menges, R. J., & Associates. (1999). *Faculty in new jobs: A guide to settling in, becoming established, and building institutional support.* San Francisco, CA: Jossey-Bass.

Wergin, J. F. (2003). *Departments that work: Building and sustaining cultures of excellence in academic programs.* Bolton, MA: Anker.

57

Navigating the Academic Environment: The Politics of Teaching

Ψ

Randolph A. Smith
Kennesaw State University

In the best of all worlds, people would be evaluated solely on their skills and abilities – on their job performance and nothing else. However, as you know all too well by now, we do not live in the best of all worlds. The truth is that there are political considerations within academia, just as there are in many careers. The key to managing politics within the academic setting is to keep them, as much as possible, from affecting your job or even sabotaging your career. A quote widely attributed to Henry Kissinger goes something like "academic politics are so bitter because the stakes are so small." When it comes to your job and career, those stakes are *not* small, so it pays to be prepared for situations you might face.

There are a few oft-cited book chapters dealing with academic politics (Capaldi, 2004; Penner, Dovidio, & Schroeder, 2004; Salancik, 1987). Although these chapters provide some useful information, they seem to be aimed primarily at faculty members in large research universities, which make up a minority of higher education institutions (see www.nsf.gov/sbe/srs/nsf04304/sectd.htm). Many faculty, of course, take jobs at institutions with more of a teaching focus. This chapter attempts to fill the gap left by those authors I have cited.

As my starting point, I will refer to an article by Bloom and Bell (1979) dealing with "superstars" in graduate school. They listed five traits of graduate students who did well in their graduate programs. I am borrowing and adapting their categories to fit new or early-in-career faculty members.

Visibility

Bloom and Bell (1979) noted that successful graduate students were around the department a lot – not simply for classes – so that faculty got to know them. Penner et al.

(2004) advised faculty to "spend time in your office over and above the time you spend meeting with students" (p. 266). Your colleagues will eventually make tenure recommendations about you; you would certainly hate for a colleague to feel that she did not really know you well at that point! In a smaller school, you may not have a colleague who shares your research interests, but your colleagues will be valuable sources of information about the culture of the department and institution, as well as the various systems and procedures you will need to know. I hope, also, that they will be fun and interesting people to get to know. After many years of narrow specialization in a graduate program, having the opportunity to talk with disciplinary colleagues outside your specialty area can be a breath of fresh air.

Your relationships with your colleagues and chair will be crucial – not only to your survival at your school, but also to your level of satisfaction. When I solicited advice on this topic from a teaching listserv, I received two relevant ideas. First, be sure to form your own opinions about your new colleagues. Some departmental faculty may be eager to share *their* impressions with you – these are probably colored by previous interactions. Similarly, some of your new colleagues may try to sway you to their perspectives on various political battles within the department or college. You would be wise to form your own opinions on these issues also.

Hard Working

Bloom and Bell (1979) pointed out that faculty members perceived graduate students as hard working because the faculty saw them working. There is no substitute for hard work in your role as a faculty member. As a new *or* experienced faculty member, you have classes to prepare, scholarship to pursue, and service obligations to fulfill. Although it may be a popular stereotype that college professors have "cushy" jobs, that perception is far from the truth. I doubt that anyone reading this book harbors any false illusions about the level of work required. An interesting notion based on the point of visibility is that if you do your hard work at home or in the library, other faculty will not see you working and may, unfortunately, form the impression that you don't work as hard as they do. Thus, early in your career, it is probably important both to be visible *and* to be working hard when visible.

Reflection of Program Values

Bloom and Bell (1979) noted that graduate superstars endorsed the values of their graduate programs fully: "Non-superstars did research because it was a degree requirement. Superstars viewed research as an integral part of the discipline and as a desirable and worthwhile activity for any professional psychologist" (p. 231). For faculty members, this characteristic may be *the most important* one on the list. It is critical for you to find out the underlying values of your department and your institution. Typically, faculty evaluations and tenure and promotion decisions hinge on your performance in the *big three areas*: teaching, research, and service. However, the weight of those three areas can vary drastically between (and perhaps even within) institutions. Discovering how your department and school weight the various elements will help you immensely with the previous category – at that point, you will know which area(s) will demand the bulk of your attention.

Many comments from my informal survey spoke to this issue. For example, one respondent said, "Do a good job, but don't let teaching overwhelm your research program (which is much more important for tenure and promotion here, despite confusing rhetoric to the contrary)." This statement underscores an interesting issue. Virtually all colleges and universities have some type of faculty handbook that details the requirements for tenure and promotion – probably revolving around teaching, research, and service. The handbook may even put these three requirements in priority order. This type of situation is why it is crucial to establish relationships with colleagues and your chair – they can give you the inside scoop on how your department and higher administrative units handle tenure decisions. If your college stresses a teaching mission but your department favors scholarship, you need to factor that information into your workload and schedule. Not only will understanding and supporting your department's mission help you in the tenure process; finding a department with a philosophy that is consistent with yours is vital to your long-term satisfaction in that department.

Professor Attachment

Bloom and Bell (1979) noted that most graduate superstars found a professor or two with whom they worked during their training. In other words, they developed a relationship with a mentor. Finding someone to serve as a mentor at your institution can be quite valuable (Boice, 1992). Just as you had an advisor or mentor to help you get through the graduate-school maze, having someone help you find the inside track at your institution can make life much simpler, particularly in dealing with the politics.

Mentors can come from different places, depending on the type of school at which you teach. In a small college, a mentor may even teach in a different department. One advantage to having a mentor outside of your department is that you may be more comfortable confiding in this individual because he or she will probably not have a say in your tenure and promotion decisions. Some schools have formal mentoring programs in which you may be assigned a mentor; some have no such program – you may have to find a mentor on your own. Regardless of how the process works, it is often helpful to have someone to whom you can turn when you have questions, when you need help, or simply when you want to unload some frustrations. A person who has been at your institution long enough to know its ins and outs and its peculiarities can be invaluable, particularly if your institution is considerably different from your graduate institution. The range of different ways to perform the same functions (e.g., parking, giving grades, purchasing items, dealing with administrative offices) at different institutions can be mind-boggling. Having a guide to turn to will simplify your life.

The W Factor

Bloom and Bell (1979) found that graduate superstars had the capability to make faculty feel *worthwhile* and rewarded. "In essence, the superstars listened, learned, grew, and produced" (p. 231). A department made a significant investment when it hired you. Although some departments are famous for "chewing up and spitting out" new faculty, the majority of departments hire new faculty because they believe those new faculty will be a good fit with the department and that they will become useful and productive members of the faculty. It is your responsibility to show your colleagues that they have not made a mistake when they selected you.

What types of behaviors are politically insensitive? What will *not* make your new colleagues feel worthwhile? Be cautious in suggesting new ideas – there is nothing wrong with change, but you should be careful about how you refer to the old practices that you would like to replace. It is likely that someone on the current faculty is responsible for putting those old practices into place. Denigrating or mocking those practices certainly will not win you any brownie points. Respect the history and traditions of the department – you may have colleagues who have invested their lives in that history and tradition. If you have moved to this department from another institution, a similar *faux pas* is to preface all your statements with "At my old school, . . ." No one wants to hear about your old school constantly – if you use this line too often, your colleagues may begin wishing you were back at your old school. It is impossible to list all the possible insensitive behaviors, so you would be wise to remember the old Indian saying: "Do not judge another until you have walked a mile in his sandals." Yes, any department can benefit from new blood and new ideas – just be careful not to go overboard.

Conclusion

I have meant no disrespect to faculty members by generating a list of good political behaviors from a list used to describe graduate-student superstars. Being wise and political in your department may gain you the label of a faculty superstar. It is far better to be labeled a superstar than a malcontent or misfit. Being politically astute in your academic career can move you along that path. Good luck!

REFERENCES

Bloom, L. J., & Bell, P. A. (1979). Making it in graduate school: Some reflections about the superstars. *Teaching of Psychology, 6*, 231–2.

Boice, R. (1992). *The new faculty member: Supporting and fostering professional development.* San Francisco: Jossey-Bass.

Capaldi, E. D. (2004). Power, politics, and survival in academia. In J. M. Darley, M. P. Zanna, & H. L. Roediger III (eds.), *The compleat academic: A career guide* (2nd ed., pp. 245–57). Washington, DC: American Psychological Association.

Penner, L. A., Dovidio, J. F., & Schroeder, D. A. (2004). Managing the department chair and navigating the department power structure. In J. M. Darley, M. P. Zanna, & H. L. Roediger III (eds.), *The compleat academic: A career guide* (2nd ed., pp. 259–76). Washington, DC: American Psychological Association.

Salancik, G. R. (1987). Power and politics in academic departments. In M. P. Zanna & J. M. Darley (eds.), *The compleat academic: A practical guide for the beginning social scientist* (pp. 61–84). New York: McGraw-Hill.

Index of Authors

Index of Subjects